FROM FUNCTIONALISTIC WILLFULNESS TO TRANSCENDENT WILLINGNESS: THE PATHWAY TO FORMATIVE HEALING

Albert A. Kuuire

En Route Books and Media, LLC
St. Louis, MO

Make the time

En Route Books and Media, LLC
5705 Rhodes Avenue
St. Louis, MO 63109

Cover credit: Dr. Sebastian Mahfood, OP

Copyright © 2021 Albert A. Kuuire

Library of Congress Control Number: 2021935121
ISBN-13: 978-1-952464-57-7 and 978-1-952464-75-1

No part of this book may be reproduced, stored in a retrieval system, or transmitted in any form, or by any means, electronic, mechanical, photocopying, or otherwise, without the prior written permission of the authors.

DEDICATION

This book is dedicated to my parents,
IGNATIUS and SYLVIA KUUIRE,
both of whom have since reached their transcendent
Transformation, and are with their Lord and Maker.

ACKNOWLEDGEMENTS

I have never encountered personally the vast majority of the people to whom I owe a great debt of gratitude for the realization of this book, the *pyramid* of the people at the top-most of which I stand. To all, I say thank you for the *of form and faith directives*.

However, there are some people I owe profound gratitude. Such sentiments of gratitude go, first to my parents who, though converts themselves to the Christian faith, are my immediate *donors* of both my *form and faith traditions*. I am also grateful to my eight living siblings who have been significant *poles* of *interformation* for me.

I also heartily acknowledge my two ecclesiastical authorities: Archbishop (Emeritus) Gregory E. Kpiebaya, and especially the late Peter Cardinal Porekuu Dery both of whom immensely made it possible for me, through their support in innumerable ways, to do the research I wanted so to do for this book.

Although there are many friends, each of whose names I cannot mention, all the same, there are a few I feel obliged, by gratitude, to mention. With all my heart I thank my friend, Archbishop Josef Erwin Ender. He gave me the initial seed-money for the project when I did not know where to turn to for that needed help. Similarly, I am most grateful to the Diocese of Pittsburgh, Pennsylvania, in the USA, which provided for me the living facility conducive for the research work.

Finally, I am most grateful to the late Adrian van Kaam, the Founder of the discipline of *Formative Spirituality*, and Dr. Susan Annette Muto, who with her sharp editorial skills, left no word nor phrase of this book un-reflected upon. To her, I truly owe a huge debt of gratitude.

As I acknowledged above, I can never enumerate the huge number of people to whom I am indebted. It is the one I am the most indebted to – the MYSTERY OF ALL FORMATION, GOD – that I entrust the task of rendering adequate thanks to all.

Msgr. Albert A. Kuuire, STD, PHD.

ABBREVIATIONS
Relative to Formation Science

FLF	Foundational life form, or founding life form
SFHF	The science of foundational Human Formation, also known as the Science of Formative Spirituality, or simply as Formation Science.

For Biblical References

NRSV:	The New Revised Standard Version
REB:	The Revised English Bible
NAB:	The New American Bible
NJB:	The New Jerusalem Bible
	Note: This translation is the one that is mainly used throughout this book; and wherever any of the other translations is used, it is otherwise specified.

Other Abbreviated Forms

Studies:	Refers to "Studies in Formative Spirituality" (Journal of Ongoing Formation).
Provisional Glossary:	Refers to the compilation of the terminologies used in Formation Science, entitled "Provisional Glossary of the Terminology of the Science of Foundational Formative Spirituality," the Catholic Catechism: *Catechism of the Catholic Church*.

TABLE OF CONTENTS

PREFACE i

General Methodological Statement of the Science of Foundational Human Formation iii
    Dialogical Selection of Topic and Event iv
    Dialogical Articulation of the Structural Coformant xii
    The Formative Action Pattern xx
    Formulation of Structural Coformants xxiii
    Dialogical Elucidation xxv
Statement of Purpose and Direction of Scientific Research xxv

DIVISION ONE: THE INCAPSULATING POWER OF GRAVE ILLNESS AND RESISTANCE TO FORMATIVE ENCOUNTER 1
Statement of Formation Problem to be Investigated 3

CHAPTER ONE: Self-Encapsulation and Resistance to Encounter in Situations of Life-Threatening Illness 7

CHAPTER TWO: Religious Persons in Grave Illness 63

CHAPTER THREE: Resistance to Graced Communion in the Face of Death 101

CHAPTER FOUR: Frustration and anger at Unfulfilled Ambitions 139

DIVISION TWO: APPRAISING IN-BREAKING DIRECTIVES 177

CHAPTER FIVE: Apprehension, Appraisal, and Application of Inbreaking Directives through Formative Questioning of Form Tradition 183

CHAPTER SIX: Discerning Faith Traditional Directives through Formative Questioning and Imagination 221

CHAPTER SEVEN: Revelation and Application of Life-Forming Directives Through Kataphatic Contemplation 253

CHAPTER EIGHT: Understanding Christian Ministry in the Light of Graced Appraisal of Inbreaking Directives 291

DIVISION THREE: SELF-ABANDONMENT TO THE MYSTERY AS FULNESS OF FORMATIVE HEALING 327

CHAPTER NINE: Movement towards a More Complete Self-Abandonment To the Mystery 331

CHAPTER TEN: Disposition of Gratitude as a Manifestation of greater Self-Abandonment to the Mystery 367

CHAPTER ELEVEN: Attaining Christian Perfection through Detachment from One's Willful Projects 403

CHAPTER TWELVE: Congeniality in Ministry through Overcoming Functionalistic Zeal 437

DIVISION FOUR: SUMMARY OF RESEARCH INSIGHTS AND CONCLUSIONS 471

Table of Contents

Statement of the Basic Formation Question... 473

Part One: Primary Obstacles to and Facilitating Conditions for the
Formation of Christian Ministers..475
Primary Obstacles to the Formation of Christian Ministers................477
Principal Facilitating Conditions for the Formation and
Transformation of Christian Ministers 479

Part Two: Affirmative-Denial Testing of the Thesis of the Research
Project... 483

Part Three: Research Project Contribution to the Science of
Human Formation...485

BIBLIOGRAPHY 487

PREFACE

STATEMENT OF THE QUESTION:

Typically, the bio-physical life-threatening illness experienced by a person is regarded as a disruption of the continuity and joy of a tranquil and peaceful life. It may even come to be considered as the inevitable end of the subject's total human existence. As the subject becomes focally aware of the weakening of his or her human powers, he or she perceives his or her ambitiously crafted projects as coming to their unfulfilled end.

However, *the human spirit*[1] is capable of transcending these limitations which the person perceives as total and meaningless disruption of his or her existence. In this process, the foundational life form[2] - FLF - of the person consonantly unfolds itself and grows towards its fullness – the fullness which one has always *prefocally*, or even *infrafocally*, desired. This spirit is the power which van Kaam and Muto describe empirically as the distinctively human capacity to move toward the "***More Than***."[3] It is what makes human formation possible.

---

[1] In Formative Spirituality, 'human spirit' refers to the empirical-experiential preformational given which the science of foundational human formation calls the foundational life form. It is this 'spirit' which makes each unique and individual person distinctively human. Conf. Adrian van Kaam, Fundamental Formation (New York: Crossroad, 1989), 306.

[2] See footnote 1. The foundational or founding life form will be more fully discussed later.

[3] In their discussion on "Becoming Appreciative," Adrian van Kaam and Susan Muto assert: "The power of appreciation starts out from the belief that people are born with the power to search for and choose in life that which appears to give

Thus, the key to human formation seems to lie in the transcending of one's *functionalistic*, willful determination. This means the free and appreciative abandonment of one's functional will to the *Mystery of Formation*. For congenial, compatible, and compassionate human formation, which consists *in* presence to the Mystery of Formation in one's everyday life, is essentially "consonance, with the Formation Mystery manifesting itself in" all of our human experiences. However, as van Kaam affirms, "to gain this consonance is to transcend our *functionalistic willfulness.*"[4] It is in this that one may find that fulfillment which one has been *preconsciously* seeking.

The basic intuition guiding this research is that, in human illness, one may attain distinctively human fulfilment only through *formative healing*. Hence, the thesis of this research is that **the formative healing of all life-threatening illness may be expedited through submission of the subject's self-encapsulated functional will to the Transcendent Will in appreciative abandonment, which allows for the congenial unfolding of the subject's foundational life-form**.

Formative healing seems to be part of that preformational *givenness* of the FLF which is called to unfold itself. It is in the consonant unfolding of this FLF that the individual can ever hope to arrive at, and to discover this perfect fullness of his or her existence. However, as the Science of Foundational Human Formation – SFHF – holds, the process of this unfolding of the person's FLF cannot be regarded as consonant unless one's *functional dimension*, together with all the lower dimensions, submits to *the executive will of the transcendent* dimension.

Using the theoretical paradigm and *constructs* of the SFHF, the research in this book will investigate and name the dynamics which operate to bring

---

them the most joy and peace, dynamism and delight." See "The Power of Appreciation, (New York: Crossroad, 1993), 21.

[4] Adrian van Kaam, <u>Fundamental Formation</u>, (opus cit.), 192. (Emphasis mine).

foundational formative healing – not necessarily physical cure – to a person in grave and life-threatening illness. This research thus intends: 1) to analyze the dissonant situation to which human illness may lead a person, and so prevent him or her from reaching formative healing. In this, it wishes to examine the contribution that a person's functional will can make to this dissonant situation; 2) It shall explore the interformational role which another can exert, both horizontally and especially vertically on the subject, and the dynamics that may ensue therefrom for the eventual foundationally formative healing of the person; and 3) It wishes to study more closely the gradual shifts of the subject's *current form of life* as he or she abandons him- or herself ever more fully to the Mystery of Formation in the unfolding of his or her FLF towards its fullness, made observable in the *reformation* and *transformation* of his or her *core disposition* of willingness.

GENERAL METHODOLOGICAL STATEMENT OF THE SCIENCE OF FOUNDATIONAL HUMAN FORMATION

The method which this research will employ is the one established by Adrian van Kaam at the Institute of Formative Spirituality in Duquesne University in Pittsburgh, Pennsylvania. This method was born out of the founding intuition[5] van Kaam had in Holland through his experience with people of different *faith and form traditions* during the Second World War. It has since then been meticulously refined over many years of study and discussion with qualified people in various fields of study who are also interested in the initiation and the pretheological development of the SFHF.

---

[5] For Adrian van Kaam's own summary of the root of his intuition – empirical-experiential research method in human formation – see the "Afterword" in Traditional Formation (New York: Crossroad, 1992), 332. His basic objective has been to establish "a program of studies about the unfolding of the human and Christian spirit in people, "329.

All these years of meticulous writing and research led van Kaam to a scientific way to study and analyze "the unfolding of the human and Christian spirit." Van Kaam summarizes this approach in his book, entitled *Scientific Formation*.[6] The following four basic steps of the methodology are described in detail in this volume referred to.

DIALOGICAL SELECTION:

The first step of the methodology is *'dialogical selection.'* To study about the unfolding of the FLF – the human spirit – and about the Christian spirit, the researcher in Formation Science selects the project he or she wants to study. An event in which the chosen topic has been experientially lived out by the researcher is then also selected. This event is narrated phenomenologically, i.e. just as it was experienced by the researcher at the time it occurred. The selection of the event is done in dialogue with the assistance of other researchers with whom the researcher wants to work; and both topic and event become thus the basis for the intended research.

DIALOGICAL ARTICULATION:

The next step is a *'dialogical articulation'* of the event. This process consists in three stages. The first stage is the prescientific description of the event. This prescientific description is a narration of the event such that its chronological unfolding is revealed. In the second stage, the foundational structures of the event are described as they were experienced as *coforming* the event. This stage is still considered prescientific articulation of the event. The third stage of this process is in which this prescientific articulation of

---

[6] Adrian van Kaam, Scientific Formation (New York: Crossroad, 1987. This fourth volume of the series of Formative Spirituality, is completely devoted to the methodology of SFHF.

the event is subsequently *put into the metalanguage of the SFHF*, in consultation with the people with whom the researcher is working. This is, indeed, the third stage, the scientific articulation of the event. In these stages of dialogical articulation, the foundational structures of the event, also known as its *coformants*, are clarified. Such articulations of the event lay bare its underlying *pattern of formative action*, and thus point out the *unique-communal* formation in it.

DIALOGICAL ELUCIDATION:

After the event has been scientifically articulated, the third step is the dialogical elucidation[7] of the formation dynamics in the scientifically articulated foundational structures of the event – its coformants. Adrian van Kaam has this to say concerning this part of the process: "Life is an exchange of polar energies in dynamic interaction."[8] The purpose of elucidating the dynamics of the event is to identify these polar energies, and so, to shed light on them as they interact with one another.

To achieve this end, the foundational structures, or the structural coformants of the event are broken down into remote foundational statements. These contain general formation dynamics and directives which may be present in other human subjects who may have experienced a similar event.[9] The analysis of these remote general formation dynamics and directives further reveal proximate dynamics and directives in them. These in their turn are elucidated by constructs of Formation Science's theory. This is done in consultation with other events which can be used as paradigms, and human sciences which are regarded as auxiliary sciences or

---

[7] For a clear understanding of what dialogical elucidation is, see Adrian van Kaam, Scientific Formation, 156, also 161.

[8] Ibid., 131.

[9] Ibid., 147.

sources to the SFHF.[10] Their findings may then be *translated* into the metalanguage of Formation Science and *transposed* into the appropriate area of formation theory where they are relevant for the elucidation of the formation dynamics and directives. The objective of all this is to dialogically integrate[11] the findings of these auxiliary sources with those of Formation Science's theory in service of elucidation of the dynamics and directives contained in the foundational structures of the formation event.

In this research, this elucidation is done for the *universal level of Human Formation*. A series of transpositions into the other three *horizons of human presence* is then made. These three horizons are: 1) the Foundational Religious Presence which, in this research, is represented by African religion as the non-adhered to faith and form tradition of the subject; 2) Christian Presence adhered to by the researcher; and 3) Segmental Human Presence made up of *priests and other Christian ministers*. These transpositions are also equally submitted to the group of fellow researchers, referred to earlier, for critical examination.

It is to be noted at this point that, in this research, the researcher intends to study each of the foundational formation structures of the event *simultaneously* in the four levels of human presence. Each of the coformants will, therefore, make up the basis for a division of the research in which the four levels of foundational human presence will form the chapters.[12]

---

[10] In this research work the auxiliary sciences will include theology, philosophy, and psychology, philosophy of religion, anthropology, medical ethics, and sociology.

[11] For the notion of scientific integration, see Adrian van Kaam, *Scientific Formation*, 201-11.

[12] This procedure, taken by the present researcher, is a slightly different approach from the initial method presented by Adrian van Kaam. He takes the methodological approach, earlier used, and inverses it, but nevertheless, making use of metalanguage of the science and the constructs therein.

PRACTICAL APPLICATION:

These steps followed by the SFHF methodology – scientific articulation; dialogical elucidation; and the paradigmatic integration of the selected event – now take us to the fourth and last step of the methodology. This fourth step summarizes and applies the insights obtained from the three other steps above. The application is to the particular formation segment of the human population for which the research is intended. This summary should outline the obstacles and facilitating conditions for consonant human formation in the event. Thus, a further elucidation of the summary of obstacles and facilitating conditions is what will make up the fourth division of this research. It will also conclude the final research endeavour which seeks to demonstrate the relevance of the project to the **Science of Foundational Human Formation (SFHF).**

SELECTION OF THE EVENT FOR THE RESEARCH

A Brief History of the Selection of Event

As has already been stated above, to research the thesis that has been described above,[13] the event has to be concrete, and one which has been experienced by the researcher himself. It should be selected according to the methodology of the *Science of Foundational Human Formation*; hence, in consultation and dialogue with other researchers interested in the topic. So it should be amenable to analysis in conformity paradigmatically with the SFHF; its constructs after its dialogical selection, articulation, and elucidation.

---

[13] See pages on "threatening human illness" which wants to bring all of one's ambitiously crafted projects in life to a sudden end, and how it can be cured.

The following event, which the present researcher will use, has been experienced and concretely lived by him. And it is entirely amenable to the rigorous analysis using the so well-crafted methodology created by Adrian van Kaam. Thus, the analysis of this event, using the methodology of Formation Science or the (SFHF) – its theoretical paradigms, dynamics and constructs, and all its methodological facets – will lead to the practical application of its findings to the segment of the human population in view; i.e. priests and other Christian ministers, through *translation* and *transposition* of these findings of the research.

Although a more detailed narration of both the **remote** and **proximate** backgrounds which lead to the event itself would have been most helpful for a greater insight to it, they will only be summarized here.

REMOTE BACKGROUND:

The remote background of the event can be summarized in the following way. As a young minister in the priesthood, even though at first the subject had plans for a completely different life, which was not the priesthood, he plunged himself all the same so enthusiastically into the ministry that was assigned to him, to such an extent that he did not take the necessary care for his health. It was nearly two years since he took up his appointment in, territorially, one of the largest parishes in the Diocese. As a result, he had to trek to nearby villages, and often to places far away from the centre, to meet people, learn their language which was new to him, preach to them about the Christian religion – the Catholic faith – and celebrate the Holy Eucharist for the few who had already received Baptism.

It was when the subject was returning from one of such treks that he was caught up in a very heavy tropical rainstorm. As a result, he became very ill, and getting to the Parish Centre, he immediately went to bed. A nun in the Parish, who was a nurse, was called in to treat him. But after a couple of days in the Parish Centre, it became necessary to rush him to the nearer Catholic hospital in the Diocese, some forty miles distance, and which happened to be less than ten miles away from his family home.

PROXIMATE BACKGROUND:

The doctor's daily visits and treatments did not seem to effect any change of his condition, and the fear that death was imminent began to be his preoccupation. So, he became depressed, morose, and despairing of any recovery. His mother, who was daily at his bed side, was not at all helpful to him, and her anxiety concerning his condition was rather a constant reminder of his imminent death.

He felt himself confronted by the **ultimate**, which he did not want to face, at least, not at the age of barely 28 years. Hence, his anger at God began to mount with every passing day and moment, and he began to question God:

> But God, why do you want me to die now? Did you let me go through all these years of seminary training for your service only to die after hardly three years of my being your priest? In the first place, you allowed me to be given as my first assignment such a tough area of ministry for so young a priest. If I am lying here in this hospital on what is now going to be my deathbed, is it not all because of those very difficult conditions of ministry which you allowed my Bishop to assign to me, as everyone is now acknowledging? Is this how you have always wanted to bring my life to its end?

And so he complained ever more bitterly to God as the days passed by. One particular morning, the nun nursing him and taking particular care of him, while feeding him, brightened up and announced to him that he would be having a visit from the Bishop who arrived the night before and was at the rectory of the parish. He did not show any interest in what she just told him and rather said to himself, "But of what use is such a visit? It is all too late now, even though I do not want to die." He thought his death was imminent, and the visit of the Bishop at this time could do nothing to bring him back from death's door.

NARRATIVE OF THE EVENT ITSELF BY THE SUBJECT:

The Bishop has come, and at first I will not as much as turn my face away from the wall to face him. I have blocked out his greetings from reaching my ears and have just ignored him. I am aware of his presence in the room, but all is silent; a silence which is all pervading. I wish it would continue to eternity.

However, it is not to be; I soon feel a warm and comforting hand come to rest on my left shoulder. In a gentle attempt to turn my face away from the wall to face the rest of the room. In spite of feeling a desire to resist, I feel myself responding to the Bishop's effort. He moves closer to the bed and is now fully engaged in making me turn sufficiently to permit my gaze to fall on his face, and he begins:

> Albert, I got back from my trip two evenings ago and the first thing I learnt about was your illness and your hospitalization here. I left the very next morning, yesterday, to be here with you and to spend some time with you. I arrived at the parish rectory very late last night, and as you know, nobody visits a sick person at night. So I sent word to the sisters to inform you that I would be coming this morning to visit you.

The Bishop concludes, telling the purpose of his presence in reflectively chosen words.

I do not make any attempt to respond. After a period of silence, the Bishop's monologue resumes, interjected by other long period of silence. I still feel very strongly depressed and angry. Because of the extreme weakness of my body, I wonder briefly whether the Bishop is able to pick up, from my bodily appearance, my deep feelings of anger both at him and at God.

After talking for some time about his trip, and the work of evangelization now going on in the Diocese, he suddenly asked me if I remember the story about Saint Aloysius Gonzaga which he told us when we were still in the elementary school. "Aloysius as a Jesuit deacon desired greatly to celebrate the Holy Eucharist, even if only once, before dying, as a result of a contagion he had contracted while helping the sick." I vaguely begin to remember the story which he used to tell us.

As I make the effort to recollect the story in detail, a certain feeling of peace begins to take possession of me, and I am no longer even following what the Bishop continues to tell me of the story. My mind is now dwelling, even if inaccurately, on Aloysius' fate; how content he was to die after being able to celebrate just one Holy Mass:

> *So even if I die now, as it is obvious I am going to do in a few days, am I not still more fortunate than poor Aloysius? People say the Pope gave special permission so that he could be ordained a priest in order to celebrate at least one Eucharist before he would die. But I have been able to celebrate the Holy Eucharist nearly every day since my ordination almost three years ago! God! You have certainly shown more love to me than you seem to have done to poor Aloysius and others like him! I am sorry for having been angry at you! I am ready to die if you want to have me come to you now.*

I heard an inner voice in me saying.

At this time, I experience all my negative feelings, especially my anger against God, and also against the Bishop, receding. I begin to feel a welling up of gratitude towards God for almost the three years of ministry. I also begin to feel similar gratitude towards everybody there in the health facility for the wonderful care I have been receiving from them.

In this deep feeling of gratitude towards God, I feel deeply within me such peace as I have never felt at any moment during the two-and-half months I have been in the hospital, nor at any other time in my life that I can remember. Presently, looking at my Bishop, I feel ashamed and sorry for having been angry at him; innocent instrument of God that he is, he has always loved me and been good to me from the first moment I knew him when he was still a seminarian. How then can he intentionally wish me any harm in life?

At this moment, I feel tired, but, nevertheless, serene and full of peace. This must be apparent to the Bishop. So, as he prepares to take leave of me, he says; "You need to have some rest. I will come back to see you sometime this evening." And with this, he blesses me and leaves the room.

As the Bishop leaves the room, I have the feeling that, deep inside me, some extraordinary change has taken place. Not only do I feel a completely different attitude towards my still impending death, but I also become aware more than at any other time that the potency of my willfulness and determination are truly contingent, indeed very limited.

DIALOGICAL ARTICULATION OF STRUCTURAL COFORMANTS

DIALOGUE WITH THE PRINCIPLES OF THE "SFHF":

Before we can go on to show the *structural coformants* of the above selected event, let us take a moment to explain some principles of the SFHF. What they are and how they correlate in the formation of the individual person leads one to the identification of the structural coformants in the formation of a person.

The intuition, born out of experience, that "Human formation is a dialogue with infrastructure forms and processes in one's own organism, and in one's surroundings,"[14] has given rise to five basic principles in the SFHF. They are the principles of 1) formability; 2) ongoing formation; 3) the formation field; 4) formation tradition; and 5) the maintenance of form potency. These five principles constitute what Richard Byrne calls the infrastructure – the foundation or the ground – of Formation Science.[15] They are applicable to all formation events, and this is quite evident in the formation event which is at the basis of this project.

Formability: The principle of *formability*, also called *form potency*, is the empirical principle of human formation. It holds that the human being is always capable of giving form to the world and receiving form from it through *form directives*. This means that the human person has the relative freedom and ability to give form to the world around him and is also open to receive and incarnate form directives coming from within and outside of himself or herself.

In the beginning, the subject in the formation event of this research receives conflicting directives which make him depressed, frustrated, and angry. These directives, which are *vital-functional*, lead him to close himself up to other more consonant and formative directives. However, other directives, such as the efforts of the other to encounter him, eventually lead

---

[14] See Adrian van Kaam, *Fundamental Formation*. Here van Kaam summarizes the essentials of human formation when he says: "In short we really experience our formation in dialogue with pre-, inter- and outer-formation powers and processes," 47.

[15] For an extensive discussion on these basic principles of Formation Science, confer Richard D. Byrne, *The Science of Foundational Human Formation and Its Relation to the Christian Formation Tradition* Ph.D. Diss., Duquesne University, Pittsburg, 1982, 166-204.

him to freely open himself up, and to cooperate with him, at least, on the vital-functional level. He is eventually able to cooperate with the other only through a series of acts which he makes. This is the **appraisal process** which consists of *apprehension*, *appraisal*, and *affirmation* of the directives in which his *mind* and *will* – his human faculties – are at work. At the end of the process, he *incarnates* the directives he is receiving through cooperating with the other who seeks to turn his face away from the wall. Even though this happens only on the vital-functional level, it marks the gradual opening up of himself to other increasingly formative directives.

Ongoing Formation (Transcendence-ability): The keyword in this principle is *transcendence*. This principle is grounded on the assumption that the foundational *life-form* is inherently capable of always transcending itself. It keeps moving from one *current form of life* towards a more *consonant* current form. This *transcendence-ability* of the human life-form is possible because of the **human spirit** which is the *distinctively* human centre of formation energy.

The principle of *ongoing formation*, or *transcendence-ability*, is made manifest in the subject of the formation event here in question. The very fact that he is depressed, frustrated, and angry about the current situation of life in which he finds himself, indicates this reality, the aspiration of his *human spirit*. He desires a better fulfilled life-form than his current one; and this makes him angry at others[16] whom he regards as obstacles to him on his way to the fulfillment of this goal. This therefore truly indicates that the subject is convinced of the possibility of a more fulfilled life-form than his

---

[16] The term "others" here refers to the world outside the subject, and includes the Mystery of Formation which he focally refers to as "God" when he says in soliloquy: "But God, why do you want me to die now?" See Proximate Background of the event.

current one, and which should be the one he should be aspiring, in life, to reach.

The Formation Field: In the SFHF, the principle of the *formation field* tries to respond to the question, "From wHence, comes form-directives?" The form directives in a formation event come from the person as a totality. This principle articulates the reality that every *facet* of the human being interacts with and influences the other in the event which the person experiences; and they do so on all the levels of presence of the person. Thus, Formation Science considers the individual to be his or her own ***formation field***. This field includes five interrelated and dynamically interacting *spheres* in four equally interrelated *dimensions*.

The five spheres of the formation field, also called poles, are the *pre-, intra-, inter-, situational,* and *mondial*. And the four interrelated dimensions in which they interact and thus manifest themselves are the *sociohistorical, vital, functional,* and *transcendent*. Furthermore, each of these poles is influenced by the *universal, common, segmental, sub-segmental,* and *personal ranges* of the individual. All of these constitute the formation field of the person, and formation takes place through the dynamic interaction of *form-directives* coming from each of them, whether the person is *focally* aware of it or not.

The *preformation sphere* of the subject in the formation event of this research is illustrated in his *biogenetic,* sociohistorical, and transcendent *preformational givens*. Besides the primordial organism with which he came into this world, he is also born into a society and a family in which his place, as first-born male with all the responsibilities usually recognized as attached to it, is reestablished. Thus, inability to live up to these responsibilities because of incapacitation by illness and imminent death at his age, is regarded in his world as failure in life. This can thus be the cause of his depression, frustration, and anger.

Secondly, survival from the malaria-hostile environment in childhood is regarded as a sign that he is to live to fulfill the role destined for him in life. Through the struggle with the unfriendly environment created by malaria, he also becomes particularly bonded with his parents.

And thirdly, the fact that the parents of the subject were new converts to Christianity, and that the father shortly after his conversion became successfully a catechist, but sooner had to quit for reasons of family responsibilities, all these nurtured his own sense of his responsibilities as first born. These preformational influences, and many others which may not be focally perceived, contribute to the dissonance of the subject in the event when such life-threatening illness has its grip on him. For in death, he will not be unable to have any of these goals of his unique life-form fulfilled.

In the *intraformation* sphere, the subject's depression, and especially his anger, blocked out the influence of directives from other spheres, and so prevent them from interacting with *facets* from his *intrasphere* – his **core**. *Infrafocally*, he is fixated in his conviction that death, which is to disrupt his life projects and so prevent him from realizing his and fulfilling his responsibilities, is imminent and there was nothing for him to open himself up to. Prefocally, however, the sudden feeling of the warm and comforting hand of the other on his shoulder is a vital directive which he receives and responds to by cooperating with it.

With regard to the *interformation* sphere, its interaction with the intrasphere of the subject is evident. Interformation takes place, at least to some extent, on the vital-functional level, when the subject receives and *appraises* the vital directive of the gentle, warm touch from an *interformative* pole – the other's warm hand. Also, it is through the vertical interformative transcendent directives from the life form of Aloysius that the subject eventually experiences the *shift* of his current life form of dissonance towards a more consonant current life form.

Preface

The influence of the *immediate situation formation sphere* is evident in practically all the dimensions in the event. It is sufficient to point out here the influence which the immediate situation of a Catholic hospital, with all its warm and delicate care, has on the subject, a young priest who is so critically ill and awaiting death. Being there among his kith and kin also has its influence on all the other spheres of his formation field, just as his actual situation of depression and anger has its own deformative directives which are conflictual to his formation.

Concerning the *mondial mediated formation sphere*, the era of independence which has gripped the entire African continent following the lead of the subject's own country fills many with much euphoria. Also, the end of the Ecumenical Council – Vatican II – with all the decisions it made in many areas of Christian and Church life is exciting. The subject perceives on all this a lot of challenges and responsibilities facing him who is nearly ordained. These challenges from the mediated world formation sphere also give directives to the subject. He is so deeply engaged in post-conciliar pastoral endeavours to implement the new directives of Vatican II. But again, soon he is not to be part anymore of these endeavours for which he was so enthusiastic.

Formation Tradition: Formation Tradition is the fourth basic principle in the SFHF. It holds that human formation does not take place in a void. Formation takes place within a particular configuration of faith and form traditions[17] to which the individual belongs in a unique way.

---

[17] Adrian van Kaam describes formation tradition as "a distinctive, overall pattern of receiving, expressing, and He has become angry giving form in one's life and world." And faith tradition as that "basic belief in some ultimate meaning and direction of their existence and the world at large" by which people live their life; see *Traditional Formation*, 2-3, and 27-8, respectively.

The subject of this formation event was brought up in the Catholic faith tradition to which his young parents had just converted and were baptised into only four years prior to his birth. As converts to a new faith tradition which was just beginning to establish itself among his people, their observance of it was very strict. Hence, the faith directives which he apprehended and appraised in the event came from his highly demanding, but sometimes misunderstood faith tradition in which he was brought up. For instance, his understanding of the goodness, justice, and power of God in his faith tradition bordered on the magical and the automatic. How can the God he has come to know in this way be anything else to him than one who rewards him for making all effort to be faithful to what he, God, has ordained? Hence, these misunderstood images of "his God" remained, at least, preconscious within him even after his higher theological studies and reflections in preparation for the priesthood. Thus, they influence him as faith directives in the way he perceives God in the event. He has become angry with such 'a god' and his representative and has lost faith in them both.

Ethnically, the subject who was born into one of the largest clans of his tribe, and as first male-born to his parents, perceives in the event the leadership role guaranteed him by his form tradition coming to an unfulfilled end. Hence, directives coming from this aspect of his form tradition influence his current life form in the event as he remembers these previously assured roles which he will no longer be able to play out.

With regard to culture, the subject grew up during a period when his traditional culture was at crossroads with Western culture in particular. Not only was his period of growing up the peak of the massive conversion of his people to the Catholic faith and religion, but it was also the period when Western-style political activity for independence was at its height. Also, as one of rather few people to have had a good dose of Western culture through its education system, the subject was further exposed to, and directed towards finding, fulfillment in his life through achievement. Hence, when it is evident that he will not see achieved the goals of his projects in life – perhaps more willfully crafted than transcendently inspired, anger became unleashed in him.

The economic formation tradition of his people, however, made him person-centred. As someone who hailed from an agrarian culture and society in which wealth of the individual is perceived in the corporate wealth of the extended family, economic values are reckoned in persons in his extended family. In this respect, the subject sees the satisfaction of his economic needs as consisting in the members of his rather very large extended family. This makes him able to apprehend and appraise divine love and blessings as people are regarded as divine gifts.

Politically, the subject came from a tradition in which party politics hardly existed. Traditional government was usually through consensus among the elders of the community. This directive infraconsciously formed in the subject a non-partisan political disposition. As such, general human development and the welfare of all form his attitude. With such disposition, he is able to apprehend and to respond appreciatively to the transcendent love which God offers to all people, even if only in different ways, as he eventually apprehends and appraises in the life of Aloysius.

Maintenance of Form Potency: This principle is based on the assumption that, in all forms, there is the inherent potency to be what they are. For the SFHF, this explains why every human life form has the capacity to influence events and things. The principle, therefore, maintains that there is inherent in the human preformation the potency to receive and donate form in events and things. That is to say, it is this power which can perceive meaning – sense of direction – in events and things, and so make possible the gradual and consonant unfolding of the human FLF. For inherent in the individual human life form is the impulse to feel good about oneself and the conviction that one can influence things and happenings. Hence, this principle is sometimes called the *principle of self-esteem*. In it the SFHF therefore upholds and articulates that every human form has the effective power to strive towards the fullness of this form[18]

This principle of maintenance of form potency is manifest in the subject of the event under research. At the beginning of the event the conflicted subject prefocally finds himself thrown into ***formation anxiety***.[19] He is so overwhelmed by his critical illness and the imminence of death that he feels powerless to give or receive form whatsoever. Nevertheless, a breakthrough moment arrives when this inherent potency, together with the innate desire to receive and also to give form manifests itself. As the subject apprehends and appraises directives from the life-story of Aloysius Gonzaga, this formation potency effectively comes alive as if from a deep sleep. Hence, the subject is able to receive form from the directives. He experiences the formative effectiveness of this inherent form potency after the event.

THE FORMATIVE ACTION PATTERN

For an event to be regarded as formative, there must be in its structural narrative a clear indication of a ***formative pattern of action*** in which is evident a movement of the person from one current form of life to another. This is what is apparent in the event which is being researched. There is observable in it a shift of the subject's current life form. In it can be traced *a movement **from** a current life form of functionalistic willfulness manifested in deep depression and anger in the situation of critical illness; **through** a profound experience of God's unique and unconditional love for him in his remembrance of Aloysius Gonzaga's willing and joyful acceptance of grave illness and death; **to** the experience of profound inner peace and serenity in repentance and gratitude as he willingly surrenders himself to God.* The

---

[18] See "Fulfillment Striving" and "Exertion Striving," Adrian van Kaam, *Human Formation* (New York: Crossroad, 1989), 80.

[19] Ibid., 195-6.

subject, energized by a series of new Inbreaking formation directives, which he apprehends, appraises, affirms, and applies, is able to make this new shift.

The Conflicted Subject:

At the outset of the event, the subject is depressed, frustrated, and angry because he is suffering from a critical illness. In this conflicted situation he does not apprehend the directives contained therein which are inviting him to a far more consonant healing than any biophysical healing can ever be. He sees only his imminent death, and the end that it will bring to his own willfully created projects in life.

Inbreaking of New Directives:

Constituted in this conflicted situation, the core of the subject which is encapsulated cannot at first be reached by any new directives. However, the other's persevering compassionate presence to him, and especially his gentle touch, gives a new directive which marks a breakthrough, however small. The subject responds by cooperating with the other, allowing him to turn him easily away from the wall. This prepares the ground for the major Inbreaking of new directives which are contained in the life-story of Aloysius. The lessening of the subject's resistance, fostered by the compassionate presence of the other, disposes him to apprehend, as he recollects the story, how Aloysius was not only to suffer in his illness, but was even very willing to die if that was God's will in his regard.

First appraisal of New Directives:

When his visitor asks him if he remembers the life-story of Aloysius Gonzaga, which he narrated to him and his friends when they were members of the Young Christian Crusaders many years ago, the subject's attention is quickly drawn to it. He begins to remember the attitude Aloysius had when he was terminally ill and knew that death was close at hand, and he appraises it. As he appraises Aloysius' disposition towards his illness and impending death, the subject feels within himself some peace taking possession of him.

Apprehension, Appraisal, and Affirmation of New Directives:

As the subject acknowledges this feeling of peace in himself, he begins to apprehend his own conflicted situation as being similar to that of Aloysius. Hence, he appraises his situation in the light of Aloysius' disposition in the face of terminal illness and imminent death. And he consequently affirms that God has manifested to him even more love than he seems to have done to Aloysius. Yet, the latter had such a joyful disposition in the face of his illness and impending death because of his belief that it was God's Will. In this affirmation of God's love for him, the subject prefocally recognises the formation which has taken place in him. This means that his life's direction has changed.

Incarnation of the New Directives:

In the event the subject expresses his immediate readiness to die if it is what God wills. This is the incarnation of the formation he has just experienced through these new directives. It is the concrete application of the directives from Aloysius' life story which he has just affirmed. He concretizes his return love for God who has always loved him, even though he may not cure him biophysically of his illness. It is after this that the subject feels profound peace and joy which is showed by his apparent serenity.

Preface

FORMULATION OF STRUCTURAL COFORMANTS

The following are tentative formulations, in common language, of the basic structural coformants of the formation event, containing all its idiosyncrasies:

First Coformant: The subject in his tense depression and anger will not turn to look at the Bishop when he comes in. He has locked out even the greetings of the Bishop, and so has ignored him. The subject wishes that the silence which now pervades the room would last forever. But his sudden feeling of the Bishop's warm and comforting hand on his shoulder makes the subject to respond to and willingly cooperate with the Bishop in his effort to turn to face him, in spite of the subject's initial desire to resist. Nevertheless, the subject still refuses to respond to what the Bishop is saying to him. However, he wonders whether the Bishop is aware of his intense feeling of anger against him.

Second Coformant: At the unexpected question whether the subject remembers the story of Aloysius Gonzaga, his mind instantaneously turns and focusses on the Saint's life-story. He becomes fully occupied with recollection of the details surrounding Aloysius' death: how he was happy to die, accepting his death as God's Will; and how he only greatly desired to celebrate the Eucharist, at least once before he would die. As the subject remembers these details of the story, he begins to feel some peace taking possession of him. The subject no longer follows what the Bishop is telling him. His mind is now entirely dwelling on the fate of Aloysius. He begins to feel that even if he would die now, he would still be more fortunate than Aloysius. He has celebrated the Eucharist practically daily for almost three years. The subject begins to feel that God has shown him more love than he has to Aloysius. So, he is also ready to die if it is what God wants.

Third Coformant: The subject feels his anger against God and the Bishop receding. At the same time, he also becomes aware of an increasing feeling of gratitude within himself. He feels a welling up of gratitude towards

God and also feels similarly grateful towards every one of the personnel of the hospital for the care they have been giving to him. The subject feels evermore strongly the immense peace which is within him. Meanwhile, he is sorry and feels ashamed for having been angry at the Bishop. But although he is still very weary, the subject presently feels himself full of peace and is serene.

The above are the coformants, unpurged of any idiosyncrasies of the formation event as narrated. Now, the following are formulations of the same basic structural coformants scientifically construed. They are the results of two years and more of dialogue with the principles and constructs of the Science of Foundational Human Formation, its auxiliary sciences, and the other interested researchers.

First Coformant: Subjects who are suffering life-threatening illness, and are vitally-functionally dissonant, may become self-encapsulated and may initially resist another's attempt at encounter. When subjects cooperate vitally and/or functionally with such attempts, they may nevertheless refuse to respond transcendently to the other's concerned presence.

Second Coformant: Subjects who are formatively questioned may remember a narrative from their own tradition. Aided by their formative imagination they may apprehend and appraise directives from the narrative. Applying such directives, subjects may begin to appreciatively abandon themselves to the Mystery of Formation and may become peaceful.

Third Coformant: As subjects transcend their vital-functional dissonance, they may now abandon themselves more fully to the Mystery, become grateful, and seek more reformation of their dissonant dispositions. While still feeling peaceful, they may also desire formative reconciliation with others.

Preface

DIALOGICAL ELUCIDATION

STATEMENT OF PURPOSE AND DIRECTION OF SCIENTIFIC RESEARCH:

From its Latin origin, *elucidation* means "bringing to light" so that what has been implied and obscure may be made clear. In this sense, dialogical elucidation is the primary methodological process of every research in Formation Science by means of which the task of bringing to light the underlying dynamics and directives in the coformants of an event is accomplished. It is thus the searchlight by means of which the scientifically articulated structural coformants of an event are broken down into remote foundational statements.

This discloses on a more general level the underlying dynamics of each coformant. These remote foundational statements are then further broken down into proximate units, each of which constitutes a formation (form) directive. Hypothetical as these directives may seem to be, in closer analysis they may reveal concrete directives at work in the coformants of the event. They are these concrete directives which, when appraised, affirmed, and applied, can consonantly ***form***, ***reform***, and even ***transform*** the human life form of the subject in the event.

This process elucidation is carried out in dialogue with the other interested researchers. When these remote and proximate statements are validated by the other interested researchers, they are transposed into the other three levels of *foundational human presence*: religious, Christian, and segmental. These remote and proximate dynamics are then put in dialogue with the relative constructs of the SFHF and its auxiliary sciences.

The purpose of elucidation in this research will be to disclose and to analyze both implicit and explicit dynamics present in the experience of a life-threatening illness. In so doing, it will also disclose the formability inherent in them. The proximate directives thus surfaced may facilitate consonant formation for others who find themselves in a similar life situation, as obstacles and facilitating conditions surfaced in the process may provide concrete ways of applying these directives.

RESEARCH FORMAT FOR DIVISIONS ONE TO THREE

The research project will employ the following format for each of its first three divisions:

a. The basic formation questions to be investigated are articulated in the context of the coformants in each of the four foundational levels of human presence.
b. The structural conformant in each of the four horizons is expressed in language appropriate to the particular horizon.
c. The appropriately stated coformant in each horizon is elucidated individually. This elucidation includes:

  i) An articulation of each remote foundational statement;
  ii) A description of each approximate dynamic to be investigated;
  iii) An application of relevant constructs and concepts from the SFHF;
  iv) A consultation with relevant auxiliary sources;
  v) A theoretical and integrational reflection;
  vi) Transitional statements connecting the research of preceding remote statements with those following; and
  vii) A summary of some obstacles to, and facilitating conditions for, consonant formation as disclosed by the research.

d. Research in each horizon in the division, and the divisions themselves, will be respectively linked to one another by transitional statements.

DIVISION ONE

THE ENCAPSULATED POWER OF GRAVE ILLNESS AND RESISTANCE TO TRULY FORMATIVE ENCOUNTER

INTRODUCTION

STATEMENT OF THE FORMATION PROBLEM TO BE INVESTIGATED

The basic problem to be investigated in this first division is the situation of self-encapsulation of a person faced with a life-threatening illness, and how interformation through encounter with another can foster the shift to a more consonant current life-form. In this situation of self-encapsulation, the person resists encounter with another. Such resistance to encounter maintains the person in isolation. Thus, it blocks prospective formative energy, which may emanate from the other and effectively influence the subject's intrasphere, and so lead him or her to formative healing.

The basic assumption here is that encounter with another fosters openness to transcendent directives which constitute the pathway to formative healing, even when the illness seems to be purely bio-physical. This is what the research in this first division will seek to disclose. Focal consciousness of this assumption is very important as it will nurture in individuals, who come into contact with persons in such situations, the compassion necessary to help them open their intrasphere to receive the form directives that these others may give them.

THE HORIZONS OF DIVISION ONE

The research in this division will investigate the dynamics of self-encapsulation simultaneously in the four horizons of foundational human presence, foundational religious presence, Christian presence, and segmental presence. It will focus on resistance to interformation through encounter on the four levels of human presence of which each will constitute a chapter in the division. It will seek in each horizon to disclose the dynamics of the dissonant dispositions which block the formative process of healing in the person through encounter with others. Hence, on the level of foundational human presence, the Division will study the dynamics of self-encapsulation, resistance to encounter, and inter-formation; and it will do the same, respectively, on the other three levels of human presence.

ARTICULATION OF COFORMANT ONE IN DIVISION ONE

In consultation with the SFHF and some other interested researchers, the first coformant of the original event is articulated in the four horizons as follows:

1. **Foundational human presence:** Subjects who are suffering life-threatening illness, and who are vitally-functionally dissonant, may become self-encapsulated, and may initially resist another's attempts at encounter. When subjects cooperate vitally, and/or functionally with such attempts, they may, nevertheless, refuse to respond transcendently to the other's concerned presence.

2. **Foundational Religious Presence:** Religious subjects who are suffering from grave illness, and who are depressed, may anxiously fear rejection by the Mystery for some wrong they believe they have committed and may initially isolate themselves from another and remain closed up to the other's attempts at encounter. These religious subjects may respond on the vital level to such attempts at encounter by the other but may remain closed up in their soul or mind to the other's compassionate presence.

Introduction

3. **Christian Presence:** Christians who are suffering from life-threatening illness and are afraid of death may feel alone and abandoned by Jesus Christ. They may initially refuse a loving attempt by a neighbour to communicate with them. Although they may respond vitally to such an attempt at communication, Christians may still refuse to open up to the graced communion offered by God through Christ in the love of others.

4. **Segmental Presence:** Christian ministers who are suffering from grave illness which threatens to bring to a sudden end their ministry may initially feel abandoned by God, and, in frustration and anger, cut themselves off from attempts by a revered superior to engage in dialogue with them. These Christian ministers may respond vitally to such attempts. But they may still refuse to enter fully into dialogue on the level of their heart through their spiritual faculties of mind and will.

CHAPTER ONE

SELF-ENCAPSULATION AND RESISTANCE TO ENCOUNTER IN SITUATIONS OF LIFE-THREATENING ILLNESS

INTRODUCTION

The object of investigation in this chapter is the first coformant of the experience of formative healing as is articulated on the level of foundational human presence stated thus below:

Subjects who are suffering life-threatening illness, and who are vitally-functionally dissonant, may become self-encapsulated, and may initially resist another's attempts at encounter. When subjects cooperate vitally, and/or functionally with such attempts, they may, nevertheless, refuse to respond transcendently to the other's concerned presence.

As stated in the outline of the methodology of the SFHF under *Dialogical Elucidation*,[1] the coformant will be divided into two remote foundational statements by which it is constituted. The dynamics of the directives inherent in the proximate statements drawn from these two foundational statements can then be further elucidated and substantiated. Thus, through exploring the directives energized by the dynamics in the

---

[1] See *Dialogical Elucidation* in the SFHF Methodology above. For more detailed information on the process of elucidation, see Adrian van Kaam.

proximate statements, we hope to elucidate and validate the directives coming from these foundational statements.

The chapter will, therefore, be divided into two parts. Each part will consist of a remote foundational statement. It is this remote foundational statement which will be elucidated by two proximate statements through a dialogical consultation[2] between the theory of the SFHF, and auxiliary sources.[3] The encounter of obstacles and facilitating conditions in this process of elucidation will demonstrate the practical application of the formation directives studied in the research.

PART ONE

INITIALLY RESISTING ENCOUNTER WITH ANOTHER

The following is the first remote foundational statement drawn from Coformant One:

Subjects who are vitally-functionally dissonant and self-encapsulated may initially resist another's attempts at encounter.

The research in this remote foundational statement will consist of two sections; **A** and **B**. While section **A** will focus on the dynamics of self-encapsulation which increase vital-functional dissonance in the subject,

---

[2] In the SFHF, the expression *dialogical consultation* is pervasive. It is generally used to refer to the conversation that is held between the theory of the SFHF, and other sources which are considered as auxiliary to the SFHF in this respect, regarding one aspect or other of a reality. Through such a conversation, more light is thrown on the truth of the aspect of the reality consideration. See Adrian van Kaam, Opus cit., 93

[3] Ibid., 21, 37, 54.

Chapter 1: Self-Encapsulation and Resistance

section **B** will study how this self-encapsulation expresses itself through the proximate dynamics of willful resistance against encounter with others.

Section A: Self-Encapsulation as Increasing Vital-Functional Dissonance

The proximate area of research here is the encapsulated current life form in which the subject is constituted in the original formation event. He had just started his third year of ministry as a young priest. Having grown up in a world in which two cultures had recently met one another, he was brought up to consider achievement and success in general, including good health and long life, as values and blessings that must be pursued in life for themselves.[4]

Thus, in his youthful enthusiasm as a priest-pastor, the subject approached his ministry with all the willful determination which he believed he needed to achieve, but to achieve it to perfection. When, therefore, he fell gravely ill in the very midst of his ministry and feared he was going to die, he became deeply depressed and angry at the sudden disruption of his life and all its projects. He perceived his willful determination for perfect achievement of success to be inadequate, and he is frustrated and powerless to do anything about it, in the face of the dissonant situation in which he found himself.

---

[4] The subject came from a faith tradition which was just still establishing itself in the society and culture into which he was born. Besides the fact that his faith tradition was still new and had not yet permeated the tradition of his ancestors on which he still heavily relied for his formation as a person, this itself was also at crossroads with Western form traditions; confer, "Formation Tradition," 24. See also Albert Kuuire, "The Christian Faith in the Dagaati Culture" (Licentiate thesis, Catholic University of Louvain, Belgium, 1972), 111-23.

From the SFHF: Formation Field in Dissonance

The Human formation Field: In the SFHF, the world in which the formation[5] of the individual human being takes place is at the very centre of the theory of human formation. Human formation is inconceivable outside of this world in which the individual person exists; it is influenced by and in turn influences the many other beings which are part of it. It is the world in which human life forms itself through receiving form directives as energy or forces destined for the formation of the person. And in turn the individual forms the world by donating appropriate form directives to the beings with which one conforms such a world.[6] Adrian van Kaam describes this process very succinctly in one sentence when he says: "Human life forms itself by its presence in the world."[7]

---

[5] The SFHF defines *formation* in the following terms: "Unconscious process of gradual realization of a characteristic form each living being, event, or thing is tending toward in accordance with its nature and conditions." See Adrian van Kaam, "Provisional Glossary of the Terminology of the Science of Foundational Formative Spirituality," *Studies in Formative Spirituality* (Studies) p1. No. 1. (February 1980): 137.

[6] Foundational human formation is achieved by the individual person through form donation and reception. Through dynamics generated by the other beings which coform the world of the individual, the person receives formation directives which enable him or her to grow towards human maturity. Essentially, this growth consists in the gradual consonant unfolding or emergence of the person's foundational life form. This growth of the person's FLF is empirically observable in the growth and change of the person from a previous current life form to a more consonant one. See Adrian van Kaam, *Fundamental Formation* (New York: Crossroad, 1989), 255-6; 265-6. For a more detail description of the coformants of the coformants of the human formation field, see Adrian van Kaam, *Fundamental Formation*, 57-92 and 145-65.

[7] Adrian van Kaam, *Fundamental Formation* (New York: Crossroad, 1989), 57.

Chapter 1: Self-Encapsulation and Resistance

The formation field of the individual therefore includes not only the cosmos in which an individual human being exists, but also the person's preformational, or pre-empirical, givenness; that means, his/her unique-communal FLF. It is this unique-communal FLF, born into a faith and form tradition, which becomes an individual person, both empirically and experientially. It is this faith and form tradition, embedded in the sociohistorical dimension of the person, that makes him or her to be one particular empirical individual and not another. Hence, it is the sociohistorical dimension of the original subject of the formation event, with his faith and form tradition as described above,[8] that made him the unique-communal individual person – with his then current life-form which became disclosed and apparent – at the time of his grave and life-threatening illness.

Speaking of foundational formation theory of personality in 1984, Adrian van Kaam asserted:

> Formation is the basic evolutionary process of the universe perceived as a formation energy field of constantly rising and falling forms. Each tends to realise, nuance, and maintain its own form potential in dialectical interaction with its formation field. Subhuman life forms give form in accordance with instinctual form directives. The human life form has to disclose and implement its own. In this process personality is born. Personality is a unique movement of disclosure and tentative implementation of receptive and creative form directives and their corresponding formation fields.[9]

---

[8] See *Formation Tradition*, 24, under *Dialogical Articulation of the Structural Coformants*.

[9] Adrian van Kaam, *Foundations for Personality Study* (Denville, New Jersey: Dimension Books, 1975), 330. This theory goes back to van Kaam's days with the "Faith Groups" in the Netherlands during the World War II.

At the centre of this individual's formation field is the Transcendent Mystery itself,[10] which is at the root of all formation. Thus, in such a field, the original subject of the formation event which is being researched has all the opportunities and possibilities to grow towards full human maturity. This process of growth is what the SFHF refers to as the unfolding of the individual person's foundational life form.[11] It is this foundational life form that van Kaam defines as

> The dynamic ground-form, foundational formation principle of human life. It inspires, directs, and moves the ongoing formation of human life. It moves human life to freely disclose and realise its ground-form. This realization gives rise to empirical forms of life that are at the same time

---

[10] Like all sciences, The SFHF has its own presuppositions upon which its theory and anthropology are grounded; See van Kaam, *Fundamental Formation*, 42-50. The SFHF assumes that, at the centre of all formation is the ***Mystery of All Formation*** which manifests itself in the cosmic, human, and transhuman epiphanies. This Transcendent Mystery is discussed at great length in the above-mentioned volume, 185-220.

[11] In his earlier writings such as *Foundations for Personality Study*, Adrian van Kaam simply refers to the *"foundational fir form"* as the "human life form." However, in his later writings, he refers to it more consistently as the ***foundational human life form***; the ***foundational life form***; or the **founding life form**; confer the volumes of **Formative Spirituality**. See also Adrian van Kaam and Susan Muto, **Formation Guide for Becoming Spiritually Mature** (Pittsburgh, PA: Epiphany Association, 1991), 41-65. This FLF is what van Kaam refers to when he is saying that it is "Dynamically speaking, our 'unique-communal life call;' See Adrian van Kaam: *Transcendent Formation*; Chap 10, under para. Heading, *Transcendent-Functional Character*.

communal and ***unique.*** If congenial and compatible, they express progressively the inherent formation principle and its direction.[12]

The foundational life form of the human being may, therefore, be described in other words as the preformational embodied spirit of each person. As Adrian van Kaam says, "The human life-form is essentially preformed as incarnated spirit." And as such, it preformed as fundamentally transcendent."[13]

In this light, the formation field of the human person is regarded as a world charged with virtually incalculable dynamics and energy. These dynamics come from the various empirical-experiential facets. But they also come from the person's preformation, especially from the Mystery of Formation which is at the centre of the person's formation field. Hence, the entirety of the field is recognised in its four basic dimensions,[14] and the five poles or spheres.[15]

---

[12] Adrian van Kaam: *Fundamental Formation*, 303. The foundational life form is a ***preempirical*** principle of life, otherwise called the "soul," not available to any empirical experience. It is not available to consciousness, i.e. to focal awareness, and so it is not available to any conscious appraisal. It is "the lasting effect of transcendent and biogenetic preformation." See also *Fundamental Formation*, 250.

[13] Ibid., 66.

[14] Confer van Kaam, *Fundamental Formation*, 260-1. These four basic dimensions of the human life form are also called horizons of human formation. They are the sociohistorical, vital, functional, and transcendent, as we already listed them, and explained them earlier. In his later presentations, van Kaam consistently listed them as *sociohistorical; vital; functional; functional-transcendent; transcendent;* and *transcendent-functional*. And in Christian articulation he added also as a dimension, the ***pneumatic-ecclesial.***

[15] Adrian van Kaam: Fundamental Formation, 248-50. Here he lists the five poles as follows: i) Pre-, ii) intra-, iii) inter-iv) extra- or outer, and v) situational. Sometimes the world itself is regarded as a pole.

Dissonance in the formation field: When these facets of the field are congenial, compatible, compassionate, and competent, they have the ability to harmoniously unfold the unique-communal foundational life form of the person.[16] However, when these directives lack any of these dispositions of consonance, they may be deformative and so create dissonance in the field. In discussing *"Living and Stilted Formative and Deformative Dispositions,"* van Kaam, after he had raised the crucial question regarding awareness of deformative dispositions we all develop and our readiness to reform them, went on to speak of the obstacles that dissonant dispositions may put on our way to formation. He says:

> For now, suffice it to say that fixation of formation energy in dissonant dispositions vitiates the open-endedness of human formation. Our formation powers may become encapsulated. If this happens, the dammed-up flow of form energy leads to exaltation of that disposition.[17]

Thus, instead of the FLF of the person being directed to a consonant unfolding of itself, the disharmony created in the formation-field-in-disarray occasions, at least, a relative loss of balance in the process of its continuous consonant self-disclosure. The formation powers have become encapsulated, and formation cannot occur until when the form energy is once again able to flow freely. This is what happened to the subject of our original formation event. He would again be able to receive consonant formation when reformation – even possibly transformation – of the

---

[16] Adrian van Kaam and Susan Muto; *Formation Guide for Becoming Spiritually Mature*, 141-6.

[17] Adrian van Kaam, *Human Formation* (New York: Crossroad, 1989), 9-10.

deformed directives coming from the dissonant (deformed) dispositions, will have taken place.[18]

From the SFHF: Self-Encapsulating Vital- Functional Dynamics

After the above discussion concerning the formation field, I would now like to consider, in the light of Formation Science, how the subject in the original formation event became encapsulated.

From what has been said above, it seems evident that self-encapsulation from the rest of the field results from the deformative, dissonant directives which have become dispositions in the subject's formation field. These directives are generated by the dynamics originating from the power centres, the coformants of the field. But what precisely may be identified in the field as the power centre from where directives may flow forth, eventually leading to the self-encapsulation of the subject?

Formation Science perceives self-encapsulation as the result of ambitious directives coming from the functional dimension of the human life form.[19] As van Kaam says with regard to absolutizing of *functional ambitions* and projects, "the functional dimension may cut itself off from transcendent aspirations, vital impulses, and sociohistorical pulsations."[20]

The functional dimension forms a bridge between the vital and the transcendent dimensions. However, since it is the transcendently pre-formed human life form which unfolds and emerges in the formation of a person, formation is not possible unless form directives from the functional

---

[18] For an elaborate discussion on the basic consonance-dissonance dynamics, see van Kaam: *Scientific Formation* (New York: Crossroad, 1987), 131-44. And for discussion on reformation and transformation, see *Human Formation*, 92-7; also 163-4.

[19] Adrian van Kaam, *Fundamental Formation*, 83-92, 293.

[20] Ibid., 87.

dimension, just as those from the sociohistorical,[21] and the vital dimensions, become submitted to the executive will of the transcendent dimension. As van Kaam consequently observes, "The forming presence of the human spirit is properly identified with the transcendent dimension of our life-form."[22]

Hence, functional ambitions which are closed off from transcendent illumination and influence may be regarded as directives which isolate a subject from the rest of the field.[23] With their organizing potency, these dynamics from the functional dimension can thus cut the subject off from the rest of the field and, in this way, create dissonance in it. This may isolate the subject, leaving it in self-encapsulation.

It is important to introduce here the notion of the **pride form** which may help us to understand still better the roots of the dynamics of self-encapsulation. Besides the FLF, the SFHF identifies in the human formation field another life-form which it calls the **pride-form**, or the **autarchic pride form**.[24] This pride form is the **counterfeit form of life**, and so is also called the **quasi-foundational life form**, "with its arrogant isolationist tendencies."[25]

As such, therefore, the pride form can be considered as one of the centres of power in the individual's formation field, able to hinder the free unfolding of the FLF. It does this by impeding the free flow of formation

---

[21] The dynamics of the sociohistorical dimension – pulsations – of the subject in the original event are clearly identifiable as have been described in his formation tradition; footnote #4 above.

[22] Adrian van Kaam, *Fundamental Formation*, 93.

[23] Ibid., 94.

[24] Ibid., 54, 188-90, 204.

[25] Ibid., 82. Van Kaam blames arrogant dispositions in us, which make us lose respect for the Formation Mystery, on the pride form. See *Human Formation*, 181.

energy from other parts of the field to the empirical core form of life.[26] Adrian van Kaam unequivocally asserts this when, after pointing out the erratic, deformative power of the pride form, says:

> Deformation manifests itself in a concentration, or imprisonment of formation powers and energies that become fixated in a proudly absolutized core or in a current or apparent life form. Our actual life-form will be similarly affected by such fixation.[27]

He considers this as the source of encapsulation of the foundational form energy, and he subsequently asserts that this is what "leads to exaltation, insubordination, and isolation of a partial, fixated formation manifestation. [And] it blocks the free flow of ongoing formation (energy)."[28]

The presence of the pride form in the subject of our original formation event, with its Insubordinate and exalting tendencies, is what is made manifest in his dissonant dispositions of anger and depression. With these vital-functional dispositions, the dynamics of which are unleashed in him by the life-threatening illness, the subject becomes self-encapsulated and so, imprisoned. Even then, it may be pointed out here that the pride form is able to bring about this self-encapsulation of the subject, thanks to his formation tradition which nurtured in him some insubordination and self-exaltation.[29] Such a disposition could also be called self-sufficiency, especially in common language.

So far, we have discussed, in the light of Formation Science, the nature of the human formation field in which the subject may be said to have

---

[26] See Adrian van Kaam, *Fundamental Formation*, 253. For concise descripttions of *the integrating forms of life*, confer 253-61.

[27] Ibid., 266.

[28] Ibid.

[29] See Preface, 24, *Formation Tradition* of the subject.

experienced his formation event. We have also discussed in what way this field may become dissonant, and how he, in his intra-sphere, may be encapsulated and so become isolated from the rest of it. With these insights from the SFHF, we may now turn to other scientists who have also explored in one way or the other, concepts which are analogous to those of the SFHF which we have explored here above. We shall examine Martin Heidegger's concept of '*Dasein*,' most particularly his concept of consciousness in its relation to the rest of reality which together constitute the totality in which a human being is, and exists. We shall also examine the source of the dynamics for the striving for perfection of a person in the '*Individual Psychology*' of Alfred Adler. The former is a philosopher while the latter is a psychologist.

Martin Heidegger: Consciousness in the context of Dasein's "Historicality"

The comprehensive philosophical work of Martin Heidegger, *Being and Time*,[30] was intended to provide an effective corrective to Husserl's concept of the human being as consciousness. Donald Polkinghorne points out: "Husserl had investigated consciousness as a pure '*region*' that could be considered in a way essentially separated from the 'facts' of the empirical realm."[31] In **Being and Time**, Heidegger understands and presents *consciousness*, not as some reality separated from the world, but rather as a lived formation of human existence in history.

Heidegger's corrective to Husserl's concept of human *consciousness* thus makes one thing particularly evident. His understanding that *consciousness*

---

[30] Martin Heidegger, ***Being and Time***, trans. and ed., John Macquarie and Edward Robinson (San Francisco: Harper & Row, 1962).

[31] Donald Polkinghorne, *Methodology for the Human Sciences* (Albany: State University of New York Press, 1983), 205.

Chapter 1: Self-Encapsulation and Resistance

is a lived formation of human existence in history strongly and clearly supports Formation Science's concept of tradition. In his discussion of temporality as a condition of *Dasein,* which it uses to manifest itself, Heidegger says:

> "Historicality" stands for the state of Being that is constitutive for Dasein's 'historizing' as such; Only on the basis of such 'historizing' is anything like 'world-history' possible or can anything belong historically to world-history. In its factical Being, any Dasein is as it already was. It is its past, whether explicitly or not.[32]

Consciousness, therefore, as a lived formation of human existence, and not some separate reality in itself, is the unfolding of human historicity. It is through such a process that the human being maintains and hands down (Latin: *trado, tradere; traditio, traditionis*) its existence from one generation to another.

Therefore, in his concept of relationship between human consciousness and the rest of the larger world in which it exists, Heidegger establishes a bridge over the chasm which Husserl tried to create in separating human consciousness from the rest of its world as if they were two distinct realities. By establishing this bridge, Heidegger thus undergirds philosophically the historicity, and so, the continuity, or "sameness" of human existence in tradition.

---

[32] Martin Heidegger; *Being and Time,* 41. Heidegger speaks of the ontological priority of *Dasein* as an entity over every other entity: "'Hermeneutic' as an interpretation of Dasein's Being, has a third and specific sense of an analytic of the existentiality of existence." See 62.

This insight of Heidegger's concept of "*Dasein*" and in particular his understanding of *consciousness* as lived formation of the *existent being*,[33] therefore vindicates Formation Science's principle of formation tradition. It helps us to perceive the subject of our original formation event as belonging to human existence through "*Historicality*." For in this light, his unique-communal individuality can be acknowledged as originating from a human tradition, which with its accretions has made him this particular individual person. Hence, as a unique individual, he stands at the very epic of the pyramid of human formation tradition to which he belongs, as formation theory would regard him.[34]

In the above rather brief discussion, we have observed the *corrective* which Heidegger provided for his friend Husserl's concept human consciousness as separate reality from the rest of the world in which it exists. We have remarked how he bridged the chasm between consciousness and the rest of the world which Husserl regarded as its contents. In doing this, Heidegger thus presents consciousness as a lived formation of human existence in history, and so, demonstrates the indispensable role of tradition in all of human existence in a person's world. In the paragraphs following, we will examine, in Alfred Adler's *Individual Psychology*, how the particular individual at the very summit of his or her human formation tradition pyramid may seek superiority in the process of his or her human formation.

---

[33] Ibid, 78-90. For an analogical view of existent being in the world, see William A. Luijpen and Henry J. Koren; **A First Introduction to Existential Phenomenology** (Pittsburgh, PA: Duquesne University Press, 1987), especially 9-52.

[34] Adrian van Kaam; Traditional Formation, (N.Y.: Crossroad, 1992), 187. Here van Kaam discusses the formation of the individual's pyramid of form traditions.

Chapter 1: Self-Encapsulation and Resistance

<u>Alfred Adler</u>: The Individual's striving for Superiority

We have earlier observed in this research how certain goals and expectations were put on our subject of the original formation event by tradition. Throughout his years of growing and maturing, the subject learned, worked, and lived his life in view of eventually fulfilling all those goals which tradition had set for him. He was striving to fulfill them to the best of his abilities.

It is when the subject perceived that he was not going to see the fulfillment of these goals – due to a life-threatening illness and thus subsequent impending death – that he became angry and depressed, and so became conflicted. In the face of this imminent death, he was convinced that he would never see the fulfillment of the goals to which he aspired so much with anticipation in his life. Hence, he considered that there was no more meaning to his striving for fulfillment, and for success and superiority in his life.

These aspirations of the subject to the fulfillment and his self-exertion for the achievement of his goals seem to be what Alfred Adler describes analogously in his psychology of the individual. In ***Superiority and Social Interest***, Adler endeavours to demonstrate that 'Striving for Superiority' is the goal of every human being. As one of the basic assumptions of his psychology of the individual, Adler says:

Individual Psychology assumes further the individual's striving for success in the solution of his problems, this striving being anchored in the very structure of life. But the judgement [sic] of what constitutes success is again left to the opinion of the individual.[35]

---

[35] Alfred Adler; Superiority and Social Interest, ed., Heinz L. Ansbacher and Rowen R Ansbacher (Evanston, Illinois: Northwestern University Press, 1964), 24.

In an earlier assumption, he asserts:

> Individual Psychology finds its firm, rational field of activity in the manner in which the always unique individual behaves towards the changing problems of life. Decisive for this behavior is the individual's opinion of himself and of the environment with which he has to cope.[36]

These two presuppositions of Adler point out the nature of, and the reason for, the individual's striving for superiority as a subject. Elsewhere, after asserting that striving for superiority is an intrinsic necessity of life parallel to physical growth, Adler expresses his conviction in this regard thus:

> The history of the human race points in the same direction. Willing, thinking, talking, seeking after rest and pleasure, learning, understanding, working and loving, all betoken the essence of this eternal melody. From this network which in the last analysis is simply given with the *man-cosmos relationship*, no one may hope to escape.[37]

These assumptions and argument of Adler cogently summarize his basic concept and anthropology of the *existent being*.

An Integrative Reflection on the Above Discussions

In our original formation event, the heart or core of the subject who is suffering from a life-threatening illness is encapsulated in himself. As a result, he is isolated from the rest of the world of which he himself is part

---

[36] Ibid.

[37] Alfred Adler, *the Individual Psychology of Alfred Adler*, ed., Heinz L. Ansbacher and Rowena R. Ansbacher (New York: Basic Books Inc., 1956), 103.

Chapter 1: Self-Encapsulation and Resistance

and parcel. However, in his illness which he is convinced is terminal, this world which is his own, is neither favorable to, nor is capable of fostering, his recovery in a formative way.

Such a world of which the subject is part and parcel but in which he is thus encapsulated is what the Science of Foundational Human Formation calls his field of formation. As Adrian van Kaam so clearly describes in formation theory:

> Human life forms itself by its presence in the world. It gives form to the world and receives form from it. This forming presence does not interact with the world as such in its totality. Rather, the world contains certain opportunities for human formation. These opportunities correspond with the unique structure of the human life-form and of its form potencies. Taken together, *they present us with the possibility of constituting a human formation field.* When people give form to that field, deepening, expanding and enhancing it, they give and receive form in their unfolding life.[38]

As the SFHF has indicated, this field, which can also be called the world of the individual, becomes dissonant when formation energy does not flow freely to all of its parts.[39] It is such fixation of formation energy in a particular dimension and or a power which may thus encapsulate the subject in the primary formation event.

Heidegger's concept of consciousness as a lived formation of human existence in history, not being a separate reality from the rest of the world in which it exists, may be considered a perfect analogy to Formation Science's concept of the human formation field. In such a concept,

---

[38] Adrian van Kaam, *Fundamental Formation*, 57. See also Foundational Human Formation Theory's definition of "formation," 40.

[39] See 'dissonance' in the formation field, 40.and ff.

Heidegger perceives the world and the consciousness of the individual human being as one reality with different characteristics. In his view, consciousness of the subject as a pure "region" and the rest of the empirical dimension are not essentially separated. He perceives consciousness and its so-called contents, according to Husserl, as ways of Being-in-the-world, in which each is a basic characteristic of *Dasein*. This is evident in the following argument which he makes: "It would be unintelligible for Being-in-the-world to remain totally veiled from view, especially since *Dasein* has at its disposal an understanding of its own Being, no matter how indefinitely this understanding may function."[40]

So, Heidegger's concept of the relationship between consciousness and the rest of the human reality confirms the relationship which Formation Science perceives among the poles and the dimensions in its concept of the formation field. If in the subject of our original formation event the bridge was maintained between his core form of life and the rest of his formation field, formation energy would have continued to flow to all its parts, thereby assuring the subject formative healing in spite of the terminal nature of his biophysical illness. However, the chasm, we may say, that separated the different spheres or poles, and the other power-centres of the subject's formation field, made it impossible for form directives to be effectively given and received by in view of his consonant formation. Hence, the subject, being in such a dissonant field, became conflicted.

Also in the light of the assertions made by Adler as quoted above, one comes to the fair conclusion that his concept of the individual striving for superiority analogously supports Formation Science's concept of "formative striving for fulfillment and exertion." However, in Formation Science, van Kaam makes a clear distinction between fulfillment striving and exertion striving. As he observes, the former "refers to our innate predisposition to

---

[40] Martin Heidegger, *Being and Time*, 86.

fulfill our receptive needs," while "striving for exertion refers to our innate predisposition to exert our potencies of form donation."[41]

Although Adler's later assumption of social interest as an innate need of all human helps mellow down his earlier rather absolute assumptions about the individual, his concept of the nature of personality still makes the individual master, and not victim, of his fate.[42] This confirms again that transcendent predisposition, which van Kaam calls, in Formation Science, the *transcendent formation freedom* in the individual person.[43]

But while Formation Science distinguishes two kinds of formative strivings in the individual, Adler, as we have remarked, simply observes this innate disposition as *striving for superiority*. He has not made the fine, and yet profound, distinction that exists between the subject's innate proclivity to fulfill his goals in life and his innate desire to exert his powers which enable him to donate form to the world in which his FLF may consonantly unfold, as the SFHF has done.

If Adler asserted only purely and simply the individual's striving for superiority and perfection, this may be because of his conviction. As he says: "we all wish to overcome difficulties. We all strive to reach a goal by the attainment of which we shall feel strong, superior, and complete."[44] As he also asserts in one of his assumptions to the merit of Individual Psychology: "It finds its firm, rational *field* of activity in the manner in which the always unique individual behaves towards the changing problems of life."[45] For Adler, the individual seems to exist in a field which serves as a separate space in which he or she strives for this perfection. If this is so, the analogous use

---

[41] Adrian van Kaam; *Human Formation*, 80.

[42] Alfred Adler; *Superiority and Social Interest*, 15.

[43] Adrian van Kaam, *Fundamental Formation*, 213-6

[44] Alfred Adler, *Individual Psychology of Alfred Adler*, 104.

[45] Alfred Adler; Superiority and Social Interest, 24. The emphasis is mine.

of the concept field by Adler, when considered in relation to the concept of the formation *field* in the SFHF, becomes even more evident.

Indeed, Adler's insistence on the individual reaching this lofty goal, all by himself or herself, narrows down the reality of this field most significantly. For, if it is the uniqueness alone of the individual person that is to be considered in the striving for success and perfection, then the field in which such a subject grows towards this goal becomes essentially limited. This would amount to isolation of the self.[46] Hence, self-encapsulation, as the self – the person – in such a field will be considered alone, infrafocally or prefocally,[47] ignoring all other centres of influence actually in its field, in its existence. Thus, given such a field, the subject of our original formation event would be left without any hope of formative healing. For, he would lack that innate potency that would give him the consonant directives he would need to reform his dispositions and to receive formative healing.

It may be true that the subject of our initial formation event had become debilitated in his striving for the fulfillment of his goals, for the reason that his formation field had become dissonant, and so formation energy could no longer move freely throughout his entire field. However, according to Formation Science theory, he, nevertheless, remained master of his own destiny. He had still the ability in his ongoing formation to transcend himself in whatever current life form he has. As the principle of *maintenance of form potency* upholds, the subject, thanks to his preformed

---

[46] John Donne; *No Man is an Island*, ed. Keith Fallon (Los Angeles: Stanyan Books, 1970). This title is selected from the writings of John Donne. See also Thomas Merton, *No Man is an Island* (New York: Harcourt Brace Jovanovich, 1978).

[47] For a fully treatment of the five horizons of the human consciousness, see Adrian van Kaam, Fundamental Formation (opus cit.), 262 – 3.

human life form, still had the inherent capacity and also the desire to receive and give form.[48]

In this integrative reflection on the above findings of our research thus far, two realities in particular have become quite evident. First, for the making of a truly formative appraisal of the reality of self-encapsulation, a *whole-field-thinking* is necessary. And, secondly, for a correct identification of the sources of formation energy, and the subsequent appraisal of the formability of the directives they give, as full and exploration of the dimensions and spheres of the subject's formation field as possible needs to be carried out.[49] No growth towards perfection, no human formation is possible unless formative directives from the lower dimensions of the field are in consonance with the Transcendent Functional Will. For growth towards perfection and striving for true fulfillment as consonant human formation denotes transcendence.[50]

The research in Section A explored the formation field and studied how vital-functional dissonance engulfs the field and so, leads the subject of the primary event to self-encapsulation and increasing dissonance. In Section B

---

[48] Adrian van Kaam, *Human Formation*, 80.

[49] Adrian van Kaam; Human Formation (opus cit.), 80-108. Here van Kaam discusses at some length the appraisal of the human formative strivings for fulfillment and exertion. In contrast, see also *The Individual Psychology of Adler*, 101-25, for more comprehensive understanding of Adler's concept of *striving for superiority*.

[50] Adrian van Kaam defines transcendence as, "The process of 'going beyond' a current life form that has been congenial and congruent in a specific life period or situation. The process implies the search for a partially or totally new current life form that is at the same time congruent and compatible with the changed life period or situation and congenial with the emergent uniqueness of the personality insofar as this uniqueness increasingly manifests itself during the journey from current life form to current life form." See Adrian van Kaam, 'Provisional Glossary,' Studies 1 (February 1980), 149.

we will focus on the willful resistance which the subject in the original formation event manifested. We shall investigate how this self-encapsulation expresses itself in willful resistance. We shall also observe how willful resistance in turn may maintain self-encapsulation and block interformative encounter with others.

SECTION B: WILLFULLY RESISTING ENCOUNTER; A RESULT OF SELF-ENCAPSULATION

In the original formation event, the subject initially refuses to enter into conversation, and so into relationship with other persons. He would not respond even to the greetings of someone who, throughout his past life, meant so much to him. He resisted having anything to do with anybody. And he would not willingly respond to any attempts to meaningfully relate to him in his actual life form. Encapsulated within himself and isolated as he was in his intrasphere from others, the subject manifestly resisted encounter and closed himself up to the possibility of interformation which might lead him to formative healing.

<u>From the SFHF</u>: Willful Resistance and Human Encounter

Willful Resistance: For the consonant unfolding of the FLF, and therefore, for the formative growth of a person, Formation Science lists three dispositions[51] of the heart as necessary. The disposition of openness is one of these dispositions for such a consonant unfolding and disclosure of the FLF in the unique-communal formation field of the individual, Adrian van

---

[51] The SFHF defines *formation disposition* as "a distinctive, relatively lasting, human formation direction." See Adrian van Kaam, *Human Formation* (New York: Crossroad, 1989), 1.

Chapter 1: Self-Encapsulation and Resistance

Kaam cogently justifies this necessary role of this disposition in describing it thus:

> It is a disposition that enables us to be as open as we can be to the formative and deformative meanings of our formation field. We can refuse to open our minds and hearts to these meanings and the feelings they engender. We can *close ourselves off* from their message and *resist* their warnings, inspirations, and subtle evocations. We can do so either unwittingly or *by willful closure.* Such a proud, deformative stance isolates us from the Mystery and makes it impossible for us to grow in consonance.[52]

One cause of such disclosure of our minds and hearts, and of refusing to open them to the formative as well as deformative meanings of our formation field, is the ***pride form***. Van Kaam explains it thus: "This quasi-foundational form of life, operative in everyone since the Fall, tends to isolate us from others, from the cosmos, [and] from the Formation Mystery itself."[53]

It is this isolation from everybody and everything else, including the Mystery itself, which truly defines our refusal to cultivate and foster the disposition of openness. So isolated, we cut ourselves off from all influences which may otherwise give us consonant directives for our growth, unfolding of our FLF, and so, formation. This refusal to disclose ourselves implies *resistance*[54] to the formative directives – "warnings, inspirations, and subtle

---

[52] Adrian van Kaam, *Formation of the Human Heart* (New York: Crossroad, 1991), 24 (emphases are mine). The other two dispositions for consonant living are appreciation, and detachment. See idem, 22.

[53] Ibid., 24.

[54] Adrian van Kaam defines 'resistance-resonance recognition' as "The acute awareness of one's spontaneous repulsion or attraction – rightly or wrongly – when

evocations" – as van Kaam has indicated. Resistance may be either an unwitting, or a willful, Hence, functional, closure of oneself.

There can be a positive, i.e. formative understanding of the term '*resistance.*' When, for instance, the dynamics of resistance offer formative directives for the formation of the disposition of firmness without which consonant life formation is not possible, resistance may be regarded as positive and formative. Adrian van Kaam gives a beautiful analogy of this positive understanding of the dynamics of resistance in the formation of the course of a river through mountain slopes and river banks. It is the sturdy, resistant rocks which help to make the formation of the river course possible. As he says, "Without these resistances the river would not be able to give form to the rushing water. It is exactly the interchange between river and resistance that grants this body of water its unique form, beauty, and disciplined power."[55]

This formative dynamics of resistance is what is understood when in Formation Science, van Kaam speaks of resistance as necessary for the formation of the disposition of firmness.[56] As he asserts, "The forming mystery manifests itself in the resistances of everyday life that invite us to rise up in nobility and strength."[57]

However, when resistance to openness of self is a refusal to disclose oneself to the manifestations of the forming mystery itself, then it is dissonant and deformative. Such a resistance may be functionally willful. In an organized and managing manner, it ambitiously refuses to open the core

---

exposed to potential formation directives." See "Glossary," *Studies* 1 (February 1980), 150. In the dynamics of resistance is, therefore, a certain spontaneous repulsion of potential formation directives.

[55] Adrian van Kaam, *Formation of the Human Heart* (opus cit. 53).
[56] Ibid., 53-66.
[57] Ibid., 53.

Chapter 1: Self-Encapsulation and Resistance

form[58] of the person to transcendent formative directives which could lead to the consonant unfolding of the unique-communal founding life call of the person towards its ultimate end. Such functional, willful resistance betrays the integrative potency of the functional dimension, whose role is to use the functional will to build a bridge between the lower dimensions and the transcendent. Such resistance is particularly deformative when it is manifestly influenced by the *pride form* which walls off consonant directives from the transcendent and prevents them from reaching the core form of life.

Human Encounter: The insights from the above discussion on willful resistance make evident the dynamics which create and also maintain self-encapsulation. As resistance to the core disposition of openness to manifestations of the forming mystery prevents formative directives from reaching the core form of life of the person, it makes the core form a prisoner. The core form of life being thus walled-off, such isolation in turn intensifies willful resistance. Hence, a vicious circle is created in which willful resistance and self-encapsulation keep re-enforcing one another. This makes impossible the consonant unfolding of the FLF. For it is the core form, or heart, which, as Formation Science asserts, "Incarnates in its palpable movement the tendencies of the foundational life form as understood or misunderstood at any given moment of life."[59]

In encapsulating and maintaining in isolation the core form of life from the other centres of formation dynamics, willful resistance thus also cuts off

---

[58] The core form or heart, as it is sometimes called, is one of the four empirical integrating human life forms Formation Science, within the context of its Christian articulation, defines it as, "The integrative centre of all global formative effects which tend to give a basic concrete form to the soul image of Christ, under the guidance of the Holy Spirit." See Adrian van Kaam, "Glossary," *Studies* 1 (February 1980):144. See also *Fundamental Formation*, 299.

[59] Adrian van Kaam, "Glossary," *Studies* 1 (February 1980), 145.

the encapsulated subject from meaningful and formative relationship with others. It is in this manner that the core form of the person is prevented from being influenced by others. Through such meaningful relationship, form could eventually be given to the person and made manifest in his current life form.

This meaningful contact between the subject and others is what the SFHF calls *human encounter*. Such encounter, which is distinguished from **fusion**, is an essentially interformative relationship.[60] While van Kaam explains fusion as a complete "identification between the intra- and the interspheres in our formation field,"[61] he defines very clearly the concept of encounter when he says: "The formation theory of personality applies the term 'encounter' primarily to interformative human relationship, as it does for the term *interformation*."[62] This is the encounter which the subject of the primary event resisted in his dissonance of self-encapsulation.

In the above analysis, the SFHF discloses the manner in which self-encapsulation expresses itself in the dynamics of willful resistance to encounter with others. In doing so, it offers some clear insights into the current life form of the subject of the primary event in dissonance. We shall

---

[60] Adrian van Kaam, *Formation of the Heart*, 128-30. Here van Kaam makes a very clear distinction between *human encounter* and *fusion*, and he asserts that the disposition of privacy is meant to foster encounter.

[61] Ibid., 128.

[62] See "Glossary," *Studies* IV (Nov. 1983); 421. Van Kaam goes on to indicate a secondary application of the term encounter: "Secondarily, however, it applies to certain formationally significant interactions with things." Interformation, as he says, "refers to the formative influences of people on one another" (See *Fundamental formation*, 249. Interformative directives come from the intersphere of the field and can be vertical or horizontal. We receive vertical formation through formation tradition directives from people who lived in the past. We continue to encounter them, and they influence us formatively through the directives they left behind in tradition. See *Traditional Formation*, 14-5.

now further explore the concepts willful resistance and human encounter in sources that the SFHF may use as auxiliaries to it. For the concept of ***resistance,*** we will turn to the psychologist, Roy Schafer; while for the meaning of ***encounter*** we will turn to the philosophers William A. Luijpen and Henry J. Koren. Their discussions of these concepts in the context of universal human presence offer an expanded understanding of them.

Roy Schafer: Resisting and Empathizing

Resistance to the analyst's empathy is considered to be one of the most powerful disturbers in the process of psychoanalysis. In order that an analysand may be seen to progress towards an amelioration in his or her currently unhealthy situation, a structural change has to occur.[63] Schafer asserts: "Structural change is shown by obvious differences in the way analysands conduct themselves in the analytic relationship as well as in other relationships."[64] He goes on to describe how this structural change is manifested in the patient or analysand:

In particular, it is shown by the way they generate independently new kinds of life situations and new ways of understanding these situations, and their doing so in ways that are better for them (in whatever adaptive sense the word "better" may be applied in each instance). This change is possible only if there has occurred a significant reduction in resistant

---

[63] Roy Schafer, *The Analytic Attitude* (Basic Books, Inc.: Division of Harper & Collins, 1983), 158-60. Here Schafer defines change of structure in his discussion of character analysis as a "change in the pattern of ego functions." He goes on to say, "This change includes lasting modification of preferred defensive measures, the direction being from more to less archaic and ego-limiting defense," 158.

[64] Ibid., 66.

activity, for then the self-imposed and self-maintained limitations on how a life is to be lived will have been fundamentally altered.[65]

This means that a structural change of the patient, from the clinically unhealthy situation to an ameliorated one, is necessary for a return towards full health. This is the truly overall goal of psychoanalysis. The maintenance of the *Status quo* of the patient, however, is manifested in the analysand's relationship with the analyst. This relationship is marked by the analysand's *resistance* to the analyst's ready-attitude to empathize. It is the form of resistance which Freud calls *transference*.[66]

Schafer sees in this concept of resistance "a force of opposition to the analyst's explanatory or interpretive aims," even though he accepts that there are other ways of understanding it."[67] Later, in discussing what he terms "the problematic Concept of Resistance,'" for example, he repeats this oppositional designation of the concept of resisting,[68] as he prefers to call it,

---

[65] Ibid., 66

[66] Ibid., 67. Sigmund Freud himself, discussing what he regards as true psychoanalysis, says: "The theory of psycho-analysis is an attempt to account for the facts of transference and resistance. Any line of investigation which recognizes these facts and takes them as the starting point of its work has a right to call itself psycho-analysis." See Sigmund Freud, 'On the History of Psycho-analytic Movement,' in *Collected Papers*, Vol 1 ed., James Strachey (New York: Basic Books, 1959), 287. See also John W. Kloepfer, **The Art of Formative Questioning: A Way to Foster Self-Disclosure**, Ph.D. Diss., Duquesne University. 1990 (Ann Abor: MI 1990), 40-2. See also R.R. Greenson, *The Technique and Practice of Psychoanalysis* (New York: International Universities Press, 1967).

[67] Roy Schafer, *The Analytic Attitude*, 67. See also 162-82 for his various conceptual understandings of resistance.

[68] Schafer regards resisting as conceptually problematic for the reason that, 'It designates opposition to the plan, consciously agreed upon, to collaborate fully and

Chapter 1: Self-Encapsulation and Resistance

using what he calls 'action language.' However, he goes on to observe the difference between this understanding as a form of resistance and Freud's transference which is also considered as a form of resistance.

There may, indeed, be varied and different shades of understanding the concept of resistance. However, most of these resistances are what Freud regarded in individual cases as "resistance against the uncovering of resistances."[69] All these seemingly varying concepts of resistance are conceived as such within the psychoanalytic context. As Schafer admits: "The work of analyzing resisting has continued to be viewed as the analysis of activity that is solely oppositional in nature; its where's, why's, how's and since when's. In this way, resisting has been isolated from the rest of the analytic material."[70]

It is through investigating all these shades of understanding *resistance* that "the analysis of the ego" may be achieved. For as Schafer once again intuits, "today we might want to say that much of 'the analysis of the ego' is accomplished around the study of resisting."[71] It seems to be in this light that Freud perceived his newly introduced adversarial term, *resistance*, when, among other descriptions of it, he referred to it saying: "Whatever interrupts the process of analytic work is a resistance."[72]

If Schafer's understanding of resistance, as a Freudian, boils down to all oppositional activities which interrupt the progress of the analytic work, and, therefore, of "the amelioration of the suffering and functional impair-

---

freely with the analyst in order to get to the bottom of things and thereby effect substantial amelioration of suffering and functional impairment." Opus cit., 164.

[69] Sigmund Freud, *Analysis Terminable and Interminable* (London: Hogarth Press, 1964), 216-53.

[70] Roy Schafer, Opus cit., 166.

[71] Ibid., 166.

[72] Sigmund Freud, *Interpretation of Dreams* (London: Hogarth Press, 1900), 517.

ment" of any patient in analysis, then resistance is indeed a central issue. Such a pervasive sense of resistance helps us to understand the sorry situation in which human encounter faces it, and the subject of our primary formation event seems to be constituted.

This discussion on resistance leads us to seek to understand more the nature of human encounter. What precisely is human encounter? William A. Luijpen and Henry J. Koren have extensively discussed this concept in what they call the ***phenomenology of intersubjectivity***. There they offer valuable insights to the understanding of human encounter. Hence, we now turn to them for more enlightenment in this regard.

W.A. Luijpen & H.J. Koren: Phenomenology of Intersubjectivity

In their extensive treatise on intersubjectivity as an existential-phenomenological reality[73] in the fourth chapter of their book *A First Introduction to Existential Phenomenology*, William A. Luijpen and Henry J. Koren discuss to some depths what could be regarded as the pivot of their philosophy. In this chapter entitled '*Phenomenology of Intersubjectivity*,' Luijpen and Koren make it abundantly clear that it is within inter-subjectivity that the human being is '*existence*'[74] and is thus capable of

---

[73] William A. Luijpen and Henry J. Koren define what they call the primitive fact of *existential phenomenology* as, "Existence or intentionality, conceived as the openness of the subject to *everything* which is not the subject itself." By this they exclude, as they say, "forms of existential-phenomenological thinking in which *existence* is exclusively understood as the unity of reciprocal implication of subject and world." See, *A First Introduction to Existential Phenomenology* (Pittsburgh: Duquesne University Press, 1969), 51.

[74] Ibid., 145-202. In *Existential Phenomenology*, Luijpen and Koren maintain the finest sense of the human being as '*existence*'. As they hold, "With spiritualism, [existential phenomenology] affirms that man is a subject; with materialism, it affirms that man is whatever he is only on the basis of matter. The subject who man

Chapter 1: Self-Encapsulation and Resistance

acquiring knowledge.[75] And as an intentionality, 'existence is involved in the world in which it is a free being.[76] This is so since an individual, completely encapsulated existent subject would be, indeed, a contradiction at best, and an impossibility of a miserable lonely existence at worst. After all, it is only within the individual human being's relationship as an existent subject with other existences that such an individual can speak of an "**I**". This may explain why Luijpen and Koren can speak of existence as *"co-existence;"* and, therefore, to exist would mean to co-exist.[77]

Such existence implies that the subjectivity of the human being is not isolated from the body, as the Cartesian divorce of subject and body makes it. It is an *openness* to *encounter*[78] – to enter into dialogue – with the other beings with whom the existent-subject co-exists. Luijpen and Koren are therefore right when they maintain that "[t]he term *co-existence* indicates that on no other level of his *existence* is man absolutely 'alone.' The presence

---

is, then, is not an Absolute Subject but an 'existent' subject. Man as subject is 'existence'." Opus cit. 33.

[75] As an existent subject the human being is consciousness – pre-reflective as well as unreflective. It is by the existent subject's consciousness that, as Luijpen and Koren say, "I am originally present to myself; by reflection I place myself in my presence," See *Existential Phenomenology*, 54. It is this potency I **am** of being present to myself – reflective consciousness – that, as consciousness and intentionality, I am capable of knowing the world in which I exist. Ibid., 53-97. For more in-depth study on consciousness and intentionality, see Edmund Husserl; *"Philosophy as a Rigorous Science"*, *Cross Current*, Vol. 6 (1956), 227-46, and 325-44. Martin Heidegger; *"The existence of Truth," Existence of Being*, ed. W. Brock, London, 1949; also Being and Time (opus cit.), 71-7.

[76] Luijpen and Koren, opus cit. 100-1.

[77] Ibid., 145.

[78] Ibid., 50-1.

of others in my existence implies that my being-man is being a being through others."[79]

It is this openness of one intentionality to other intentionalities which makes human encounter possible. And such an encounter of intentionalities is a distinctively human relationship since it becomes, not just a relationship between the existent subject and the world, but a relationship between existent-subjects. Luijpen and Koren, after identifying and distinguishing from one another terms that may be used to explain co-existence, make the following assertion: "Here, however, 'encounter' and 'presence' lie on a more personal level: they refer to a person-to-person relationship in the stricter sense of the term."[80] It is this kind of relationship that the subject of our primary formation event seems to resist.

Integrating Formation Science Concepts and those of the Auxiliary Sources

The above insights offered by Formation Science and the two auxiliary sources, psychological and philosophical, disclose several details relative to the current life form of the subject in the original formation event. They reveal the universal nature of the dynamics in his willful disposition of resistance which he shares with other human beings, and how these dynamics of willful resistance may block any encounter with others. The deformed disposition of resistance manifested in the subject, in the light of these insights, seems to originate from his isolation from the rest of his field. Thus isolated, he is present to himself alone in his current life form which is dissonant. Hence, he refuses to open himself up to the other centres of the

---

[79] Ibid., 145-6.
[80] Ibid., 158; emphases are mine.

Chapter 1: Self-Encapsulation and Resistance

field which, otherwise, have the potency to influence his core, or heart, formatively.[81]

This refusal to open to the rest of his formation field is itself resistance. It is a rejection of potentially formative directives which come from centres of formative dynamics of the field.[82] A further examination reveals, and makes evident in the subject, a more fundamental source of his resistance to encounter. The dynamics of resistance may easily be perceived as originating from the pride form which blocks the human ability to listen to the consonance of the heart because of dissonant dispositions[83] from his functional will.

Such resistance of the subject in the original formation event seems to be what Schafer also describes in psychoanalysis as, 'a form of opposition to the analyst's exploratory or interpretive aims," as we have observed.[84] In psychoanalysis which seeks to restore health to the analysand, the patient, who is functionally impaired, it is resistance as oppositional activity which can disrupt and prevent the attaining of such a goal. Analogically, this seems to be what happened to the subject in the original formation event. He actively resisted any encounter, and thus any influence which might lead him to some formative healing.

When, therefore, resistance is established and re-enforced in the subject, encounter with others who are part of his field in the interformative sphere

---

[81] Adrian van Kaam; *Formation of the Human Heart*, 24. Such presence to oneself, such isolation of oneself from the rest of reality, is what the SFHF describes as *exclusive introspection*; see van Kaam: Foundations for Personality Study (Denville, New Jersey: Dimension Books, 1983), 373. See also John W. Kloepfer, The Art of Formative Questioning: A Way to Foster Self-Disclosure. Ph.D. Diss., Duquesne University, 1990 (Ann Arbor: UMI, 1990), 25-9.

[82] See footnote 62 above.

[83] See Formation event, Preface to this Book, viii-xii.

[84] Opus cit., 67.

becomes impossible. This is precisely what occurred with regard to the subject in the primary formation event. As the subject confesses in his narration of that part of the event when the Bishop came into his room: *"At first I will not as much as turn my face from the wall to face him. I have blocked out his greetings from reaching my ears, and have just ignored him."*[85]

Encounter, as the SFHF points out, is a meaningful and therefore formative relationship which a person may enter into with another. Adrian van Kaam makes this evident when he defines encounter as being applied by formation theory of personality to interformative human relationship. This insight regarding encounter as a meaningful and distinctively human relationship is supported by Luijpen and Koren in the arguments they put forward in their discussion on the phenomenology of intersubjectivity. As they demonstrated in their discussion on existence and co-existence, encounter, and also presence, refer to a person-to-person relationship[86] as intentionalities. This is the type of encounter which the subject, in the primary formation event, refused to enter into with the other.

Transition to the Second Remote Foundational Statement

In the above research – first part of chapter one, we have investigated *'resistance manifested in encounter with others'* in a situation of life-threatening illness. We have studied and discovered directives which may lead persons, who are faced with life-threatening illness, to isolate themselves from others and to willfully reject encounter with them. In part two, we will explore to find out what formative potency's cooperation on the vital and functional levels alone may or may not have.

---

[85] See Formation Event, 10 ff.

[86] William A Luijpen and Henry J Koren; Opus cit., 148-60, and in particular, 158.

PART TWO

FORM IMPOTENCY OF MERE VITAL AND FUNCTIONAL COOPERATION

The Second Remote Foundational Statement which was formulated from Coformant One is the following:

Subjects who cooperate vitally and/or functionally with another's attempts at encounter may refuse to respond transcendently to the other's compassionate presence.

Like in Part One, the research in this remote foundational statement will also be carried out in two sections, Sections **A** and **B**. Section **A** will investigate to find out why the level of mere vital-functional cooperation alone is inadequate for human encounter that will be able to give form. Section **B** will focus on the transcendent level, where human encounter is capable of form donation.

SECTION A: COOPERATING ON THE VITAL-FUNCTIONAL LEVEL WITH ANOTHER'S ATTEMPTS AT ENCOUNTER

In the original formation event, the subject initially resisted encounter with, and refused to relate meaningfully to, another. He eventually cooperated with the other only on the vital-functional levels as the other gently tried to make him turn round so that they may face each other. However, even though the subject cooperated with the effects of the other to turn him round, he still would not open up himself to respond meaningfully to the other as human being, and so, encounter him.

In this section, we wish to investigate the intuition that vital-functional cooperation alone cannot be encounter in the formative sense. It lacks the dynamics contained in a true encounter capable to give form. We shall, therefore, explore the concepts of the vital and functional dimensions, and the interformation pole in Formation Science. It is hoped that the insights thus gained will lead to the understanding of why cooperation on the vital-functional levels alone is insufficient for formation.

From the SFHF: The vital-functional Dimension

We have already made mention of the vital and functional dimensions of the human life form among others when we discussed the formation field.[1] Formation Science regards them as opportunities by which human life is present and forms itself in the world.

> These opportunities correspond with the unique structure of the human life-form and of its form potencies. Taken together, they present us with the possibility of constituting a human formation field. When people give form to that field, deepening, expanding, and enhancing it, they give and receive form in their own unfolding life.[2]

In this sense, both the vital and functional dimensions, like the socio-historical, are empirical-experiential, and they make the integration of the

---

[1] For the distinction among the five poles, particularly between intra- and inter-formation, see above, under paragraph-head, *Intra-formation and Interformation Poles*.

[2] See *Fundamental Formation* (Opus cit.), 57.

Chapter 1: Self-Encapsulation and Resistance

human life possible. They are the opportunities by which the embodied [human] spirit[3] is in the world.[4] As van Kaam says of the spirit form,

> The foundational life-form unique in each person is preempirical. In order to form the rest of life, it needs the mediation of the **human spirit**. The human spirit – mind and will as illuminated by the transcendent dimension of the mind – must form itself in congeniality with the foundational life-form and in compatibility with the providential communities and life situations in and through which one has to form one's life and world.[5]

With this understanding of the unique foundational life-form of the individual, we can perceive how the vital and functional dimensions become opportunities by which the preempirical human life form integrates itself in the human core form of life, and subsequently, in the other three: current, apparent, and actual.

---

[3] In describing the human spirit as the core if the human-self, and so, in contradistinction of it from spirit as graced by the Holy Spirit, van Kaam says: "by spirit is meant not only spirit as graced by the Holy Spirit, but the human spirit as it manifests and unfolds itself even before its elevation by grace." And further on, to explain human formation as spirituality, he insists: "The core of man's existence is his spirit and the primary force of man's unfolding is his spirituality." See *The Dynamics of Spiritual Self Direction* (Pittsburgh, PA: Epiphany Association, 1992), 9. See also *Foundations for Personality Study* (Opus cit.), 466. And for more on the nature of the human spirit, see Adrian van Kaam, In *Search for Spiritual Identity* (Denville, NJ: Dimension Books, 1975).

[4] Adrian van Kaam; *Fundamental Formation*, 198-200. Besides being the physical epiphanic manifestation of all forms in it, the world is also "a continuous flow of ongoing formation," 198. See also the world as one of poles within the formation field, 290.

[5] Ibid., 306.

It is in the vital dimension that there resides the potency of the human life to receive and give form to impulses from our biogenetic vital life. And similarly, in the functional dimension is the potency by which human life may give form to ambitions through functioning in life situation and world.[6] Therefore, while the vital dimension of the human life form refers to the biogenetic make-up of the human being, the functional dimension refers to the functioning managerial powers. This latter "articulates itself in an individual, technical, social, and functional aesthetic presence to its forma-tion field."[7]

However, the vital and functional dimensions, together with the sociohistorical, are not capable by themselves alone to donate or receive formation in the individual. And although the vital and functional are two of the three forming and unifying power centres, van Kaam categorically asserts that they must be subordinated to the unique and distinctively human spiritual centre which manifests itself in each of them.[8] This refers to the transcendent dimension which is the most essential of the three power centres. As van Kaam would say later, discussing distinctively human formation,

---

[6] Ibid., 261. Adrian van Kaam describes very well the structure of the heart, which he calls its basic model of configuration, as essentially "historical, vital, functional, transcendent, and pneumatic." See "Provisional Glossary," *Studies in Formative Spirituality*, 1 Feb. 1980): 145.

[7] See Fundamental Formation; 261.

[8] Ibid, 65. See also 53-6 where van Kaam discusses the necessity if the three mutually integrating power centres of formation. Hegel's concept of the spirit differs essentially from that of the human spirit in Formation Science. Hegel identifies spirit *consciousness*, i.e., knowledge – *Scientia* - with reason. See G.W.F. Hegel; *Phenomenology of Spirit*, trans. A.V. Miller (Oxford: Oxford University Press, 1977), 14-5, and 263 ff.

Chapter 1: Self-Encapsulation and Resistance

The forming presence of the human spirit is properly identified with the transcendent dimension of our life-form. We aspire to spiritually meaningful life directives that transcend the limitations of our merely vital and functional concerns.[9]

It is therefore clear that in Formation Science theory, the dynamics from the vital and functional dimensions alone cannot effect distinctively human formation. Formation can only take place when all three power centres – vital, functional, and transcendent – mutually integrate.

From the SFHF: Intraformation and Interformation Poles

As we already mentioned, in the formation field, formation theory has identified five spheres. These are the pre-, intra-, inter-, extra- or outer situational, and world formation poles.[10] They all regularly interact with one another in a dynamic relationship for the formation or consonant unfolding of the person. In contradistinction of the poles from one another, van Kaam defines intraformation and the other spheres of human life form in this way:

> [Intraformation is] Formation that takes place by the interaction of formation processes within the human person. Intra-formation is distinguished from inter-formation and from extra- or outer-formation. Inter-formation refers to formation processes that happen in the interaction with other persons and communities of persons. Extra or outer formation refers to formative processes that result from inter-

---

[9] *Fundamental Formation*, 98.

[10] Ibid., 248; see also Formation-polarity Diagram, 296.

action with the life situation and the wider world beyond the immediate life situation.[11]

With regard to the interformation pole, van Kaam insists elsewhere that, it "refers to the formative influences of people on one another."[12] Such interformation takes place between individuals, especially in a tradition, and can be horizontal or vertical.[13]

As the persons exerting such influence on one another are humans – embodied spirits, their influence on one another can be on the transcendent level,[14] since they share in the same human spirit, though each in a unique manner. It seems, therefore, evident that cooperation on the vital and functional levels alone cannot effect interformation; and so, one can firmly and rightly assert that interformation may occur only where there is genuine human encounter.

As it seems clear, the above investigations of the vital and functional dimensions, and also of the interformation pole, have demonstrated how cooperation on the vital-functional level alone is inadequate for formation.

We now wish to discuss what the psychologist and philosopher Ken Wilber calls *"The Levels of Identity."* His intuition seems to support the presence of another dimension of the human life form which is not usually so readily perceived as such by other scientists. And after a brief study of Wilber's intuition, we shall examine *relationship* in *the hermeneutical experience* of Hans Georg Gadamer. This may further explicate for us the formative potential of encounter with the interformative pole.

---

[11] Adrian van Kaam, "Provisional Glossary," *Studies in Formative Spirituality*, 1 (Feb. 1980): 138.

[12] *Fundamental Formation*, 249.

[13] Adrian van Kaam, *Traditional Formation* (New York: Crossroad, 1992), 14.

[14] Adrian van Kaam, *Fundamental Formation*. Opus cit., 148. It is on the transcendent level that human beings share spiritual identity.

Chapter 1: Self-Encapsulation and Resistance

Ken Wilber: Levels of Human Identity

In his investigation of the complex, yet fundamental question, "Who am I?" Ken Wilber outlines several basic levels of human identity.[15] Observing first the pervading difficulty of an answer to how a person might identify himself or herself, Wilber quotes R.M. Bucke to underscore the suddenness with which the awareness of our complex being can break upon us:

> All at once I found myself wrapped in a flame-colored cloud. For an instant I thought of fire, an immense conflagration somewhere close by in that great city; the next, I knew that the fire was within myself. Directly afterward there came upon me a sense of exultation, of immense joyousness accompanied or immediately followed by an intellectual illumination impossible to describe. Among other things, I did not merely come to believe, but I saw that the universe is not composed of dead matter, but is, on the contrary, a living Presence; I became conscious in myself of eternal life. It was not a conviction that I would have eternal life, but a consciousness that I possessed eternal life then; I saw that all men are immortal; that the cosmic order is such that without any peradventure all things work together for the good of each and all; that the foundation principle of the worlds, is what we call **love**, and that the happiness of each and all is in the long run absolutely certain.[16]

Wilber's comment on such an experience leaves no doubt that he sees in such human awareness the unity of all reality in which the individual human consciousness is taken up. As he attests:

---

[15] Ken Wilber, *No Boundary: Eastern and Western Approach to Personal Growth* (Boston: Shambhala, 1985), 1-14.

[16] Ibid., 1.

The most fascinating aspect of such awesome and illuminating experience – and the aspect to which we will be devoting much attention – is that the individual comes to feel, beyond any shadow of doubt, that he is fundamentally one with the entire universe, with all worlds high or low, sacred or profane. This *sense of identity* expands far beyond the narrow confines of his mind and body, and embraces the entire cosmos.[17]

In such an awareness, the identity of the individual reality seems to have '*no boundaries.*' Yet it is in the interior of such a widespread experience this *supreme identity* – "the nature and condition of all sentient beings"[18] – that the individual has to respond to the question, "Who am I?" The response to this question cannot but consist in identifying the individual, i.e. progressively limiting our world turning from one true nature in order to embrace boundaries.

In all, Wilber identifies five levels of human identity by which the individual can respond to the question, "Who am I?"[19] He admits that these levels are not the only correct "*types of self-maps.*" As he observes, "There are indeed several major types of self/not-self boundary line."[20] However, besides the close analogy that exists between Wilber's concept of *boundaries of the individual* and Formation Science's concept of the formation field, it also seems to support, in the same analogous manner, Formation Science's concept of the dimensions of consciousness.[21] Wilber's boundaries of "the

---

[17] Ibid., 3.

[18] Ibid., 3.

[19] These five levels of human identity contained in the *supreme identity* of the individual are the *self, total organism, self-image, persona, and transpersonal.*

[20] Ibid., 8.

[21] For the definition of Formation Science's concept of 'dimensions of consciousness', see Adrian van Kaam, *Fundamental Formation*, 300.

Chapter 1: Self-Encapsulation and Resistance

total organism" and "the self-image" also offer powerful insights relative to formation theory's concepts of the vital and the functional dimensions.

Hans-Georg Gadamer: Relationship and the Hermeneutical Experience

After Hans-Georg Gadamer had argued that the historicity of experience[22] has been neglected by science which only aims at objectifying it, he described what he regards as genuine experience – *Erfahrung*.[23] As he asserts, "Every experience worthy of the name thwarts an expectation. Thus, the historical nature of man essentially implies a fundamental negativity that emerges in the relation between experience and insight."[24] In this light, therefore, it is experience which has not lost its historical content which leads to insight. And insight, as Gadamer maintains, always involves an element of self-knowledge; thus constituting a necessary side of experience in the proper sense.[25]

It is in this that the hermeneutical method comes to the service of experience. As he is convinced; 'the classical discipline concerned with the art of understanding texts,' hermeneutics gives meaning to the historical experience of the human person. This, Gadamer points out, is how Aeschylus

---

[22] Hans-Georg Gadamer, Truth and Method, 2nd ed. Trans. Joel Weinsheimer and Donald G. Marshall (New York: Continuum, 1993), 346-55. He writes, critical of human sciences; "The main deficiency in theory of experience hitherto – and this includes Dilthey himself – is that it is entirely oriented toward science and Hence, takes no account of the inner historicity of experience. The main aim of science is so to objectify experience that it no longer contains any historical element." 346.

[23] Ibid., 355-62.

[24] Ibid., 356.

[25] Ibid., 356.

came to recognize the metaphysical significance of experience as expressing its inner Historicality of "learning through suffering."[26]

In this light, hermeneutical experience is concerned with tradition; for, as Gadamer claims, "This is what is to be experienced."[27] However, he observes that tradition is a language and that it expresses itself like a **Thou**. And he lists three kinds of experience of the **Thou**.

Gadamer enumerates the three experiences of the Thou in the following way. The first experiences of the *Thou*, as he perceives it, is knowledge of human nature. "We understand the other person in the same way that we understand any other typical event in our experiential field." The second is that the *Thou* is acknowledged as a person. Although in this experience is still understood as a form of self-relatedness, Gadamer explains that 'such self-regarded derives from the dialectical appearance that the dialectic of the "*I-Thou*" relation brings with it.' And he goes on to explain the third kind of hermeneutical experience of the *Thou* as 'openness to tradition, characteristic of historically effected consciousness. Gadamer claims this to be the highest of the three. It is a fundamental reality, not only in the person who speaks, but also in the one who listens. So, he explains that 'without such openness to one another there is no genuine human bond.' Hence, he concludes after all these arguments by affirming that openness to the other then involves recognizing that I myself must accept some things that are against me, even though no one forces me to do so."[28]

---

[26] Gadamer's comment on Aeschylus' recognition of the metaphysical significance of experience is to the point; "What a man has to learn through suffering is not this or that particular thing, but insight into the limitations of humanity, into the absoluteness of the barrier that separates man from the divine. It is ultimately a religious insight – the kind that gave birth to Greek tragedy." *Truth and Method*, 357.

[27] Ibid., 358.

[28] Ibid.,See page 361 where all these arguments are so clearly made.

Chapter 1: Self-Encapsulation and Resistance

Our assumption here is that the relationship implied in such openness is one in which persons meet at the core of their being. It is only at that level that the hermeneutical experience of their relationship can have any meaning to them as humans. This, we surmise, is why Gadamer contends that without openness to one another there is no genuine human bond.

An Integrative Reflection

In the primary event, the subject eventually cooperated with the other person who was trying to enter into a meaningful relationship with him; i.e. to encounter him. When the visitor finally physically tried to turn him around to face him, the subject let go, so that he was turned round as the visitor wished him to do.

However, this cooperation with the other in turning round to face him did not denote encounter with him. Although this other could now see his face, the subject still did not open himself to the visitor. Thus far, the relationship between the subject and his visitor was only on the vital level, and at best, functional level. As the insights gained from Formation Science make evident, relationship on these levels alone is not sufficient to allow encounter to take place, and which, therefore, can effect formation. Encounter may take place, and so, formation become possible only when all three centres of power mutually integrate.[29] But the presence of the third formation power centre may only be fostered through ***openness***. Hence, though the subject in the original event cooperated with the other trying to encounter him, the relationship remained only on the vital-functional levels, and so there was no encounter.

The fact that the subject in the primary event could not experience encounter with the visitor seems to be strongly supported by the ***self/not-self boundaries*** of Wilber. In his understanding of the five levels of indivi-

---

[29] Adrian van Kaam, *Fundamental Formation*, 65.

dual identity, not any single one of them, not even two of them, would sufficiently respond to the question, "Who am I?" For, as Wilber observed, "[The human being's] sense of identity expands far beyond the narrow confines of his mind and body.[30] Therefore, if the subject of the original event is to encounter his compassionate visitor, he would have to be present to him beyond the boundary line of his total organism, self-image, and even his persona, and relate to him within what Wilber describes as the **transpersonal boundary**. It is in embracing all these levels that the totality of his being would be open to the totality of the other as a human individual.

Formation Science perceives the failure of encounter between the subject and the other at this point as the place where the subject might have been able to receive form from this other. In this light, the other, regarded as opportunity of formation to the subject, is constituted in the subject's field as his interformation pole, and thus could exert formative influence on him.[31]

Here again, Formation Science is not alone in having this intuition. Gadamer makes clear, in his analysis of the three kinds of *hermeneutical experience of the Thou,* that the third kind, which he considers as the highest, is the experience of openness to another. Without it, no genuine human relationship of encounter is possible. Thus, as long as the subject of our original formation event remains closed up and cannot be encountered, the other, as interformation pole, cannot exert any formative influence on him so as to give him formation directives.

The insights from the above analysis have, therefore helped us to see clearly that the cooperation with another on the vital and functional levels alone by a self-encapsulated subject, is not adequate to effect true human encounter capable of giving form. Openness of the subject is necessary for formative influence from the other. Such openness is what Formation

---

[30] Opus cit., 3

[31] See Adrian van Kaam, *Fundamental Formation*, 249.

Chapter 1: Self-Encapsulation and Resistance

Science calls *transcendence presence*. This is what we shall now focus upon in Section **B** of the research on human formation.

SECTION B: REFUSING TO RESPOND TO ANOTHER'S COMPASSIONATE PRESENCE ON THE TRANSCENDENT LEVEL

So far, the research has discussed the reason why the subject in the original formation event was not able to encounter the compassionate other. We had observed the fact that the subject was only vitally and functionally, but not transcendentally present to the other. We had also discussed the fact the three power-centres of formation – the vital, the functional, and the transcendent – must mutually interpenetrate in the consonant unfolding of the human life form. However, the transcendent remains the most important of the three, as we indicated earlier.[32] As the SFHF asserts, the directives of both vital and functional, also of the sociohistorical, must always submit to those of the transcendent if formation is to take place. Hence, encounter, which might have led to form donation and reception between the subject of our primary formation event and the compassionate other, could not take place since the subject remained closed up and encapsulated. The question which one may now ask is this: In what does transcendence consist? So, in this section, transcendence and its dynamic is what our inquiry will now seek to elucidate.

From the SFHF: Transcendent Form Potency

In his book *The Transcendent Self*, Adrian van Kaam speaks of how the return to transcendence, in the height of our functional life, "is an invitation to break out of the chains we have forged for ourselves, to relinquish the

---

[32] See texts of footnotes nos. 94 and 95 above.

thought of functional efficiency as an ideal in its own right."[33] This implies that when we are present to ourselves only on the functional level, we become tied down to that dimension of our life form and are imprisoned therein. We need to break out of the prison, "going beyond" the limits of our presence in the functional, and *a priori*, vital dimension of our life, so that we may be present to ourselves in transcendence. Adrian van Kaam defines transcendence more comprehensively in these terms:

> [It] is the process of "going beyond" a current life form that has been congenial and congruent in a specific life period or situation. The process implies the search for a partially or totally new current life form that is at the same time congruent and compatible with the changed life period or situation and congenial with the emergent uniqueness of the personality insofar as this uniqueness increasingly manifests itself during the journey from current life form to current life form.[34]

This is what it means to grow towards the fullness of one's being. In this definition of transcendence is implied *the principle of ongoing formation*. In it is articulated the *transcendence-ability* of the human life form which, as ground form, freely and progressively discloses itself.[35] Van Kaam asserts in chapter 13 of *Fundamental Formation* (p. 166) that this is the very nature of every human life form. As he says, "Our whole life can be seen as a demand

---

[33] Adrian van Kaam, *The Transcendent Self* (Pittsburgh, PA: Epiphany Association, 1991), 145.

[34] Adrian van Kaam; "Glossary," Studies I (Feb., 1980), 149. For a fuller discussion on transcendence, see *Fundamental Formation*, 145-84

[35] Confer the definition of the foundational life form in *Fundamental Formation*, p.303. See also Marie L. Baird, *The Role and Dynamics of Conversion in Human and Christian Formation*, Ph.D. Diss., Duquesne University, 1993 (Ann Abor: UMI. 1993).

to disclose and implement our call to transcendence." And he insists on the following page that the ability to achieve this goal is not something that we have, but it is something that we are. The power to always go beyond our current life form, the transcendent form potency that we are, precedes transcendent formation: and it is precisely the transcendent dimension of our life that makes us human.

It is, therefore, when this disclosure of the unique-communal life form is congenial and compatible, that the empirical forms of life, among which is the current life form,[36] progressively express the inherent ongoing formation dynamic and its direction. The founding life form as ground-form of the human being has the power to transcend itself as it goes on unfolding itself in consonance. And it expresses this self-transcendence empirically through its integrating life forms, particularly in the current form of life in which the change may be observed.

Through the above insights from Formation Science we believe that some illumination has been brought to the concept of transcendence – its nature and dynamics. We shall now turn to the ***transpersonal psychology*** of Abraham H. Maslow which arose from his humanistic psychology – the "Third Force" – and became the "Fourth Force" of psychology. Insights from transpersonal psychology may help us to further elucidate the concept of transcendence in this proximate statement.

---

[36] Formation Science understands the current life form of a person to be "the provisional form that life assumes in implies a modulation of the core-form of life and offers an opportunity for a more refined disclosure of the uniqueness of one's life." See *Fundamental Formation*, p. 300. The whole of life is truly a search for our original consonance, and it is this continuous search which gives rise to our successive current life form; Albert A. Kuuire, "Transcendence Crisis as Invitation," *Studies* XIV (Nov. 1993): 370.

Abraham H. Maslow: Transpersonal Psychology

In the preface of his book *Toward a Psychology of Being*, Abraham Maslow, after a brief assessment of humanistic psychology, known as ***The Third Force Psychology***, declared:

> I consider Humanistic, Third Force Psychology to be transitional, a preparation for a still "higher" Fourth Psychology, transpersonal, transhuman, going beyond humanness, identity, self-actualization, and the like. There will soon be a *Journal of Transpersonal Psychology*, organized by the same Tony Sutich who founded *The Journal of Humanistic Psychology*. These new developments may very well offer a tangible, usable, effective satisfaction of the "frustrated idealism" of many quietly desperate people, especially young people. These psychologies give promise of developing into the life-philosophy, the religion-surrogate, the value-system, the life-program that these people have been missing. Without the transcendent and the transpersonal, we get sick, violent, and nihilistic, or else hopeless and apathetic. We need something "bigger than we are" to be awed by and to commit ourselves to in a new, naturalistic, empirical, non-churchly sense.[37]

This declaration can be considered as none other than a recognition of the reality of the transcendent dimension of the human life form. That this would be made by someone like Maslow who, as a psychologist of "The Third Force" of which he was the founder,[38] is a clear statement that,

---

[37] Abraham H. Maslow, *Toward a Psychology of Being*, 2nd ed. (New York: Van Nostrand Reinhold Company, 1968), iii-iv.

[38] R.B. Hergenhahn, *An Introduction to Theories of Personality*, 3rd ed. (Englewood Cliffs, NJ: Prentice Hall, 1990), 469-71.

towards the end of his life, Maslow had come to realise how humanistic psychology did not embrace all of the human life potential. There was much more left out which ought to be considered for a wider understanding of the human being than just "his needs and interests."[39]

Maslow and Sutich debated a lot about the most appropriate name they would give to the new journal which was to coordinate and publicize the findings of 'The Fourth Force Psychology.' It was not until in February, 1968, that Maslow wrote to Sutich, recommending the use of the term "*transpersonal*," after he had met with Stanislav Grot. Among other things he wrote:

> The main reason I am writing is that in the course of our conversations we thought of using the word "transpersonal" instead of the clumsier word "transhuman" or "transhumanistic." The more I think of it, the more this word say what we are all trying to say, that is, beyond individuality, beyond the development of the individual person into something which is more inclusive than the individual person, or which is bigger than he is.[40]

Even if Maslow was a humanist and believed in the self-actualization of the individual, it is evident from the above that he came to the conviction that the human being is larger than his purely empirical-experiential dimension demonstrable in 'The Third Force Psychology.' The human being is "beyond individuality."

---

[39] For Maslow's various meanings of transcendence, see his book *The Farther Reaches of Human Nature* (Viking Penguin Inc., 1971), 259-69.

[40] Anthony J. Sutich, "The Emergence of the Transpersonal Orientation: A Personal Account," *Journal of Transpersonal Psychology*, VIII (1976): 12-8.

Integrative Reflection on the Above Findings about Transcendence

The above investigations of transcendence have shed light on what had taken place as the subject in the original formation event refused encounter with the compassionate other. Although he eventually related to the other on the vital-functional level, he had refused to open himself in his totality as a human being.

The totality of the subject as a human being does not consist in his sociohistorical, vital, and functional dimensions alone. And he is not directed to the fulfillment of his life form by their dynamics. For the subject to become open in his fullness as a human being to the other, he had to "go beyond" his empirical-experiential presence, to enter into what Ken Wilber calls his "not-self boundary," and for Maslow, his transpersonal self. Although this presence may not be familiar to him, it is, nevertheless, a dimension of him as a human being with the inherent ability to "go beyond" what he may be familiar with of himself. This dimension is what Formation Science very appropriately calls his *transcendent dimension*.

Formation Science, as we have observed above, has clearly demonstrated that every human being is capable of this transcendence through our preformational transcendence potency.[41] It has identified and demonstrated how in the individual founding life form is inherent and is the dynamic which would progressively unfold itself, giving expression to this process in its integrative life forms, and is observable in the changing current life form.

This progressive unfolding of the founding life form in formation becomes possible only when the person opens himself to the transcendence which is, indeed, the very centre of his being as embodied-spirit. But this is

---

[41] For a more complete discussion on the "transcendent form potency," see the entire chapter 13 in *Fundamental Formation*, 166-84. Here van Kaam succinctly explains how the transcendent form potency operate in the individual on various situations.

what the subject in the original event was unable to do, due to the fact that his intrasphere resisted openness to transcendence. This is implied in what he said: *"I do not make any attempt to respond. After a period of silence, the Bishop's monologue resumes, interjected by other long periods of silence. I still feel depressed and angry."*[42] Thus, he had continued to close himself up and would not open himself to transcendence and the possibility of its inspirations through the influence of the other. His refusal to encounter the other made futile the opportunities of transcendent formation of the subject through the directives contained therein.

It can be said that the above reflection brings to some conclusion the elucidation of Chapter One. However, before we can go on to Chapter Two, we wish to identify some potential obstacles to, as well as some facilitating conditions for consonant unfolding of human life in the remote and proximate dynamics we have explored.

OBSTACLES TO AND FACILITATING CONDITIONS FOR FORMATION

Two primary obstacles to consonant human formation and reformation have become evident in the remote foundational and proximate statements explored in this chapter. The first of these is the vital-functional dissonance of depression, frustration, and anger[43] created by the life-threatening illness from which the subject is suffering. This life-threatening illness unleashed in the subject the fear of imminent death and triggered the dissonant

---

[42] See the narrative of the Formation event, Preface to this Book, viii-xii.

[43] Concerning frustration and anger, see the fourth basic assumption of Abraham Maslow in the context of human sickness and health in *Toward a Psychology of Being*, 3. Functionalistic willfulness is a dissonant disposition of the functional dimension.

directives of depression, frustration, and anger, and thus led him ultimately to isolation and self-encapsulation.

A second potential obstacle is the disposition of functionalistic willfulness.[44] This is what seems to have maintained the subject in his initial dissonance. Such a disposition of unbridled ambition which the subject refused to submit to the transcendent will blocked disclosure of his intrasphere. The subject could only see in what he believed was his approaching death, the sudden disruption of his willful ambitions.

Equally illuminated in this chapter are several facilitating conditions for formation. Here we can indicate three of them. The first is the compassionate, formative presence of the other. Through such a presence, undergirded by patience, the other was able to gently remain with the subject, even in the face of what seemed to be the subject's obvious rejection of him.

The second facilitating condition is silence.[45] When silence is abiding, it has the power to increase the subject's attention, as Muto rightly describes it, and so can open his intrasphere to transcendence.

And the third facilitating condition well-elucidated here is the vital cooperation of the subject. Although such vital directive may not be formative in itself; nevertheless, it can predispose and prepare the subject for an eventual opening up of himself to transcendence, and so to formation when that would happen.

---

[44] Functionalistic willfulness of the subject comes from his inordinate ambitions in his ministry as a young, overly enthusiastic priest. Prefocally, these ambitions were not submitted to the transcendent will.

[45] Susan Muto defines *silence* in varying formulations in her book: *Pathways if Spiritual Living* (Petersham, MA: St. Bede's Publications, 1984), 51-9.

Chapter 1: Self-Encapsulation and Resistance

Transitioning to Chapter Two of the Research

The foregoing chapter has elucidated the dynamics of resistance in vital-functionally dissonant and encapsulated subjects on the level of universal human presence. It has illumined the dynamics in resistance which hinder encounter with others, and thus frustrate the opportunity of interformation. It has made evident that, even though subjects may cooperate with another's compassionate presence on the vital-functional level, their intrasphere may remain closed up to formative directives coming from this same other. It has also elucidated the transcendence dynamic as the privileged power-centre of all human formation.

Chapter Two will seek to disclose dynamics of fear of rejection that religious subjects may develop and how that may lead them to refuse to open themselves for encounter with another. It will further seek to elucidate the dynamics of the apparent openness of such religious, but which dynamics are impotent to give them form directives congenial and compatible with their religious life form as long as their spirit or mind remains closed.

CHAPTER TWO

ENCOUNTERING RELIGIOUS PERSONS IN GRAVE ILLNESS

INTRODUCTION

As it is indicated in the last paragraph of Chapter One, this chapter of the research will focus on Coformant One, which will be directed towards religious persons or subjects. This coformant is stated as follows:

Religious subjects who are suffering from grave illness, and who are depressed, may anxiously fear rejection by the Mystery for some wrong they believe they have committed, and may initially isolate themselves from another, and remain closed up to the other's attempts at encounter. These religious subjects may respond on the vital level to such attempts at encounter by the other but may, however, remain closed up in their soul or mind to the other's compassionate presence.

As in the First Chapter, we shall draw two remote foundational statements from this coformant. We shall then proceed to study some of the significant proximate formation dynamics and directives which are inherent in these two remote foundational hypothetical statements.

PART ONE
ILLNESS AS A SIGN OF REJECTION BY THE MYSTERY

This part of the research will seek to elucidate the following remote foundational statement which is the first formulated from the coformant above:

> Religious subjects who are suffering from grave illness and are depressed may seriously fear rejection by the Mystery for some wrong they have done, and so may also remain closed up to encounter with another.

The investigation of this remote foundational statement will concentrate on two proximate dynamics and the formative directives that they give. **The first section** will focus on the anxious fear of rejection that religious subjects may manifest for some wrong they believe they have committed. And **the second**, which will study proximate dynamic two, will explore the refusal of such religious to open themselves up to another so that interformation may take place.

Section One: Anxiously fearing Rejection for Some Wrong Done

The life-threatening illness from which religious subjects suffer may not only lead them to frustration, depression, and anger because of the imminent disruption it brings to their personally crafted life's projects through death. They may also become anxiously fearful that they are being rejected by the divinity for some wrong they must have committed. Thus, in their conviction that they are abandoned by God, they find no more meaning in life itself, nor in other people who might previously have meant a lot to them. We shall examine the religious dynamics of rejection by the divinity – the Mystery – first in the intuitions that Formation Science may give, then in intuitions that some of its auxiliary sources may also offer.

Chapter 2: Encountering Religious Persons in Grave Illness

<u>From the SFHF</u>: Appreciative and Depreciative Abandonment

Besides the feeling of frustration, depression and anger that religious persons may experience in suffering a life-threatening illness, fear that they may be rejected by the divinity – God, the Mystery – for some wrong they have done, brings on them the most intense anxiety. This means that such religious subjects in this life-threatening situation believe themselves to be rejected, and so abandoned by the Radical Mystery of All Formation because they have committed some morally wrong and unpardonable deed, either with a focal or a prefocal consciousness of it. In this situation, they consider that it is God who abandons them.

Formation Science, however, holds a more comprehensive yet very specific view about the concept itself and the phenomenon of abandonment.[1] In a detailed discussion on "abandonment option" with regard to the Mystery of Formation, van Kaam explores in depth the issue of what he calls the foundational formation option. In this, he succinctly distinguishes between "primordial appreciative abandonment" and "primordial depreciative abandonment." After he has asserted and established that there is an alternative in "primordial formation," he defines this primordial alternative as "a pre-reflective or reflective yes or no to the Mystery of Formation." This means that the decision for either alternative is made on the level of prefocal or focal consciousness. Thus, he further explains:

---

[1] See Adrian van Kaam, *Fundamental Formation* (New York: Crossroad, 1989), 221-42. Van Kaam discusses abandonment to the Mystery in many other places in his writings. Thus for example, see also *Human Formation* (New York: Crossroad, 1989), 14 in connection with fundamental features; 53, in the context of the triad of faith, hope and love: and 193 where he discusses the importance for the counselee in 'Formation Counseling' to abandon himself or herself in awe to the Mystery of Formation. See also his book, *The Transcendent Self*, in which he uses more the constructs *'detachment-attachment'* and *'surrender'* in the sense of abandonment.

It is the choice of a willingness either to abandon ourselves to, or feel abandoned by the seemingly ambivalent processes of formation. One or the other conviction cannot be forced upon us or proven conclusively by means of mere functional logic or by the methods of the proximate sciences.[2]

This underscores the freedom with which the individual person makes this choice. He or she abandons himself or herself to the Mystery of Formation, or to feeling abandoned *by* this Mystery. Even if, as van Kaam observes, the "primordial abandonment option" is not completely free because of various factors,[3] as he subsequently admits, "Most people come to the abandonment decision spontaneously, implicitly, and pre-reflectively in the midst of their ongoing daily formation."[4]

Therefore, abandonment of oneself either **to** the Radical Mystery, or to one's feeling that one is abandoned **by** this Mystery, is a decision which the religious subject has the innate potency to freely make, however limited that freedom may be. Abandonment never comes from the Radical Mystery, but from the religious who may, in freedom, either positively and appreciatively entrust themselves to the formative care of God, the Radical Mystery, or falsely, negatively and depreciatively believe themselves to be rejected and abandoned by their divinity for some wrong they might have done. They despair and lose hope that they will ever be loved again by God.

---

[2] Ibid., 231.

[3] *Fundamental Formation,* Opus cit. 221-2. Here van Kaam lists the three following reasons as examples of sources from where the limitation to complete freedom in the primordial abandonment option for some people can come: i) innate deformative predispositions from genetic preformation; ii) deformative interformation in childhood; and iii) succession of meaningless formative life situations.

[4] Ibid., 226.

Chapter 2: Encountering Religious Persons in Grave Illness

<u>From the SFHF</u>: Awe and the dispositions of Anxiety and Fear

If religious people, in the unfolding of their FLF, arrive at abandoning themselves either positively or negatively vis-a-vis the Radical Mystery of Formation, it is perhaps because of the ***foundational predisposition of awe*** which has a primordial place in the hierarchy of dispositions in the heart of every human being. As Formation Science assumes, not only is awe primordial, but it is also transcendent since it has the Transcendent Mystery itself for its very source and object.[5] Van Kaam makes very powerfully this point when he asserts:

> Human life is called from within its formation field by the Formation Mystery. This call is the ground of our personal relation to the Mystery. The invitation to share in the epiphany of the Mystery and its forming potency in our life fills us with *awe* for our own participant form potency. *Awe is the source of our transcendent dignity* within the scheme of life and history. This call resonates in our hearts mysteriously. It makes the heart, the inspired core of our formation and its disposition.[6]

The statement which regards the nature and origin of the disposition of *awe* paves the way for one of the best definitions of *awe* enunciated by van Kaam. Further in his discussion about the disposition of awe in relationship to the other core form dispositions of the human life form, he writes, "The disposition of awe is a mysterious force in the core of our being; it is a principle of consonance and unity." Further, he goes on to describe it thus:

---

[6] Ibid., 165. The emphases are mine.

Awe gives new and profound meaning to the other formative dispositions, not by making the partial meanings of these dispositions superfluous, but by rooting them in our deepest center. Awe helps us to be truly alive in all these dispositions without becoming their captive. It is the secrete source of our consonance, our peace of heart, mind and body; it is the spring of faith, hope, and love, of fairness and courage in the midst of adversity.[7]

Such a description of the essence of *awe* demonstrates very well its transcendence, and also the primordial form disposition of the heart that it is. It is such *awe* which "disposes us to be present to the Formation Mystery and its epiphanies in the universe, and in history as well as in our daily life."[8] But *awe* can become inverted in a person. This is the case when the person is isolated, and so is imprisoned the functional satisfactions of his or her ambitions.[9]

In chapter eleven of *Human Formation*, the second volume of his seven-volume series on Formative Spirituality,[10] van Kaam speaks of *formative wisdom* which he regards as leading to realistic appraisals, relative liberation from deformative self-consciousness, and experiences of consonance with the Mystery. He also calls it *wisdom-in-awe* and traces *formation anxiety* to it. It is this *formation anxiety* which van Kaam contra-distinguishes from *formation fear*. While in "formation fear we are afraid that we cannot give or receive form in regard to this or that specific formation event," formation

---

[7] Ibid., 182.

[8] Ibid., 183.

[9] For a more detailed description of inverted awe, see Ibid., 193-4. John Kloepfer also discusses it and gives some light to it in his Ph.D. dissertation: *The Art of Formative Questioning: A Way to Foster Self-Disclosure* Duquesne University, 1990 (Ann Abor: UMI, 1990), 240-1.

[10] Adrian van Kaam, *Human Formation*, 191-202.

Chapter 2: Encountering Religious Persons in Grave Illness

anxiety in us "emerges when we are faced with the threat of absolute formlessness and form impotency."[11]

Hence, for Formation Science, both the dispositions of formation fear and formation anxiety have their origin in the primordial core disposition of awe. This reality appears to be the undergirding reason why, although the disposition of fear initially seems to diminish the formative power of formation opportunities of religious subjects, and formation anxiety brings an all pervasive fear of formation impotency, formation anxiety still has the power, and "generates a wisdom that entrusts itself to the veiled form direction of evolution and history," as van Kaam affirms.[12] That is to say, formation anxiety still maintains in itself power to call us forth from an existential paralysis to transcend the situation of form impotence to formation. Thus, van Kaam does rightly conclude that wisdom-in-awe rests in ultimate abandonment in faith, hope, and consonance to the Formation Mystery.[13]

In this view of Formation Science, therefore, it is difficult to perceive illness as an abandonment of the subject by the Mystery of Formation for whatever reason. For, in the light of the above discussion, even bio-physical illness is considered an opportunity for and an invitation to formation. However, having established this intuition, we want to turn to other sources for further enlightenment on the nature of the abandonment that religious subjects suffering life-threatening illness may feel. We shall discuss what John Mbiti, a writer and expert in African religions, considers to be the cause and meaning of death in African religious thought and philosophy; and subsequently, we shall discuss with Jack Goody, an anthropologist who did a lot of ethnographic studies among the Dagaaba of West Africa, the

---

[11] Ibid., 195.
[12] Ibid., 195.
[13] Ibid., 196.

belief among the Lo-Dagaa that illness as an immediate cause of death is symptomatic of a moral or mystical cause of death.

John Mbiti: Causes and Meaning of Death

We made the observation earlier that the subject of the primary formation event of our research was born to young parents who were, themselves, new converts to the Christian faith.[14] But although the subject was born into and raised and raised in the Christian faith tradition, the faith, and especially the formation tradition of his ancestors, which in fact cannot be dichotomized from the former, retained, at least *infraconsciously*, a great influence on him, as it still gave pulsation to his society in general. In such a society, illness and death are attributed to some moral, mystical cause.[15] This seems to be the same religious reality which John Mbiti observes in his book *African Religions and Philosophy*. Speaking about the causes and meaning of death, Mbiti writes:

> Man has since accepted death as part of the natural rhythm of life; and yet, paradoxically, every human death is thought to have external cause, making it both natural and unnatural. People must find and give immediate causes of death. By far the commonest cause is believed to be magic, sorcery and witchcraft.[16]

---

[14] Confer *Formation Tradition*, under Dialogue with the Principles of The SFHF, 25 & ff.

[15] Confer Albert A Kuuire, "*Dagaati Solidarity and Salvation in Christ in the Light of 'Gaudium et Spes'*" (S.T.D. Diss., Rome: Pontificia Universitas Lateranensis, 1976), 182. The mythical and moral cause of sickness and death was already taken note of here.

[16] John Mbiti; African Religions and Philosophy (Portsmouth, New Hampshire: Heinemann Education Books Inc., 1969), 151.

Chapter 2: Encountering Religious Persons in Grave Illness

Mbiti claims that this is attested to in every African society, though in varying degrees and emphasis. He enumerates four general causes to which the death of any person is attributed. These are: a powerful curse; the living-dead;[17] spirits; and God-self. As he points out, the fourth cause, God, on which death is blamed, would be responsible for all other deaths for which no satisfactory explanation can be found.[18] In this category would be included the death of a person who may have broken an important injunction which is believed by the tradition to have come from God. This would apply most especially to the death of persons who are considered to be still rather "too young to die."

Death itself, as Mbiti observes after he had analyzed various terms used all over Africa for describing actual dying, is perceived as a departure. The person who has died is not annihilated but goes on a journey that takes him to join the company of the departed, his ancestral congregation.[19]

The above discussion on the causes and meaning of death sheds light on some of the core form dispositions of the subject of our primary formation event. It makes more intelligible, within a tradition in which the cause of death must always be identified and its morality determined, that, faced with death at his age, he would pose such a question: "But God, why do you want me to die?" However, most causes of death are preceded by sickness which is always believed to be symptomatic of its moral or mystical cause.

---

[17] The living-dead, as Mbiti explains, "applies to those of a given family, particularly the living-dead who may have been offended before they died, or may not have been properly buried, or may have a grudge against someone; see opus cit. 151.

[18] Ibid., 151. See also Jack Goody; Death, Property and the Ancestors (London: Tavistock Publications, 1962), 208 & ff.

[19] Mbiti, Opus cit. 152-3. See also Albert A. Kuuire, Opus cit. 238-44; Edward Kuukure, *The Destiny of Man*, 108-15: In his presentation of Dagaaba beliefs about life after death, Kuukure describes their belief as a journey.

Among many other researchers, this is one of the issues which Goody eloquently discusses in his book *Death, Property and the Ancestors,* and to which we would now like to turn.

Jack Goody: Illness as Symptomatic of a Mystical Cause of Death

While Mbiti gives four general causes to which death is attributed in most African societies, Jack Goody, the social anthropologist, describing the causation of death among the Lo-Dagaa, indicates three levels of death. After he analyzed and found death among the Dagaaba[20] to be a social phenomenon attributed to some conflict in the social system, either with living persons or past members of the society – ancestors – he viewed most deaths as causes of homicide.[21] Hence, he came to the following conclusion:

> There are thus three levels of causation [of death], i) the immediate; ii) the efficient; and iii) the final. The immediate is the technique used to kill the deceased: disease, snake bites, or other "natural" causes as well as forms of mystical aggression. The efficient is to be found among the members of the community itself, the person who was behind the act of

---

[20] The people that Goody calls the Lodagaa is a collection of different groups of the same generic tribe but with significant linguistic expressions depending on where in the territorial boundaries one lives. Thus, they are variously designated as Dagara, Dagaaba, Lowville, etc., and they inhabit the North-western part of present-day Ghana and the adjacent areas of Burkina Faso and Cote d'Ivoire.

[21] Goody points out that there are two main exceptions to this view. These are; i) the case of children who die before they are weaned, and ii) the case of old persons who are considered to have reached their allotted span of life, and have begotten children who have, in their turn, also begotten children. See Opus cit. 208-9.

killing. The final cause is an ancestor, the Earth shrine, or a medicine shrine.[22]

If disease or illness is regarded only as the immediate level of the cause of death as Goody indicates, then it is evident that the real cause of a particular death lies deeper and is something of which the disease is only symptomatic. As it is clear from the above quote from Goody, illness which immediately causes the death of a person is, itself, efficiently caused by some person. This person, who represents the second level of the causation of death, is either a member of the community of the deceased or some "natural" or mystical being. But still, the ultimate causation of every death is always traced to a third level, a divinity to whom the death is finally attributed. This divinity is either an ancestor, or the Earth shrine, or a medicine shrine.[23]

Illness or disease, therefore, becomes the perceivable symptom of the real cause of death. It is what immediately appears, and so indicates that there is some moral or mystical reality which is responsible for the death of a person. Divination, which we shall discuss later in this chapter, is the means by which the real cause of a person's death may be determined.

---

[22] Jack Goody; opus cit. 210. Goody himself admits that this list does not exhaust all the possible causes of death, as the ancestors, the Earth shrine, and the medicine shrines are sometimes said not to have the power to kill a person unless allowed to do so by the person's tutelary.

[23] The Earth shrine is a designated ritual area or a parish division or the countryside to which the persons who settled there and have become its local congregation owe allegiance. The persons in the settlement are all thus bound together in that they all have to observe certain prohibitions, especially the shedding of blood of another member of the settlement. This is what Goody speaks about in his book (Opus cit., 7. For the cause of illness associated with medicine shrine, see Benjamin C. Ray, *African Religions* (Englewood Cliffs, N.J.: Prentice-Hall, Inc., 1976, 103.

In this first section of our research in chapter two, we have investigated the anxious fear of 'abandonment *by* God' which the religious subject of the primary formation event was experiencing. We also sought to shed some light on the primordial disposition of *awe* to which both the *fear* and *anxiety* can be traced; and we have pointed out how the subject's disposition of *awe* can be deformed and so become *inverted*. The second section, B, will concentrate on the repercussions of *such inverted awe* in the formation of the subject. It will study the deformative dynamics of isolation of the intrasphere of such a religious subject, as opposed to its openness which makes interformation of the subject possible.

SECTION B: REFUSAL TO OPEN ONESELF TO ANOTHER FOR INTERFORMATION ENCOUNTER

As the religious subject in the original formation event is locked up in fear and anxiety of being abandoned by the Divine Mystery and is thus in despair, he will not encounter another. He feels no one can be confirming to him in his current life situation. This area of the research will therefore study the dynamics of openness to another and will examine the potency of interformative confirmation by this other.

From the SFHF: Isolation of the Intrasphere

In Chapter One of the research, we discussed the disposition of openness as one 'that enables us to be as open as we can to the formative and deformative meanings of our formation field.' Hence, when a person's disposition of openness is deformed, it leaves his or her intrasphere in isolation. The core of the person becomes cut off from the rest of the poles and dimensions of his or her formation field into which formation energy could flow.

Chapter 2: Encountering Religious Persons in Grave Illness

It becomes evident, therefore, that when the intrasphere of a person is encapsulated, he or she is incapable of receiving any formation. This is what van Kaam makes clear in his discussion of the preformation of the human life form and of the poles of the formation field. In reference to the processes of organic and vital formation as dependent on a common source – intraformation,[24] he writes:

> This vital formation does not develop in *isolation* from other aspects of emergent life. An intraformation process unfolds within the human life form itself. Hence, the term intra- (within) formation. This process brings the vital intraform into forming interaction with other inner modalities of human life.[25]

Van Kaam has consistently insisted on the impossibility of the formation of a human life form in any way if it is isolated and cut off from the rest of its inner modalities. As he warns, "The isolation of our intrasphere excludes from form reception and donation in relation to our intersphere and outer sphere.[26]

From the SFHF: Confirming Interformation

The religious subject who thus isolates his or her intrasphere from other persons also cuts himself or herself from what the SFHF calls their confirming interformation. To begin with, the intrasphere of every person unfolds consonantly through formation directives which he or she also receives from others. But one can only receive form from another in this

---

[24] Adrian van Kaam, *Fundamental Formation*, 304.
[25] Ibid., 250.
[26] Adrian van Kaam, *Formation of the Human Heart* (Opus cit.), 165; see also 44-5.

way through this other's confirmation of what one's own form potency already tries to realize consonantly. And he or she can confirm these consonant attempts of one's form potency only when, in trust, he or she communicates such attempts at the formation of his or her intrasphere to the person. Van Kaam states this quite succinctly when, in reference to communication of one's interiority, he affirms:

> How sure I am about my form potency depends largely on my interformative experiences in the past. If my parents were appreciative, if they confirmed attempts to exercise my form potency in my own consonant way, this initial confirmation will be part of my formative memory, imagination, and anticipation. Hence, I will be inclined to risk the expansion of the intra- into the inter- and outer spheres. I do not feel as alone as when facing communication unsympathetic strangers. My intrasphere is filled with confirming interformative memories of the past.[27]

This quotation puts in perspective the necessity of the confirmation of my intraspheric attempts at formation by others for the truly consonant unfolding of my foundational file form.

In the above paragraphs, the SFHF has elucidated the formation dynamics of the intrasphere, and how the deformative disposition of isolation can obstruct its interformation. It further illuminated the necessity of the formation of the individual's intrasphere through confirming interformation by others. To understand better the African religious subject's concept of the Radical Mystery, and that of the individual *vis-à-vis* such a Mystery, we would like to explore with Gregory E. Kpiebaya and again John S. Mbiti, respectively.

---

[27] Ibid., 163.

Chapter 2: Encountering Religious Persons in Grave Illness

Gregory E Kpiebaya: Dagaaba Beliefs about God

In his Licentiate thesis entitled *God in the Dagaaba Religion and in the Christian Faith,* Kpiebaya devoted all of the first part to a thorough exposition of Dagaaba beliefs about God. After he had given in Chapter One what he calls a 'bird's-eye-view' of Dagaaba life before the arrival of the Christian missionaries, he went on to describe in Chapter Two how they discover God in the six principal areas of their life.[28] In conclusion to his exploration of these six principal areas of Dagaaba life's activities through which they came to know God, Kpiebaya asserts the following as their belief in God, and in his existence:

> God's existence is simply taken for granted. He (God) is one of the facts of life man cannot escape. The Dagaaba do not claim any special revelation from God concerning himself. All they know about him, everything they do in reference to him, comes from the ancestors and the traditions. These are the supreme authority of truth.[29]

---

[28] Gregory E. Kpiebaya; *God in the Dagaaba Religion and in the Christian Faith* (Licentiate thesis, Universite Catholique de Louvain, 1973), 34-114. He lists these six areas of religious activities through which God becomes manifest as: i) divination; ii) ancestral veneration; iii) the Earth shrine cult; iv) medicine shrine cult; v) the Barge cult; and the Rites of Passage in life.

[29] Opus cit. 109. In his "Essai sur la Religion des Dagara," Louis Girault also attests to such existence of God for the Dagaaba as unquestionable; "Il est incontestable que c'est l'idée de Dieu qui domine et coiffe l'ensemble de la religion des Dagara. Elle est tellement encrée en eux qu'il ne leur viendrait même pas à la pensée de mettre en doute son existence. La vie quotidienne en est imprégnée et au milieu de l'ensemble complexe de fétiches et de superstitions, Dieu émerge toujours et a sa place nettement a part.» see IFAN, Bulletin, 1959, p. 331.

In the light of this exploration of their life's activities in which God is manifested, Kpiebaya came to an overall conclusion that in the Dagaaba religion God has a geographical area where he inhabits, but which habitation is considerably less important than the location of the Earth shrine, the Medicine shrine, and the habitation of the ancestors.

If these three centres where God can manifest himself seem therefore to be arrogated more importance than where God lives, it is because of Dagaaba belief that the 'Supreme Being' – God – relegates the daily affairs of the cosmos to these other beings which are, nevertheless, part of God's creation.[30] The fact that God remains "*Naangmin*," occupying the most central place in the Dagaaba religious thought, is sufficiently evident in their in their cult and worship, even if he receives his due honour mainly through these others who, indeed, serve as intermediaries.[31] As Kuukure rightly puts it when explaining why the Dagaaba religion is in such close contact with the cosmos, "It is in and through nature that he communicates with the divinity."[32] This reality has also been pointed out by Ray in his affirmation of the one creator-God in African religions as he asserts: "[God] is usually remote in the daily religious life."[33] But as he earlier claims in his discussion on archetypal symbols, ritual, and community, "Through ritual man

---

[30] Albert A Kuuire; "The Christian Faith in the Dagarti Culture" (Licentiate thesis, Catholic University of Louvain, 1972), 58-9.

[31] Ibid., 64-77. The Dagaaba designate God as, **Naangmin**, a composite of two terms, **Naa**- and ***ngmin***. Naa, meaning 'chief,' someone with authority; and 'ngmin', signifying a deity, a superior being, and therefore more powerful than the human being. So the term '**Naangmin**'is the name which the Dagaaba attribute to the chief and most powerful of all the divinities.

[32] Edward Kuukure, "*The Destiny of Man: Dagaare Beliefs in Dialogue with Christian Eschatology*" (Frankfurt am Main: Peter Lang, 1985), 55-6. He had already earlier asserted the uniqueness of the place of God, see p.50.

[33] Benjamin C. Ray; *African Religions* (Englewood Cliff, New Jersey: Prentice-Hall Inc. 1976, 50.

transcends himself and communicates directly with the divine."[34] If such then is the African's belief about God, what can we say is the African's perception of the human being?

John S. Mbiti: The Original State of Man, and God's Provision for Him

In Chapter Nine of his book, African Religions and Philosophy, Mbiti delineates three beliefs that African Religions have about the human person. They concern man's origin – creation; his original state of being and God's provision for him – nature; and the separation that came to be between God and the human being – dissonance.[35] From his analysis of various creation myths, Mbiti depicts the human being's original state in this way:

> According to many stories of creation, man was originally put in a state of happiness, childlike ignorance, immortality or ability to rise again after dying. God also provided him with the necessities of life, either directly or through equipping him to develop them, and lived more or less in a state of paradise.[36]

This analytical description of the human being's original state at his creation makes evident the African's perception of himself as an existent being. In the ignorance, purity, and simplicity of his or her being endowed with immortality, he or she is thus fitted out by God, his or her creator, with all that is needed for his or her ongoing development in life.

However, the happy state at the beginning and the cordial relationship between the human being and God, and also the gift of immortality, came

---

[34] Benjamin C. Ray, opus cit., p.17.
[35] John S. Mbiti; opus cit., 90-7.
[36] Ibid., 93.

to an end, and God and man separated, as various stories demonstrate.[37] After his analysis of these stories, Mbiti draws several conclusions, but all concern "the lost paradise." In the light of these stories, he wonders if it would not be legitimate to suggest that African acts of worship are only a search for "the lost paradise." Hence, he reasons thus: "Since in these acts people are searching for something past, something in distant *Zamani* period, it follows that there cannot be myths about the future recovery of 'the lost paradise,' or reversal of the *fait accompli*."[38]

In any case, in the faith, as well as form tradition of the Dagaaba to which the subject of the formation event belongs, the actual world in which God and man have become estranged, man continues to enjoy the pristine endowments God had provided man with – the means of survival in life. Hence, after the loss of the paradise, the Dagaao redefines for himself a central position in the cosmos which continues to be God's provision for him on his journey to the world *(Teng)* of God where all the ancestors have already congregated.[39] In this light, acts of worship are not a mere search for a paradise lost. They are carried out especially to catch the continuous provision by God, through the ancestors and the lesser deities, for man's needs in life on the journey to God's world for which he is destined and fitted out with the means to take him there. Furthermore, discussing the inalienable importance that archetypal symbols and ritual have in the community, Benjamin Ray seems to register support for this line of thought when he says:

---

[37] Ibid., 94-7. Mbiti cites stories from the Ashanti of Ghana, the Mende of Senegal, the Bambuti, the Banyarwanda, the Bushman, etc., of Central and Southern Africa to demonstrate the different ways in which this original state of man is thought by different societies to have come to its end. See also Edward Kuukure, opus cit., 53-9.

[38] John S. Mbiti, opus cit. 96.

[39] Edward Kuukure, opus cit., p. 56

The coming of divinity to man and of man to divinity happens repeatedly with equal validity in almost every ritual occasion. The experience of salvation is thus a present reality, *not a future event*. The passage from the profane to the sacred, from man to divinity, from moral conflict to moral unity occurs *Here and Now*. In short, almost every African ritual is a salvation event in which human experience is re-created and renewed in the all-important ritual Present.[40]

An Integrative Reflection

With the deterioration of his illness which he now believes will lead to his certain death, the subject of our primary formation event anxiously manifests deep fear that he has been abandoned by God, the Radical Mystery of Formation, for some wrong that he has committed. Hence, he has no more hope that he can ever fulfill his life's projects, including that final one, reaching the abode of the ancestral congregation where God himself is the centre. This explains the subject's agonizing question in which he asks God why he wants his death.[41]

In his book *When Bad Thing Happen to Good People*,[42] Kushner exemplifies in his own life the fundamental question, "Why do bad things happen to good people?" This question is not only fundamental, but it is also universal; and people pose it, not only as a theoretical question, but one for which they genuinely seek an answer. The following is one of such events which Kushner encountered in his ministry, the question to which there, indeed, is no answer on human level:

---

[40] Benjamin C. Ray, opus cit., 17.

[41] See Proximate Background to Formation Event, p. 16.

[42] Harold S. Kushner, *When Bad Things Happen to Good People* (New York: Avon Books, 1983).

I was a young rabbi just starting out in my profession, when I was called on to try to help a family through an unexpected and almost unbearable tragedy. This middle-aged couple had one daughter, a bright nineteen-year-old girl who was in her freshman year at an out-of-state college. One morning at breakfast, they received a phone call from the university infirmary. "We have bad news for you. Your daughter collapsed while walking to class this morning. It seems a blood vessel burst in her brain. She died before we could do anything for her. We are terribly sorry." Stunned, the parents asked a neighbor to come in to help them decide what steps to take next. The neighbor notified the Synagogue, and I went over to see them that same day. I entered their home, feeling very inadequate, not knowing any words that could ease their pain. I anticipated anger, shock, and grief, but I didn't expect to hear the first words they said to me: "You know, Rabbi, we didn't fast last Yom Kippur."[43]

Devastated as these parents are of their young and beautiful daughter's sudden death, they immediately began to look for a response to this fundamental question, "Why this has happened to us?" They came out with the response that it is because they did not fast during the last Yom Kippur.[44] Although Kushner does not go on to explain psychologically how they could arrive at such a response, the obviously implied explanation is that "we have done something wrong." So, it is for this wrong that God is punishing them in letting their daughter meet such an early and sudden death.

As both Mbiti and Goody observe in most African societies, such an event which brings pain and suffering is only symptomatic of some deeper, mystical cause. In this light, it could be surmised with good reason that the couple to whom Kushner ministered saw the sudden death of their daughter

---

[43] Ibid., 8.
[44] Yom Kippur is the Day of Atonement for Jews. It is a Jewish fast day.

as a symptom of God's abandonment of them for the wrong they had done, in not having fasted on the last Yom Kippur. God has rejected them for the wrong they have committed, even if they were not focally conscious of it at the time.

If the couple arrived at such an answer to the question of pain and suffering, it is because, in their appraisal of the dynamics of the event, they apprehend God as the one who has abandoned them. However, John Carmody, in his reflection on living with a terminal illness in his book *Cancer and Faith*, exemplifies the ability of still appreciatively appraising the dynamics which come from a tragic event such as brutally facing death in a lethal illness.[45] After he was diagnosed as having multiple myeloma, a cancer of the bone marrow for which there is no cure, Carmody could still apprehend the dynamics of such lethal illness as a great opportunity and a more urgent invitation to abandon himself to God in what he calls "this death sentence," of which he accuses God. As the CAT scan confirmed his fears, he acknowledged both the necessity of, and the love in, abandoning himself to God in the following words:

> I want to abandon myself, as all lovers do, even though I am afraid. I cannot do it myself. You must continue to do it in me, as you have been, O God, you are not too strange to be believed but too good. Who could think you love us, scrubby shabby sinful us, and make us divine? Who has been your counselor, God?[46]

In the light of the SFHF, what led the grieving couple to such a depreciative appraisal of the dynamics in their daughter's death is their disposition of awe which has become ***inverted***. Unlike Carmody whose

---

[45] John Carmody, *Cancer and Faith* (Mystic, Connecticut: Twenty-Third Publication, 1994).

[46] Ibid., 5.

disposition of awe enables him to see his lethal illness as an opportunity and an invitation to embrace ever more firmly the transcendent will of God through self-abandonment, their deformed disposition of anxiety and fear *inverted* their innate awe for the Radical Mystery, and so led them to such a depreciative appraisal of the form directives which the death of their daughter offered them. It is only when these parents reform their individual dispositions of *awe-in-wisdom*, through reforming their deformed anxiety and fear of being abandoned by God, like Carmody, that they will each be able to appraise appreciatively the form directives contained in the event of their daughter's death.

These insights make it clear that, similarly, it is only when the religious subject of the primary formation event reforms his primordial form disposition of *wisdom-in-awe* that he will be able to appraise appreciatively his dispositions of fear and anxiety, in his life-threading illness. It is only then that he will be able to consonantly apprehend the formative directives in his life-threatening illness as an opportunity and an invitation to abandon himself to the unconditionally loving and caring God, the Radical Mystery of all formation. For his disposition of depreciative abandonment comes from *inverted awe*, **not** *wisdom-in-awe*, even though it is in essence a contradiction in the existent-being in formation.

If the subject of the original formation event arrived at the conviction that God has abandoned him, it is also because his intrasphere is isolated from the rest of his field, including the Mystery – God. Hence, consequently, he refuses to encounter another persona who would have influenced him consonantly to formation and healing. This means that he refuses to use the necessity of life with which God provided him and fitted him out with at the moment of his creation, as Mbiti intuited.

In *When Bad Things Happen to Good People*, Kushner has pointed out that it is the bereaved who sought help from a neighbour. At first, they make it appear that they are well connected with others who are their inter-formative poles, and that they may therefore not be isolated from their field, but when we examine more closely their response to that fundamental question, which answer Kushner himself never expected to hear, we can apprehend therein an expression of their separation, and hence their isolation from the Mystery itself – God, however prefocal it may have been to them. The fact that they refused to fast during the last Yom Kippur is symptomatic, and therefore symbolizes empirically their separation from God. Thus, they were living in a state of self-isolation from God, closed upon themselves and not open to inspiration of the Radical Mystery, lest they might abandon themselves to God.

Kushner did not say whether later the grieving couple used the event of their daughter's death as an opportunity and an invitation to reform their dissonant disposition of self-isolation or not. However, Carmody, in *Cancer and Faith*, demonstrates that there is potency in the individual human being which enables him or her to remain open to another in interformative encounter. He himself is an exemplification of this reality. Even when he is in shock, angry, and aggrieved, and openly accuses God of being the one who pronounced "this death sentence" on him through such a lethal illness, Carmody remained open to God and did not cut himself off from God. On the contrary, he could conclude in his first reflection, which he made upon hearing that his illness cannot be cured:

> My life has been sinful, imperfect, nothing I am ready to let you judge. If you are not the father of prodigal children, the mother who can never abandon the child she has nursed, I have no hope. Give me hope, my God. Let my tears not flow in vain.[47]

In this light, therefore, the validity of the assertion by Mbiti, Kpiebaya, and Kuukure for all African societies, that in God's creation of the individual he also provided him and fitted him out with that which is

---

[47] John Carmody, opus cit., 3.

necessary for the consonant growth and development of his life, supports formation theory of the principles of *form potency* and *ongoing formation*, which hold, respectively, that every person in his or her preformation, is capable of giving form and receiving form, and that the *founding life form* also has the ability to continually transcend itself. Thanks to this primal endowment, one could still hope that the subject of the formation event might still reform his deformative disposition of intrasphere isolation, and thus allow confirming interformation to take place on all levels. In this way, like in the case of Carmody, the subject would be able to go beyond the dissonance of his current life form which has its source in that sad separation between God and the primal human being, and which the SFHF calls the *mystery of iniquity*.[48]

Transiting to the Second Remote Foundational Statement

The foregoing research examined the religious subject's fear of being rejected by God, and of which rejection the terminal illness he is suffering from is symptomatic. It also investigated how, because of this, the subject was refusing to encounter another. In this second part, the second remote statement will focus on the dynamics of refusal to open up to communication with another. This will help to discover how the subject will be persuaded to open up himself to encounter with another so that he may receive transcendent directives for eventual reformation.

---

[48] The theory of Formation Science attributes the reality of the mystery of iniquity to *the autarchic pride form:* See van Kaam, *Fundamental Formation*, 53-6.

Chapter 2: Encountering Religious Persons in Grave Illness

PART TWO
REFUSAL TO OPEN UP MIND AND SOUL TO ANOTHER

The second remote foundational statement, derived from Coformant One on the religious horizon is formulated as follows:

Although such religious subjects may manifest apparent readiness to encounter another who is compassionately present to them. They may remain closed up to this compassionate other in their soul or mind.

As in Part One, the exploration in this part of the Coformant will also be carried out in two sessions: **A** and **B**. Section **A** will explore the proximate dynamics of the encounter on the apparent level while Section **B** will examine the dynamics coming from the proximate directives of closing one's spirit to another.

SECTION A: being open to encounter on the apparent level alone

Though the religious subject may cooperate with the compassionate other who is visiting him, allowing this other with his warm and comfortable hands to turn him to face him, it does not necessarily mean that he is truly open to him, or that he may be influenced interiorly by his concerned visitor. This area of the research therefore is to investigate and to find out whether or not such cooperation is only on the apparent level.

From the SFHF: Apparent Form of Life

We have already discussed at some length in Chapter One, Formation Science's construct of the *unique-communal founding life form*.[49] In

---

[49] See chapter one.

Transcendent Formation, van Kaam refers dynamically to this unique-communal founding life forma as our "unique-communal life call."[50] It is this preformationally given unique-communal founding life form which "concretizes itself in the emergent core form or heart."[51] This core form, which is the relatively enduring ground form of one's empirical life, "is what gives rise to the other three integrative forms of life: the current, the apparent, and the actual."[52]

Van Kaam describes the apparent life form as "the integrational manifest form which life assumes in reaction and response to real or imagined expectations of others."[53] However, commenting on what he calls *pseudo-gentility*, or the "lie of gentleness," he warns:

> We may try to shorten the road by cultivating pseudo gentility or the lie of a gentleness not really felt. To keep this lie alive, we may deform our apparent form by pasting on the mask of kindness. When this tactic fails, we may resort to that of affective isolation. Avoidance of involvement with people seems to enable us to maintain our status. We can stay nice on the surface by escaping any chance of conflict.[54]

However, in spite of the fact that the apparent form of life can be an imagined expectation of others which a subject might assume, the formative

---

[50] Adrian van Kaam, *Transcendent Formation*, opus cit., 133.

[51] *Fundamental Formation*, opus cit., 251.

[52] Ibid., 253-5.

[53] Ibid., 256-7.

[54] Adrian van Kaam; *Formation of the Heart*, 97. To distinguish between real or imagined expectations of others which a subject may assume, van Kaam gives some examples of consonant form structures of the apparent life form. He does this in contradistinction to the allowing of its exclusive domination by pulsations, pulsions or ambitions on the personal level of our intrasphere; see 180.

disposition of privacy allows a person to assume such an apparent form of life which does not represent the reality that these others may expect. For such a life form can create opportunities for the consonant disclosure of our FLF since it protects in this way our privacy, thereby creating a favorable ambiance – an emergent private life – where, in our intrasphere, the unfolding of our FLF takes place. As van Kaam clearly points out, such an emergent private life is our personal partner in the dialogue in which the ongoing disclosure of our FLF may occur.[55]

From these insights on the apparent form, it is implied that a disposition of openness which remains only on the apparent level of the vital dimension of life cannot create sufficient opportunity for a true encounter with another. As we have earlier demonstrated, human encounter is a meaningful and interformative relationship between persons. And through such a relationship a subject allows another to reach his or her core form and to influence his or her intrasphere for the consonant unfolding of his or her FLF. This consonant unfolding of the subject's founding life form, which would include true formative healing of the person, can be regarded in the SFHF as the fruit of interformation and the overall objective of true encounter.

This fruit of interformation and the overall objective of encounter are what divination in practically all African societies seeks to provide for the individual who requests it. For, by means of divination the diviner is credited with the ability to encounter the individual in his or her intrasphere in order to disclose the deformities therein, so that he or she may heal the person through reformation of the subject's intrasphere. In dialogue with R.S. Rattray, and especially with Gregory E. Kpiebaya, we will explore the meaning and objective of divination which is also commonly known as soothsaying.

---

[55] Ibid., 140-1.

R.S. Rattray and Gregory E. Kpiebaya: Divination or Soothsaying

In the second volume of his over 600-page work on the tribes of Northern Ghana, Robert Sutherland Rattray says of the religious activities of the people: "If I were asked to name the most conspicuous though not necessarily most important feature in Northern Territory religious practices, I would, I think, select the cult of the soothsaying with their consulting shrines."[56] This observation by Rattray is indeed true, not only of all the different tribes in Northern Ghana, but of most African societies.

Soothsaying, more descriptively called divination, is not just popular and conspicuous feature in African religious practices. It is, indeed, an important feature in their life; it is essential for the disclosing of the interior condition of the individual, particularly in his or her relationship with God, and the interior depths which the individual may never get to know by him or herself without the help of a diviner. This explains in part Ray's correct affirmation that, in the traditional context, religion plays an enormous role in African societies, and so cannot be left to the individual as his or her personal affair. The African considers the relationship to the sacred to be a communal one. And in listing the offices which serve the community in this respect, Ray includes the diviners.[57] This conclusion concerning the diviners demonstrates the important role that divination plays in these communities and societies.

What precisely then is divination? To underscore the reality that soothsaying is not only a conspicuous religious practice, but also a truly important and even necessary feature in the religious practices of the people referred to by Rattray, Kpiebaya claims that divination constitutes the

---

[56] R.S. Rattray, *The Tribes of the Ashanti Hinterland* (Oxford: Clarendon Press, 1932), 313.

[57] Benjamin C. Ray, *African Religions*. 17.

preamble to many religious activities of these people.⁵⁸ It is the tool by which the hidden causes of events, either in the life of an individual, family, or community, are brought to light. Kpiebaya referred to an earlier affirmation he made, that people always try to find the connection between an event and its repercussion, and goes on to describe the objective of, and define divination in, these terms:

> Among the Dagaaba, "Baga-bugebo" [divination] is the means by which they can establish this link; at the same time it is through it that they can know what action to take in given circumstances. Divination is the technique by which we can know the hidden meanings or causes of events that happen in our lives.⁵⁹

Through divination, therefore, the deformities which may be in the intrasphere of a subject are not only disclosed, but the diviner also indicates and gives directions as to what is to be done to redress the dissonance in the subject.

Hence, if the subject of the primary formation event still belonged to the faith tradition of his forefathers, it is the diviner who would have been called in to minister to him before the 'medicine-man.' For it is a diviner who would have had to reach into his deep interior to find out the cause of his illness and to give directives for what action would have to be taken for his healing. But what is happening when the interior of the person is proving to be inaccessible to the diviner? Our objective in the following section will be

---

⁵⁸ Gregory E. Kpiebaya, *God in Dagaaba Religion and in the Christian Faith*, 38.

⁵⁹ Ibid., 38. After giving the objective of, and defining divination, Kpiebaya discusses in detail its various aspects and practice among the Dagaaba. See 38-52. See also Edward Kuukure's concept of who the diviner is; opus cit., 106.

to inquire into how someone's mind, or spirit and will, may be closed up to another.

SECTION B: CLOSING ONE'S MIND/SPIRIT AND WILL TO ANOTHER

The religious Subject who may cooperate only on the apparent level with a compassionate visitor by his hospital bed may still keep his core/heart closed to this other. His human spiritual faculties of mind and will are not open to the other visiting him. Our exploration in this area of the project will focus on the intraformative sphere, its potencies and dispositions.

From the SFHF: The Intraspheric Formation Potencies

So far, our research has come to the practically evident conclusion that any consonant interformation takes place in a person's intrasphere.[60] We have also sufficiently demonstrated in Section A above that if the intrasphere remains insulated from all influences and particularly interformation directives, formation of the individual cannot occur since true formative human encounter must include the intrasphere.[61]

In his discussion of the *Intraformative Sphere and the Origination of Dynamic Directives*, van Kaam claims, "At the centre of this sphere, there is a core of central dynamic potencies and dispositions, to be distinguished from the auxiliary Intraspheric form potencies of memory, imagination, and anticipation."[62] This core of central dynamic potencies has as its origin

---

[60] Adrian van Kaam defines Intraspheric formation as "formation that takes place by the interaction of formation processes within the human person." See *Fundamental Formation*, 304.

[61] See chapter one, under *Human Encounter*.

[62] Adrian van Kaam, *Scientific Formation*, opus cit., 135.

the FLF which, according to van Kaam, "hides the secret of our transcendent identity."[63] Thus in this light, van Kaam describes the FLF as "a source of congeniality or integrity dynamics," and he adds compatibility to this quality of congeniality.[64]

Central Formation Powers: The FLF itself being preempirical, its dynamism is latent and therefore is not directly available to focal apprehension and appraisal. However, the core form of life, which is the empirical and is known as the secondary foundational form of life, consists of the mind or spirit and the will. These, together with the dispositions of the core form or heart – attention, apprehension, and affirmation, which are the direct activities of mind and will – are the central powers of formation of the human person. It is by them that the formative appraisal process of form directives can be completed.[65]

Auxiliary Intraspheric Form Potencies: The process of appraisal of the form directives is not carried out by the central powers of formation alone. As van Kaam indicates: "*This kind of inquiry is not merely logical; it is dialogical. This approach implies the use of our central and auxiliary intraformative powers.*" As we have observed ourselves, these auxiliary intraformative potencies are the memory, imagination, and anticipation. Van Kaam describes them in these terms:

---

[63] Ibid, 147.

[64] Ibid., 149; See also Adrian van Kaam and Susan Muto, *Formation Guide*, 90 and 141-2.

[65] The appraisal process consists of formative attention, apprehension, and appreciation. Simplistically put, the mind becomes aware of or attentive to the presence of a formative directive; it apprehends such a directive and examines it various aspects, thus giving its appreciation of it. It is then the task of the formative will to affirm or not to affirm the directive so appraised, and also eventually to affirm its incarnation or practical application. See Adrian van Kaam, *Scientific Formation*, 156.

Memory helps to concretize dissonant directives by recalling their influence in our past. Imagination gives concrete shape to motivations and situations in which the desired consonant directive could be implemented. And Anticipation enables us to project situations in which our resolve will be put to the test.[66]

It is all these formation power centres which, according to the SFHF, the religious subject of the original formation event enclosed within his intrasphere when he refused encounter with his compassionate visitor. As his intrasphere, i.e., his core form of life or soul, remains insulated and cut off from the influence of any directives from the other areas of his field, the central powers of formation characterizing his heart – mind and will – together with its dispositions and auxiliary formation powers are all locked up, and so out of reach of the formation directives from the other.

Formation directives, which reach the core of the individual and are appraised appreciatively by the Intraspheric powers, make possible the consonant unfolding of the personality of the individual. This process is what van Kaam defines as follows:

> An empirical-theoretical elucidation of human life and its unfolding as disclosed by a critical appraisal of experiences, empirical data, explications and theoretical explanations in the light of the spiritual formation perspective and in dialogue with unfolding formation anthropology."[67]

Benjamin Ray presents an African concept of the person which may enable us to expand the Science of Foundational Human Formation's insight on the Intraspheric formation powers in the light of the original formation event.

---

[66] Ibid., 135.
[67] Adrian van Kaam, "Provisional Glossary" *Studies* 1 (May 980), 288.

Chapter 2: Encountering Religious Persons in Grave Illness

Benjamin C. Ray: **Concept of the Person**

Although several authors, including Benjamin Ray himself, hold that in African philosophy persons tend to be defined in terms of the groups to which they belong,[68] he still acknowledges that African thought gives a definition to the individual person. As he admits: "African thought also recognizes that each individual is a unique person endowed by the creator with his own personality and talent, and motivated by his own particular needs and ambitions."[69] Ray goes on to express his perception of this African concept of the person as an acknowledgement of the transcendence of the individual person over his or her sociohistorical dimension, even though this concept may always be balanced against the sociohistorical dimension of the individual.

Ray may be right in his perception of the African concept of the individual as being always balanced against the sociohistorical (which he calls the social and historical context or the sociocultural context). Nevertheless, there are others whose concept of the person in African thought may be regarded as differing from, yet complementary to, the one enunciated by Ray. For example, after a brief survey of a host of definitions of the person in African thought, Edward Kuukure warns that one should not be led astray by the well-publicized traditional body-spirit constituents by which the human has often been defined.[70] He affirms what he considers as the Dagaaba concept of the human person in these terms: "Man is not a loose confederation of these parts, i.e. body and soul, but a unity, a person, a conscious responsible self-capable of communicating and relating to others.

---

[68] See John S. Mbiti, *African Religions and Philosophy*, 106; Maurice Delafosse; Haute-Senegal-Niger (Paris: Emile Larose, 1912), vol. 3, 95.

[69] Benjamin C. Ray, *African Religions* (opus cit.), 132.

[70] Edward Kuukure, opus cit., 81-2.

Whatever happens to any part happens to the whole person."[71] He supports this concept of the person by pointing to the abundant Dagaaba metonymic expressions which regard the human faculties and sentiments.

An Integrative Reflection

The theoretical discussions in this section have led us to some light on the current life form of the subject of the original formation event on the religious horizon. When the religious subject of the primary formation event felt the gentle touch of his visitor's warm and comforting hand, he responded vitally to it, cooperating with its movements. This could easily have been mistaken by an untrained observer as an absolutely unmistakable sign of openness of the subject's intrasphere to his visitor. However, this cooperation was only on the surface. For, as it seems evident from the narrative of the event, the subject was still rather depressed and angry, and did not want his visitor to reach his intrasphere, his core form of life.[72] This makes his vital response to the gentle touch of his visitor to qualify only as apparent. It does not come from the core form of his life which is the immediate empirical concretization of his preempirical *unique-communal founding life form*.

If we allege then that the cooperation which our religious subject of the original formation event gave to his visitor was only a vital and, therefore, an appearance of a response which remains only on the surface, we are saying that his turning around to face his visitor did not in itself denote an act which came from his core form. But to verify such an allegation concerning the religious subject, it would require in his faith tradition a diviner who has that technique by which, as Kpiebaya claims, the hidden meaning or cause of the event of the subject's life-threatening illness. However,

---

[71] Ibid., 83.
[72] Confer the Narrative of the Formation Event, viii-xii above.

knowing whether the religious subject in allowing himself to be guided by the hand of his visitor indicates openness for a human encounter at the level of his intrasphere or not, is an empirically verifiable phenomenon which seems to be common among people of various faith traditions.

In her autobiography, Thérèse of Lisieux speaks with great pain of how no one knew of her vocation except her deceased mother from whom she was already *separated* for five years.[73] Her mother was, in fact, the one responsible for her vocation, which remained undisclosed in her intrasphere, and now disclosed to only her sister, Celine, who has become her confidante in that respect. She had not disclosed it to even her father who referred to her as his *Queen*. As Therese herself writes in her biography:

Celine became, then, the confidante of my struggles and sufferings, taking the same part as though it were a question of her own vocation. From her I had no fear of opposition. I didn't know what steps to take to announce it to Papa. How should I speak to him about parting from his Queen, he who'd just sacrificed his three eldest? Ah! What interior struggles I went through before feeling courageous enough to speak![74]

From this description of her interior struggles and sufferings about her vocation, unknown to her father, it is clear that Therese had, until then, refused to disclose the treasures of her soul/mind to her father, even though she was his "Queen." In Formation Science language, we can say her apparent life form before her father shielded what was in her intra form, at least with regard to her vocation. She gives the pain her father would suffer in having to part from his "Queen" as the reason for refusing to open up her soul and mind to him.

---

[73] Saint Thérèse of Lisieux, *The Story of a Soul*, trans. John Clarke (Washington, D.C. ICS Publications, 1975).

[74] Ibid., 107.

Although the apparent form of life, as we have observed, can be used in a deformative way,[75] we also remarked that, on the other hand, *formative disposition of privacy* allows its use in order to protect one's privacy in view of creating favorable conditions for the consonant disclosure of one's FLF. Our presumption here, therefore, is that, if Therese did not disclose, open up her mind and soul to her father in this respect, it is in view of the undisturbed and consonant unfolding of her FLF. As she said of her sister, Celine, the confidante of her struggles and suffering, "From her I had no fear of opposition." This implied that she feared she might meet opposition from her father in, at least, his pain of having to part with his Queen. For this in turn would disturb, to some extent, the joy in her vocation, as she had so much affection for her father, and did not want to see him suffer such pain in having to let go also his Queen. Hence, this explains the assumption of her apparent form of life before her father, and which protected the consonant unfolding of founding life call until such time as she could then disclose it to him.

It is also appropriate to observe here that, as Therese was already opened up to her Lord,[76] and was experiencing the consonant unfolding of her FLF, she did not need in any way the help of a *diviner*. As both Rattray and Kpiebaya so clearly assert, the diviner is only called upon to help an individual in the consonant unfolding of his or her founding life call.

However, returning to our original formation event, although the diviner could not be called in, for the reason that the subject belonged to the Christian faith tradition, the theoretical question can still be raised out of curiosity. What would have been the nature of the subject's response had his compassionate visitor been perceived as a *"Christian diviner?"* Hypothetical as such a question may indeed seem to be, the religious practice of divination aims at encounter between the subject and the diviner

---

[75] See footnote #54 above.
[76] Thérèse of Lisieux, opus cit., 105-6.

through focally conscious placing of the subject directly before the divine.[77] In this context, the subject more readily opens up his core form to the other – the diviner – who is thus able to give consonant form directives to him for his true formative healing.

It is for this reason that Therese did not need a diviner since she was already directly before her Divine Lord himself. Her Intraspheric powers of formation – her mind and will – though closed to her father in this respect were in formative openness before her God. This was not the case with the subject of our original formation event whose mind and will were closed up to the compassionate visitor.

With the above reflections, we consider the important dynamics of this remote foundational statement of the coformant sufficiently elucidated on the religious horizon. However, before we go on to Chapter Three, in which we shall examine the role that Grace can play in this situation, we will point out some potential obstacles to, and also facilitating conditions for, consonant human formation on the religious level, that may be inherent in the event.

OBSTACLES TO, AND FACILITATING CONDITIONS FOR, RELIGIOUS FORMATION

In the coformant on the foundational religious level of presence, the main obstacle to consonant formation and reformation is the fear which takes control of the subject. This is the fear that the subject may consider himself as rejected by the Divine Mystery for some wrong that he believes he must have committed and of which the grave illness and impending death are symptomatic.

---

[77] Edward Kuukure; opus cit., 105. Here Kuukure describes the diviner as "the most esteemed personage with a most important role in the life of the community."

Besides this fearful anxiousness that he is abandoned by his God, and which makes him feel he must be abandoned by all other human beings, the closure of the intrasphere of the religious subject to all formative influences coming from consonant directives leaves his current life form in an abyss of despair. There is no hope of receiving form that would lead to the reformation of the deformed and dissonant life disposition, and thus eventually bring him formative healing.

A principal facilitating condition for consonant formation is the caring presence of the other. This other who is closely associated with the divine Mystery itself – God – through persistent care and concern for the subject, can promote appreciative appraisal of the divine Mystery in the subject.

Also the silence – which the religious subject of our original formation event observes as pervading the room – can again be a facilitating condition for religious formation and reformation. Even though it may seem purely externa, all the same, it is favourable and conducive to formative attention, and can create the consonance necessary for the appreciative appraisal process whenever the time for it would come.

A Transitional Note to Chapter Three: Foundational Christian Presence

The above investigations concentrated on the fear of divine rejection and retribution, in which the religious subject in grave illness, and facing imminent death, is locked in. It also sought to explain such a religious subject's refusal to open up to others. The following chapter which will research on the same coformant but will do so on the level of foundational Christian presence, will focus on the Christian subject's resistance to graced communion with God through Jesus Christ and the neighbour, in the face of terminal illness and imminent death.

CHAPTER THREE

RESISTANCE TO GRACED COMMUNION IN THE FACE OF DEATH

INTRODUCTION

In Chapter Two, we examined the anxiety and fear which a religious person may experience in time of grave and life-threatening illness. We studied the dynamics which characterize his or despair at the feeling of being abandoned by God. In Chapter Three, we will seek to elucidate similar dynamics which come to the fore in a Christian in the same coformant stated thus:

> Christians who are suffering from life-threatening illness and are afraid of death may feel alone and abandoned by Jesus Christ. They may initially refuse a loving attempt by a neighbour to communicate with them. Although they may respond vitally to such an attempt at communication, Christians may still refuse to open up to the graced communion offered by God through Christ in loving others.

Two remote foundational statements will be drawn from and investigated in this coformant. They are *Self-Isolation from the Triune God and Neighbour in the Face of Death* and *Refusing to Open Oneself to Graced Communion*.

PART ONE
SELF-ISOLATION FROM THE TRIUNE GOD AND NEIGHBOUR IN THE FACE OF DEATH

This first part of the chapter will seek to explore the following remote Foundational statement:

Christians who are suffering from life-threatening illness and are afraid of death may feel abandoned by God in Jesus Christ, and they may initially refuse to open to a neighbour's loving attempt to communicate with them.

The research in this first remote foundational statement will be done in two sections and will elucidate two dynamics inherent in it. Section A will explore what is entailed in the feeling of being abandoned by Jesus Christ which the Christian may experience while Section B will examine the refusal of the Christian, who is facing death, to cooperate with the loving attempt of a neighbour who desires to communicate with him or with her.

Section A: Feeling Abandoned by Jesus Christ

In his illness, which he believes is leading to his imminent death, the Christian subject of the primary formation event may not understand why Jesus Christ, to whom he has been so willfully faithful, would not deliver him from it. Such a Christian may feel that God, in the person of Jesus Christ, has abandoned him. This area of the research will endeavour to disclose the deformed conception that the Christian subject may have about the dynamics of the transcendent/pneumatic will.

Chapter 3: Resistance to Graced Communion in the Face of Death

<u>From the SFHF</u>: The Eternal Radical Mystery of Formation

In Chapter Two of this study, the fear and anxiety experienced by the religious subject of being abandoned by God is identified as "depreciative abandonment," which has its origin in ***inverted awe***.[1] This God whom the religious subject, through inverted awe, fears to have abandoned him is the same God that formation theory in its Christian articulation of pretheological Formation Science[2] designates as the Radical Mystery of All Formation – the Divine Forming Mystery. Van Kaam and Muto obviously intuit this reality when, in their discussion of our on the source of our being, they made the following statement:

> The Lord God reaches down to our fallen humanity; the Divine Forming Mystery, revealed as the Holy Trinity of Father, Son and Spirit, released into a fallen world the Incarnate Word; through his death and resurrection Christ restored the right relationship between us and the Father; thus was god's grace fully revealed.[3]

They arrived at this conclusion regarding "fallen humanity"[4] based on Formation Science's presupposition that "ours is an originality willed by our creator from all eternity."[5] As they explain, "Formation Science uses the

---

[1] See chapter two.

[2] See Adrian van Kaam, *Preliminary Glossary of Christian Articulation of Formation Science*, TS Epiphany Association, Pittsburgh, PA, 1-3.

[3] Adrian van Kaam and Susan Muto, *Formation Guide for Becoming Spiritually Mature* (Pittsburgh, PA: Epiphany Association, 1991), 36.

[4] The term "fallen humanity" used here may also remind one of Heidegger's construct of "Verfallen Daseins" in which the term "Verfallen means more decaying, deterioration; see Martin Heidegger, *Being and Time* (opus cit.), note 2, 42; note 1, 172; and note 1, 219.

[5] Adrian van Kaam and Susan Muto, *Formation Guide* (opus cit.,), 35.

phrase '*Divine Forming Mystery*' to signify God in whom we are sourced and from whence our life receives its direction."[6]

It is this same Divine Forming Mystery – God, the Radical Mystery of Formation – which Formation Science puts at the very centre of the formation field.[7] Rooted in the centre as origin and source of the field, the Divine Forming Mystery becomes evidently the eternal power of formation, and "in the free formation will of the human person."[8]

From the SFHF: The Christ Form

However, as van Kaam and Muto describe above, this Eternal Radical Mystery of Formation who is our source reaches down to us even in our "fallen-ness," and has revealed itself as a Holy Trinity of Father, Son, and Spirit. Hence, in the light of pretheological Formation Science,[9] God is not only at the origin and centre of all creation, but in the very formation will of the individual.

Such presence of the Eternal and Divine Forming Mystery in his creation, also of the human, is particularly through his Incarnate Word as the Judeo-Christian faith tradition reveals. It is this Word that God used to create.[10] And from this Word man continues to receive and give form, thus

---

[6] Ibid., 35. Van Kaam's Formation Theory of Personality starts with the discovery that God "is the unfathomable mystery in whom we live and move, and have our being." This echoes the words of Paul to the Areopagites in Athens (Acts 17:28).

[7] Confer Adrian van Kaam; "Preliminary Glossary of Christian Articulation of Formation Science," opus cit., 27.

[8] Ibid., 28.

[9] Ibid., 19. Here van Kaam points out that the basis of *pretheological Formation Science*, like *formation anthropology*, is empirical-experiential-formational reason.

[10] Gen 1: 1-2; the chapter details anthropomorphically how God, the Mystery of all Formation, gave form to everything including the human being. In fact, he

Chapter 3: Resistance to Graced Communion in the Face of Death

forming and reforming, and gradually unfolding himself, thereby responding to his foundational life call.

Therefore, while pretheological Formation Science helps us to know that the unique-communal founding life form of the individual has its origin in the Mystery, formation theology reveals to us that this FLF of the individual – the soul – is formed from all eternity, in the image and likeness of God. Furthermore, it reveals that each FLF has been formed from all eternity in the likeness of the Word who, in time, empirically and experientially became one like us – Jesus Christ. Thus God, the Divine Forming Mystery, presents to us the Christ-Form in, by, and through which our preforma-tional founding life form was created as the being that we are called to be formed after. Hence, the congenial unfolding of our FLF consists in living the Christ-form in the basic Christian character which is modelled after the heart or character of Christ himself.[11] In this way, we are receiving the graced Christ-Form which makes us share "in his consonance with the will if the Father within our formation field," as van Kaam conceives it. This seems to be what Paul brings home in his letter to the Galatians: "My children, I am going through the pain of giving birth to you all over again, until Christ is formed in you" (Gal 4: 19). Earlier in the same letter, Paul had stated emphatically his own transformation into the Christ-form (Gal 2: 19-20).

---

formed the human being in his own image and likeness. In his Gospel, John makes it clear that the Word God used to create refers to Christ; see Jn 1: 1-5, 14, and 16-7.

[11] Adrian van Kaam, *Transcendent Formation* (New York: Crossroad, 1995), 103-30. See also *Preliminary Glossary of Christian Articulation of Formation Science* (*PGCA*), 67-9. For more on congeniality with the Christ-Form, see also *PGCA*, 66.

Such is the God of the Christian – the Divine Forming Mystery, hidden from all eternity.[12] And who has manifested himself empirically in the human being, Jesus Christ, his Eternal Word. This is the Christ in whose image the Christian believes he has been formed (Col 1: 15-20). However, this is the same Christ by whom the Christian now fears he has been abandoned in his current life form of death-threatening illness, and so left in despair. With Karl Rahner and Gerald May, we shall investigate this reality in order to approach more closely the true character of Jesus Christ after which all human beings, especially the Christian who explicitly believes in him and is assured in the Christian tradition, are formed.

Karl Rahner: The Will for the Cross

Adrian van Kaam, who equates character with core-form, defines the construct, Christian character, in Christian articulation of Formation Science as: "A hierarchical constellation of consonant dispositions, identified as the infused-theological (faith, hope, and love); the cardinal (prudence, justice, fortitude, and temperance); and the moral (humility, patience, moderation, love of neighbour, charity) virtues."[13] Later on in the same Preliminary Glossary, he asserts that the Christian formation tradition provides us with graced directives and dispositions or virtues, some of which are ultimate, and others proximate, directives and character dispositions.

---

[12] Rom 16: 25-6; Eph. 1: 9, 3: Col 1: 26; 2:2; 4:3. Note 'a' of Col chapter 4 in the Jerusalem Bible, referring to verse 3 says that the phrase "the Mystery of Christ" is a variant of the phrase "the Mystery of God" in Colossians 2:2.

[13] Adrian van Kaam, "Preliminary Glossary of Christian Articulation (opus cit.)," 67. See transcendent Formation (MS, *Formative Spirituality*, vol six, Pittsburgh, PA), in which he devotes the whole of chapter ten to the anthropology of transcendent conscience and character formation.

Chapter 3: Resistance to Graced Communion in the Face of Death

All these consonant character dispositions and directives are together the spiritual founding life form of the Eternal Word in time – the Christ-form – after which we are formed and called to disclose in ourselves. One of the most outstanding of such character dispositions in the Christ-Form is what Rahner calls [Christ's] Will for the Cross." In one of his best theological works, Rahner says this of 'Christ's Will for the Cross:'

> It is the will for the Cross, the obedience onto death, the voluntary sacrifice of his life by the one who has power to give his life or keep it, by the one who gave it because this was his Father's Will. It was therefore a will for sorrow, for the chalice of bitterness, for destruction, because God was to be glorified precisely by such a voluntary acceptance of suffering.[14]

Rahner calls this *'the sacrificial disposition of Jesus himself.'* It is this disposition which one can say characterizes the core-form of Jesus Christ; that core-form assumed by the Eternal Word of God through whom all forms come to exist and in the likeness of which we are formed. The reality of the Cross – experiencing such suffering and dying – is the best and most empirically powerful manner by which God's Only Begotten Son could reveal his Father. In this way, he manifests to us the best character disposition which we need to cultivate and nurture in imitation of him in view of our relationship with God in the unfolding of our FLF.

In the light of such powerful character form of Christ, our life and well-being – Salvation – consists in nothing short of complete surrender and abandonment of the self to God as the Eternal Word manifested in his will for the Cross. Such understanding of this character of the Christ-Form leads Rahner to make this yet very powerfully insightful assertion:

---

[14] Karl Rahner, *The Content of Faith*, eds. Karl Lehmann and Albert Raffelt (New York: Crossroad, 1992), 297.

No amount of suffering, death, dark night, and denial of the unruly will to live could have forced God to come down to man. But such active renunciation of one's own happiness as is contained in surrender to pain and sorrow is still the clearest practical confession of the fact that the person, conscious of his own powerlessness in the face of the God of forgiveness and elevating grace, expects his salvation from above and not from himself, and hence, can and will sacrifice his ego and its values, those values which are powerless to procure his salvation.[15]

This most radical assertion made of Jesus by Rahner succinctly describes Christ's absolute submission, surrender, and abandonment of his will to God as Father. And it is, indeed, absolute because it is a surrender of the will of the Word of God from all Eternity, and therefore surrender of the will of the Absolute – God – empirical form, to the Absolute – God the Eternal Divine Forming Mystery.

Gerald G. May: Willingness and Willfulness

At the head of his chapter on Willingness and Willfulness in his book entitled *Will and Spirit*, psychiatrist Gerald May quotes the following from Dag Hammarskjöld's diary:

I don't know who – or what – put the question. I don't know when it was put. I don't even remember answering. But at some moment I did answer Yes to Someone – or Something – and from that hour I was certain that existence is meaningful and that, therefore, my life, in self-surrender, had a goal.[16]

---

[15] Ibid., 297.

[16] Dag Hammarskjöld, *Markings* (New York: Alfred A. Knopf, 1966), 1.

Chapter 3: Resistance to Graced Communion in the Face of Death

The obvious reason for which May took this particular quote from Dag Hammarskjöld's remarkable journal is to disclose to his readers one of his own heart's secrets; his entire life's longing "to say Yes, to give myself completely, to some Ultimate Someone or Something."[17] By this, May means he has been longing all of his life to surrender his will to Some Ultimate Being. Just as Dag Hammarskjöld found meaning in his existence the very moment he answered Yes to Someone or Something higher than himself, so also did May have the intuition that his life would be more meaningful when he would at last be able to say Yes to some Ultimate Someone or Something, to freely abandon his will to an Ultimate to take charge of, and to which something in him has been searching for such self-surrender from his childhood.

May affirms that even though it is difficult, "there is something in our hearts that calls for reconciliation of the individual, autonomous qualities of will with unifying and loving qualities of spirit."[18] This surrender of oneself may, therefore, come only after really difficult questions such as this: "Even if it is to God to whom I surrender, how can I trust that this God is true and good and will not abandon me?"[19] In all of this, May sees the paramount role of the human will, which he asserts "has more to do with personal intention and how we decide to use our energies."[20] As he concludes his contrast between human faculties of spirit and will, the "[w]ill has qualities of independence, of personal freedom, and of decision making."[21] It is, therefore, the will of the person which can say this "YES."

But just as the will can say, "Yes, I surrender myself in a truly significant way to the Ultimate, to be mastered by it," it [the will] can also say NO. The

---

[17] Gerald G. May, *Will and Spirit* (San Francisco: Harper & Collins, 1982), 1.
[18] Ibid., 3.
[19] Ibid., 2.
[20] Ibid., 3.
[21] Ibid., 3.

former is what May calls *willingness*, and the latter, *willfulness*. And though he admits that the two concepts cannot be explained in a few words, he nevertheless describes and defines them in this way which can be considered concise.

> ***Willingness*** implies a surrendering of one's self-separatedness, an entering-into, an immersion in the deepest process of life. It is a realization that one already is a part of some Ultimate cosmic process and it is a commitment to participate in that process. In contrast, ***Willfulness*** is the setting of oneself apart from the fundamental essence of life in an attempt to master, direct, control or otherwise manipulate existence. More simply, ***willingness*** is saying yes to the mystery of being alive in each moment. ***Willfulness*** is saying no, or perhaps more commonly, Yes, but…"[22]

Thus, a willing person is one who abandons his or her will to the Absolute Other in his or her life to control and to direct; while by being willful, a person separates and isolates himself or herself from the very source and ground of his or her life form, whether he or she is focally conscious of it or not.

An Integrative Reflection

If the Christian in the original formation event is feeling himself abandoned by Jesus Christ, it is most likely because of one of three reasons, or any two of them, or even all three taken together. It is either because the Christian's *pride-form*, which may still envelop his unique-communal FLF, hampers thus its consonant disclosure; or such a Christian may be

---

[22] Ibid., 6.

ignorant[23] of the Christ-Form after which he is formed and given, in time, as the Ultimate transcendent directive for the consonant unfolding of his FLF, and in his response to his unique-communal founding life call: or he may still be struggling within himself as to whether to say "yes" to the Divine Forming Will of God in imitation of the example of the Christ-Form, or to hang onto his own functional will which wants to remain the master.[24]

In his seventh reflection, after the diagnosis which confirms that he has bone cancer, Carmody muses on what the pill, which he takes on days during his chemotherapy, does inside his body. As he visualizes the good cells eating up the bad ones, according to some people, he expresses his deep gratitude to God for the fact that Jesus always put the spirit first and has thus, in his body, become for us myriad sacraments[25] of our Origin and Source. He puts it in the following terms:

> I'm grateful for Jesus' emphasis on the spirit. You have given us myriad sacraments. O God, all illumined by your Word made flesh. The understanding of Jesus expressed in John's Gospel has always pleased

---

[23] In the context of what he calls *A Contemplative Epistemology*, de Wit discusses in detail two types of knowing – **conceptual** and **perceptual** – and goes on to delineate different types of *ignorance* and *confusion* in relation to the two types of knowing. See Han F de Wit; *Contemplative Psychology* trans. Marie Louse Baird (Pittsburgh, PA: Duquesne University Press, 1991), 81-93.

[24] See Gerald G. May; opus cit, pp. 3-4. See also Karl Rahner, opus cit., 297. Here Rahner also attests to the struggle in the following terms: "surrender does not come easily. It has long been treated as a noxious concept in our society. We are taught never to give up, never to allow ourselves to be determined by anyone or anything other than our own self-will."

[25] *The Catechism of the Catholic Church* (Libreria Editrice Vaticana: Ligiori Publications, 1994) defines *Sacraments* as "perceptible signs (words and actions) accessible to our human nature. By the action of Christ and the power of the Holy Spirit they make present efficaciously the grace they signify" (p. 282 #1084)'

me most: very God and very man. I do not understand those who shy away from Jesus' divinity. To safeguard his full humanity they go mute about his openness with you, the Absolute Mystery. Surely that was settled hundreds of years ago, when canonical Christian faith insisted on both full humanity and full divinity. Surely we have no absolute fulfillment of our humanity and history, if Jesus is no more than the best of our mortal kind.

Feeling completely mortal these days, I am greatly consoled By Christ on the Cross. His vulnerability and courage would teach me all I need to know, were I faithful.[26]

In this emphatic declaration of his gratitude to God for what Christ is to him, Carmody reveals not only his profound trust in God, even in his terminal illness, but he reveals also the sacrament that Christ is to his unique-communal founding life-form. In God's Eternal Word made flesh, Carmody perceives the only form upon which his founding life-form has been modelled. If as he says, "there is no absolute fulfillment of our humanity and history, if Jesus is no more than the best of our mortal kind," the fundamentally implied conclusion is, how can I cease to trust in and depend on him even if in my body I am suffering pain and faced with imminent death? Precisely, as I feel so deeply my existential predicament – mortality – I experience consolation in Christ's vulnerability and his courage so clearly manifested on the cross."

Such trust in and dependence on the model form that Christ is to him, not only in spirit but also in his body, strengthens Carmody's continuous faith in God. Thus, in spite of the pain and suffering he is subjected to by his illness, he, nevertheless, believes that God, in Christ, has not abandoned him. On the contrary, the Christ-Form which suffered pain, and eventually died on the cross, inspires him to accept his suffering and his imminent

---

[26] John Carmody, *Cancer and Faith*, opus cit., 14.

death in abandonment to the will of God, now that he has been more profoundly awakened to this aspect of the Christ-Form by this stark reality of his own mortality.

The insights which Rahner offers on Christ's will for the cross, and the distinction that May makes between *willingness* and *willfulness*, all help us to understand better Carmody's abandonment of himself to God in imitation of the Christ-Form after which he has been preformed in his FLF. If the Christian in our original formation event feels abandoned by Jesus Christ, it may indeed be that he is still struggling within himself as to whether to say "yes" to the Divine Forming Will of God in imitation of the Christ-Form, like Carmody in his experience, or to say "no," being greatly influenced by his *pride-form*.

SECTION B: REFUSING THE LOVING ATTEMPT OF A NEIGHBOUR TO COMMUNICATE

As the Christian feels unjustifiably abandoned by Christ in terminal illness and impending death, he may also refuse to communicate with a neighbour who, in genuine love, tries to communicate with him. Such a Christian subject, who is thus frustrated, may have lost hope and may be despairing. In this section, we will like to explore the transformative potential of the neighbour and the channel of Christ's saving grace that such a neighbour may be to the subject.

From the SFHF: Negative Phase of Formative Transcendence

Not only did the Christian in our primary formation event feel himself abandoned by Christ, and so become alone and isolated from God, this feeling of abandonment by Christ led him also to isolation from others, and to refusal to have anything truly Intraspheric to do with them. All this is so because he is thrown into a ***transcendence crisis***. In the face of his imminent death caused by grave illness, the Christian is suddenly confronted by the limitations of all his human faculties, including his spiritual powers of mind and will. He is brutally faced by what van Kaam describes as "the disclosure of our finiteness in the very experience of our confinement manifested to us by a loss of opportunities, relationships, vital and functional strength and endurance."[27]

This manifest dissonance in the current life-form in the Christian makes, at least, temporally ineffective all consonant formation as the person becomes impervious to all formation directives, including directives from interformation poles. This dissonance in the current life-form of the subject is what the SFHF paradoxically regards as the ***negative phase of formative transcendence***. It is paradoxical because it is the negative part of that significant transcendent or spiritual formation stage which, in a negative way, positively and unmistakably calls for a redirection of the subject's current form of life. To quote directly from van Kaam's succinct and apt description of the redirection desired:

> Such redirection is meant to attune a person more finely towards the graced form he or she is called to live uniquely. The spiritual crisis that both renews and deepens transcendence involves in turn death and resurrection. The death experience is the negative stage of the crisis of transcendence. If one becomes fixated in this phase, he may be unable to experience the resurrection which normally follows the working through of the death experience.[28]

---

[27] Adrian van Kaam; *The Transcendent Self* (Pittsburgh, PA: Epiphany Association, 1991), 45. See also his *Human Formation*, p. 195. Here van Kaam describes ***transcendence crisis*** as crisis "marked by the destruction of one's current form, primarily functional appraisals, on which one has built one's life formation."

[28] Adrian van Kaam; *Transcendent Self*, 177.

We can therefore conclude that, although the negative phase of formative transcendence may, at first, be perceived as dissonant and undesirable, it is part of the journey to the full transcendent formation that every individual desires and eloquently demonstrates.

From the SFHF: Roadblocks to Transcendence-Grace

The negative phase in the formative transcendence stage of a person, which "is an invitation to breakout of the chains we have forged for ourselves, [and] to relinquish the thought of functional efficiency as an ideal in its own right,"[29] can become fixated. Thus, instead of becoming an opportunity and an invitation, it turns into a persistent series of roadblocks to transcendence, which prevent all transcendent formative energy, including energy from another, from reaching the central formation powers of the subject. The reality of such roadblocks is what van Kaam and Muto describe so clearly when they say: "We need the grace of transcendence to escape the dead-end streets of dissonance and depreciation. One main hindrance to flowing with grace is the automatic directive of self-protection at any price. This measure is partly instinctual, partly learnt from birth through our environment."[30] They insist that, for consonant formation to take place in the subject, "liberation from such reactions is necessary to release the floodgates of transcendent formation."[31]

Essential to the removal of the roadblocks on the journey towards transcendent peace (and formative healing) is "our ***willingness*** to respond to the invitations of grace to relinquish reliance on our insulated self or

---

[29] Ibid., 145.

[30] Adrian van Kaam and Susan Muto, *The Power of Appreciation* (New York: Crossroad, 1993), 57.

[31] Ibid., 57.

pride-form alone."[32] It is only in eventually removing these roadblocks on his journey to transcendence formation and healing that the subject may thus allow the loving attempts of the other to communicate with him to become truly effective through the flow of consonant formation directives.

For the Christian, a true understanding of who the other is may foster in him the willingness necessary to respond to the invitation of grace coming to him through this other and to relinquish his reliance on his own insulated self. This other is who is also known in the Judeo-Christian tradition as the *neighbour*. We will seek the Christian understanding of the neighbour which the Spanish mystic of the first half of the 16th century, Teresa of Avila, so well manifested in her writings. We shall also explore the Christian understanding of the concept "neighbour" with the distinguished German moral theologian, Bernard Häring.

Teresa of Avila: Love for One Another

Throughout the second volume of her Collected Works,[33] Teresa of Avila has consistently used the phrase "one another" in her instructions and exhortations to her sisters, whom she also addressed as friends and daughters. In *The Way of Perfection,* she frequently exhorted them to love **one another**.[34] In her instructions to them about the three pillars of their constitutions, Teresa considered love for ***one another*** to be the most

---

[32] Ibid., 58.

[33] Teresa of Avila, *The Complete Works of St. Teresa of Avila*, vol. 2, trans. Kieran Kavanaugh, and Otilio Rodriguez (Washington D.C. Institute of Carmelite Studies, ICS Publications, 1980). This volume consists of: *The Way of Perfection*, Meditations on *the Song of Songs*, and *The Interior Castle.*

[34] See, for example, *The Way of Perfection*, pp. 28, 29, 35, 56, 58, 165, and 200.

important.[35] And she takes care to explain to them what true love for the neighbour is. True Christian love for 'one another' is neither in excess nor in defect. Thus, Teresa warns her sisters in the community about the dangers of 'excessive love' in the following terms:

> Excessive love gives rise to the following: failing to love equally all the others; feeling sorry about any affront to the friend; desiring possessions so as to give her gifts; looking for time to speak with her, and often, so as to tell her that you hold her dear and other trifling things rather than about your love for God.[36]

From this description of excessive love, it becomes already clear that true Christian love for one another has God for its Ultimate object and centre. As Teresa explicitly says in conclusion to her description of excessive love for the other. "For when it is in service of His Majesty, the will does not proceed with passion, but proceeds by seeking help to conquer other passions."[37]

In the Christian Scriptures, tradition[38] on which Teresa's instructions and exhortations to her sisters are firmly based, the *neighbour*, the *other*, is perceived implicitly as image of His Majesty to whose service one is called in life. God is seen through the neighbour, the other; and this other becomes

---

[35] Ibid., 28. Teresa regards love of the neighbour and the other two – *detachment* and *humility* – to be the coformants of the foundation of prayer.

[36] Ibid., 55.

[37] Ibid.

[38] The Judeo-Christian Scriptures, most especially the N.T., are replete with the formula "love one another," or Love your neighbour." For example: see John 13:34; 15: 12, 17; Rom 12: 10; 1 Thess 4: 9 also Lv 19: 18; Mt 5; 43; Mk 12: 31; Rom 13: 9; Gal 5:14; Jas 2: 8; etc. All references are made from the New Revised Standard Version (NRSV).

thus the means through which God, His Majesty, can also direct us in our life and fill us with his favours – his graces. Within the context of Christian love, we shall explore with the theologian Bernard Häring who will offer further insights to understanding of the concept *"neighbour."*

Bernard Häring: "Neighbour" within the context of Christian Love

In the second of his three-volume Magisterial Work entitled *Free and Faithful in Christ*, Bernard Häring discusses in Chapter Nine, what he calls "Actualizing the Truth in Love."[39] Here in the article, "The Truth of Love Revealed in Jesus Christ," he explores under the paragraph-head 'Unity of divine love, love of neighbour, and oneself (425-30). Under the paragraph-lead, "Love of Self and Love of Neighbour," he writes:

> No biblically grounded person would speak of the "true self" outside of a genuine relationship with the other, with the Thou. Man exists in word and love; he becomes a spiritually conscious and free being only by opening himself to the love and acknowledgement coming from others and by responding in acknowledgement and love, by word and action.[40]

In these words, Häring makes it very clear that it is only within a genuine opening up of "himself" or "herself." It is only when a person opens himself or herself up, both to receive love from and to give love to another empirically, that such a person can mirror his or her "true self."

---

[39] Bernard Häring, *The Truth will Set You Free*, vol. 2 of *Free and Faithful in Christ* (New York: The Seabury Press, 1979), 419-91.

[40] Ibid., 428. Bernard Häring makes reference to F. Eibner's works: *Das Wort und die geistigen Realitat* (Innsbruck, 1921); *Wort und Liebe*, (Regensburg, 1935); also Martin Buber, *I and Thou* (Edinburgh, 1971); and R.O. Johann, 'The Making of Love' (Westminster, Md, 1959).

In the perception of one's true self in this way, Häring draws strong support from the behavioural sciences. Inspired by R. Volkl through the latter's works,[41] he strongly asserts: "The behavioural sciences make it even more evident than a legitimate self-affirmation, ego-strength and genuine love of self goes hand-in-hand with love of neighbour, just as the Bible teaches."[42]

At this point, it seems sufficiently clear that Häring uses the terms "other" and "neighbour" as synonyms; "true self" can only be perceived in "genuine relationship with the other," and "ego-strength and genuine love goes hand-in-hand with love of neighbour." The question that one may pose here is: "To whom can we refer as neighbour?" This is the question which Häring responds to when, after he quoted from The Second Vatican Council the following, "Everyone must consider his every neighbour, without exception, as another self,"[43] he went on to declare:

> We cannot honour and love ourselves as persons if we honour only those who are rich, who can reward us. If we despise other people or refuse them honour and love because of their colour, culture, social status or religion, we become unable to affirm our personal dignity and to love ourselves.[44]

In this light, it becomes evident that *neighbour* for the Christian, refers to all other persons without exception.

---

[41] R. volkl, *Selbstliebe in der Heiligen Scrift und bei Thomas von Aquin* (Munchen, 1956). See also *Fruhchristliche* and *Botschaft und Gebot der Liebe nach der Bibel* (Freiburg, 1964)

[42] Bernard Häring; Opus cit., 428.

[43] Vatican Council II, *Pastoral Constitution on the Church in the Modern World* – "Gaudium et Spes," 27a.

[44] Bernard Häring, *opus cit.*, 428-9.

An Integrative Reflection on the Above Section

Insights from the above discussions in Formation Science, with collaboration from the auxiliary scientists, Teresa of Avila and Bernard Häring, offer a specifically foundational understanding of the concerned and compassionate visitor to the Christian in the primary formation event, lying in his hospital room. In the light of these insights, the terms **_other_** or **_neighbour_** for the Christian, takes on a meaning different from the ordinary sense in which they are commonly used.

The image of the neighbour which comes out from all of the above illumination seems to be the *neighbour*, the *other* whose loving attempt to communicate with him is being rejected by the conflicted Christian. In the Holy Scriptures of the Judeo-Christian tradition, the concept of *neighbour*, experientially, gradually underwent different perceptions until the time of Christ, when it reached its finest and universal application to all human beings.

In the Old Testament (OT) period, and even at the time of Christ, the term only fellow Jews whom one was obliged to love as neighbours.[45] But it was not even all the members of the community of Jews that one had to regard and love as neighbours. Although it was not a law to hate the enemy, as Jesus is interpreted to have quoted from the law (Mt 5:43),[46] all those who did not live according to the law of Yahweh, and were thus considered wicked sinners, could not be regarded and treated as neighbours. They did

---

[45] Leviticus 19:18 – "You will not exact vengeance on, or bear any sort of grudge against, the members of your race, but will love your neighbour as yourself."

[46] See in NJB. Footnote "r" to Mt 5:43 explains Jesus' quote of the law of Old.

not deserve to be loved as neighbours; "For the Most High himself detests sinners" (Si 12:6).[47]

In the New Testament (NT), concept of the term *neighbour* reached the peak of its understanding as universally applicable to all human beings without exception. This New Testamentary image of the *neighbour* finds vivid and experiential expression in the parable of **The Good Samaritan** (Lk 10:29-37). In the NT, Christ in his teaching about who the neighbour is, did not only extend the OT's understanding of it to include fellow Jews alone, even if they are wicked, but also to all human beings. All are to be loved as neighbours just as the "Heavenly Father" loves all unconditionally (Mt 5:43-8).

This is, indeed, what makes *the Parable of the Good Samaritan* to be the most classically experiential and all-time valid definition of the term, *neighbour*. In it, Jesus concretely demonstrates the unlimited boundaries of who the *neighbour* is. This Samaritan who was not a Jew, and therefore not a neighbour according to the Jewish application of the term, is considered by Jesus, and also admitted by his audience, to have demonstrated all the marks of a true neighbour to the Jew who had fallen into the hands of the robbers. Thus, this obviously is the most powerful representation of who the neighbour is when one remembers the fact that Jews and Samaritans were actually enemies and hated one another most vehemently.

The love that the Good Samaritan manifests towards the unfortunate Jew who is an enemy defines best, most especially for the Christian, who the **neighbour** is. If therefore the Christian of our original formation event would perceive the *other* who is at his bedside as a neighbour in the image of the Good Samaritan, he most likely would not refuse to open himself to him, so as to allow the other to encounter him, and would not have even

---

[47] Ben Sira/Ecclesiasticus in 11:29 – 12:18 clearly defines the wicked, evildoers as sinners, and so are enemies who are to be detested and avoided by the God-fearing and just ones.

been regarding him as a contributor to his death-threatening illness. This is to say, if such a Christian is seeking the disclosure of his "true-self," he will not be able to find it "outside of a genuine relationship with the other, [and] with the Thou," as Häring attests.[48] Through encounter with the neighbour, he could open himself more so as to receive the grace of transcendence which would remove the roadblocks and thus open the floodgates, thereby liberating him to go consonantly and appreciatively on his journey towards formative healing, and so, transcendent peace and joy.

Transiting to the Second Remote Foundational Statement

Our exploration of the remote foundational statement above, concentrated on the feeling of abandonment by the Triune God, experienced by the Christian in his life-threatening illness. It also examined who the neighbour is and the role that he could play as the channel of Christ's saving grace to the subject. Research of the following remote statement will focus on the dynamics of graced communion with God to which the Christian may still be refusing to open himself or herself to.

PART TWO
REFUSING TO OPEN ONESELF TO GOD'S GRACED COMMUNION IN CHRIST THROUGH A LOVING NEIGHBOUR

This second part of the Chapter will examine the following remote foundational statement drawn from the coformant on the Christian horizon of human Presence:

Even though they may respond to such a communication on the vital level, Christians (suffering from life-threating illness and are afraid of

---

[48] See footnote #40 above.

death) may still refuse to open themselves to graced communion with God, offered through a loving neighbour.

Though several proximate dynamics can be found at work in this statement, two clear proximate directives come most directly to the fore. These are i) *Being offered God's graced communion in Christ through a loving neighbour*, and ii) *Refusing this graced communion with God*. However, because their dynamics are so interwoven. The results of the research in this part will be considered valid for both directives. We shall, therefore, endeavour to elucidate the dynamics of graced communion with God in the Christ-Form, which is offered through the neighbour, but to which the Christian, threatened by death and despairing, is refusing to open himself. He closes the door of his heart to Christ and his healing/saving grace which may come to him only through the neighbour. Hence, the study will focus on the neighbour as epiphanic manifestation of God, The Radical Mystery of All Formation. It will also examine how the presence of Christ in the neighbour may be communicated to the Christian subject as graced formation power.

From the SFHF: Epiphany of the Mystery of Formation

As the Christian subject, despairing of God's having abandoned him, refuses to respond to the compassionate neighbour visiting him, he implicitly rejects God himself, the Divine Forming Mystery, who may be manifesting himself to him through the visiting neighbour. For, as the SFHF affirms, "The mystery of formation manifests itself everywhere. It is like a never ending dance of rising and falling forms in cosmos, humanity, culture, and history."[49] In the self-isolated state in which he is, cut off from God, the Christian subject becomes blinded to all the other areas of his formation

---

[49] Adrian van Kaam, *Fundamental Formation*, 187.

field. He is encapsulated within "a self-constructed world of functional formation" where he is alone and feels he has either to succeed, doing it all by himself, or to fail to grow in formation.[50] The inherent "givenness" of his FLF, that "every event is related to every other,[51] is blunted by the quasi-FLF – the pride-form, as far as the rest of the cosmos and, indeed, the universe is concerned.

Although the cosmos is regarded as the epiphany of the Formation Mystery, the human being, in a most special way, is the epiphany of God. Adrian van Kaam echoes Einstein who declares that the basis of his scientific research rests on the inescapable conviction that the world is ordered and comprehensible, and not a thing of chance. In this declaration, van Kaam finds a vindication of Formation Science's assumption that a transcendent power is responsible for change and growth in everything, and provides elemental structure, order, and direction for all. After assuming that it is this power which is the source of what appears to be an inexhaustible variety of forms and expressions, he asserts the unique and special way in which human being manifests this transcendent power which, for the Christian, is the Divine Forming Mystery. As he says, "Human life too, is called to be a *manifestation of the formative power* of this formation mystery. This distinctively human epiphany of the formation mystery is a call to be personal-social and yet in harmony with the overall transcendent direction of universe and evolution."[52]

In this light, the individual human life-form is one of congenial and compatible consonance which has its source in the Formation Mystery itself.[53] As we observed in the Judeo-Christian Scriptures, this Formation

---

[50] Ibid., 194.

[51] Ibid., 198.

[52] Ibid., 208.

[53] The four dispositions of consonance by which we each mirror the Mystery of Formation – God – are congeniality, compatibility, compassion and compe-

Mystery, God, formed the human being in his own image and likeness (Gen 1:26). It is a "given," a grace which the unique yet communal life-form of the Individual receives. Hence, every human life form is, by its formation, in graced communion with the Divine Mystery that formed it. In this sense every individual human being is, in himself, an epiphany of God, and he shares this disposition of graced communion with the others. Thus, being in graced communion with the Divine Mystery, and therefore endowed with the potency to become a true epiphany of God, the individual also becomes God's graced communion to others.

From the SFHF: Graced Power of Formation

If the Christian subject, like all human beings, is endowed with the potency to mirror God in Christ, and thus to be the epiphany of the Divine Forming Mystery among the others, implicitly he also cooperates in the ongoing formation of these others, as they disclose their distinctively human life form. This is because the Christian participates in the graced power of formation. In Formation Science's language, van Kaam eloquently describes this reality in these terms:

> As power of incarnation, graced formation power discloses and implements – in the light of pneumatic-transcendent presence – congenial and compatible life forms that express in unpredictable and creative ways the foundational Christ-Form of the soul and that appropriate

---

tence. To these four dispositions is added courage, which "enables us to persevere, to press on towards the goal of becoming spiritually mature in Christ so that we may mirror the mystery of peace and joy for which all creation longs." See Adrian van Kaam and Susan Muto, Formation Guide, 141-2.

progressively the final transcendent and transparent self-forgetful form of life.[54]

In this light, it can be inferred that in one's empirical life form created after the Christ-Form, the Christian subject is, indeed, the incarnate power of formation for others. In this congeniality or compatibility with the graced formation powers of the Christ-Form, the Christian in turn becomes the source of such power with the ability to help others to disclose their own unique-communal life form through the concrete form directives that may emanate from it.

This Divine Forming power in oneself and the other is what the Christian needs for apprehending and appreciating both himself and the other. For once the Christian is focally conscious of the Christ-Form that the other can be to him or to her, he or she will be more disposed to be open to the other in order to share more effectively in the graced communion with this other.

From the SFHF: Willing openness to Divine Manifestations, and Willfulness

Our discussion on the graced power of formation with which the individual in his founding life-form is endowed has made it clear that the Divine Forming Mystery thus enables the individual to freely cooperate and participate in his own ongoing formation, and in that of others. This free cooperation on the part of the person is the function of his will. The will affirms the apprehended directives and thus cooperates in one's own ongoing formation and that of others, or it does not affirm them – the directives, and so refuses to cooperate.

---

[54] Adrian van Kaam, "Provisional Glossary," *Studies in Formative Spirituality* 1 (May 1980), 298.

Chapter 3: Resistance to Graced Communion in the Face of Death

We discussed in Part One of this Chapter the concepts of willingness and willfulness which Gerald May presented in his book, *Will and Spirit*. However, in the light of what Formation Science explains, when the Christian chooses to freely participate in his own ongoing formation or that of others, he effectively chooses to use the forming image of Christ inherent in his FLF. This is the *willingness* or *willing openness* to experience God on one's level of existence. Hence, it is a disposition of the transcendent will. This is evident in the example which van Kaam gives after defining *willing openness* as the permanent source of manifold ways of particularizing one's fundamental openness: "If I decide to grow to a truly religious existence, I become increasingly a *willing openness* for all manifestations of the presence of God in the reality which surrounds me."[55] *Willing openness* as a disposition therefore comes from the functional transcendent will of the person, which the SFHF also calls *existential* and *religious will*.[56] We may therefore conclude that *willing openness* is graced potency of formation which is given to the individual through the Christ-Form and which the person freely uses both for his own and others' ongoing formation.

Contrary to *willing openness*, and also analogous to its concept as is delineated above by May, is *willfulness*. Formation Science distinguishes three ways in which religious persons may understand the nature and task of the will in their religious growth.[57] Besides willingness which it also calls *existential will*, as we have already discussed, Formation Science identifies *willfulness* and *willlessness* as the other two. Both of these two are at the exaggerated extremities of the true nature and function of the will as *existential*.

---

[55] Adrian van Kaam, *Religion and Personality* (Pittsburgh, PA: Epiphany Association, 1991), 106-7.

[56] Ibid., 112-3. Here van Kaam offers a summary definition of both existential will and religious will.

[57] Ibid., 92.

If the existential will is one's openness to reality as it reveals itself and is also one's "subsequent personal option and execution of behaviour which integrates all relevant meaning of [one's] situation,"[58] willfulness is the ignoring of the working of grace in oneself in the belief that one alone by oneself can make it all work. Adrian observes that "Willfulness emerges in man when he loses the experience of his unity. He separates his will, as it were, from other elements of his personality."[59] Such dissonant disposition of the will leads a person to ignore even the transcendent dimension in one's formation field. And a Christian can similarly ignore the Christ-Form in his life-form.

These realities – the special manifestation of God in the Christ-Form after which the human is formed, and the graced communion with God which the Divine Forming Mystery offers to every person, especially the Christian – are all indeed a gift; i.e. grace[60] also offered to the Christian who may accept it or reject it. A rejection of such grace and communion with God comes from the despair that the Christian's current life-form may be in because of his dissonant conviction that he has been abandoned by God. With the help of *the Catechism of the Catholic Church*,[61] and Søren

---

[58] Ibid., 112

[59] Ibid., 92.

[60] The term 'grace' comes from the Latin, *gratia, gratiae*. Cassell's Latin-English Dictionary gives five shades of the English understanding of the term *gratia, gratiae*: that which is pleasing; favour with others; a kindness or favour done; indulgence towards an offence; and thankfulness. It is in especially this last sense of it that the term grace is used here, and in Christian theology. In its ablative plural form – *gratiis* or *gratis*, it means "without recompense," "for nothing," "gratis:" see "gratia, gratiae," *Cassell's Latin dictionary: Latin-English, English-Latin* (New York: Macmillan, 1968).

[61] The *Catechism of the Catholic Church* is currently the most recent comprehensive compendium of Christian Doctrine prepared by the Catholic Church under the instructions of Saint John Paul II, Pope, after the Second Vatican

Chapter 3: Resistance to Graced Communion in the Face of Death

Kierkegaard, we shall briefly discuss the "refusal of grace" and its root-cause, despair, respectively in the following paragraphs.

From the Catholic Catechism: Refusal of Grace

Before we go on to discuss the refusal of grace in the *Catechism of the Catholic Church,* let us look a bit more closely at grace itself. In his book, *The Craft of Theology,* Avery Dulles, in Chapter One, under the paragraph heading, "Anthropology: sin and grace," discusses the divination of man through Christ. He writes: "In Christ man is God as other. By contemplating the incarnate Word, we can learn that humanity is, in its inmost reality, a capacity to share in the divination preeminently realized in Christ."[62]

In reference to grace, Dulles affirms logically and ontologically that "in Christ, therefore, grace expressed itself through a human and bodily form, which became the 'realizing symbol' of God's redeeming action."[63] He makes this affirmation after his assertion that the theology of grace may be developed on the same principles as the theology of sin which he had earlier sketched out. He conceives the relationship between grace and its outer manifestation in terms of the two affirmations of Piet Schoonenberg.[64] And

---

Ecumenical Council, and published through the Apostolic Constitution, *Fidei Depositorum* on October 11, 1992. The English translation used here is the one for the United States of America: Citta del Vaticano: Libreria Editrice Vaticano, for the United States Catholic Bishops' Conference, 1994. Henceforth, it will be referred to simply as *Catechism of the Catholic Church.*

[62] Avery Dulles, *The Craft of Theology: From Symbolism to System* (New York: Crossroad, 1992), 30.

[63] Ibid., 31.

[64] Piet Schoonenberg formulates his two affirmations as follows: "First, each contact by which a person communicates his interior life to another person is, explicitly or not, a testimony about his relation to grace. Next, on account of our being human and especially on account of the humanity of God's Word there is no

with that he concludes saying: "Grace therefore has an influence on the way individuals relate to one another."[65]

Earlier, we mainly referred to grace as a participle qualifying the communion in which the Christian may live with the Holy Triune God through the Christ-Form. However, even the very communion in which the Christian may live with God is itself grace.[66] Thus, after defining grace as a participation in the life of God which introduces us into the intimacy of Trinitarian life in Baptism in the grace of Christ, the head of the body,[67] the *Catechism of the Catholic Church* goes on to declare:

> God's free initiative demands man's free response, for God has created man in his image by conferring on him, along with freedom, the power to know him and love him. The soul only enters freely into the communion of love. God immediately touches and directly moves the heart of man. He has placed in man a longing for truth and goodness that only he can satisfy.[68]

This declaration makes it clear beyond any ambiguity that, for the Christian, grace is a completely free gift which God, the Divine Forming Mystery freely offers to the Christian, and indeed to all humans. This offer which God makes does not compel the person to accept it. Because of the

---

granting of God's grace in which the world and one's fellow man do not have a part." See Piet Schoonenberg, *Man and Sin* (Notre Dame, IN: University of Notre Dame Press, 1965), 119.

[65] Avery Dulles, opus cit., 32.

[66] Speaking about preparing for the reception of grace, the Catechism of the Catholic Church holds "The *preparation of man* for the reception of grace is already a work of grace," 484 (#2001).

[67] Ibid., 483 (#1997).

[68] Ibid., 485 (#2002).

image of God as an Eternally Free Being in which the human person is formed, the person shares in the potency of freedom, however limited, to decide either to accept God's offer of loving communion with him, or to refuse it. If, therefore, the individual chooses not to accept God's loving communion offered to all humans, and focally and consciously offered to the Christian, then such an individual refuses grace.[69]

Søren Kierkegaard: Despair is "the Sickness unto Death"

In our discussion on the inverted awe which may lead a religious to the feeling of being abandoned by God, we observed that the deformative disposition of despair may be the undergirding reason for that.[70] As the person despairs in his or her conviction that he or she has been abandoned by God, he or she does not see what more there is for him or her in life. Thus, the person closes and folds up any further formation of his or her life-form.

In reality, however, the despair which the Christian experiences in this way, even though it may be only temporal, is what Kierkegaard calls *the Sickness unto Death*. Hearing such an expression the first time, one may easily be led to think that **"despair as Sickness unto Death"** means that despair itself is the mortal illness which will lead the one despairing to death. In metaphysical, and hence, transcendent concepts however, Kierkegaard explains what he means when he says that *despair is sickness unto death*:

> The concept of the sickness unto death must be understood in a particular sense. Literally it means a sickness the end and outcome of which is death. Thus one speaks of a mortal sickness as synonymous with a sickness unto death. In this sense *despair* cannot be called the

---

[69] Quentin Quesnell, "Grace," in *The New Dictionary of Theology*, eds. Joseph A. Komonchak, Mary Collins and Dermot A. Lane (Collegeville, Minnesota: The Liturgical Press, 1991), 437-50.

[70] See chapter two.

sickness the sickness unto death. For in the Christian understanding of it, death itself is a transition unto life. In view of this, there is from the Christian standpoint no earthly, bodily sickness unto death. For death is doubtless the last phase of the sickness, but death is not the last thing. If in the strictest sense we are to speak of a sickness unto death, it must be one in which the last thing is death, and death the last thing. And this precisely is despair.[71]

The despair, therefore, which Kierkegaard is speaking about as a "sickness unto death" is despair in the transcendent dimension. It is not an illness which would lead the subject to mortal, bodily – vital-functional – death, since, especially for the Christian, such death which may be regarded as only the end of the empirical form of life of the subject is indeed not the end, but the assuming of a Preface for the Dead, "Lord, for your faithful people life is changed, not ended."[72]

Understood in this light, the death unto which despair is said to be the sickness, is the torment into which such a disposition of despair plunges the person. In this disposition, the person is not able to die so that everything might come to an end. For, as Kierkegaard reasons: "If one might die of despair as one dies of a sickness, then the *eternal* in him, the self, must be capable of dying in the same sense that the body dies of sickness."[73] But this is, indeed, not possible, since "the self," the preempirical FLF shares in the image and likeness of the Eternal Divine Forming Mystery – the Triune God.

---

[71] Søren Kierkegaard; "The Sickness unto Death," in *A Kierkegaard Anthology*, ed. Robert Bretall (Princeton, NJ: Princeton University, 1973), 341.

[72] See the first Preface in the Mass of Christian Death in the Sacramentary of the Roman Missal (New York: Catholic Book Publishing Co., 1985).

[73] Søren Kierkegaard, opus cit., 342.

Chapter 3: Resistance to Graced Communion in the Face of Death

An Integrative Reflection

Both Formation Science and its auxiliary sources, through the above discussions in this section, have given us more clear insights in this horizon. They have elucidated the very nature of grace, and so, have given us greater understanding with regards to the refusal of graced communion with God by the Christian subject in our original formation event.

From the insights offered us by the SFHF, it is evident that God, who the Christian in the primary formation event believes has abandoned him, is in reality present to him. God is truly present to him, offering him formation in his graced loving communion with him through the compassionate neighbour who is visiting him, and has not abandoned him. As the SFHF observes, besides the fact that the infraformation of the human life-form[74] in the universal unconscious process of the cosmic epiphany of the Mystery of Formation,[75] the life form of each person "is called to be a manifestation of the formative power of this Formation Mystery."[76] Hence, the concerned and the compassionate visiting neighbour is the epiphany of God himself – the Divine Forming Mystery, but whom the Christian subject, in these circumstances, fails to recognize. As Jesus clearly indicated, he is identified with, and is to be recognized in, the neighbour, in whatever his or her unique-communal life call may be.[77]

This reality of the neighbour being the epiphany of God himself, through whom God bestows graced power of formation, is very well illustrated in the well-known conversion story of the Apostle Paul as he was

---

[74] Adrian van Kaam, "Provisional Glossary," *Studies* 1 (Feb 1980): 137.

[75] Adrian van Kaam, *Fundamental Formation*, 209.

[76] Ibid., 208.

[77] This is the criterion which Christ, "the Son of Man" will use to judge each person at end of time and history; Mt 25: 31-46. See also 10: 40; and Lk 10:16; Jn 13:33-5.

on his way to Damascus (Acts 9: 1-19). Even though Paul saw the light which shone around him and subsequently heard the voice which identified itself as that of Jesus whom Paul was persecuting, it is only later in Damascus that the meaning of the epiphany became fully clear to him through the visit of the disciple, Ananias.

When, for reason of his own, Ananias wanted to object to the Lord sending him to Paul who was then living in Straight Street, the Lord made it clear that he wanted to give his *graced power of formation* to Paul through him, Ananias. As Luke, the author of the Acts of the Apostles makes it clear: "The Lord replied, 'Go, for this man is my chosen instrument to bring my name before gentiles and kings, and before the people of Israel; I myself will show him how much he must suffer for my name'" (Acts 9: 15-16). Ananias did eventually go to visit Paul as directed by the Lord; and though he had regarded Paul as an enemy of the Church who was coming to Damascus to persecute it, he addressed Paul as "Brother Saul" and invited and gave to him the graced and formative power of healing, which comes from the Holy Spirit. As Paul willingly opened himself up and encountered a *neighbour*, a "*brother*," whom he did not know earlier, he was able to receive true "formative healing," and recovered his sight: "It was as though scales fell from his eyes and immediately he was able to see again. So he got up and was baptised, and after taking food he regained his strength" (Acts 9: 18-19). It was only when Paul recognized the disciple, Ananias, as a neighbour and the epiphany of the Lord, Christ, that he was able to receive *graced formation* and *healing*. He would not have received sight and healing had he refused to open himself up to Ananias and to recognise in him the epiphanic manifestation of Christ, the Lord himself.

In the light of the above, the opposite seems to be what happened in the case of the Christian of our original formation event. As he is refusing to recognise in the *other* the epiphany of God, and so, would have opened himself to encounter this other, the Christian refuses God's grace of unconditional loving communion with him. This is because the disposition

Chapter 3: Resistance to Graced Communion in the Face of Death

of his *existential will* has not been one of *willing openness*, but rather the deformed disposition of *willfulness*. And if such a Christian is to receive God's graced and loving communion, which he offers him unconditionally in Christ through the concerned neighbour, he will have to reform his disposition of ***willfulness*** and to allow it to be transformed into one of *willing openness*. For it is only in this latter disposition which is congenial and compatible with the *existential will* that he can apprehend, appreciate, and so, be able to encounter God's loving communion in Christ offered to him through the neighbour.

Formation Science has also led us to a better understanding of what this grace of communion, of which the neighbour is the epiphany, truly is. This graced communion of God with the Christian is the graced power of his formation itself, sourced by the pneumatic-transcendence presence incarnated in the neighbour. As Formation Science tells us, this power of formation incarnated in the neighbour is able to disclose and also effect congenially the life forms that express the foundational Christ-Form in the soul of the Christian, thereby progressively making the soul approach the final transparent or transcendent disclosure of itself.[78] This potency for the full disclosure of his life form is therefore precisely what the conflicted Christian in the formation event refuses when he refuses God's graced communion with him offered through the neighbour.

This is the same graced communion that God offers to the Christian, which the *Catechism of the Catholic Church* describes as God's free gift that has the power to make the receiver ever more transparent. As it states: "Grace is first and foremost the gift of the Spirit who justifies and sanctifies us. But grace also includes the gifts that the Spirit grants us to associate us with his work, to enable us to collaborate in the salvation of others and in the growth of the Body of Christ, the Church."[79] It is the nature of this grace

---

[78] See footnote #53 above.

[79] *Catechism of the Catholic Church*, 485 (#2003).

of communion with God which Dulles so clearly brings home to us, pointing out the special manner in which it can influence the relationship of individuals to one another.

Kierkegaard, in the explanation of his affirmation that "despair is the sickness unto death," helps us to understand better the nature of the dissonance in the disposition of despair which led to the current life form of the Christian in the primary formation event and to his refusal of graced communion with God. This despair is the torment that the Christian experiences of not being able to die and so rest away from everything.[80] It is an existential disposition which, when taken in a literal sense, is an ontological contradiction. And this, in my view, is the current life form the Christian, in the primary formation event, is experiencing.

With such an in-depth understanding of the dissonance into which the Christian in the original formation event is plunged, we consider the investigation in this chapter completed. However, before we go onto the next chapter, we wish to conclude the present chapter with a summary of potential obstacles to, and facilitating conditions for, a more consonant unfolding of the Christian's life form.

OBSTACLES TO AND FACILITATING CONDITIONS FOR CHRISTIAN FORMATION

It may be observed from the outset that several obstacles to the consonant formation and transformation of the Christian are identifiable in the coformant on this horizon of the human presence. However, presently we will point out just two primary obstacles which come to the fore. i) The first of these is the feeling that the subject has, *that he is abandoned by Jesus Christ*. This feeling is responsible for the isolation of our Christian subject from Christ and makes it impossible for him to receive directives from the

---

[80] Confer footnote #72 above.

Christ-Form. ii) The second obstacle is the Christian's subsequent refusal to communicate with the loving neighbour. He is also unable to encounter the neighbour, and to communicate with him at the level of his core form of life because of his *willfulness*. This *willfulness* makes him refuse to be open to the neighbour.

Unless such a Christian overcomes these two obstacles, there is virtually no hope that he can enter into a graced communion with God through Christ, but which he desires so much infrafocally and even prefocally.

As with regard to potential formative conditions for facilitating the reception of graced communion with God in the Christ-Form, besides *transparent grace itself which is initially freely given* by God in the Christ-Form, the most obvious other facilitating condition is *the concerned and loving neighbour.* With his persevering and consonant presence, *his attempts to go beyond the subject's apparent form to his core* offers a principal facilitating condition for the reformation of the latter's **existential will** as a Christian. For, thus formed, the Christian's *existential will* may become disposed to *willingly open* him to encounter with the loving neighbour who is the potential channel through which he may receive God's graced communion in Jesus Christ. And thirdly, although not featuring so prominently, the respect that the Christian subject has always had for such "an-other" is also a potentially facilitating condition.

A Transiting Note to Chapter Four: Christian Ministers

The research in the foregoing horizon of consonant Christian formation, in Coformant One, focused on transcendent dynamics which come from the graced communion with God in Jesus Christ, offered through another. It investigated the dissonant directives in the situation of grave illness which may block the Christian from encounter with a compassionate other, thereby preventing him from graced communion with God in the Christ-Form of which the other is the epiphany.

From Functionalistic Willfulness to Transcendent Willingness

In Chapter four, we shall investigate, on a segmental level, the dynamics which are present in the situation of life-threatening illness and which may lead a Christian minister to frustration and anger at unfulfilled projects.

CHAPTER FOUR

FRUSTRATION AND ANGER AT THE UNFULFILLED AMBITIONS

INTRODUCTION

In Chapter Three of this research on the Christian horizon level of human presence in Coformant One, we explored the dynamics of graced communion inherent therein. This Chapter will investigate, in the same Coformant, on the segmental level of Christian minister, the dynamics behind the frustration and anger at unfulfilled ambitions which Christian ministers may suffer. The Coformant to be elucidated is stated as follows:

> Christian ministers suffering from grave illness which threatens to bring to a sudden end their ministry may initially feel abandoned by God and, in frustration and anger, cut themselves off from attempts by a revered superior to engage in dialogue with them. These Christian ministers may respond vitally to such attempts, but they may still refuse to enter fully into dialogue on the level of their heart through their spiritual faculties of mind and will.

Like the ones before it, this Chapter will also be divided into two parts. Each part will consist of a remote formational statement drawn from the Coformant. In the first part, A, we will study the imminent end ministry perceived by the subject as a sign of abandonment by God; and in the second part, B, we will seek to disclose the dynamics involved in engaging in a transforming dialogue in such a dissonant current form of life.

From Functionalistic Willfulness to Transcendent Willingness

PART ONE
IMMINENT END OF MINISTRY PERCEIVED AS A SIGN OF ABANDENMENT BY GOD

The first remote foundational statement drawn from the Coformant on the segmental level of Christian ministers is articulated in the following these terms:

> Christian ministers suffering from grave illness which threatens to bring to a sudden end their ministry may feel abandoned by God and, in frustration and anger, cut themselves off from attempts made by even a revered superior to engage with them in dialogue.

We shall study this foundational statement in two sections. Section A will focus on the proximate directive of *sensing an imminent end to one's ministry* while in section B we will explore the proximate dynamic of *cutting oneself off from communication with a revered superior*.

SECTION A: SENSING AN IMMINENT END TO ONE'S MINISTRY

As the Christian minister suffers from grave illness in which death appears to be imminent, he may perceive the end of all the ministry to which he believes he gave himself so completely. In this area of research, we will endeavour to discover the formation dynamics which give form directives to the Christian minister as he feels that the end of his ministry is imminent.

From the SFHF: Transcendence Crisis

Before the Christian minister of the original formation event fell gravely ill and felt his life, with all his supposed ministerial projects, disrupted and coming to a sudden end because of what he perceived to be his approaching death, everything seemed to be going very well and according to his plans in life. He enjoyed good health; he was able to master the new language in his parish sufficiently to be able to preach in it within a rather short period of time, and all the projects he had so enthusiastically embraced, or willfully and ingeniously drawn up for himself, seemed to be going on so well – and he was highly regarded in his ministry. Now, suddenly, the end of all this success in life looms all round him. He is thus thrown into an *existential crisis* of his life which he had never before experienced nor anticipated.

This is an experience in the current form of a human life which the SFHF calls *transcendence crisis*, and to which we have already referred above.[1] In discussing the current life-form which marks the moment of the awakening of *wisdom-in-awe*[2] in people, van Kaam observes the following:

> People who are captivated by naïve trust in the powers of functional formation alone may be shaken out of their complacency by transcendence crisis. These crises are marked by the destruction of one's current, primary functional appraisals on which one has built one's life formation. The shattering of current appreciations, memories, anticipations, and imaginations brings one face to face with a void of formlessness and form impotence. One does not know any longer how to give form to life functionally in a way that makes sense. The exper-

---

[1] See chapter three, under the paragraph-heading, '*Negative Phase of Formative Transcendence.*" Van Kaam defines *transcendence crisis* as "A period of basic insecurity due to the structural weakening of a no longer effective life form and deepened by the uncertainty about appropriate directives for a new current life form more congruent with the changing life period or situation and more congenial with the Christ-form of the soul as it increasingly discloses itself." see *Studies* 1 (Feb. 1980), 149.

[2] See chapter two.

ience of threatening formlessness and form impotence evokes formation anxiety.³

This, indeed, seems to be the mark of the awaking of *wisdom-in-awe* which the Christian minister in the primary formation event is experiencing. Transcendence crisis is nothing less than what the SFHF also calls *originality crisis*. If, for the Christian, transcendence is one of the fundamental dynamics of formation, a crisis in our transcendent dimension moves and directs us towards our very original source, which is God in whose image and likeness we are formed. Hence, van Kaam rightly underscores this reality when in these words after he has observed that transcendence crisis accompanies each transition to which God calls us in life. He says: "Note again that because *this transcendence crisis* is in fact the Spirit's invitation to disclose and implement more of our original life call in Christ, it can also be called an *original crisis*.⁴

From the SFHF: Form Impotence

Being so brutally confronted with such utter contingency of himself in which he is completely helpless makes the reality of his form impotence overwhelming. The subject finds himself to be in a void of formlessness. He is incapable of either giving or receiving form. He is in a current life form which is one of impotence, as van Kaam points out.⁵

Yet, paradoxically, it is this experience of threatening formlessness and form impotence which evokes formation anxiety the origin of which is in the primordial core disposition of awe, as we observed earlier in Chapter

---

³ Adrian van Kaam, *Human Formation*, 195.

⁴ Adrian van Kaam, *Religion and Personality*, 183.

⁵ Adrian van Kaam, *Human Formation*, 195.

Chapter 4: Frustration and Anger at the Unfulfilled Ambitions

Two.[6] It is precisely when the person is in this current life form of formlessness and form impotence that he or she stands in front of the opportunity and is invited and made to perceive himself in *wisdom-in-awe*, beyond his formlessness and impotence. For, at this point of his current form of life, *transcendent wisdom* takes over and offers the person the opportunity to allow himself to be guided by transcendent directives. In this disposition of formation anxiety which brings the person to the type of despair of which Kierkegaard speaks, his dormant predisposition of awe for God – the Divine Forming Mystery – whom he serves may awaken. Adrian van Kaam sums all this up beautifully when, discussing formation anxiety and wisdom he says:

> Formation anxiety generates a wisdom that entrusts itself to the veiled form direction of evolution and history. No longer does the cleverness and astuteness of our functional, logical, scientific mind prevail. Transcendent wisdom is rooted in awe whose object cannot be controlled by logic and science. This wisdom is neither antirational nor dissonant with the factual findings of the sciences. It transcends naïve trust in our power to function well in the formation field. It lifts us beyond the anxiety generated by formlessness and form impotence when our formation field seems totally shattered.[7]

It is in this light that form impotence becomes paradoxically an indisputable opportunity for, and a clear invitation to, transcendent formation, and the experience of the threatening formless disposition becomes a transcendent formation potential.[8]

---

[6] See "Awe and the Disposition of Anxiety and Fear" in chapter two.

[7] Adrian van Kaam, *Human Formation*, 196.

[8] See van Kaam, "Provisional Glossary," *Studies* 1 (Feb. 1980), 147. Here, van Kaam defines transcendent formation potential as "The potency and tendency of

The Christian minister in the primary formation event does not seem to have apprehended the potency in his current form of life; i.e. he seems to ignore that the transcendent wisdom is what could have awakened in him the dormant predisposition of awe for the Divine Forming Mystery in Christ whom he serves. He might have been serving himself and his own personally willfully crafted projects, instead of those of the Divine Mystery of Formation which [projects] are made manifest in the Christ-Form. If this is so, the basic question which may need to be examined here is the existential disposition of such a Christian minister towards God whom he presumes to be serving in Jesus Christ in that way. What kind of faith does he have in the God to whom he presumes to be ministering in others? To help us in our true understanding of faith which the Christian minister should have, we will now turn to Paul Tillich whose little volume *Dynamics of Faith* is described by Reinhold Niebuhr as a "Little Classic."[9]

Paul Tillich: "What Faith Is Not"

In his small but highly charged volume, *Dynamics of Faith*, Tillich, after he has superbly described and analyzed the nature of faith,[10] goes on to present what I would call in this context, "the anti-thesis of faith." He calls this *anti-thesis of faith*, "What Faith is Not," and summarizes his description

---

all human life to be formed by and to give form to aspirations emerging from the transcendent nature of human life.

[9] See Reinhold Niebuhr's evaluation of Paul Tillich's *Dynamic of Faith* (New York: Harper and Row, 1957), on the back of cover design, by Marian Ebert.

[10] Paul Tillich, *Dynamics of Faith*, opus cit. pp.1-29. Tillich defines faith in these pages as an Ultimate *Concern* and a Centered Act. And after describing its source, he delineates its rapport with *the Dynamics of the Holy* and distinguishes the difference between it and *doubt*. He finally concludes his compacted outline of the nature of faith by identifying [it] as the *Ultimate Concern of the Believing Community*.

Chapter 4: Frustration and Anger at the Unfulfilled Ambitions

of the *anti-thesis* under three paragraph-heads.[11] Under what he calls "the intellectualistic distortion of the meaning of faith," Tillich writes:

> The different distorted interpretations of the meaning of faith can be traced to one source. Faith as being ultimately concerned is a centered act of the whole personality. If one of the functions which constitute the totality of the personality is partly or completely identified with faith, the meaning of faith is distorted. Such interpretations are not altogether wrong because every function of the human mind participates in the act of faith. But the element of truth in them is embedded in a whole error.[12]

What Tillich seems to be pointing to here is that if the subject of the act of faith is totally or even partly identified with the personality of the believer, it cannot actually also be at the same time the pure and absolute subject in which one believes. For the subject of faith and the believer cannot be identified as one and the same thing. This is what happens if someone has identified certain projects in his life with his whole person and turns round to think of them as the will of the true subject of faith – God. In this case, the person indirectly makes himself the subject of his faith, and not God.

Tillich regards the consideration of an act knowledge that has a low degree of evidence in our scientific age as the most ordinary misinterpretation of faith. This he rejects as faith. Similarly, he points out the *voluntaristic*, and also *emotionalistic, distortions* of faith cannot be what faith truly is.[13] Faith as ultimate concern is an act of one's total personality and

---

[11] Ibid., 30-40.

[12] Ibid., 30-1.

[13] Tillich holds that the intellectualistic distortion of the meaning of faith is the basis for the voluntaristic distortion of it. He distinguishes between the Catholic perception of this voluntaristic interpretation in which the lack of knowledge is basically complemented by an act of the will; and the Protestant perception in

therefore is characterized by: 1) the unconditional demand of total surrender to the subject of one's ultimate concern; 2) the promise of ultimate fulfillment; and 3) the threat of exclusion from the promised fulfillment.[14] It is the growth of faith thus characterized that Fowler discusses in his book entitled *Stages of Faith*.

James W. Fowler: Growth and Development in Faith

In *Stages of Faith*, James Fowler argues that faith matures through crisis. Using as an analogy the structural-development theories of psychologists Jean Piaget and Lawrence Kohlberg, both of whom basically maintain that structural development occurs when the subject – in his interaction with the environment – has to construct new modes of knowing and acting in order to meet new challenges of the environment. Fowler claims that "[g]rowth and development in faith also result from life crisis, challenges and the kinds of disruption that theologians call revelation."[15] Thus, according to Fowler, the increase of faith in an individual can be attested to empirically in crises which are observable in the current life form of the person, but which bring the person to beyond what is empirical and points to his transcendent origin and source.

From the insights offered by both Tillich and Fowler, one thing really seems to become evident. This is the necessary link that exists between faith

---

which the content to believe is supplied by the intellect; see *Dynamics of Faith*, 35-6. With regard to the emotionalistic distortion of faith, Tillich points out that Schleiermacher's description of religion as "the feeling of unconditional dependence" is what "induced many people to believe that faith is a matter of merely subjective emotions, without a content to be known and a demand to be obeyed." See ibid., 38-9.

[14] Ibid., 2.

[15] James W. Fowler, *Stages of Faith: The Psychology of Human Development and the Quest for Meaning* (San Francisco: Harper & Collins, 1981), 100.

and crises of transcendence which people experience in their current form of life. Such transcendence crises are existential opportunities and are truly moments of invitation to rise up to their graced Divine life form to which they have been called in their preempirical form of life.

Integrative Reflection

The above insights gained from both Formation Science and its auxiliary sources of Christian theology, philosophy, and psychology bring much light to the Christian minister's perception of the imminent end of his ministry. As it seems obvious, the Christian minister in the original formation event is profoundly shaken out of the complacency of his earlier achievements and successes in life by what Formation Science would call the destruction of his current primary functional appraisals.[16] It is on the basis of the power of his current primary functional appraisal that he built what he believes to be his ongoing formation – what seems to him to be the consonant unfolding of his founding life call.

Hence, when this basis begins to fall apart with what seems to be his approaching death, which is certain to bring an end to all of this seeming consonant unfolding of his life's call, it brings him face-to-face with the naked reality of the contingent nature of these powers. This is what the SFHF calls *transcendence crisis*. Adrian van Kaam states elsewhere that in the context of what is often referred to as mid-life crisis, the crisis of transcendence "is thus negatively the disclosure of our finiteness in the very

---

[16] The construct "functional appraisal" in Formation Science refers to the judging of one's life potencies only in the light of what is empirically demonstrable. Such judgement is limited to only the sociohistorical, vital and functional dimensions of the human life form, and it excludes the transcendent dimension. See Adrian van Kaam, *Human Formation*, 66; also 95 where he defines *exclusive functional appraisal*.

experience of our confinement manifested to us by the loss of opportunities, relationships, vital, and functional strength and endurance."[17]

This precisely is what has become clear in the subject of the original formation event. In his life-threatening illness, the Christian minister begins to experience the impotence of his vital and functional strength and endurance. And he who so far had always been effective and successful in realizing projects which he might have willfully crafted for himself has confused them with the true ministry of transcendent origin to which he is called. Hence, in his imminently approaching death, he perceives the disruption and end of his crafted projects which he has confused with his divine call to ministry in Jesus Christ. It is only when he will be able to see the finiteness, and so, the impotence of his current primary functional appraisals in such transcendence crisis, that he may come to recognise the opportunity and the invitation to transcendence offered him therein. For such impotence, which comes from his contingency, ironically points to the transcendent level of formation to which he is foundationally called. And it is evident that his sociohistorical, vital, and functional levels cannot be the source of power for such transcendent formation as they are of his own willful and contingent projects.

The confusion of the Christian minister's personal and willful projects with those of his divine ministry after the model of the Christ-Form may come from a distorted interpretation of his faith. As we observed what Tillich says, **faith is ultimate concern**. In this light, *it is a centred act of the entire personality of the one who makes it*. If, therefore, one of the functions constituting the totality of the person becomes identified with the subject of this ultimate concern, the meaning of faith becomes essentially distorted.

What, therefore, seems to have occurred is that the Christian minister in the primary formation event identifies his own willful projects and their goals with the project and goal of his ministry which is willed by God in and

---

[17] Adrian van Kaam, *The Transcendent Self*, 45.

through Christ. In so doing, he distorts the very subject of his faith,[18] because in this way he makes his own voluntaristic projects, God's. Hence, he implicitly identifies himself with God at that point and thus injects his contingency into the very subject of his faith – God – who should be the *Other*, his *Ultimate Concern* who is transcendent and cannot be contingent.

When that is so, surrender of the Christian minister's willful projects, and, indeed, appreciative abandonment of his entire will to the subject of his faith by himself, becomes practically impossible. He cannot see how God should not be already working on his side in what he believes is willed by [God], but rather would want to bring everything to such an abrupt end in willing his imminent death. It is only when the Christian minister consonantly experiences such "life crisis, challenges and kinds of disruption," as Fowler calls them, that his faith, as "a centered act of Ultimate Concern," grows consonantly towards maturity in transcendence.

Such consonant faith truly centred in the Christian minister's Ultimate Concern may enable him to perceive even the imminent approach of his death with the consequent abrupt termination of his own willful projects, not as the disruption of the will of God who has called him to minister, but as another way in which God may want him to exercise the ministry to which he has called him. Thus, in such a disposition, he may seek to surrender and appreciatively abandon his own willfulness to God instead of cutting himself off from God in Christ and others. In the following section, we shall examine how the Christian minister in such a current form of life does not only cut himself off from God, the Ultimate Concern of his misinterpreted faith, but also from others, even from a revered superior.

---

[18] See Paul Tillich, in pp. 171-2.

SECTION B: CUTTING ONESELF OFF FROM A REVERED SUPERIOR

In perceiving that his ministry is about to end abruptly, the Christian minister in anger and despair cuts himself off from all dialogue, not just with God, but also with even a superior he has always revered. He feels that the superior could have prevented this fatal illness from befalling him. This area of research will seek to delineate the dynamics which direct the relationship between the Christian minister and his superior.

From the SFHF: Form Delineation through Interformative Mediation

As one observes the dissonant current life form which has become apparent in the Christian minister of the primary formation event, one wonders if he has been aware of the direction of his life form and how he came to appraise himself and to know the direction his life form might be taking. The question here may be posed neutrally this way: How can someone depict his or her own life form so that he or she might know whether it is consonantly disclosing itself or not? This question is not so theoretical or hypothetical as it may sound. If, for example, the Christian minister in the formation event has been able to delineate from the beginning his current life form, he might have been able to know earlier the general direction that his life formation was taking.

The SFHF offers a serious response to this question in its construct, **form delineation through interformative mediation**. In an entry in his "Provisional Glossary" under this same title, van Kaam says:

> People initially disclose their basic form direction through the *interformative mediation* of people, events and things that manifest to them who or what they are not and cannot control. This accumulation

of formative experiences of who or what they are not, *delineates* indirectly and progressively what they are or may be.[19]

Such a description of form delineation through interformative mediation demonstrates an indirect manner by which people may get to know who they truly are, and what their life form potency may be. In their interaction with other people, event and things, people get to receive form from and donate form to others and the world in various ways. In this way, the structures of their current life form are gradually formed. In speaking of the constitution of the structures of the current life form of people, van Kaam observes: "[These structures] are constituted by consistent reactions and responses of people to the characteristic manifestations of inter- and outer poles of their *formation field* during a certain prolonged period of their formation history."[20] It is through getting to know who they are not, and what they are not capable of doing in their interformative[21] experiences with the inter- and outer poles, that they gradually become able to depict what their life form is or may be later.

Thanks, therefore, to the interformative reactions and responses that people make between themselves, and in events and things, they are gradually able to delineate the structure of their current life form and what they may become in the future.[22] Hence, for a valid delineation of one's life

---

[19] *Studies*, IV (Nov. 1983), 420.

[20] *Fundamental Formation*, 258.

[21] The term *interformative* is used here in a broader sense to embrace the other poles of the formation field other than the interformation pole; see Adrian van Kaam, Ibid., 249.

[22] See *Human Formation*, 139-64. Here, and in fact, already earlier (5, 14, 16, and 44), van Kaam speaks of *anticipation* as a *formative disposition*, and its relationship to *formative memory*, and also *formative imagination*. All three together with the mind and the will, are the auxiliary formation powers.

form, interformative mediation is necessary. If this interformative mediation through the other poles of the formation field is blocked, even temporally,[23] consonant delineation of one's current life form and its structure may prove difficult during that time. As van Kaam continues in his description of form delineation through interformative mediation, "While this delineation process starts in childhood, it remains part of one's ongoing formation during a lifetime."[24]

From the SFHF: Distinctively Human Interformative Communication

If form delineation concerns the disclosure of people's basic life form direction in the years through interformative mediation of other people, events, and things, *distinctively human interformative communication*[25] refers more directly to interformation between people through interactions and responses.[26] Distinctively human interformative communication is particularly important for the consonant unfolding of the individual's FLF. In communicating with others, people become like a mirror in which the persons they communicate with mirror themselves. Thus, we do not only mirror the Mystery to one another.[27] Through communication with others whom we encounter,[28] we are able to see and to delineate our own current life form in them as if in a mirror. We are able to perceive mirrored back to us the image and likeness of God which we share together through Christ. Hence, distinctively human interformative communication becomes indis-

---

[23] See Adrian van Kaam, and Susan Muto, *The Power of Appreciation*; under "Growing in Epiphanic Sensitivity," 60.

[24] *Studies*, IV (Nov. 1983), 420.

[25] See "distinctively human formation," in *Fundamental Formation*, 93-102.

[26] See footnote #2&3 above in the same chapter.

[27] Adrian van Kaam and Susan Muto; *Formation Guide*," 121-46.

[28] See chapter one: "Human Encounter."

pensable for the consonant disclosure of the individual's life form. Adrian van Kaam brings home the crucial importance of such a distinctively human interformative communication in his description of it in the following terms:

> Interformative human communication is the primordial indispensable means of life-forming delineation and subsequent disposition formation. When children, because of some handicap, cannot benefit from such communication, their life-form delineation is delayed. The pre-empirical life direction, form or image, symbolized by the soul, is released into the basic disposition formation of the core form of the empirical life, symbolized by the heart, mainly via interformative communication. Once the phase of distinctively human encounter begins, it soon prevails over the forming influence of the phase of the functional and vital affiliation with things in one's formation field. The former means to delineation and communication remain in the background as a possibility. Human encounter and interformative communication by play, work or other symbols awaken the transcendent dimension of the human life-form.[29]

From the above description of "distinctively human interformative communication," its indispensability for the consonant unfolding of the life-form of the individual, and also for the delineation of this progressively disclosing life form, is obvious. The lack of such interformative communication between a particular individual and others is symptomatic of the self-severance of such an individual from others. This denotes

---

[29] *Studies*, IV, 424.

stagnation of the particular individual in a current form of life in which ongoing formation is no longer possible.[30]

The above discussions in Formation Science disclose to us ways in which the individual can cut himself off from others, and so, from consonant ongoing disclosure of his or her founding life call. A genuine Christian knowledge of a revered superior in particular, as depicted by the Apostle Peter in his First Letter, could foster in a Christian minister more formative dispositions for both form delineation and interformative communication.

Philo Judaeus of Alexandria: A True Elder

The *HarperCollins Encyclopedia of Catholicism* defines an elder as "a respected leader of a community."[31] This definition of the term is inspired by biblical understanding and usage of it. Since the naming of the elders of Israel at the time of the Exodus (Ex 3:16), they have often been mentioned as leaders in the communities of Israel. Philo Judaeus of Alexandria, a historian of the Early Church, considers the term to be used for a person, not because of his age, but because of his "desire (for) the elder opinion;" i.e., he is "the perfect man, who thinks nothing honourable but what is good."[32] As he observes with regard to Moses' choice of *elders*:

---

[30] Ongoing unfolding of the individual's FLF is impossible without the dialogical free flow of formation energy throughout all the spheres of the person's field. Hence, when interformative communication between a particular individual and others who are interformative poles to him or to her is broken, ongoing formation is not possible anymore. It is as if the current in a wire to a bulb has been switched off, and therefore a disconnection has taken place.

[31] "Elder," *Encyclopedia of Catholicism*, ed. Richard P. McBrien, 1st ed. (San Francisco: HarperCollins, 1995)

[32] C.D. Yonge, trans., The Works of Philo: New updated ed. (Peabody, Massachusetts: Hendrickson Publications, 1993), 228.

It has therefore been proved, that in many passages Moses is in the habit of calling a person young, having regard not to the age off the body, but to the desire of the soul for innovation; and also we will now proceed to show that he calls some persons elders, not because they are oppressed by old age, but as being worthy of honour and respect.[33]

Such elders continued to function in Jewish society in the time of Christ (Mt 15: 2; 21:23 and parallels).

Besides the Apostles, elders were appointed as leaders in the early Church communities. In the Acts of the Apostles, for example, the controversy over the Gentiles in Antioch, to be obliged or not to follow the Mosaic tradition of circumcision, was taken to Jerusalem by Paul, Barnabas and others, where "they were welcomed by the Church and by the Apostles and *elders*" (Acts 15:4).[34]

The role that the elders had to play in the Christian community is clearly well-defined. Obviously, it is delineated as none other than the Christ-Form itself; the image of Christ as the "chief shepherd" whose supreme goal is to lead, guide, and direct God's flock on its journey back to him. This confirms Philo's observations of the elder among the Jews and also in the early Church, as one who, most of all, is "worthy of honour and respect" in the guiding and directing of the followers of Christ – the flock that "Christ the Good Shepherd" entrusts to the elders as his substitutes. Thus, Peter urges the community, of which the elders are the shepherds, to trust their guidance of such elders in obedience and humility (1 Pet 5:5-11).

---

[33] Ibid., 228. See also 704.

[34] For more references on the Judeo-Christian nature of elders, see Acts 14:23; 1 Pet 5: 1-4

Integrative Reflections of the Above

In the primary formation event, we observed that the Christian minister in his anger and despair, does not only isolate and cut himself off from God in the person of Christ in whom he had so much faith as to become his minister. He also severs communication with others, and even with the *elder*[35] in the Christian community in which he serves as minister, through self-encapsulation. In such a disposition, the Christian minister is unable to appreciatively appraise his current life form. And so, he could not anticipate the form direction it is taking.

As the insights offered by Formation Science in the above paragraphs show, a clear and appreciative perception, or formative apprehension of a person's current life form is not possible without interformative mediation. It is through such interformative mediation that one's basic form of life can be disclosed. If for example, Saul did not allow the disciple, Ananias from Damascus, to encounter him, interformative mediation might never have taken place leading to his conversion (Acts 9: 10-19). It is, therefore, through interformative mediation in general that the Christian minister, like every other individual person, can assess or delineate his current life form as a Christian minister in his actual situation. But if he cuts himself off from people, events, and things, it is clear that there is no medium left through which could be manifested to him "who or what [he] is not and cannot control,"[36] even as minister.

More importantly, Formation Science makes it clear that distinctively human interformative communication is crucial for the ongoing and consonant unfolding of the Christian minister's founding life call. As it affirms, such "interformative human communication is the primordial indispensable means of life-forming delineation and subsequent disposition

---

[35] See first paragraph of the formation event itself.

[36] *Studies*, IV (Nov. 1983): 420

formation[37] In cutting off communication with especially the elder and, therefore, leader of the Christian community in which he himself is minister, the subject of the original formation event deprives himself of the best mirror in which he could see his own current life-form. Looking into it, he could be able to assess whether his current life form is consonant and progressively unfolding consonantly or not.

The elder, visiting and seeking to encounter and communicate with the Christian minister, may be regarded as one of those privileged and revered mirrors whose life call Peter describes as "the caring shepherd of God's flock." Hence, the visiting elder shares deeply in the Christ-Form, "Chief Shepherd" of the flock of God. In this light, the compassionate, caring elder would not seek to misdirect any one sheep of the flock of God that has been entrusted to him.

If the conflicted Christian minister is able to heed the urging of the chief Apostle Peter to trust in obedience and humility such an elder, he may be led to distinctively human interformative communication with him. This could subsequently direct him to consonant delineation of his current life form, and so to reform his disposition towards his own willfully crafted projects in his ministry. The consonant and appreciative appraisal of such a visiting elder would therefore have led him to competently delineate his current form life and have also presented him with the Christ-Form of the Good Shepherd in the likeness of which he himself has been called as a Christian minister. As Richard Rohr says in his reflection on 'The Pain of Rejection,' "Love is a humbling experience, as we learn in interactions with intimate friends. That is why the proud person cannot love or grow."[38]

---

[37] Ibid., 424.

[38] Richard Rohr, *Radical Grace*, ed. John Bookser Feister (Cincinnati, OH: St. Anthony Messenger Press, 1993), 367.

Transition to Second Remote Foundational Statement

In the first remote foundational statement of the Coformant on the horizon of Christian ministers, our research focused on dynamics which, in the face of death-threatening illness, lead angry and despairing Christian ministers to perceive the end of their ministry as imminent, and the result of being abandoned by God. The research also sought to delineate consonant directives which may guide such Christian ministers in inter-formative communication with their superiors. The second remote statement will discuss, in Part two, concentrating on the dynamics of a truly transforming dialogue in which such ministers could engage with their superiors.

PART TWO
ENGAGING IN A TRANSFORMING DIALOGUE

The following is the remote foundational statement which will be explored in this second part of the Chapter:

On the level of the senses, Christian ministers may appear willing to enter into dialogue with the other, but they may still refuse to engage in it on the level of their heart through their mind and will.

The research in this remote foundational statement will investigate two directives from the dynamics of dialogue. While section A will examine the proximate directive of *dialogue on the level of the heart*.

SECTION A: Entering into Dialogue on the Apparent Level

In their despair and feeling of being abandoned by God, Christian ministers who suffer from life-threatening illness may seem willing to dialogue with superiors. But such a dialogue may remain only on the superficial level, and so may have little formative potency. This area of research will examine the dynamics of apparent dialogue.

From the SFHF: Levels of Dialogical Relationships

In the primary formation event of this research project, the Christian minister expresses, vitally and functionally, some willingness to dialogue with the respected elder. This seems evident when the minister cooperated with the latter who gently attempted, with his warm and comforting hand, to turn him round to face him. Whether such a dialogue at the vital-functional level is formative or not is something that would still have to be determined. From the Greek origin, *dialegein, dialegesthai* (*dia + legein, legesthai*), to converse, Webster's International Dictionary defines the substantive *dialogue* as "a written composition in which two or more characters are represented as conversing or reasoning on some topic." It goes on to define it in a second sense as "[a]n instance of conversational exchange."[39]

In his use of the term *dialogue* which, with its derivative, *dialogical,* is pervasive in Formation Science,[40] van Kaam clearly attests that human formation is a *dialogical* process which takes place in the formation field of every human individual.[41] To unfold and disclose one's founding life form, the individual donates and receives form. This is, analogically speaking, an

---

[39] "Dialogue" Webster's Third *New International Dictionary*.

[40] See Adrian van Kaam, *Scientific Formation*. The pervasive character of the term 'dialogue,' and its derivatives in Formation Science's methodology is quite evident in this volume which discusses in depth the *science of foundational human formation*. This is particularly so, beginning from chapter seven of the volume onward.

[41] *Fundamental Formation*, opus cit., 158.

instance of conversational exchange – a dialogue. This conversational exchange in this case takes on a more generic application and extends to all the spheres and dimensions of the individual's formation field. Dialogue, therefore, is a process which [inalienably] has to be entered into between the core of the individual and the other formation centres of his field. This is what van Kaam seems to imply when he says that *dialogical field thinking*, "instead of focusing on a particular cause or reason for a happening, tries to comprehend it as emerging from life as a whole. [And that] it considers each event to be open to the influence of other facets of the field."[42]

But dialogue, just like conversation, can be entered into on different levels or dimensions. In the light of the discussion above, we can say that a dialogue is a form of relationship. And as we observed earlier, for a relationship to be formative, it has to be one in which encounter occurs.[43] Hence, a truly formative dialogue can be considered as a formative relationship within which may be empirically expressed a true human encounter. However, this dialogue can also be only on the apparent level in which no encounter has taken place. Thus, such a dialogue may remain formationally ineffectual, just as when a relationship is only on the sociohistorical and vital-functional levels alone, and therefore has no formative power.[44]

Such a dialogue is formationally ineffectual because, similar to what van Kaam says of the disposition of formative gentleness, it is only a "make-believe" *dialogue*.[45] Although it may appear to the observer as a true conversational exchange between a subject and another person, it remains only on the surface. It is only an apparent dialogue because whatever formative directives may ensue from such a dialogue, they are not able to reach the core, the heart, the intra-form of the subject. So, even though there may

---

[42] Adrian van Kaam, *Scientific Formation*; opus cit., 62-3

[43] See chapter one.

[44] Ibid.

[45] Adrian van Kaam, *Formation of the Human Heart*, 106-7.

seem to be a dialogue going on, such a dialogue may have rather little formative potency.

From the SFHF: Defensive Distance

The subject who so willfully enters into an apparent dialogue assumes an apparent form of life through which he maintains a distance between himself and the other with whom he *makes-believe* he is in dialogue. This is what Formation Science calls ***defensive-distance-keeping***. As van Kaam asserts, "To protect ourselves against others as potential invaders of our threatened inferiority, we form compulsive, anxious, suspicious safety directives that may solidity into excessive security dispositions. We lose the natural rhythm between distance and encounter."[46] He goes on to remark: "When defensive distance prevails, it [is] between our inner and outer spheres." Hence, a relationship by which a person may keep such a defensive distance, so that another may not invade his interiority, can only be called, as we have done above, an apparent dialogue which has minimal formative power.

From the SFHF: Insertion of the Demonic

The above dynamic of defensive distance may be responsible for the disposition of the *make-believe-dialogue* – dialogue on the apparent level, which deceitfully keeps the core, or the interiority of the subject closed to any formative dialogue and encounter. The origin of such a dynamic may be the pride form – the quasi-foundational life-form, and certainly not his or her founding life-form. Through the pride-form of the subject, the demonic is able to act on the functional dimension of the person and distort the personalization of pneumatic inspirations obtained even through Holy

---

[46] Ibid., 165.

Scripture. This is what van Kaam refers to as ***insertion of the demonic***. Here is a warning he gives in reference to the *personalization of pneumatic inspirations*:

> This process of personalization of the inspirations of the Spirit always carries with it the danger of distortion, especially for committed Christians. In demonic mini-obsessions there is always an attempt by the demonic to distort also the pneumatic dimension and its structure of unique inspirations by suggesting through the imagination deformative directions as if they were pneumatic inspirations.[47]

Thus, in its action to block and to prevent a formative dialogue from taking place between, for example, the Christian minister and the revered elder visiting him, the demonic, through a distortion of the pneumatic disposition of silence,[48] could distance him from any truly formative dialogue.

All of the above discussions which centre on constructs of Formation Science have proffered us deeper insights concerning especially the nature of apparent dialogue. These constructs so elucidated help us to understand better how a person can enter into a make-believe-dialogue with another, but which dialogue has no formative power that could lead to consonant disclosure of the person's founding life call. One thing which must, however, be taken absolutely into consideration is the foundational

---

[47] Studies 2 (Nov. 1981): 522. In Luke's Gospel, Jesus warned his seventy-two disciples, who returned from the mission on which he sent them, rejoicing because they had power over even the devils (Lk 10: 18-20).

[48] For true formative silence see Susan Muto; *Pathways of Spiritual Living* (Peters ham, Massachusetts: St. Bede's Publications, 1984), 51-9; also *A Practical Guide to Spiritual Reading* 2nd ed. (Petersham, Massachusetts: St. Bede's Publications, 1994), 115-6.

assumption that God the Divine Mystery of formation himself has, in the preformation, already been working in the soul of the person in mysterious ways which are beyond our observation.

Having said this, therefore, it is evident that there still exists a huge margin of "non-knowing" of what is truly going on in the life form of the subject. In my estimation, this margin of *ignorance* on our part, as to what is going on in the soul of the person in similar situations, is what Saint John of the Cross attempts to put into human language in his mystical and most beautiful poem, "Dark Night." Although it will not be possible to discuss in any depth the contents of this poem here, the simple brushing of what St. John of the Cross observes as essentially taking place in a human soul on its journey to union with God vindicates the presence of the paradox we are referring to.

Saint John of the Cross: "Dark Night"[49]

In the introduction to her book *John of the Cross for Today: The Ascent*, Susan Muto holds that *The Ascent of Mount Carmel* is John's own commentary on his poem, "Dark Night." This commentary, she says, is continued in another of his books, *The Dark Night*.[50] St. John of the Cross

---

[49] Saint John of the Cross describes his mystical poem, **Dark Night**, as "A song of the soul's happiness in having passed through the dark night of faith, in nakedness and purgation, to union with its beloved;" see St. John of the Cross, *Collected Works*, trans. Kieran Kavanaugh & Otilio Rodriguez (Washington, D.C.:ICS Publications, 1979), 68.

[50] Susan Muto, *John of the Cross for Today: The Ascent* (Notre Dame, Indiana: Ave Maria Press, 1991), 14. In fact, the two books, *The Ascent of Mount Carmel*, and *The Dark Night* are treated as on single piece of work, Ascent-Night, as Kieran Kavanaugh says in his introduction to the two works. Both of them are commentary to the same poem, "Dark Night;" see *Collected Works*, 43.

himself confirms this in the prologue to his book, *The Ascent of Mount Carmel*. He says, for example:

> The darkness and trials, spiritual and temporal, that fortunate souls ordinarily encounter on their way to the high state of perfection are so numerous and profound that human science cannot understand them adequately; nor does experience of them equip one to explain them. He who suffers them will know what this experience is like, but he will find himself unable to describe it.[51]

In Muto's opinion, *The Ascent of Mount Carmel of St. John of the Cross* contains "[i]n its timeless, timely fashion the wisdom people need to hear, especially if they have reached one or the other stage of ego-desperation and if they have undergone an initial awakening experience."[52]

This wisdom, contained in *the Ascent of Mount Carmel*, St. John of the Cross' commentary to his poem, "Dark Night," is what Muto claims, has the answer for those who have reached ego-desperation and have undergone an initial awakening experience. But to have reached "ego-desperation" means to have reached some moments of crisis in one's life. Hence, if Muto is right, this wisdom, which is the subject of John's commentary in *The Ascent of Mount Carmel*, is especially for people who are in crisis situations.

Let us refresh our minds with the claim we already made above, that a crisis moment can provide an opportunity and invite a human person to formation and transformation.[53] This seems to be what the 'Dark Night' experience of St. John of the Cross does. It contains that wisdom which is the answer to particularly the person in his or her crisis moment in which he or she looks for a solution. Keith Barron asserted in a lecture that all of

---

[51] Saint John of the Cross, opus cit., 69-70.
[52] Susan Muto, opus cit., 14.
[53] See above under paragraph heading "form potency."

Chapter 4: Frustration and Anger at the Unfulfilled Ambitions

our life is surrounded by conflicts. In his estimation, there is no security in this world, no escape from conflicts and crises. As soon as our secure way of doing things changes, we are challenged, and we find ourselves in some conflictual situation in which we no longer feel secure.[54] This, in the language of the SFHF, is transcendence crisis for which the person – in his primordial disposition of "transcendence-ability," and in accordance with Formation Science's principle of maintenance of form potency – would seek a resolution.

In this light, the "Dark Night" of St John of the Cross is truly a transcendence crisis which contains the wisdom capable of offering the most radical of all solutions to the conflictual situation in which the person is. It is the crisis which leads the way of the mystic to the ultimate goal of his FLF – union with God through total abandonment of self in humility to [God];[55] it is a transcendence crisis in which faith itself is a **dark night**. Yet in all of its darkness, this night, paradoxically, becomes most capable of guiding; it is lovelier than the dawn; it is the night that unites the Lover with the beloved; it is, indeed, the night that transforms the beloved into the Lover. Thus St. John of the Cross could say in the fifth stanza of *Dark Night*:

> O guiding night!
> O night more lovely than dawn!
> O night that has united
> The Lover with His beloved,
> Transforming the beloved in her Lover.[56]

---

[54] Keith Reeves Barron, "unpublished lecture Notes," in *Christian Formation and the Life of Prayer* (Pittsburgh, PA: Duquesne University – IFS, Spring Semester, 1993 – January 11, 1993).

[55] St. John of the Cross, *Collected Works*, 70-1.

[56] Ibid., entire poem, 68-9; also 295-6.

Saint John of the Cross perceives all this as "sheer grace," as he asserts in both the first and the second stanzas.

Reflectively Integrating All of the Above Regarding the Christian Minister

The above investigations have led us to deeper insights about the dialogue which the Christian minister of the original formation event seems to have entered into with the respected elder. In the first instance, it seems obvious that there is, at least, a *make-believe-dialogue*. It seems that the communication between the Christian minister and the elder remained only on the apparent – the vital-functional level. As we observed in the primary formation event, the response by the Christian minister to the attempts of the elder to engage with him in dialogue was not forthcoming until the moment when the elder touched him with his warm comforting hands. But even after he allowed himself to be turned round so that the elder could behold his face, his intrasphere still seems to have remained impervious to any interformative influence from the visiting elder. For as the Christian minister himself admitted, "I do not make any attempt to respond."[57]

It is in this light that the vital-functional cooperation, which the minister demonstrated in turning to face the elder, can be considered as being in dialogue only on the apparent level. And if that is all the level of his response, it cannot be understood as a dialogue in the proper sense, since a true dialogue implies an encounter in which process formation may take place through donation and reception of form directives.

From our theoretical discussions above, not only do we come to a clearer understanding of the nature of the dialogue between the Christian minister and the elder who is visiting him. We also came to intuit the possible origin

---

[57] See Formation event, Preface to this Book, viii-xii.

of such a disposition of dialogue. As we discovered in Formation Science's concept of *"defensive distance,"* the minister, in his anger and despair from feeling abandoned, might have wanted to distance himself from everyone, even from an elder. But the elder being someone he had always respected, he seems to have felt himself confronted with two conflicting dispositions arising from within him. On one hand, how can he, in his current life form of anger, despair, and feeling of abandonment – hence, of being cut off – remain congenially open to an elder, even if that elder is a revered one? Yet on the other hand, how can he refuse to dialogue with such an elder whom he has always respected?

It seems evident, then, that it is the conflict between these two dispositions – self-isolation, and respect for an elder – which led to the deformed disposition of the *make-believe-dialogue* which the Christian minister eventually assumed and manifested in the formation event. In this way, he could maintain a defensive distance, even from such a revered elder; and he could thus continue, in the current life form, to cut himself off from interformative influences, especially those which could come from the revered elder.

The concept of *demonic insertion* in Formation Science's theory strongly points to the source from where such a dynamic, which could keep the intrasphere of the Christian minister closed up, could have come. As he personalized the inspirations of the Spirit in his ministry, the minister could fall victim to the danger of distorting such pneumatic inspirations, bending them to suit his own willful projects in his ministry. Thus *demonic insertion* could in this way distort his personalization of, for example, the otherwise true pneumatic disposition of silence, thereby using it in its deformed sense to defensively distance him from all interformative influences, including those coming from the visiting elder.

However, as much as we become enlightened by the insights from the above discussions concerning the nature of the dialogue that went on between the Christian minister and the revered elder, the *Dark Night* experience of St. John of the Cross indicates that his human life form could be, indeed, paradoxical to the one we have so far delineated. The *Dark Night* experience of the soul makes it evident that although, on the empirical level, the dialogue between the Christian minister and the elder may be manifestly only apparent, and therefore formatively ineffectual, the soul of the former, through the "sheer grace" of God, could actually be experiencing a *Dark Night* on its journey to union with God.[58]

SECTION B: ENGAGING IN DIALOGUE ON THE LEVEL OF THE HEART – MIND & WILL

As dialogue between despairing Christian ministers and their superiors remain only on the vital level, the heart[59] - mind and will – may not become truly engaged in such a relationship. When that is the case, a formative dialogue will not be possible since the core form of life cannot be influenced. In this area of our investigations, we wish to underscore the importance of the human mind and will in the appraisal process of a truly formative dialogue.

From the SFHF: Mind and Will in Formative Appraisal

In Chapter Two of our research, we discussed how a religious subject may keep his core form or heart closed up to another.[60] From the insights therein, it became clear that the core form which is the integrating and

---

[58] St. John of the Cross, *Collected Works* (opus cit..), 68.

[59] In the SFHF theory, the core form of life is often referred to as the heart; See Adrian van Kaam, *Fundamental Formation*, 253-7.

[60] Confer chapter two.

relatively enduring ground form of the human life,[61] is the empirical expression of the *human spirit*.[62] The powers or faculties, which are preformationally "given" together with his human spirit are the mind, which is sometimes simply called the spirit, and the will.

These two spiritual faculties are the means by which the spirit may generate responsibility feelings in the heart or core form. As van Kaam explains in the process of *ascendance and descendance of dimensions into the human heart*:

> Formation Science views the transcendent responsibility feeling of the heart as a fruit of the spirit. The spirit may directly generate responsibility feelings in the heart. It does so as a messenger of the soul or foundational life form with which the heart is also directly affiliated. The spirit may also influence the heart via mind and will, which the spirit itself makes possible and illumines.[63]

The way in which the spirit may influence the human heart or core form of life is what Formation Science also calls *formative appraisal*. Through the appraisal process, the human spiritual faculties of mind and will, illumined by the spirit, formatively influence the core form or heart of the human being.

The process of appraisal, therefore, is the collaborative work of the mind and the will. The mind with its two-fold potency of appraisal – transcendent

---

[61] Adrian van Kaam, *Fundamental Formation*, 299. Note how van Kaam articulated the core form of life from the Christian point of view. He writes: "In the Christian view, the core form or heart, of life becomes the integrative responsible-sensible centre of global formative affects, which tend to give a basic concrete form to the soul's image of Christ, under the guidance of the Holy Spirit."

[62] See footnote #1 under *Preface*, 17.

[63] Adrian van Kaam, *Human Formation*, 170.

and functional – is able to functionally apprehend the concrete conditions in the particular individual's formation field, in a transcendent manner, by means of the human spirit.[64] This process in which the mind is engaged in formative appraisal is what van Kaam and Muto so succinctly explain in their book, *Formative Guide*.[65] First of all, the primordial awe inspires an abiding presence of the transcendent in the concrete condition and brings the mind to attend to it and to apprehend it. Then follows the functional appraisal of the concrete condition with the help of questions which concern the consonance of the said condition for formation.[66]

However, as van Kaam remarks, "Appraisal by the transcendent and functional mind is not sufficient to bring us to a final decision."[67] The transcendent and functional will of the person becomes formed and informed by the above activities of the mind, and is thus prepared, in freedom, to make a decision, affirming or rejecting the concrete condition presented to it by the formative mind, thereby unfolding the FLF of the person. Besides this, a last function of the will in this process is the application of incarnation of the decision thus arrived at. Then it falls back to both functional mind and will to carry out the practical execution of what has been so appraised for the ongoing consonant disclosure of the foundational life form of the person.

---

[64] Ibid., 66.

[65] Adrian van Kaam & Susan Muto, *Formation Guide for Becoming Spiritually Mature*, 118-9.

[66] Formation Science has worked out eight principal criteria to facilitate scientifically this stage of the appraisal process. These criteria are openness; appreciation; congeniality; compatibility; compassion; joyousness; competence; and effectiveness. See *Human Formation*, 67.

[67] Ibid.

Chapter 4: Frustration and Anger at the Unfulfilled Ambitions

Thomas Aquinas: The Intellectual Powers of the Soul

The functional and transcendent mind and will which we have just described above are what Thomas Aquinas, the thirteenth century scholar and saint, calls the intellectual powers of the human soul. As we have already observed, the soul is what Formation Science also designates phenomenologically as the foundational life form of the individual human being, the empirical principle of life.[68]

In his *Summa Theologiae*, Thomas Aquinas identifies the powers of the soul as the intellect and will.[69] In his answer to the four objections that the intellect cannot be a power of the soul, he affirms with Aristotle, whom he always called the Philosopher, that the intellect, which is also called the mind, is a power of the soul – the foundational life form. He expounds:

> I answer that, in accordance with what has been already shown (Q. LIV., A.3; Q. LXXVII., A.1) it is necessary to say that the intellect is a power of the soul, and not the very essence of the soul. For then alone the essence of that which operates is the immediate principle of operation, when operation itself is its being: for as power is to operation as its act, so is the essence to being. But in God alone His action of understanding is His very Being. Wherefore in God alone is His intellect

---

[68] See chapter one, footnote #12.

[69] Thomas Aquinas, *Summa Theologiae* 2nd.ed. trans. Fathers of the English Dominican Province (London Burns Oates & Washbourne LTD., 1922), I. QQ77,79 and 82. The first objection in particular and its response list three powers of the soul. According to St. Augustine, they are memory, understanding (or mind/intellect), and will.

His essence: while in other intellectual creatures, the intellect is a power.[70]

Hence, for Thomas Aquinas, the human mind or intellect is only one of the powers of the soul which is itself a participation in what is the essence of God. And in a similar way, the human will is also one of the intellectual or spiritual powers of the soul. With the help of the memory[71] – which Formation Science theory regards, together with imagination and anticipation, as auxiliary powers of the soul – the mind and will become the principal power centres of operation in the human soul. They cooperate in formatively appraising the concrete conditions which the soul – the foundational life form – encounters in the ongoing disclosure of itself.

An Integrative Reflection

The above discussions on the central powers of the core form or heart may seem rather theoretical, and therefore, irrelevant to this part of our study, or even to the entire research. However, when we apply the insights gained from these discussions to our Christian minister of the primary formation event, much light is shed on the reasons why he cannot engage in a formative dialogue with his visiting elder.

---

[70] Ibid.,I. Q.79, A.1. Previously in Q. 54. A.3, Aquinas already established that there is a distinction between power and essence when he discussed the power and essence of the Angels. He repeated this distinction in Q.77, A1 when he discussed and demonstrated that the essence of the human soul is also distinct from the powers inhering in it.

[71] Being strongly influenced by the formula of the Trinity, St. Augustine conceived most of transcendent reality in threes. Thus, he considered memory, not as an auxiliary, but a main power of the soul on the same degree with the mind and will; see St. Augustine, *De Trinitate*, IX, 2.

Chapter 4: Frustration and Anger at the Unfulfilled Ambitions

The main insight gained from such discussions points to the fact that the Christian minister of the formation event is unable to enter into a formative dialogue with the other because his heart is closed up.[72] It is within this heart, which is the empirical expression of his human spirit, that his spiritual powers – mind and will – reside. But as Formation Science discloses to us in the above discussions, it is through these powers that his spirit could influence his heart and so disclose his founding life call by means of formative appraisal of his current form of life. Hence, as long as he remains cut off, and his intrasphere closed, no degree of dialogue on the vital-functional level alone can ever lead him to that consonant unfolding of his founding life form. For the agents of formative appraisal, which is the fruit of formative dialogue, are the spiritual powers of the mind and will. But being locked up in his heart, and unable to be reached through a make-believe dialogue, they become unavailable for their collaborative task of formative appraisal of his current life form.

Another major insight from our above discussions is the indication of the deformative apprehension that the Christian minister, in the original formation event, has of the ministry to which he believes he has been called. If he is angry, despondent, and despairs because he perceives the end of all his so-called ministerial projects approaching – as he feels God has abandoned him to die leaving them unfulfilled – it is because he does not have a consonant apprehension of the true nature of his founding life call. Indeed, it is evident that if the Christian minister had a clearer understanding of his founding life call, this would have contributed more purposefully towards the appreciative appraisal of his dissonant current form of life. It is here that Thomas Aquinas' understanding of the powers of the Christian soul – intellect or mind and will – as we have learnt above, might have

---

[72] See above footnote #60.

expedited the activation of his inherent ability and desire to maintain his *form potency*.[73]

OBSTACLES TO AND FACILITATING CONDITIONS FOR THE FORMATION OF CHRISTIAN MINISTERS

The main obstacles to consonant formation and reformation in this horizon of the Coformant – the level of the Christian minister – despair at the imminent end of the subject's ministry, and the subject's subsequent refusal to enter into a true dialogue with another. Unless the subject is able to overcome his despair, which comes from his deformative understanding and perception that God has abandoned him, and that his own willfully crafted plans in his ministry are God's, he will not be able to re-establish hope and absolute trust in God which reality will lead him to self-abandonment to God, and so to consonant growth. Such desired consonant growth is not possible without the opening of the subject's interiority to formative dialogue and encounter with especially revered others. So, consonant formation and reformation of his current life form will become more necessary if the subject is to be able to overcome these obstacles. The ministry he exercises could then be perceived as Christ's, and his imminent death regarded as part of that ministry to which he has been called.

Two principal facilitating conditions for consonant formation and reformation are also here present. The first is the inherent form potencies of mind and will by means of which the subject can enter into formative dialogue. But even with these powers, if there would not exist the proper interformative sphere in which they could operate, consonant formation and reformation of the subject's core would still be impossible. Hence, the compassionate and loving presence of the superior provides the second main facilitating condition for this consonant formation and reformation

---

[73] See, 'the principle of maintenance of form potency,' 26.

of the Christian minister, and even to lay the conditions for his eventual ***transformation.***

TRANSITING TO DIVISION TWO

In investigating the four horizons in Division One, our research has studied simultaneously the dynamics of self-encapsulation which originates from life-threatening illness, and the imminent death accompanying it, and hence, the disruption of life which, it is perceived by the subject, to bring. The Division also focused on resistance to interformation through encounter with others. The foregoing research therefore examined in depth the formation dynamics in the conflicted subject in all the four horizons in the first Coformant.

In Division Two which follows, we will concentrate on the elucidation of the dynamics in the second Coformant of the formation event. It will study the influence which form-tradition directives, through formative questioning, may exert on the subject in all the same four horizons of human presence.

DIVISION TWO

APPRAISING INBREAKING FORMATION DIRECTIVES

INTRODUCTION

STATEMENT OF THE BASIC FORMATION QUESTION TO BE INVESTIGATED

The basic question to be investigated in the Division concentrates on form tradition narrative and its evocative power to bring about a consonant shift of the current life-form of subjects who may be conflicted by life-threatening illness and impending death. The assumption here is that subjects who are encapsulated by vital-functional dissonance and are seemingly resistant to horizontal encounter with others, as is demonstrated in Division One, may be consonantly influenced by their form tradition narrative to change.

Thus, on all four horizons of human presence, form tradition narrative may have the inherent power to unlock and so free the self-imprisoned subjects, and thereby foster in them the conditions which may lead to a more consonant shift of their current life-form. The formative dynamics which may bring about this shift within the current life form of the subjects come from the second Coformant of the original formation event. The insights obtained from this Coformant, first formulated in the Division for the universal human presence, will then be respectively and appropriately transposed to the other three horizons – religious, Christian, and segmental human presence.

ARTICULATION OF THE SECOND COFORMANT OF THE EVENT IN DIVISION TWO

The second Coformant of the primary formation event is articulated in the four horizons of the Division as follows:

1. **Foundational Human Presence**

Subjects who are formatively questioned may remember a narrative from their form tradition. Aided by their formative imagination they may apprehend and appraise directives from the narrative. Applying directives, subjects may begin to appreciatively abandon themselves to the Mystery of formation and may become peaceful.

2. **Foundational Religious Presence**

Religious subjects who are formatively led through questioning to reflect on their faith tradition may recall a narrative therefrom. Aided by their imagination they may, in meditation, become aware of and appraise life-directives which arise from the narrative. Inspired by such life-directives, religious subjects may become focally aware of the Radical Mystery of Formation and may begin to submit themselves to His transcendent will and feel peaceful.

3. **Foundational Christian Presence**

As these Christians are formatively questioned in their faith tradition, they may contemplate a story therein. Aided by Kataphatic contemplation, life-forming directives may be revealed to them from the story. Such directives may inspire Christians to renew their faith in Jesus Christ and begin to humbly abandon themselves to the pneumatic will, and they may enjoy peace.

4. Foundational Segmental Presence of Christian Ministers

Christian ministers, when formatively questioned in their tradition, may recollect the historic life-story of a minister-saint. Their formative imagination may help them to perceive, with greater clarity, Christ-Form directives inspired by the life-story of the saint. As they incarnate these directives, they may be further inspired with new zeal and dedication to imitate, in their own lives, the example of true Christian ministry given to them in the narrative and are humbly led to abandon their own will in obedience to the will of God who has called them to them to be ministers.

CHAPTER FIVE

APPREHENSION, APPRAISAL, AND APPLICATION OF INBREAKING DIRECTIVES THROUGH FORMATIVE QUESTIONING OF FORM TRADITION

INTRODUCTION

The task which will be undertaken in this Chapter will be to enquire, on the universal human level of presence, the Inbreaking formation directives inherent in the Second Coformant of our original formation event. On this horizon, the Coformant is articulated as follows:

> Subjects who are formatively questioned may remember a narrative from their own tradition. Aided by their formative imagination, they may apprehend and appraise directives from the narrative. Applying such directives, subjects may begin to appreciatively abandon themselves to the Mystery of Formation, and may become peaceful.

In two remote foundational statements drawn from the Coformant, our investigation in this chapter will seek to disclose, through formative questioning, the Inbreaking form directives which come from a formation tradition narrative of the subject. These two foundational statements will focus on, first, *the power that formative questioning about a form tradition narrative has to evoke formative memories in subjects*; and secondly, *the role of imagination in the appreciative appraisal of what is thus evoked in the subjects.*

PART ONE
EVOCATIVE POWER OF FORMATIVE QUESTIONING

The first remote foundational statement is articulated as follows:

Subjects who are formatively questioned may remember a narrative from their tradition.

In this remote foundational statement, we shall explore two proximate dynamics. While we shall discuss in the first one – section A – how formative questioning may evoke formative memories in the subject, and we will address in the second on – section B – the formative potency which may be inherent in a tradition narrative.

SECTION A: FORMATIVE QUESTIONING AS EVOKING FORMATIVE MEMORIES

In the original formation event, the subject continues to resist any disclosure of his intrasphere to another. However, as the other continues, in his gentle way to be compassionately present to the subject through formative questioning, the intrasphere of the subject begins gradually to open up. He begins to receive Inbreaking directives which come from the memories evoked by the formative gentle questioning of the other. We intend to study in this proximate area of research, the power that formative questioning has to evoke formative memories.

Chapter 5: Apprehension, Appraisal, and Application

From the SFHF: Formative Memory

In the discussion on engaging in dialogue in the last chapter, we identified memory as one of the intellectual faculties of the human being.[1] Formation Science has demonstrated that formative memory, together with formative imagination and anticipation, is a secondary or auxiliary power in the process of human formation.[2] In his explanation of what Formation Science calls *formative memory*, van Kaam says: "Each of us has a history of formation and deformation. What happens to us during that history is not totally lost. Certain residues remain to affect the present direction and formation of our life, its dispositions and actions. This affect can be actual or potential."[3]

This seems to be precisely what Thomas Aquinas says, as he agrees with Aristotle (*De Anima*, iii. 4) that, when the memory, as passive intellect, ""*is identified with each thing as knowing it, it is said to be in act, and that this happens when it can operate of itself. And even then, it is in potentiality, but

---

[1] See chapter four, footnote #71. However, while St. Augustine considers memory to be equally a central power of the soul – FLF – just as the intellect or understanding and will, thus making a trilogy of the central powers of the soul (*De Trinitate*, IX, 2), Thomas Aquinas, in his *Summa Theologiae*, identifies memory as belonging to the passive power of the intellect, and hence, secondary or auxiliary to the intellect as a central power of the soul of which it is part (I. Q. 79, A.7).

[2] For detailed discussion on memory and anticipation, see Adrian van Kaam, *Human Formation*, 139-64. Formative imagination is discussed in relation to disposition formation in the preceding chapter in the same volume, pp.100-38. Van Kaam discusses the three powers again auxiliary intraformative powers to the central powers of the heart – the mind and the will – in the appraisal process; see *Scientific Formation*, 143.

[3] Adrian van Kaam, *Human Formation*, 143.

not in the same way as before learning and discovering."[4] It is indeed such memory that van Kaam calls, in Formation Science language, "formation memory." For the passive intellect in identifying itself with the subject of knowledge – the form that it had given to our life – passes again from its disposition of potentiality to that of act. Thus, van Kaam is right when he says of formative memories: "They have given form to our lives in the past, and they continue to give form to them in the present."[5]

From the SFHF: Formative Consciousness

Just as formative memory is indispensable for the giving of form to our lives both in the past and the present, and hence, for the ongoing formation of the individual, so is formation consciousness essentially and intricately connected with our entire human life, and for the maintenance of our formation potency. Human formation, as we have observed all along, is essentially in the transcendent dimension.[6] Formation consciousness which, like formative memory, has the unique-communal FLF as its source and ground, must also be transcendent in its nature.

Speaking about what he calls *"psychodynamics of spiritual presence of the human being"* in his book entitled *In Search of Spiritual Identity*, van Kaam implicitly underscores this transcendent origin of the human formation consciousness. After he has asserted our human presence in reality as being constituted by five dimensions of our life form, he observes:

---

[4] Thomas Aquinas, *opus cit*. I Q.79, A.6. The same reasoning is used in his response in article 7, where he argues that the passive intellect – formative memory – although distinct from the active intellect, "is not differentiated by any difference of being."

[5] Adrian van Kaam, *Human Formation*, 143.

[6] See, for example, chapter one, part two, under section B.

In this summation we note especially the terms *supra* and *infra* conscious. They are not found in self-theories that do not start from the principle of the fundamental spiritual nature of man. In our self-theory both the *supra* and the *infra* conscious are unconscious. This means that my presence on these levels is not available to my actual awareness; neither can I make these levels available at will. Other self-theories usually use the word *unconscious* to identify only what we call here infra-conscious.[7]

As he would later affirm, "Experience teaches us that human life is spiritual through and through. Certain acts of the human person are in some measure free and conscious. This means that they transcend the immediate sociohistorical and the vital-functional determinations of human life.[8]

In this light, human consciousness can rightly be said to share essentially in the formative process undertaken by each unique-communal individual FLF. In the unfolding of the individual founding life call, all five levels of

---

[7] Adrian van Kaam, *In Search of Spiritual Identity* (Denville, N.J.: Dimension Books, 1975), 109. Here van Kaam lists the five dimensions of human presence or consciousness as "the natural and the divinely illuminated supraconscious, the infraconscious, preconscious, and conscious," which he then gives detailed explication of each in the pages that follow – 110-37. In *Studies* 1 (Feb. 1980), 149, however, he identifies four dimensions of consciousness; these he lists as: the focused, pre-, infra-, and trans-consciousness. But again, in his first volume of his seven magisterial works on **Formative Spirituality** – *Fundamental Formation*, he distinguishes "five dimensions of formative human consciousness in relation to life formation." And he lists them as: focal (or focused); pre-; inter; infra-; and trans-consciousness; see *Fundamental Formation*, opus cit., 262-3.

[8] Adrian van Kaam, *Human Formation*, 54.

consciousness are involved, whether explicitly or implicitly.[9] Hence, Formation Science calls it formation consciousness.

From the SFHF: Formative Questioning

In his Ph.D. dissertation in Formative Spirituality, John W. Kloepfer has very well presented the formative value that is contained in artful questioning of a subject who is before a reality to the truth of which he or she is prejudiced. The entire objective of Kloepfer's dissertation, precisely entitled *The Art of Formative Questioning*, is, as he says in the introduction, "to reveal some of the formative dynamics that are present when people are enabled, through a process of formative questioning, to move from one level of self-awareness to another."[10] Truly artful questioning indeed has the power to facilitate, in a person, the process of thinking formatively. And this formative thinking is what can lead the person to "formative shifts in self-knowledge," as Kloepfer acknowledges.[11]

Right here, the question can be asked as to what may be described then as formative questioning, or formative questions? Kloepfer basically responds to this question in the first five chapters of his research, and he adds to this responds in the tenth chapter. In Chapters one to five, he respectively describes as formative, questions which are objective, reflective, maieutic, and simple. Then in Chapter Ten, he adds to this description as formative, **questions which spark the human imagination**. All these are

---

[9] As van Kaam distinguishes among the levels of consciousness, focal consciousness is *full awareness*; while the rest in varying degrees do not comprehend "the fully aware concentrated disposition and acts of attentiveness" of the human life form; see *Fundamental Formation*, 262-3.

[10] John W. Kloepfer, *The Art of Formative Questioning: A Way to Foster Self-Disclosure*, Ph.D. Diss., Duquesne University, 1990 (Ann Arbor: UMI, 1990), 1.

[11] Ibid., 2.

qualities which, if inherent in a question, would vest such a question with the potency to lead an individual standing before a reality to the truth of which he or she may be prejudiced, to think formatively, and so, to arrive at a formative shift in self-knowledge with regard to that reality. If therefore a question does not have, at least, one of these qualities, we may rightly conclude that it is devoid of any formative power since it will be incapable of leading the subject to any formative shift in self-knowledge.

All the above discussions on formative questioning as evoking formative memories are the viewpoint of formative science. We shall now for a brief while turn again to Gadamer who brings a philosopher's acumen to the discussion relative to questioning.

Han-Georg Gadamer: Understanding and Question

In his extensive research for a theory of hermeneutic experience, Gadamer, either by constraint or by design, had to address the issue of raising questions. In discussing the understanding of the meaning in aesthetics, for example, he holds that reconstruction and integration are hermeneutic tasks. This implies that the goal of hermeneutics is the understanding of the reality with which one is confronted. For it is in view of understanding something that one would seek to reconstruct it so that, eventually, one would integrate it in one's own life. As Gadamer therefore contends, "The classical discipline concerned with the art of understanding texts is hermeneutics."[12]

Discussing Heidegger's disclosure of the fore-structure of understanding[13] within the general background of what he calls "the hermeneutic

---

[12] Hans-Georg Gadamer, *Truth and Method* 2nd ed. (New York: Continuum Publishing Company, 1993), 164.

[13] Heidegger's *fore-structure of understanding* to which Gadamer refers is what Heidegger himself describes in his concept of the hermeneutic thus: "It is not to be

circle[14] and the problem of prejudice" in relation to the historicity of understanding, Gadamer says in opposition to Heidegger: "Our question, by contrast, is how hermeneutics, once free from ontological obstructions of the scientific concept of objectivity, can do justice to the historicity of understanding. Hermeneutics has traditionally understood itself as an art or technique."[15] Later, in his discussion on the concept of *the "classical,"* Gadamer further asserts what **understanding** is in terms of historical movement. Thus, he says: "*Understanding is to be thought of less as a subjective act than as participating in an event of tradition*, a process of transmission in which past and present are constantly mediated."[16]

If hermeneutics is an art of understanding, or a technique by which one may go beyond the aesthetic object, or historical event to the meaning behind them, its technique must include a way by which the particular meaning inherent in them may eventually be evoked to stand out crystallized though interpretation. This way, in its finest form, is what Kloepfer calls the art of questioning. As Gadamer, still discussing the problem of prejudice, says:

---

reduced to the level of a vicious circle, or even of a circle which is merely tolerated. In the circle is hidden a positive possibility of the most primordial kind of knowing. To be sure, we genuinely take hold of this possibility only when, in our interpretation, we have understood our first, last, and constant task is never to allow our fore-having, fore-sight, and fore-conception to be presented to us by fancies and popular conceptions, but rather to make the scientific secure by working out these fore-structures in terms of the things themselves." Martin Heidegger, *Being and Time*, trans. and ed., John McQuarrie and Edward Robinson (San Francisco: Harper & Row, 1962), 195 (H. 153).

[14] See Schleiermacher's concept of *the hermeneutic circle*, in *Truth and Method*, 190.

[15] Ibid., 265.

[16] Ibid., 290.

It is impossible to make ourselves aware of a prejudice while it is constantly operating unnoticed, but only when it is, so to speak, provoked. The encounter with a traditionary text can provide this provocation. For what leads to understanding must be something that has already asserted itself in its own separate validity. Understanding begins, as we have already said above, #229 **when something addresses us.** This is the first condition for hermeneutics. We now know what this requires, namely **the fundamental suspension of our own prejudices.** But all suspension of judgements and hence, *a fortiori*, of prejudices, has the logical structure of a *question*.[17]

It is therefore this insight that must have led Gadamer to address the issue of raising questions, the essence of which, he says, "is to open up possibilities and keep them open."[18]

A Reflection Integrating the above Discussions

When we take into context the subject of our original formation event in this light of the insights to which the above discussions have revealed, i.e., on the role that formative questions can play in evoking memories that lead to formation, a number of issues become clear. In the original formation event, the subject in his self-encapsulation, seemed to have been insulated, and thus to have become impervious to all influences, even those that may have come from a compassionate other. There seemed to be no way in which his intrasphere could be penetrated by another who might eagerly

---

[17] Ibid., 299. The emphases by way of bold print are mine. The #299 within the quoted text refers to pages 290 and 295 of *Truth and Method*, where Gadamer already discussed the issue of when we begin to have understanding of an historical event.

[18] Ibid., 299.

seek to encounter him through a veritable dialogue. As the visiting other talked about various issues, including his recent trip from which he had just returned, all what seemed to preoccupy the subject were his feelings of anger at both God and his visitor. He even wondered, at a point, whether these feelings were not being observed by his visitor.[19]

As the subject admits, it was not until when "he [the visitor] suddenly asks me if I remember the story about Saint Aloysius Gonzaga, which he told us when we were still in the elementary school,"[20] that he [the subject] feels provoked and begins to think of the life-story of Saint Aloysius appreciatively. This means that the question which the visitor finally asked the subject, in his faith tradition, had such power that it penetrated all the defenses and blocks which previously prevented any outside influence form reaching his core form.

In his "reflections on living with a terminal illness," John Carmody demonstrates very clearly how formative questions have the potency to evoke formative memories. Confronted with imminent death through myeloma, Carmody was led to abandon himself to God who, he had come to the conviction, knows best what "true living and good dying" is. He arrived at this self-abandonment to God only when he posed himself, and responded to the question, "Who knows what is true living and good dying?"[21]

Logically, it is in his deliberation for the response to this question that Carmody must have begun to remember what various spiritual masters had said about abandonment. He himself formulates it thus in his eighteenth reflection:

---

[19] See Formation event, Preface to this Book, viii-xii..
[20] Ibid.
[21] John Carmody, opus cit. 40.

> The lesson I am hearing today concerns abandonment. You make a chorus, if not a single voice, of the *Cloud,* Saint John of the Cross, Teresa, Brother Lawrence, and de Caussade. I hear them telling me that my life is your doing, as my being is your giving. The more I give my life and death, myself and being, over to you, the better for everyone. Who knows what is true living and good dying? You alone, Socrates going to his death remains a consoling figure: Arguably he was doing a far, far better thing than the senators who condemned him.

Carmody goes on to make more maieutic his question, the response to which is already contained in the above reflection, and which he then makes more explicit in the following:

> Should I pray for a remission, if the price would be a lesser death? Have I even the right to ask this question? The question fades when abandonment takes center stage. I should pray for what should most honor you, what you know is best for me, and for all for whom I'm responsible.[22]

In the light of the above, the formative question, as to whom he should abandon himself, evoked the memories Carmody had about abandonment from the Cloud of Unknowing: John of the Cross, Teresa of Avila, Brother Lawrence of the Resurrection, and Jean-Pierre de Caussade. Memories of what all these spiritual masters taught him in his past readings of them, together with his historical knowledge of the dramatic condemnation of Socrates to death, reformed in him a consonant disposition of self-abandonment to God.

The power unleashed by formative questions, therefore, put into operation the memory of a subject, leading such a subject to appreciatively

---

[22] Ibid.

appraise the immediate life situation with which he is actually confronted. This becomes the consonant moment when knowledge of himself begins to shift formatively away from his conflicted current life form. In the following section, we will discuss the formative powers thus unleashed through the question concerning the form narrative in the subject's faith tradition.

SECTION B: *FORMATIVE POTENCY OF FORM TRADITION NARRATIVE*

The memories which contain the Inbreaking directives, with formative powers for the subject, come from a narrative of his formation tradition. These directives in his faith tradition. The study in this proximate area will concentrate on the evocative power of formation narrative.

From the SFHF: Formation Potential of Form Tradition

In the previous section, we investigated into how formative memory is the human mind which, as passive intellect, identifies itself with the form that it had given to our life in the past and now reactivates the knowledge with which the mind previously identified itself remained thus in potency. And now it passes into act, giving us form again through that same object of knowledge with which it was identified in the past.[23] Van Kaam describes such formative power of the memory in this very clear manner:

> The formative power of memory represents the unavoidable potential and actual impact of one's whole past formation and deformation. It can be raised partially or totally to the level of a main power of present and future formation and direction by means of meditative, formative

---

[23] See Formative Memory above.

remembrance. It can decisively influence actual formation events by means of formative focal recall.[24]

We also gained the insight that formative questions about the object of knowledge with which the mind as formative memory identifies itself, may consonantly facilitate human presence – formative consciousness. It is this object of knowledge thus formatively present to the subject, through mediation of his or her form tradition that may lead him or her to a formative shift in his or her current formative memory. This is what van Kaam describes as "[t]hose past shared or personal formation events that contribute to the current formation and direction of life, independent of their degree of availability to formative remembrance, focal recall or meditative remembrance."[25]

In the primary formation even which we are investigating, the object of knowledge with which the subject is identified, and which is now a potential giver of form to him, as it was in the past, comes from a form narrative in his faith formation tradition. It is contained in a narrative of the life story of one of his ancestors in the tradition of his faith. This form narrative concerns the exemplary life of one of such an ancestor and has the potency to give formative inspiration to the subject. In this respect, the ancestor becomes a vertical formative pole[26] whose life in the faith tradition has the

---

[24] *Studies* 2 (Feb. 1981), 118.

[25] Ibid., 119.

[26] See Adrian van Kaam, *Fundamental Formation*, 99. Formation theory considers interformation to be fundamental to human formation. Here van Kaam distinguishes between vertical and horizontal interformations. After lamenting the fact that we humans tend to live in formation ignorance, he asserts that, to overcome it, we need help from others, from whom we can become the beneficiaries of interformation. He says elsewhere that "Horizontal interformation may happen in an encounter with truly enlightened people in our times or

potential to influence and give form to the subject. As van Kaam affirms, with regard to *formative anticipations and form traditions*, "Our anticipations are especially affected by form traditions because they constitute the realm of a vertical interformation, which stretches over centuries. They bring us in touch with whoever and whatever gave form significantly to life and world long before our generation."[27]

This therefore makes it evident that form narratives which come from the subject's formation tradition may exert vertical interformational influence on him. As such, it is this form narrative which, in its capacity as the object of knowledge, has the vertical formation power as form tradition to renew in a consonant way the formation directives of the subject. This explains why van Kaam insists that "[f]ormation scientist[s] or practitioners must try to help people become better aware of the *formation potential* of the foundations of the form tradition they have chosen."[28] For formation traditions which have such aspirational and inspirational potencies are essentially transcendent. They have the source of their origin in the Mystery itself.[29]

From the SFHF: Language and Form Tradition

In connection with the formation potential of formative narrative in form tradition is **language**. In evaluating the potency of form narrative, which comes from a form tradition, the importance of language as the instrument for ordering the formation field of the subject cannot be

---

surroundings," while vertical interformation is "WITH THOSE WHO LIVED BEFORE US"; SEE Adrian van Kaam, *Human Formation*, 92.

[27] Adrian van Kaam, *Human Formation*, p. 161.

[28] Adrian van Kaam, *Fundamental Formation*, 113.

[29] Adrian van Kaam, *Traditional Formation*, opus cit., 111-3. Also *Human Formation*, 92.

exaggerated. Van Kaam implies this important character of language when he says: "Our traditional ways of need fulfillment are maintained for the most part by our use of language. Language is a direct or indirect product of the significant traditions that over the centuries *have given form* to a culture. Our use of language coforms what we experience."[30] In fact, we can say that in this sense, it is language which preserves or conserves, in narrative form, the object of knowledge – the memories of past formation events of others that can inspire us today, and thus make it possible to pass them on. It is in language that we encounter these others who thus become for us poles of vertical interformation. This is what van Kaam points out when he says: "Through use of language and other symbols, some form traditions can deform human life from infancy on."[31]

From the SFHF: Appraisal of Traditional Directives

In the light of the above discussions on the formative potency of form tradition, and the importance of language as the instrument of accumulating wisdom, experience, and knowledge in narrative, the importance of consonant appraisal of traditional directives becomes evident.[32] Since form traditions are accumulations of wisdom, experience, and knowledge of past generations,[33] and may, through language by way of narrative, also contain deformative directives, in order that one's form tradition be considered effectively formative, the directives contained in it must be consonantly appraised. To facilitate such consonant appraisal, Formation Science considers it necessary to develop form dispositions for their wise appraisal.

---

[30] Adrian van Kaam, *Traditional Formation*, 45.
[31] Ibid., 45.
[32] For the appraisal of directives in general, see chapter four.
[33] *Traditional Formation*, 296.

Hence, van Kaam proposes six different aspects by which the process of such appreciative appraisal may be realized.[34]

We have referred to language as the instrument through which form traditions are preserved from past generations and handed down to us in the form of narratives. Under the following two paragraph-leads, we will discuss briefly, with Donald Polkinghorne and Janet Riffing, the relationship that exists between narrative and the self, and narrative as metaphorical expression of experience.

Donald E. Polkinghorne: Narrative and the Self

One of the questions which comes up in the above discussion regards narrative through the use of language. We came to the conclusion that narrative contains the object of knowledge with which the formative memory becomes identified in the past as a formation potentiality in the future. How does such a vehicle relate to the **self** of the subject?[35] It is

---

[34] The six aspects of the appraisal process for traditional for directives proposed by van Kaam could be summarized as follows: i) an appraisal and appreciation of opportunities for transcendent formation in the light of transcendent traditions; 2) an appraisal guided by both traditional directives and insights into one's own life call; 3) appraisal of directives modulated in order to adapt them to the unique particularity of the formation event; 4) appraisal of basic congeniality of both content-directives and implementation-directives; 5) appraisal of competence directives in the light of formation traditions during projection or execution of implementations; and 6) appraisal of new questions in response to attempts at implementation. See *Traditional Formation*, pp. 296-7

[35] Confer footnote # 8 above. See also van Kaam's explanation of the construct "ex-sistence" which he says, "includes the original '**wholeness**' of **self**, experience, measurable behaviour, body and environment; See *Foundations for Personality Study* (Denville, New Jersey: Dimension Books, 1983), 176. ***The Self***, intended by van Kaam in the construct, "existence," is what he describes in the text referred to

Chapter 5: Apprehension, Appraisal, and Application

towards a valid response to this question that insights offered by Donald Polkinghorne may be perceived.

In Chapter Two, "Narrative Expression," of his book entitled *Narrative Knowing and the Human Sciences*, Polkinghorne defines the term *Narrative* as "the fundamental scheme for linking individual human actions and events into interrelated aspects of an understandable composite."[36] Later, he draws attention to the equivalence of the term "narrative" and goes on to point out to his readers his use of the term "narrative" as equivalent to the term "story," not in the fictional sense, but in reference to a "true story" – "such as the *story* of one's life."[37] In this light, a narrative is, therefore, a linguistic expression of the '*self*', i.e. it is an empirical expression, by way of language, of the unique and communal life-form of a particular individual.

Later, discussing the *self as a substance – substratum –* in relation to narrative, Polkinghorne, who first distinguishes two primary identities of the *self*: identity of the body, and identity of the memory, asserts that there is a third form of identity in response to the perennial and basic question, "Who am I?"[38] After a clear description of the first two identities as response to the question, "Who am I?" he follows suit with a third response:

---

by the footnote #8. For a more comprehensive consideration of the *Self*, see *Fundamental Formation*, pp. 53-6. See also 65; in the latter, it becomes more evident that the communal and unique life-form of an "existence" is the Self of that "existence."

[36] Donald E. Polkinghorne, *Narrative Knowing and the Human Sciences* (Albany, New York: State University of New York Press, 1988), 13. Donald E. Polkinghorne, *Narrative Knowing and the Human Sciences* (Albany, New York: State University of New York Press, 1988), 13.

[37] Opus cit., 13-4.

[38] Ibid., 146-7.

Beyond these two recent answers to the question, there is a third, historically significant answer. This position is based on the idea that ultimately each of us is an incorporeal self, or mental substance, rather than a mere body. As a consequence, personal identity must be related to the mental subject that experiences and remembers, not to experience itself. The substratum that underlies the series of mental or psychological states is a soul, unique self, and each of us has absolutely certain, although private, knowledge of this self and its states whenever they occur.[39]

In the light of formation theory, what Polkinghorne describes as the identity of *self* seems to be non-other than what Formation Science calls the founding life-form of the individual – the soul, the heart.

Janet Ruffing: Narrative and Metaphorical[40] Expression of Experience

Narrative, which is therefore a linguistic way of expressing events in relation to the *self*, is a mode by which people usually share an experience. The question which seems obvious here is, "What is intended by '*experience?*'" Janet Ruffing explains: "Human experience is an interpretive encounter with someone or something and a reflective, conceptual awareness

---

[39] Ibid., 147.

[40] In psychological terms, *Jacques Lacan* holds that "metaphor consists in the substitution in a signifier-signified relationship of a new signifier, S, used as the signifier of the original S, which now becomes a signified;" see Anika Lemaire, Jacques Lacan, trans. David Macey (London: Routledge, 1979), 96. *Webster's Third New International Dictionary* defines *metaphor* as "A figure of speech in which a word or phrase denoting one kind of object or action is used in place of another to suggest a likeness or analogy between them." As Ruffing makes it clear, a metaphor is essentially interpretive.

of this encounter."[41] She substantiates her concept of human experience by quoting Denis Edwards' definition of experience.[42]

It is experience seen in this light which leads Ruffing also to affirm that "[n]arrative form, then, is the ordinary way people share an experience or report its actuality."[43] Hence, she further asserts:

> Narrative by its nature, invites the imaginative participation of its hearers in the events narrated. It can offer opportunities for new experiences to the auditors as well as concretize those experiences for the narrator. Narrative is a primary form of communicating a tradition even as narratives of original experiences of faith embody that tradition anew or challenge it to change.[44]

It is therefore obvious that narrative metaphorically expresses the experience of a *self* to others. It represents the true story of a person, the communal and unique foundational life form of the individual. In itself, the narrative is a strong invitation to the imaginative participation of its hearers.

---

[41] Janet Ruffing, *Uncovering Stories of Faith* (New York: Paulist Press, 1989), 73.

[42] See Denis Edwards, *The Human Experience of God* (New York: Paulist Press, 1983), 7. Edwards defines human experience in these terms: "Experience is best seen as encounter with something or some person which has become available to consciousness through reflective awareness. It refers to an encounter that is interpreted within human consciousness. This second element, interpretation, has always already occurred whenever we know we have experienced something."

[43] Janet Ruffing, *Opus cit.*, 75.

[44] Ibid., 76.

Integrative Reflection

If the subject of the original formation event, reflecting on the question about his ancestor in the faith, is able to arrive at the conclusion in which he can say to the Mystery, "I am ready to die if you want to have me come to you now,"[45] it is because of his formative power inherent in the *formation narrative* from his form tradition. In the light of what Formation Science demonstrates, the knowledge of his ancestor's life story with which the subject's mind previously identified itself is an empirical experience. It is something which was concretely experienced by his ancestor in the faith. And now, as formative memory in him, it becomes again a power which has "the unavoidable potential"[46] to effect a *formative shift of dispositions* in him. It now actually gives form again to the subject just as it did in the past to his ancestor in the faith.

It is therefore obvious that the life story of the subject's ancestor, which has been preserved in a narrative, becomes for him *a vertical formation pole*. In this respect, the narrative which comes from the ancestor's faith tradition, becomes impregnated with formation potency which is capable of reforming the subject's dissonant dispositions and bringing about a *consonant shift* in his current life form. Hence, contrary to his previously dissonant current form of life, he can now say to the Mystery, as we observed above, "I am ready to die."

The potency that tradition narrative has, to effect a formative shift in form disposition of persons, is not peculiar to the subject of our original formation event. In the preceding integrative reflection, we referred to the question which led Carmody to the *re*formation of his disposition of self-abandonment to God. As we observed then, he might never have arrived at that point of shift of his disposition had it not been for the evocation of his

---

[45] See Formation event, Preface to this Book, viii-xii.
[46] See footnote #26.

memory – his auxiliary intraformative power of the teachings of the spiritual masters concerning abandonment of oneself to God.

It is necessary to remember that the teachings of the spiritual masters in their classics are conservations, in language, of faith and form traditions. Preserved in this way, they are handed down to successive generations in narrative form. This is how the teachings of the spiritual masters on the formative disposition of abandonment of oneself to the Radical Mystery of Formation – now a form tradition – could reach Carmody in his situation of illness and could reform in him his own disposition of self-abandonment to God. If, therefore, the evocation of his memory about the disposition of self-abandonment of God – as handed down in the teachings of the spiritual masters – eventually led Carmody to abandon himself to God in his illness, it demonstrates the formative potency that is inherent in form tradition narrative.

Therefore, just as the form tradition narrative about self-abandonment to God, as contained in the teachings of the spiritual masters, gave consonant form to Carmody, so did the narrative of the life story of the ancestor of the subject of our original formation event give consonant form to him. For, as Polkinghorne observes, the narrative of his ancestor's life story is "true" linguistic expression of his – the ancestor's – life,[47] and not some empty fiction. As such, this expression of the empirical life experience of the subject's ancestor has metaphorically[48] the power to lead the subject of the original formation event to the reformation of his deformed dispositions. Hence, ultimately, the form tradition narrative – the expression of the subject's ancestor's life story – contained from the beginning, the potency to effect consonantly the shift of his current life

---

[47] Donald E. Polkinghorne, opus cit., 13-4.

[48] See under paragraph-head above, "Janet Ruffing: Narrative and Metaphorical Repression of Experience."

form, just as the form tradition narrative about self-abandonment disposition reformed the deformed abandonment disposition in Carmody.

Transition to Second Remote Foundational Statement

The first remote foundational statement in this second Coformant focused on the evocation of subjects' formative memories of a narrative in their faith and form tradition when they are formatively questioned. It further examined the form-ability inherent in one's formation tradition. Investigation in the second remote statement will concentrate on the role of formative imagination in the appraisal of the directives which come from the form tradition narrative of subjects and are capable of initiating subjects' self-abandonment to the Mystery.

PART TWO

IMAGINATION IN THE APPRAISAL PROCESS LEADING TO APPRECIATIVE ABANDONMENT

Below is the articulation of the second remote foundational statement on the universal level of human presence, drawn from the Second Coformant:

Subjects who are aided by their formative imagination may apprehend, appraise, and apply directives to begin to abandon themselves appreciatively to the Mystery of Formation in peace.

In this remote foundational statement, we shall be investigating in Section **A**, the role that formative imagination plays in the appraising of directives from the form tradition narrative. And in Section **B**, we shall explore the beginning of appreciative abandonment to the Mystery that the subject may manifest.

SECTION A: FORMATIVE IMAGINATION AND THE APPRAISING OF DIRECTIVES FROM TRADITION NARRATIVE

The memories of the subject of our original formation event concerning a narrative in his formation tradition are awakened. He feels himself aided by his formative imagination to consonantly appraise the directives which emerge therefrom. The research in this proximate area will seek to identify the power of formative imagination which enables it to enhance the appraisal of the directives coming from a narrative of the subject's form tradition.

From the SFHF: Formation Reason

We have observed already the fact that formative imagination is one of the secondary, or auxiliary powers of human formation.[49] As both primary and secondary formation powers are expressions of the human intellect, which is also sometimes referred to as **human reason**,[50] the following

---

[49] See Part One above, Section A, under "Formative Memory." See also chapter two, part one, under "Confirming Interformation;" and Part Two, Section B, under "Auxiliary Intraspheric Form Potencies." For more extensive discussion on *Formative Imagination* as secondary or auxiliary formation power, see Adrian van Kaam, *Human Formation*, 108-43; and *Scientific Formation*, 156.

[50] Thomas Aquinas, *Summa Theologiae*, Q. 79, Art.8. Hegel uses the terms "consciousness" or "self-consciousness" for *reason*, instead of the scholastic term *intellect*. As it is clear in his philosophy, the term *reason* is comparable to the term *spirit* in the SFHF. But the *human spirit* can be considered the immediate source of the *human reason*: *Phenomenology of Spirit*, trans. A.V. Miller (Oxford University Press, 1977), paragraphs 13-22 & 232.

question may be posed: In what way can human reason be said to be formative?

After distinguishing between transcendent reason and functional reason – each of which he considers as part of human reason in general[51] - affirms that human reason itself "is endowed with the predisposition to attend to, apprehend, appraise, and argue meaningfully about the form reception and donation to be given to life."[52] It is therefore this predisposition which enables us to give direction to the way we receive and donate form in our field. This innate capacity to give and receive form, i.e., to consonantly unfold our FLF, is what the SFHF calls formation reason. Hence, van Kaam summarizes it in these terms: "We can describe formation reason as a universal predisposition of transcendent and functional reason that enables people, focally or prefocally, to attend to, apprehend, and appraise distinctively human formation directives that foster the consonance of their existence.[53] It is in this sense, therefore, that the SFHF perceives the human reason as formation reason.

From the SFHF: Imagination and Apprehension in the Appraisal of Directives

If the human reason, as formation reason, is what predisposes the individual, focally or prefocally, to attend to, apprehend, appraise, and meaningfully argue about the reception and donation of form directives, it is evident that this is the task which falls upon all of his or her formation powers – central and auxiliary, or primary and secondary. In Chapter Four

---

[51] Adrian van Kaam holds the human transcendent reason operates by a type of higher affinity and intuition while the human functional reason works by means of concept formation and conceptual argumentation. See *Scientific Formation*, 192.

[52] Ibid., 193.

[53] Ibid., 194.

above, we already discussed the role of the two primary or central powers of formation. Earlier in this Chapter, we also discussed, to a certain extent, the auxiliary power of formative memory. Although allusion has been made to the other two auxiliary formation powers – imagination and anticipation – we want to focus briefly again on the role that formative imagination plays as part of formation reason in the process of the appraisal of formation directives.

As we made mention of, Kloepfer, in researching the qualities of truly formative questions, devotes the entire tenth Chapter of his work to the description of "Questions which Spark the Imagination."[54] He demonstrates very well, particularly on the Christian horizon of human presence, how such questions have the potency to draw a person to the Mystery, and hence, to transcend himself, through transcendent and pneumatic meditation.

The power that formative imagination has for achieving this comes from its ability to enhance the appraisal process through *imaginative apprehension* of the form directives which is being appraised.[55] In the apprehension of directives by the mind, formative imagination can magnify in images, or even fictitiously create formation situations in which the form directives become, in consonance, more clear and attractive to the formative will of the person. Van Kaam contends that formative imagination is able to operate in this manner in all the five spheres of human formative presence.[56]

It is not only Formation Science which acknowledges the power of imagination in the ongoing formation or maturation of the human person. In the following paragraph, short as it may be, we shall observe insights concerning the power of imagination from the psychologist, Karen Horney.

---

[54] John W. Kloepfer, opus cit., 440-79

[55] Adrian van Kaam makes it clear that not all imaginations are formative. Hence, by the construct "formative imagination," the SFHF refers to imagination which relates to distinctively human formation; see *Human Formation*, 108.

[56] Adrian van Kaam, *Human Formation*, 109.

Karen Horney: Idealized Image – The Power of Imagination

In strong terms, Karen Horney underscores the power of imagination when she points out that it can be the last resort and the only way through which a person who has grown under inner conditions unfavourable for healthy realization of his or her needs can have them fulfilled. After enumerating the three basic needs for the self-realization of every person from childhood, and after a summary of the unfavourable conditions that create basic anxiety in the child, thus frustrating his or her achievement of the goal of self-realization,[57] she concludes:

> Provided his inner conditions do not change (through fortunate life circumstances), so that he can dispense with the needs I have listed, there is only one way in which he can seem to fulfill them, and seem to fulfill all of them in one stroke: through imagination. Gradually and unconsciously, the imagination sets to work and creates in his mind an *idealized image* of himself. In this process he endows himself with unlimited powers and with exalted faculties; he becomes a hero, a genius, a supreme love, a saint, a god.[58]

---

[57] Karen Horney, *Neurosis and Human Growth: The Struggle towards Self-realization* (New York: W.W. Norton and Company Inc., 1950), 17-23. The three basic needs for the creation of favourable conditions for the healthy growth of the child are: 1) an atmosphere of warmth for inner feeling of security and freedom; 2) the good will of others to guide and encourage him or her towards maturity; and 3) healthy frictions with the wishes and wills of others. Horney summarizes thus the unfavourable conditions which others may create against the self-realization of the individual: "They may be dominating, overprotective, intimidating, irritable, over exacting, overindulgent, erratic, partial to other siblings, hypothetical, indifferent, etc." (p.18).

[58] Ibid., 22.

Chapter 5: Apprehension, Appraisal, and Application

In this brief recall of Horney's comprehensive analysis of the potency of imagination to create an idealized image, it is evident she is concerned about hurtful imagination.[59] As she affirms after presenting other grandiose images that neurotics are able to create with their imagination, "The more injurious work of imagination concerns the subtle and comprehensive distortions of reality which he is not aware of fabricating."[60] However, it needs to be pointed out that, as Formation Science and others indicate, imagination can be a truly formative power which is able to enhance and foster consonant apprehension of form directives and of the entire appraisal process.[61]

Integrative Reflection

The findings of the above theoretical investigations help us to understand more clearly what happened in the subject of our original formation event, as the formation question was put to him. In the formation event itself, we observed at one point how the subject's attention is drawn to the life story of an ancestor in the faith. He is suddenly asked if he remembers the life story of Saint Aloysius, and he finds himself remaining with the question, attending to it, and not letting it go by as he has done earlier with other issues.[62]

---

[59] See footnote #55 above.

[60] Karen Horney, opus cit., 33.

[61] See footnote #57 above. See also Sir Karl R. Popper, *Popper Selections*, ed. David Miller (Princeton University Press, 1985), 37, 44, 55, 83, and 172 for instance. A relentless critic of Plato and Marx, and also of inductive reasoning, Popper distinguishes himself in emphasizing the way in which we learn through making and correcting mistakes, and also on the role imagination plays in creating new possibilities.

[62] See Formation event, Preface to this Book, viii-xii.

In beginning to remember the life story of his ancestor, however vaguely, the subject is no longer only attending to the story. His functional reason or mind has begun to apprehend, through his formative memory, the life story of his ancestor. As he vaguely remembers, then recollects in detail, "Aloysius desired greatly only to celebrate the Holy Eucharist, at least once, before he might die of his terminal illness." In this respect, the subject is well into the process of appraising the directives contained in the life story of his ancestor.

If the subject's apprehension of the life story of his ancestor reached such clear details, it is thanks to his formative imagination. As his functional mind apprehends the life story of Aloysius with the help of his formative memory, his formative imagination enhances the contents that are apprehended – the form directives – by recreating and magnifying them in images. This is what van Kaam remarks in an example about the formative imagination of the woman who may choose to devote her life to teaching the art of formative living.[63]

Throughout the entire life story of Aloysius, what seems to be the undergirding reality is his profound disposition of prayer. Cepari has made this the fine line which runs through all his narration of Aloysius' life. In Chapter two, titled "The Perfect Novice,"[64] in the second part of the American Edition of his life, a detailed account is given of Aloysius' practice of the virtues, especially humility and obedience. However, what is outstanding here is his extraordinary gift and devotion to prayer. His biographer underlines: "The saint although he lived in an atmosphere of prayer, was in the habit of preparing himself carefully for his morning meditation."[65] Later, he lists the principal themes on which Aloysius medi-

---

[63] Adrian van Kaam, *Human Formation*, 109.

[64] Virgilio Cepari, *The Life of St. Aloysius Gonzaga of the Company of Jesus*, American Edition (New York: P.J. Kenedy & Sons, n.d.), 173-99.

[65] Ibid., 193.

tated. As he reveals, "The chief subjects of his meditation were the Passion of our Lord, the circumstances of which he always vividly renewed at midday; the Divine attributes, in the contemplation of which he became always singularly absorbed: and the Most Holy Eucharist."[66]

This disposition of prayer was already present in Saint Aloysius from a very early age. In the account of his early boyhood, Cepari speaks of how he would try to hide away from his personal attendants and spend virtually the entire day in prayer.[67] He describes the manner in which the attendants would find him:

> They would behold their young Lord, prostrate before the crucifix, where for hours he would remain, or praying with his arms extended or crossed over his breasts; and all the while, the perennial fount gave forth its stream from eyes riveted on the image of the Lord, and his bosom heaved with deep sobs and sighs.[68]

If Aloysius, in these circumstances, was able to demonstrate such genuine emotions coming from his very depths, it seems obvious that it was because of the very vivid and concrete manner in which he was able to apprehend the directives which came from his contemplation of the crucifix or the Passion of Christ. Therefore, it can legitimately be assumed here that Aloysius' power of imagination enhanced his apprehension and subsequent appraisal of the form directives which he received in prayer from his contemplative presence before the Crucifixion and Passion of Jesus. Agreeing with Popper's acknowledgement of the creative power of imagination,[69] it can be assumed that Aloysius' formative imagination vividly recreated the

---

[66] Ibid., 195

[67] Ibid., 53.

[68] Ibid.

[69] Sir Karl R. Popper, Popper Selections (opus cit.), 83

scenes of the Passion and the Crucifixion of Jesus each time he meditated on them. Hence, the Passion and the Crucifixion, and indeed, all the other themes on which he usually meditated, became really present to him and was not just some empty fiction.

So, if in the light of the example above, the subject of the original formation event is able to arrive at such an appreciative appraisal of these directives, it is thanks to the role played by his formative imagination. For, through its creative way of apprehending the form directives, his formative imagination was able to truly enhance his entire appraisal process.

SECTION B: THE BEGINNING OF APPRECIATIVE ABANDONMENT TO THE MYSTERY

As the subject in appraisal reflects upon the directives coming from the narrative of his form tradition, he begins to be aware of a movement of surrender of his functionalistic will to the Mystery in an appreciative manner. He also begins to feel peaceful. The fact that the subject begins to appreciatively abandon himself to the Mystery is an indication that a shift has occurred in his current form of life. It is on this shift in the subject's current life form that this proximate area of research intends to focus upon and to explore.

From the SFHF: Abandonment to the Formation Mystery

In the original formation event, we learnt, in the subject's own words, that as he recollected details of his ancestor's life story, he began to experience a feeling of peace taking hold of him. The question which may be lurking in the reader's mind can be the following: "How could feelings of peace begin so suddenly to take possession of someone who has reached such depths of frustration, depression and anger with the Mystery whom he considered as having abandoned him? How could he so suddenly begin to feel peace in the very presence of one whom he regarded, a moment ago, as part of the reason for his current dissonant situation and disposition of life?"

If the subject of our primary formation event suddenly began to feel such peace shortly after appreciatively recollecting details of his ancestor's life story, it seems obvious that his current life form had undergone some shift. After he appreciatively appraised the disposition of willingness of his ancestor in the faith, to abandon his own to that of the Mystery, the subject's own intrasphere was attained by it. Thus, his awakened or reformed *disposition of loving trust*,[70] affirmed by his will, moved him also to entrust himself to the loving Mystery in the same way as his ancestor. This is what the SFHF calls **abandonment to the Formation Mystery**.[71] As van Kaam clearly asserts:

> When we speak about the foundational triad of faith, hope and consonance as *the root of appreciative abandonment,* we do not mean particular disposition of faith, hope and consonance toward certain people, events or things. We mean this threefold disposition as a basic orientation of the whole person toward the Formation Mystery as a whole.[72]

---

[70] The phrase, '*disposition of loving trust,*' here sums up the primordial triad of faith, hope and love or consonance, which is innate in each person. It is the basic disposition of **sensibility**, the development or gradual awakening of which, in the individual, is through what Formation Science calls *parental benediction*. This parental blessing is expressed in the loving appreciative and confirmatory presence of the parents or their substitutes and varies in degrees in the individuals. For some people, unfortunately, the expression of such blessing may have been virtually non-existent. See Adrian van Kaam, *Human Formation*, 59-60.

[71] Adrian van Kaam, *Fundamental Formation*, 221-42.

[72] Ibid., 230.

Formation Freedom

In Chapter Two of this research, we discussed in some length the notion of abandonment, especially the difference between appreciative and depreciative abandonments.[73] We observed that whichever alternative abandonment a person chooses, he or she would always do so with his or her ***formative freedom***.[74] This freedom, van Kaam is convinced, "is not exclusively a characteristic of this or that particular act of formative willing, made here-and-now at this moment. We sense that it must have deeper roots in our foundational human life form."[75]

It is this formation freedom, as fundamental choice, which sanctions in consonance the abandonment of oneself to the Mystery of formation. For, in freely abandoning oneself to the Mystery, one responds positively and with the innate freedom from the very centre of one's being to the meaningfulness of this Mystery which is responsible for one's formation.[76] Through *formative freedom*, the individual, in his or her positive self-abandonment to the Mystery of formation, therefore expresses appreciatively his or her foundational *disposition of loving trust* – the triad of faith, hope, and consonance – in this Mystery.

Influence of Consonant Form Tradition

After the above discussion on abandonment to the Mystery, we believe it will be sufficient to bring to focal awareness that, in the process leading to self-abandonment of the individual to the Mystery, *consonant form*

---

[73] See pages 108-12.
[74] Ibid., 110.
[75] *Fundamental Formation*, opus cit., 225.
[76] Ibid., 225.

Chapter 5: Apprehension, Appraisal, and Application

tradition plays an enormous role. In his discussion concerning cultural obstacles to awe, van Kaam observes:

> The greatest benefit for any culture or civilization is the all-pervasive presence of consonant form traditions. They purify the cultural unfolding of humanity by silently exposing mere self-centered interests through fostering a fundamental presence to the transcendent meaning of culture.[77]

In this light, there is no doubt that consonant form tradition does display great inspirational influence on their adherents. Such traditions have the potency not only to reform their adherents, but even to transform[78] them.

However, transformation will only take place in an adherent when the consonant form tradition, by means of its form directives, is able to tap into and arouse the innate or preformationally given power of ongoing formation in the person. For as the two first principles of Formation Science theory respectively assume, every individual is in his or her preformation fitted out with form-ability for his or her ongoing formation – transcendence.[79] This innate potency for reforming, and even transforming oneself seems to be what Edgar A. Levenson calls '***the homeostatic power of the patient***' in psychoanalysis.

---

[77] Adrian van Kaam, *Human Formation*, opus cit., 224.

[78] See Adrian van Kaam, *Fundamental Formation*, 146

[79] Adrian van Kaam, *The Art of Existential Counseling* (Denville, New Jersey: Dimension Books, 1966), 28-40.

Edgar A Levenson: The Homeostatic Power of the Patient

In his article "The Purloined Self,"[80] psychoanalyst Edgar A. Levenson very crisply describes and points out homeostatic power,[81] which is inherent in the system of the patient in psychoanalysis. After he has illustrated – with two examples similar to Edgar Allen Poe's famous story of *The Purloined Letter* – how the most "*hidden*" data in psychoanalysis is often sitting right under the analyst's nose, he went on to make the point that change in the patient's condition becomes possible when he starts listening to himself and not anymore to the therapist. The presumption here is that, as he stops listening to the therapist who may think that he knows what is wrong with him, the patient takes up his own responsibility. He begins to draw from that inner power, which has always been there, but was never before utilized to bring about the needed change which will be for the better in his situation of illness.

This is precisely where the paradox in psychoanalysis lies. As Levenson, in reference to the relationship between patient and therapist succinctly states: "Psychoanalysis works because the therapist can show the patient that it **cannot** work because what is occurring between them is the same as what they are talking about. Psychoanalysis works because it is *unwork-*

---

[80] E.A. Levenson, "The Purloined Self," in *Journal of the American Academy of Psychoanalysis*, 15, no. 4 (1987): 481-90.

[81] *Webster's Third New International Dictionary* defines homeostasis as "A tendency toward maintenance of a relatively stable internal environment in the bodies of higher animals through a series of interacting **physiological** processes." The term is similarly applied to the **psychological** condition of an individual with respect to contending drives in him. And thirdly, it is also applied to the social conditions among groups with respect to various factors and competing tendencies and powers within the body politic. In this light, *homeostatic powe*r can easily be perceived, in terms of formation theory, as the preformational form potency in the "existent being."

able."[82] It is for this reason that, for Levenson, the real issue in psychoanalysis is not in deciding what is relevant data, but is "rather any detailed deconstructive inquiry (free-associative or detailed inquiry) matched against the development of an *isomorphic* pattern in the therapy relationship"[83]

An Integrative Reflection

We have remarked the shift that took place in the current life form of the subject of our original formation event. This shift is empirically manifested in the sudden feeling of peace in him, a peace-feeling which accompanied the initial surrender of his functionalistic will to the Mystery. As he appreciatively acknowledged how happy and willing his ancestor in the faith was to die, for his unconditionally loving God, whom he trusted and believed in, willed it; the subject's deformed disposition of **willfulness**, which earlier made him resist the transcendent will, began to give way to a consonant disposition of **willingness.** This enabled him to **abandon himself *to*** the Radical Mystery, and to say: "I am ready to die if you want to have me come to you now."[84]

In his seventeenth reflection, 'Feeling Good Again' – in *Cancer and Faith*, Carmody seems to insinuate more strongly a similar formative shift that has been progressively taking place with regard to his disposition of self-abandonment to God. He has been receiving chemotherapy treatment for his bone marrow cancer, the diagnosis of which initially left him utterly devastated. Now, he is also feeling physically better. His temperamental proclivity – not to worry – also kept him away from depression. In this

---

[82] E.A. Levenson, opus cit., 488.

[83] Ibid., 488. *The American Heritage Dictionary* defines *isomorphism* as, "Similarity in form, as in different kinds of organisms."

[84] See Formation event, Preface to this Book, viii-xii.

actual life form, he describes how he perceives and accepts God's will for him in his journey through illness, and recognizes, in his life form, the shift that has occurred as a result in his reforming of his disposition; submitting himself more to God's will each day as he describes it:

> As my illness takes its course I see much benefit in imagining that God is disposing my time quite intimately. It feels properly religious to feel this way, and it seems to bind me closer to God. I sense the workings of the divine Spirit more finely. I pray more simply and feel more intensely that I am covenanted to God and should let God travel with me day by day.
>
> Has God a stake in my shift to a more naked encounter with my illness? Does God want this new phase of my little drama to occasion close contact, fuller intimacy? I cannot know God's mind, but my faith suggests that this could be so. Simply accepting the fact that I have a terminal disease tends to sharpen my mind and stretch the proportions of my life more clearly.[85]

From the above quote alone, it is obvious that Carmody is experiencing a certain measure of peace and tranquility deep in himself, as the caption for this reflection number seventeenth – Feeling Good Again – suggests. This good feeling is not just from the relief that the medical procedure must have been able to bring him. As he acknowledges, it comes especially and essentially from God. Hence, in conclusion to what we can call his appreciative appraisal of God's directives in his current life form, he responds with a clear sense of complete self-abandonment to these divine directives – the expression of God's will – and addresses God thus: "Come God, my death (or my life). Do with me what you will, what the love of your heart prompts. Help me to trust that this has to be good."

---

[85] John Carmody, opus cit., 64.

Chapter 5: Apprehension, Appraisal, and Application

In Carmody's response, we recognise the inner voice of the subject of our primary formation event. Thanks to his *Intraspheric* power – his *formative freedom* – he was eventually able to become **willing** to abandon himself to the transcendent Mystery and so began to experience the feeling of peace and tranquility in himself.

OBSTACLES TO AND FACILITATING CONDITIONS FOR FOUNDATIONAL HUMAN FORMATION

The investigations in this chapter have revealed several obstacles to consonant human formation in this Coformant on the universal horizon. Here, however, we wish to indicate three such obstacles:

1) The first obstacle is the ***dissonance of the immediate life situation of the subject***. This situation of dissonance greatly diminished, or even, if only temporally, blocked the effectiveness of the dispositions of relaxation and openness. These dispositions are necessary for making operative the dynamics of formative imagination, and ultimately, for applying and incarnating the directives coming from formative memory;

2) A second potential primary obstacle is ***deformed formation traditions***. Such deformed traditions could be the source of dissonant images and forma directives. These, instead of leading the subject to consonant human growth and transcendent formation, would rather keep him in dissonance, and so delay the reformation of his dispositions; and

3) A third potential obstacle would be the ***absence of truly formative questions which could spark the formative imagination of the subject***. For, without such objective, reflective, interpretive, simple, and maieutic questions, the intrasphere of the subject would remain

closed upon itself and cannot be stimulated to appraise appreciatively any formation directives.

Similarly in the Coformant, the investigations also revealed to us especially three major conditions which can facilitate consonant formation and reformation on the foundational level of human presence. We can enumerate them as: 1) The ***ability of formative questioning*** in the subject's form tradition, to evoke formative memories in aspect of his faith; 2) The ***inherent power of form tradition*** to give transcendent directives to the subject; and 3) ***formative freedom***, which is the preformational inner power of the subject to freely abandon himself to the Mystery.

Transition to Chapter Six

The objective of the foregoing exploration on the level of foundational human presence has been to elucidate the formative dynamics inherent in form tradition narratives through formative questioning, so as to evoke formative memory. The study also disclosed to us the formative power of imagination.

On the foundational religious level of human presence, we intend to explore in the following chapter, Chapter Six, how faith tradition directives may be discerned through formative questioning and imagination.

CHAPTER SIX

DISCERNING FAITH TRADITIONAL DIRECTIVES THROUGH FORMATIVE QUESTIONING AND IMAGINATION

INTRODUCTION

This chapter will research the dynamics in Coformant Two of our primary formation event – faith traditional directives, formative questioning, and the power of imagination. We shall study the Inbreaking formation directives on the religious level of human presence as formulated in the following terms:

Religious subjects who are formatively led through questioning to reflect on their faith tradition may recall a narrative therefrom. Aided by their imagination they may, in meditation, become aware of, and appraise life-directives which arise from the narrative. Inspired by such life-directives, religious subjects may become focally aware of the Radical Mystery of be peaceful.

The research in this area will be carried out, as usual, in two parts, each of which will be an exploration of a remote foundational statement derived from the Coformant. Each part will be elucidated through the articulation of two inherent proximate form directives.

PART ONE

RECALLING MEMORIES OF A RELIGIOUS FAITH TRADITION

The remote foundational statement which constitutes this part of the research we shall be making in this chapter is articulated in these terms:

> Reflecting on their faith tradition through formative questioning and meditation aided by their imagination, religious subjects may recall a narrative within it and appraise the life-directives which arise from the narrative.

In two separate sections, **A** and **B**, the research on this remote foundational statement will study two proximate dynamics and the formative directives they give. Section A will study how evocative questioning can help one to reflect formatively on one's faith tradition; while Section B will explore the fostering of this formative reflection – in meditation – through the help of imagination.

<u>SECTION A</u>: REFLECTING ON FAITH TRADITION THROUGH FORMATIVE QUESTIONING

The compassionate and gentle presence of the other eventually takes the form of evocative questioning. He asks the subject whether he could recall a particular story in his faith tradition which was narrated to him earlier in his life. This open-ended question may lead the subject, not only to remember the content of the life-story of an ancestor in his faith tradition, but also to begin to reflect on its meaning for him in his current situation of life. In this proximate area of research, we wish to explore the concept of faith tradition, and the capacity that religious subjects have to reflect upon it formatively.

Chapter 6: Discerning Faith Traditional Directives

From the SFHF: Reflection and the Distinctively Human

The ability to reflect on events, either in one's own life or on life in general, is a power which is inherent in only the *existent being*. It is a power which only the distinctively human person can exercise. This is one of the basic assumptions of the SFHF. It is what Adrian van Kaam means and asserts in the following terms:

> Persons begin to emerge as distinctively human when a minimum of reflection enters their life. Reflection implies the possibility of humanly appraising our life direction. Such appraisal goes beyond instant vital reaction. It creates room for some choice or response. Shall I or shall I not?[1]

Earlier, in his discussion on *the emergence of science of formation*, van Kaam already brings to light the nature and origin of the distinctively human power of reflection when he distinguishes between prereflective and scientific knowledge.[2] After asserting that our life formation is primarily preformation, and also that the science of formative spirituality assumes the Mystery of formation to be at the root of all formation,[3] he maintains the existence of preformative knowledge in all humans. Thus, he argues: "The fact that we can ask questions about formation means that we must already have a dim knowledge of what we are asking."[4]

---

[1] See Adrian van Kaam, *Fundamental Formation*, 76. Van Kaam has made it clear that instant vital reaction, which he associates with the vital dimension, "does not yet share (even) the response potency of the functional dimension of life." 75).

[2] Ibid., 5-11.

[3] Ibid., 6.

[4] Ibid., 8.

With this insight, van Kaam is able to make the logical distinction between prereflective knowledge that we all have of our life direction and the scientific – explicit – knowledge which we can obtain of the implicit knowledge about such life direction – our formation – through reflection. Hence, he holds:

> Our reflective knowledge of them, [i.e. our *unfolding life directions*, current life-forms, and formation phases] is open to a continuous correction and refinement in the light of new imaginative intuitions, date and theoretical insights. The science of foundational [human] formation starts out, therefore, from the fact that we have a prereflective a priori awareness of foundational formation.[5]

In van Kaam's view, therefore, it is abundantly clear that scientific or reflective knowledge of our formation – hence, our life direction – is only possible because of our transcendent origin. This, it seems obvious, is what he means when he affirms that such a science "can be illumined by transcendent, imaginative formation intuition." As he further states:

> The science of formation can emerge only as a proximate science by means of reflection upon concrete formation experience. In this reflection we become present to our formation. We begin to see it as an incarnation of **the transcendent dynamic inherent in human life**. We begin to discover that the dynamic is awakened in us by our interaction with a formation field. This field is reflected in our successive situations and by interaction with our communities and form traditions.[6]

---

[5] Ibid., 9.
[6] Ibid., 9-10. Bold emphasis mine.

Chapter 6: Discerning Faith Traditional Directives

It is by virtue of our participation in the Transcendent Radical Mystery of All Formation, the origin and source of our FLF,[7] that our power of reflection becomes a quality which is distinctively human.

From the SFHF: Transcendence Dynamic and Faith Tradition

The distinctively human power of reflection, which is a *transcendent dynamic* inherent in our life, is a means by which we can incarnate our formation. The question is: How best may reflection be fostered so that it may serve to embody formatively within a person his or her faith tradition? The above discussion on "reflection and the distinctively human" makes it clear that this power can bring to concrete realization the actual experience of our life direction – our ongoing formation.

In the process of making concrete our experience of formation, reflection which participates in our transcendent *being-ness*, makes us "become present to [this process]," as van Kaam has already asserted.[8] Thus being present to our life direction through reflection, the *transcendent dynamic* inherent in our life-form becomes awakened by virtue of the interaction we have with our formation field. The formative quality of this presence to our life direction depends very much on questioning the means by which such interaction takes place among the different form dimensions and spheres of the field. Hence, when our questions are truly formative,[9] they dramatically awaken the transcendent dynamic of our human life form and greatly foster formative reflection. In this way, we become qualitatively present to our formation as unfolding, and to all the spheres of the field.

In *Traditional Formation*, Adrian van Kaam describes the **transcendent dynamic** as "The supreme potency and tendency to integrate transfor-

---

[7] Ibid., 93. See also chapter four.
[8] See footnote #6 above.
[9] Confer chapter five, Formative Questioning.

mationally all of human life in light of its rootedness in the Mystery of Formation."[10] He elaborates:

> Such transformation happens in the light of a transcendent or quasi-transcendent meaning. Our transcendence dynamic mores us to adopt such a meaning as our ultimate direction. It elevates it above all other directions, and points to a transcendent mystery as the source and end of all formation.[11]

Here is where faith tradition has its origin and source. As van Kaam unequivocally states in response to the question regarding the common criterion that determines the variety of transcendent form traditions in pluralistic culture:

> These traditions are about the empirical-experiential art and discipline of implementing the general human transcendence dynamic in our everyday concrete fields of human presence and action in the light of a specific faith tradition.[12]

The transcendence dynamic which points to the transcendent Mystery as the source and end of all formation in each of these transcendent form traditions potentially constitutes each of these as a faith tradition.

Faith tradition, van Kaam earlier observed, is the underlying source of various form traditions. The different form traditions are its many ramifications.[13] It is this observation which leads him to make the following

---

[10] *Traditional Formation*, opus cit., 30.

[11] Ibid.

[12] Ibid., 29-30.

[13] Ibid., 26-7. See also "Discrepancy between Faith and Form Traditions," in *Studies*, 4 (November 1983), 411.

claim with regard to the nature of the construct, *faith tradition*: "Deep down, most people tend to live their life on the basis of their belief in some ultimate source of meaning and direction of their existence and the world at large."[14] It is therefore the **transcendence dynamic** inherent in our human life-form which makes belief in and adherence to a faith tradition possible.

Formation Science has offered us the above insights on the human power of reflection, faith tradition, and formative questioning. Now we want to examine briefly in what ways the foundational religious presence of the subject of our original formation event may be influenced in this regard.

Bekuone-Some Der Joseph-Mukassa: "Le Vivant Spirituel"[15] – The Living Spirit

If the question from his visitor – as to whether he remembers a particular story from his faith tradition – evoked such a dramatic and engaging response from the religious subject of the original formation event, it is due to that psychic and spiritual vital principle in him, called *sie*, in Dagara,[16] which distinguishes him from animals. After he has identified

---

[14] Ibid., 27.

[15] Bekuone Some Der Joseph-Mukassa, "Les Dagara : Leur Ecosystème et Son Fonctionnement Interne Face à la Modernité » (PhD. diss. Institut Catholique de Paris, 1989), vol. I. 128-30. For the term 'Dagara', see chapter two, footnote #20.

[16] Although the concept, *sie*, in Dagara philosophy may not be simply translated into English as the 'soul,' this rendering will however be the closest to it. See the concept, sie, in "Les Dagara: Leur Ecosysteme," as referred to in footnote #15 above. See also opus cit., vol. III, p. 30 the concept *ya* in the Dagara language would be more commonly translated as *intelligence*, in English. Although its specific application as such is to the human being, it is also generally applied to animals. But still in a more general sense, it is considered as the principle of life in the cosmos; see ibid, Vol. I, 127-8; also Vol. III, 31.

various principles of life in the constitution of the cosmos in general and of the human being in particular,[17] Bekuone Some Der summaries the Dagara concept of the human person in the following manner:

> Dans la pensée philosophique Dagara, l'homme est en tout compose de plusieurs principes vitaux en interaction les uns avec les autres qui le font vouloir et désirer. Le «*ya*» (principe biologique vital) associe au « *sie* » (principe spirituel psychique et vital) constitue le siège de la volonté humaine. La philosophie de l'homme n'est donc pas dualiste (corps et âme) comme dans d'autres philosophies main globale.[18]

Earlier, Der observed that the Dagara put in hierarchical order all living things and that they believe in the existence of a vital principle in material/corporeal beings, in biological and sensible beings, and in the psychical and spiritual beings – the human person. It is in this light that he then asserts the priority of *ya* over both biological life and corporeal living beings endowed with vital breath.[19] He further asserts: "Ainsi l'homme est un animal dote d'un souffle vital (nyovuuru) et d'un principe biologique sensible, '*ya*' associé a un principe vital psychique et spirituel '*sie*' qui le fait vouloir et désirer, »[20] and he concludes by affirming:

---

[17] Der, opus cit., Vol I, 126-8.

[18] Ibid.,vol. I. 129. This may be translated into English thus: "In Dagara philosophical thought, the human being is a composite of several vital principles, interacting with each other, which make this person to will and to desire. Ya (a vital biological principle) constitutes the seat of the human will. The philosophy of the human being is therefore not dualistic (body and soul) as in the philosophies, but global."

[19] Ibid., 128.

[20] Ibid., 129. This can be rendered in English thus: "Hence, the human being is an animal endowed with a breath of life, and with a sensible biological principle '*ya*' associated with a vital psychic and spiritual principle '*sie*' which makes him or

Chapter 6: Discerning Faith Traditional Directives

Dans la pensée Dagara, le sie c'est l'essentiel du tout matériel qu'est l'homme (homo). Il a un corps (*yagan*) sans poil comme les animaux. Il est lisse (saa) d'où « nir-saal » qui a donné « *nisaal* » (l'homme) au sens générique.[21]

This *nisaal*, though communal in so far as it is shared by many others of the same species, it can also refer uniquely to an individual in as much as it is said of a particular person. For, as Bekuone Some Der writes:

Dans l'ideogie animiste Dagara, il n'y a fondamentalement pas de différence ontologique entre le vivant humain Der et l'être humain désincarné (kpiin) de Der. C'est la même personne (*nir*) de Der qui vit selon les modes différente d'existence.[22]

In the light of all the above insights regarding "le vivant spirituel" of the Dagara of West Africa, the '*sie*' of the human person is what distinguishes him or her, not only from all material, corporeal living beings such as plants and even animals,[23] but also from all other animals. It is because the Dagara perceives the human being as being endowed with a *sie* that such a being is

---

her to will and desire." The term nyovuuru may be rendered as 'breath of life," Hence, *life* itself; Ibid, vol. III. 25.

[21] Ibid., Vol. I., 132. '*Yagan*' means the body in Dagara. The English translation would be the following: "In Dagara thought, the *sie* is the most important element of the human being. It has a body which does not have hair like the animals. It is 'smooth,' Hence, the generic designation of the human being as "nisaal."

[22] Ibid., Vol. I, 129. This may be rendered in English as follows: "In the animist ideology of the Dagara, there is fundamentally no ontological difference between the living human being, Der, and the spirit of Der. It is the same person, Der, who lives according to these different modes of existence."

[23] Opus cit., 126.

regarded as a person. Bekuone Some Der claims the following to be the best definition of the human '*sie*': "Ce qui fait que le vivant corporel humain est une personne, c'est la realite du '*sie*.'"[24]

For the Dagara, it is therefore the sie which makes the human being "stand-out – ex-sto, ex-stare – from among all other corporeal beings and as distinct from them all. Thanks to the same given with which he or she is endowed, the human person can "bend-back-upon" – "re-flect on" – himself or herself, becoming aware of his or her own being. He or she is able to recognize that the same unique person can assume different modes of existence.[25] Through his or her *sie*, he or she is thus endowed with the potency to reflect upon the direction of his or her life (nyovuuru) both in its uniqueness in himself or herself, as well as its communality, i.e., as it has been lived by others here and now, or by the ancestors and the generations past.

The theoretical investigations above have shed much light in the source of the inherent potency of the religious subject, to reflect on the direction of his life. With these inherent dynamic principles, not only is he equipped to reflect on his life direction as he is formatively questioned, but also "bend-back-upon" the faith tradition which his ancestors and the past generations have bequeathed him. In Section B, we shall explore how best this takes place.

SECTION B: MEDITATING WITH THE AID OF FORMATIVE IMAGINATION

In his reflection upon the content of the life-story of an ancestor in his faith tradition which he is evoked to remember, the religious subject is aided by vivid imagination of the heroic life of this ancestor. He meditates on these

---

[24] Ibid., 129. English rendering of the French: "What makes the 'living' human being to be a person is the reality of the *sie* (the soul)."

[25] See footnote #22 above.

images in the light of his own current life form. This proximate area of research will study the role that images play in such meditation.

From the SFHF: Meditation in Motion

As we have observed, Formation Science clearly demonstrates the formation potential of formative questioning.[26] One of the most effective results formative questioning has on the subject is the evocation and the leading of him to a serious reflection – "bending back" – on his current life-form. This is what we may also call **meditation**. Discussing the importance of formative anticipation for disposition van Kaam insists on how disposition formation can be fostered through meditative attention.[27]

In her book *Meditation in Motion,* Susan Muto succinctly and dynamically captures the nature of meditation and the daily opportunities we have for it. In the beginning of the first chapter, titled "Food for Thought," Muto gives such a clear description of how to engage oneself in meditation that, at the same time, she reveals its very nature. For beginning the first meditation, she presents to her reader how one can effectively enter into it, as she instructs:

> Close your eyes for a moment. Think of one event that happened to you today, this week, or during the past month that really touched your heart. Call this event to mind as vividly as possible. It may be a sad or joyful encounter, a humorous exchange, a warm greeting on a cold day.

---

[26] See John W. Kloepfer, *The Art of Formative Questioning.*

[27] Adrian van Kaam; *Human Formation,* 160. Van Kaam also makes it clear that "creative reflection," and especially "dwelling in meditative presence on the mystery," are primary means of formation, as they are more capable of evoking and nurturing the triad of faith, hope, and consonance. See *Formation of the Human Heart,* 316-7.

> Move back into this moment as fully as imagination will allow. Meditate on it. Let the event give rise to meditation. What is its meaning for you? Why did it touch your heart? Think about it for a while, thank God for it, and if you wish, record the event and your responses to it in your journal.[28]

This preparatory phase to meditation to which Muto invites her reader reveals not only how best meditation can be effectively made, but it also reveals the purpose of meditation itself; i.e., as a means by which one can be truly in touch with one's deep self – reflecting and seeking the meaning of events with the help of one's imagination – through formative questioning of oneself. As it is evident in the meditation itself, the many questions which Muto suggests to the one meditating to ask himself or herself are all deeply thought-provoking and need the help of one's imagination to respond to them effectively and formatively:

> Who am I most deeply? What has become of my youthful ideals? Am I in tune with my sacred origins? Is life slipping through my fingers day by day, or does it have some purpose? Am I using my gifts and talents to the fullest?[29]

I cannot experientially, effectively, and formatively respond to such questions without the aid of my imagination. It is only with the help of my imagination, which can recreate concrete situations in my life that I can keep on reflecting formatively, and meditating on the questions regarding them. In this respect, meditation will always be in Motion in us since there

---

[28] Susan Annette Muto, *Meditation in Motion* (Garden City, N.Y.: Image Books, 1986), 17.

[29] Ibid., 17-8.

will always be a continuous flow of events[30] in our life form, which keeps unfolding itself.

From the SFHF: Fantasy and Imagination

In indicating the important role that imagination can play in meditation, it is necessary to point out that not all imagination can be regarded as consonant, and therefore, formative. Adrian van Kaam rightly holds that the reality of deformative imaginations in the following terms after he has given examples of such imaginations, especially in the field of human sexuality: "From the preceding examples and discussions, it may be clear that we can distinguish a consonant and a dissonant imagination. Formation Science refers to dissonant imagination also as fantasy." He goes on to explain: "Because fantasy does not have a pejorative connotation for all researchers in the auxiliary sciences, the term dissonant imagination is often used instead."[31]

After he has pointed out the fact that not all images and imaginations are consonant, van Kaam underscores once more the immense power with which images impact on the formation of individuals in the following terms:

> From the point of view of formation, images are far more powerful than concepts. Most of our life is guided by focal, pre-, trans-, and infrafocal imagery. Imagery can exert either a consonant or a dissonant influence. It can be our greatest friend or enemy. It can channel the flow of formation energy in consonant directions by means of like images and symbols, or it can also dissipate the energy flow in the dissonant ruminations of our fantasy life.[32]

---

[30] Ibid., 122.

[31] Adrian van Kaam, *Human Formation*, opus cit., 129.

[32] Ibid.

The discussions of the SFHF's constructs above offer us further insights about recalling memories. They also shed light on how such recalled memories can become formative through meditation. Memories which came from religious faith tradition may become similarly formative. In the following short paragraphs, we shall explore, with Benjamin Ray, how archetypal symbols can be sacred images.

<u>Benjamin C. Ray</u>: Archetypal Symbols as Sacred Images

After explaining the reasons for the polymethodic perspective which he has used in his study of African religions, Ray lists the three major themes around which he has organized his book.[33] He enumerates these three themes as: ***archetypal symbols; ritual; and community***. Describing what he intends by "archetypal symbols," he writes:

> By "archetypal symbols" I mean sacred images, whether they be gods, ancestors, sacred actions or things, which make up the traditional universe. Such images, enshrined and communicated in myth and ritual, provide a network of symbolic forms, uniting social, ecological, and conceptual elements into locally bounded cultural systems.[34]

By means of such enshrined images, communicated through myths and ritual, the religious subject is aided to vividly bring back to memory, for example, the persons and lives of his or her ancestors in symbolic forms. In this way, these enshrined images become a concretely perceivable background against which he or she may reflect on his or her current life form in a particular situation. These images which are thus enshrined, and re-

---

[33] Benjamin C. Ray, *African Religions*, 16-20.
[34] Ibid., 17.

communicated through myths and ritual, as Ray asserts, have assumed concrete forms, even if still only symbolically and are therefore no longer just concepts.

As such, the religious subject does not merely conceptualize these memories, but perceives them in their mythical and ritual symbolic forms as if in visions. In visualizing them as images rather than mere concepts, the influence they thus exert on the person becomes obviously more powerful. This power of sacred images communicated through myths and rituals is what Ray so forcefully captures when, with regard to the salvific value of ritual, he summarily observes: "In short, almost every African ritual is a salvation event in which human experience is co-created and renewed in the all-important ritual present."[35] Thus, it becomes clear that images as archetypal symbols, like rituals, are so powerful that, for the African religious, their sphere becomes fused with the reality he or she experiences. The two become one – non-dichotomized – reality.

An Integrative Reflection

The assumption that the above discussions on the recalling of memories have greatly elucidated the formative potency of religious faith tradition seems well-founded. In the original formation event under investigation, the religious subject, who previously seemed impervious to all influences from an elder visiting him, suddenly becomes deeply engaged in remembering, reflecting, and meditating on the life-story of an ancestor in his faith tradition, evoked by an appropriate question.[36] One may wonder why the subject suddenly enters into such deep reflection on the life story, which could also be called a myth,[37] about an ancestor. It is to this question

---

[35] Ibid.

[36] See Formation event, Preface to this Book, viii-xii.

[37] Benjamin C. Ray, opus cit., 17.

that the above theoretical discussions, in both Formation Science and its auxiliary sources, bring to light.

The SFHF has indicated that if in the first place the religious subject can recall to his memory and reflect on these memories of the life story of this ancestor in his faith tradition, it is thanks to his distinctively human power of reflection. The source of this power is the founding life form in which it inheres as a preformational given. This ground of the distinctively human power of reflection is also what Bekuone Some Der designates as '*sie*' in the Dagara philosophical thought. It is this distinctively human capacity to reflect on what is past, either in one's own life-form, or in the life-forms of other human generation or events, which predisposed the religious subject of our primary formation event to recall memories of an ancestor's life form. He is predisposed by a preformation *transcendent dynamic*.

If, secondly, the religious subject is able to attain such depths and concreteness – beyond mere concepts – in his reflective meditation on the details of his ancestor's life story, it seems obvious that it is due to his formative imagination. As Muto makes it evident in her invitation to preparation for meditation, the more fully the subject retreated into details of his ancestor's life story as his imagination would allow him,[38] the more clearly defined the details of the story became for him. Hence, as these details became so clear to him, the subject could say to God in his soliloquy: "God! You have certainly shown more love to me than you seem to have done to poor Aloysius and others like him. I am ready to die if you want to have me come to you now."[39]

The subject of our primary formation event can say this because, helped by his formative imagination, he is able, in his reflective meditation, to see very clearly in [concrete] images, and not just conceptually, the life story of his ancestor. As Ray points out, these images are sacred to the religious

---

[38] Susan Annette Muto, *Meditation in Motion*, 17.

[39] See Formation event, Preface to this Book, viii-xii.

subject. Thus, as *archetypal symbols,* they have become enshrined and fused with his actual living world and are thus communicated to him in the form of myth.[40]

These theoretical insights on the recalling of memories and the meditative reflection on them can be verified in many instances. As Ray says of African religions, among the Dagara of West Africa, who do not have a written tradition, traditional beliefs, moral truths, and philosophical presuppositions and realities are usually commonly enshrined, and thus preserved in proverbs, stories, myths, and rituals. In this way, the memories of these realities become concrete **images** which are readily recalled as the current life form of a particular individual may so warrant. In such a situation, the more vivid one's power of imagination may be, the more impelling the images communicated from the enshrined stories or myths may become.

In a story titled *"Small People Cannot Dream,"* Sebastian K. Bemile demonstrates the powerful way in which the Dagara belief in the equality of all human beings is enshrined.[41] The setting of the story is in "The Animal Kingdom." One day, all the animals, in a historic meeting, decided and passed a law that any animal who would dream about another animal would have this other animal killed for it to feast upon. That same evening, following the passing of this historic law, the wolf went early to bed and dreamt about the deer. Thus, according to the law enacted earlier that same day, poor deer was captured and slain for the wolf to eat all alone. The following evening after the wolf had justice done on his behalf according to that newly enacted law, but at the fatal expense of unfortunate deer, the wolf once again went very early to bed and dreamt again. This time, his dream concerned his feasting with lion flesh. Again, according to the new law, the lion who

---

[40] Benjamin C. Ray, Opus cit., 16-7.

[41] Sebastian K. Bemile, ed., *The Wisdom which Surpasses that of the King's: Dagara Stories* (Heidelberg; p. Kivouvou Verlag – Editions Bantoues), 1983.

was strong enough to fight against being killed, agreed and let himself be slaughtered and given as meat to the wolf to feast upon.

However, occasion for the testing of the law as applicable to all the animals in fairness soon came. The third evening after the new law was enacted, it was someone else's turn to dream; and this animal's dream was about the wolf. The narrative continues in the following manner:

> For once the Hare, too, decided to go to bed very early, while all other animals were still very feverishly discussing many social issues. A very, very short while after laying itself on its mat, the Hare began to shout in a shrill voice: "Waaai! Waaai! Waaai!" All the animals, including Mr. Wolf got frightened and ran to his rescue. The Hare explained: "I've had an extremely horrible dream. You see, I dreamt, illusionary though it may seem, that I was given the skin of a wolf for my personal ornament and decoration!" "That is not true at all!" Snapped the wolf. "It cannot be true. How can you, of all tiny beings, a Hare, dream? No, it's a lie: Small people cannot dream!" However, the wolf's vehement protests could not save him from being killed and skinned. For no animal was above the law made in general consensus. No animal was invulnerable.

As this story makes it evident, it is the Dagara belief of the equality of all human beings which is enshrined in these vivid images of the story. Thus, concretely enshrined, the Dagara belief that all human beings are equal and should be treated as equals accordingly, easily comes to the imagination of the particular individual who may find himself or herself seductively led by something to such a belief in his or her current life form. Such vivid images, because of their power, sharply awaken the person to the moral reality that all human beings are equal.

Hence, images which are products of the auxiliary intraformative potency of the imagination, demonstrate themselves as being more powerful than pure concepts. This powerful role of formative imagination can be seen in what van Kaam underlines as follows in formation theory: "imaginative memory helps us to make dynamics stand out as distinct from the background of the field as a whole." He insists on this reality saying: Only in looking back reflectively on what transpired can we apprehend and appraise various facets of the formation flow as distinct from one another."[42]

We can, therefore, conclude that, it is in the light of such definitive role played by his imagination that the religious subject of the original event could arrive at the decision he did. As he is led through questioning to recall and to reflect meditatively on the details of the life story of an ancestor in his faith tradition, his imagination intensified and eventually facilitated for him the process of formatively discerning the aspects of his ancestor's life. This discernment process led him to acknowledge in turn that God obviously loves him unconditionally. Hence, in return, he is willing to submit himself completely to God, even to die, if that is what God wills.

Transition to Second Remote Foundational Statement

In the first remote foundational statement in this Coformant on the foundational religious level, our exploration concentrated on recalling memories of the faith tradition of religious subjects. Through formative questioning, and aided by their imagination, religious subjects may discover life-directives which are contained in a narrative of their faith tradition. In remote foundational two, we shall study how such religious may be inspired through these life-directives and may thus be led to submit themselves to God's divine will.

PART TWO

INSPIRATION THROUGH VERTICAL INTERFORMATION

---

[42] Adrian van Kaam, *Scientific Formation*, opus cit., 143.

The second remote foundational statement of the Coformant on the religious level is formulated as follows:

> Religious subjects may become inspired by such life-directives and begin to submit themselves to the transcendent will of their God, and feel peaceful.

Like the first remote foundational statement of the Coformant, two separate proximate statements will also be elucidated in this statement. In Section A, we shall briefly examine how a religious may be *inspired by life-directives* in a narrative from his or her faith tradition. Then in Section B we shall study how such a religious may *submit himself or herself to the transcendent will of God*.

SECTION A: BEING INSPIRED BY LIFE-DIRECTIVES FROM A FAITH TRADITION NARRATIVE

As the religious who is being formatively questioned about a narrative in his faith tradition by another is aided by his imagination to discern life-directives therefrom, he or she may become inspired by them. Hence, the current life form of such a religious may receive a new life direction, to move in consonance towards the original life-form to which he or she may have been aspiring all his or her life as a religious being. This proximate area of research will investigate the dynamics of life-directives which come from faith tradition.

From the SFHF: Aspiration and Inspiration Directives

Chapter 6: Discerning Faith Traditional Directives

In Chapter Four, we discussed at some length about inspirations within the context of the *pneumatic* and the *insertions of the demonic*.[43] Also, discussing the *formation potential of form tradition* in the last chapter, we underlined the essentially transcendent origin of **aspirations**, as well as of **inspirations**. After asserting that spiritual ideals are transcendent, van Kaam explains:

> They appeal to us from the beyond; they are not made by us but are given to us. Rather than allowing us to grasp them, they grasp us. Surpassing us, they unite us with the horizon of the spirit. They embody the call of a spiritual identity, which is a mystery that only gradually discloses to us what we are most deeply called to be.[44]

This explanation actually makes it clear that *spiritual ideals* are transcendent, and that they come from the Mystery of Formation itself. So, as they grasp us and unite us with the *horizon of the spirit,* they fill our human spirit with essentially formative ideals. These imbue us and inspire our distinctively human existence, beckoning and directing us to grow towards what we are formed to be. Hence, in this light, van Kaam rightly affirms: "The transcendent ideal that calls us forth is truly an **inspiration**."[45] What is inspired in us becomes a directive, which dynamically leads us to consonantly unfold our founding life-form as our preformational given. Adrian van Kaam says in summarizing the transformation of such transcendent ideals: "Briefly, an ideal on the spiritual level is transformed into a *practical project* on the functional level."[46] What precisely then do we understand by *aspiration and inspiration directives?*

---

[43] See pages 188-9 and 194.

[44] Adrian van Kaam, *Fundamental Formation*, 168.

[45] Ibid.

[46] Ibid.

Discussing the fundamental difference between mere gratification directives and aspiration/inspiration directives, van Kaam also offers a foundational understanding of the last two directives – aspiration and inspiration. Comparing the two to purely gratification directives, he writes:

> Aspiration and inspiration directives transcend directives for gratification. They direct us to rise above mere need fulfillment; they enable us to appreciate the need-transcendent preciousness of persons, things, and events in themselves. Even if they can no longer fulfill our needs, we keep appreciating them for what they are.[47]

When we look at them in this light, it becomes evident why both aspirations and inspirations are far more fundamental in their effectiveness than the mere gratification of needs. In an attempt to give a greater clarification, van Kaam states: "Human life is distinctively human insofar as it is marked also by aspirations and inspirations and not only by needs."[48] It is no wonder that distinctively human life form should also be marked, and I would say essentially so, by aspirations and inspirations; for both distinctively human life form and aspirations/inspirations have the same transcendent source – the Radical Mystery of Formation. It is to this Mystery, the Source of the human preformation, that the distinctively human being is led by such aspiration and inspiration directives. The faith tradition of each human being is always replete with narratives of things, events, and persons, all of which are capable of inspiring the individual's life form as directives.

Although formation theory presents in one of the best ways the reality of the formative *direction-ability* of inspiration and aspiration, it is not alone in observing this reality. In discussing what he calls *the original state of man* in the many African stories of creation, Mbiti wonders if one might not

---

[47] Adrian van Kaam, *Traditional Formation*, 111.
[48] Ibid., 112.

legitimately suggest that African acts of worship are ways of searching for the paradise which man lost.[49] From its strongly imaginative stance, African religious thought perceives in particular the ancestors and totems to be truly formative sources of inspiration.

Albert A. Kuuire: Ancestors and Totems, Sources of Inspiration

In my study of the origins and role of **solidarity and co-responsibility in the moral life of the Dagaaba**, I discovered that totem and the ancestor are the sources and mainstay of unity and solidarity among them.[50] The unity of the clan,[51] which is the more important group of belonging within each tribe, is believed to be effective through both the ancestor and a totem.[52]

That the ancestor is the origin and mainstay of such unity and solidarity within a clan is easy to understand. For the ancestor, from whom an entire lineage of people descend, is believed by his or her descendants to continue to live among them, and to exert a lot of influence in their lives.[53] Hence, in

---

[49] See chapter two.

[50] Dagaati Solidarity and Salvation in Christ in the Light of "Gaudium et Spes" (S.T.D. diss., Academia Alfonsiana, Pontificia Universitas Lateranensis, Rome, 1976), 152-67.

[51] Among most African societies, the more important clan is the group of people who belong together through descent from the same patrilineage. They are often referred to as people of the same *patri-clan*; but more often, simply as the *clan*. However, there are tribes in which descent from the patrilineage is considered more important. In them, reference to the clan denotes the matri-clan; See Peter K. Sarpong, *Ghana in Retrospect* (Accra-Tema Ghana Publishing Corporation, 1974), 36-60.

[52] Albert A. Kuuire, opus cit., 152-4.

[53] Ibid., 163-7.

this way, and especially in their veneration of him or of her,[54] he or she continues to be an inexhaustible source of inspiration to each member of the clan through the deeds by which he or she is especially remembered. In their responses to such inspirations, each member of the clan aspires to form and reform in himself or herself the virtues or character[55] of their worthy ancestor.

Although a totem may not be given the same status as an ancestor as I demonstrated,[56] the totemic object is, however, considered as a concrete and practical source of inspiration to the individual member of the given clan. Besides the fact that unity and solidarity among the members of a particular clan may be empirically observable in the respect they show towards the same animal or totemic object,[57] the totem is also believed to have miraculous and mysterious powers. By means of these powers, it inspires members of the clan who may find themselves in certain unhealthy situations, just as it inspired their common ancestor in similar circumstances.[58] In this way, it may lead them out of such dissonant situations. Knowledge of these practical responses towards both ancestor and totem are handed down from generation to generation orally. It is done through the faith tradition

---

[54] For a long time, Western anthropologists have designated the veneration of ancestors in Africa in particular as ancestral worship. Peter Sarpong, among many others, asserts that the belief in the spirits of the dead and their influence over the living is found among all peoples. As he writes, "When Christians call their dead, saints, and refer to those of pagans as ancestors, they are not expressing different ideas. Both words express ideas about people who once belonged to their religious group, and are supposed to be in a position of influence over the living;" see *Ghana in Retrospect*, 33.

[55] Confer Adrian van Kaam, *Transcendent Formation* (opus cit., 1995), 103-30.

[56] Albert A. Kuuire, opus cit., 158.

[57] Ibid.

[58] Ibid., 158-60.

Chapter 6: Discerning Faith Traditional Directives

narratives of the clan, tribe, and the people in which these practical ways of responding to the inspirations are codified and thus preserved.

The above discussions on the ancestors and totems as sources of inspiration have offered us many insights on reality of inspiring life-directives. However, before we may make any integrative reflection on them, we would like to explore further how inspirations from one's faith tradition can lead the religious subject to self-submission to the transcendent will of God.

SECTION B: SUBMITTING ONESELF TO THE TRANSCENDENT WILL OF GOD

The inspiration, which the religious may receive from the life-directives contained in the faith tradition narrative, may lead him or her to recognize in these directives the will of his or her God. This recognition of the divine will may further lead such religious submit his or her own ambitious, functional will to God's divine will. This section of the proximate Coformant will seek to disclose the dynamics which may lead the religious to self-submission to God.

From the SFHF: Primordial Abandonment Option

In Part One of Chapter Two, we discovered that the African religious may fear illness to be a sign of rejection by the Mystery – *a depreciative abandonment*. However, in our discussion we also arrived at what we consider to be the *consonant abandonment* of oneself to the Mystery which leads one to formation.[59] As we established, such abandonment, which is also called *appreciative abandonment* of oneself to God, is an alternative choice which the individual is capable of making in view of his or her consonant formation. This capacity to choose between the two alternatives

---

[59] See chapter two.

– appreciative abandonment and its opposite, depreciative abandonment – is a potency which is primordial and innate in all human beings, even if it is not entirely free. It is what the SFHF therefore calls a **foundational formation option.**[60]

It is this foundational formation option of the religious – to submit himself or herself appreciatively to the transcendent executive will of God – which van Kaam further designates as a *primordial abandonment option*. He describes its origin within the framework of a *foundational formation option* thus:

> People are called to participate in the Mystery of formation in their lives. Their first response to this, is called *foundational formation decision*. In this basic option they choose to believe in the meaningfulness or meaninglessness of their life formation. It is a choice either to abandon themselves to this Mystery or to feel abandoned in this cosmos as in a meaningless and careless system closed in upon itself. Our primordial formation decision is thus a *faith option* for positive or negative abandonment.[61]

In this light, it is evident that *primordial abandonment option* is, indeed, a potency, an innate disposition, which is part of the "preformational given" of every human being. It is the *foundational freedom*, however limited it may be,[62] that the individual exercises, either to submit himself or herself to God, or to nurture feelings of meaninglessness of his or her formation, and so feels abandoned in a meaningless and careless world. In the first alternative, one will have freely chosen *appreciative abandonment* of oneself to God for one's foundational formation. In choosing the second alternative, however,

---

[60] Ibid.
[61] Adrian van Kaam, *Fundamental Formation*, 221.
[62] See chapter two, footnote #3.

Chapter 6: Discerning Faith Traditional Directives

one will be exercising one's freedom to choose a *depreciative abandonment* of oneself to a meaningless cosmos, which one feels does not have any foundational potential for him or for her, nor does it care for such foundational formation in the person.

It seems that the main reasons why someone may make the second of the two options is because one is either oblivious of the Radical Mystery of Formation and its epiphanic manifestations in the cosmos, or because one simply and willfully pays a blind eye to these divine manifestations. In "Moving into Meditation,"[63] Muto succinctly indicates how much a dissonant disposition may be reformed through formative thinking or reflective meditation. After asserting that formative thinking gives us courage "to surrender to the Mystery of life we cannot master," she says this of the *spiral approach* in meditation:

> The spiral approach often helps us, that is, it breathes forth and breeds spirit-filled thoughts in the center of our heart. We are mindful of the mystery of everydayness, of the gifts embedded in the simplest experiences, like smelling a rose. We want to stay with these things, to mine their meaning, to be affected by them.[64]

The above quote from Muto helps us to clearly see that to arrive at the choice of appreciative abandonment of oneself to the transcendent will of God, Mindfulness of the mystery of everydayness is indispensable in one's current life form. According to Mbiti, the awareness of this mystery of everydayness, which is indispensable for the eventual appreciative abandonment of oneself to the transcendent will of God, seems to be a reality which is a common experience of the African religious. We shall briefly examine

---

[63] Susan Annette Muto, *Pathways of Spiritual Living* (Petersham, Massachusetts: St. Bede's Publications, 1984), 81-92.

[64] Ibid., 85.

this reality in Mbiti's concept of God's *omnipotence,* which the African religious so commonly experiences.

John S. Mbiti: The Omnipotence of God

For the African religious, the assumption that God manifests himself in their everyday life-experiences is substantiated by all that they perceive going on in the cosmos. Kuukure tells us that the entire cosmos is the epiphany of God which is apprehended by the Dagao as his ongoing action of creation.[65] In this way, God incessantly announces his omnipotence in the cosmos.

Among the five intrinsic attributes of God which Mbiti presents in the very first chapter of his book *Concepts of God in Africa,* he discusses *the omnipresence of God* as the second of such attributes.[66] In his interpretation of the Kananga people's metaphor of "the Great Pool, contemporary of everything," which they use in reference to God, Mbiti cites the following hymn they address to God:

> Great Spirit…
> Waters of the pool that turn
> Into misty rain when stirred.
> Vessel overflowing with oil…
> Thou bringest forth the shoots
> That they stand erect…
> Thou givest of rain to mankind…[67]

---

[65] Edward Kuukure, opus cit., 57-9.

[66] John S. Mbiti, *Concepts of God in Africa* (New York: Praeger Publishers, 1970), 5-8.

[67] Ibid., 5.

In his explanation of this hymn, Mbiti makes it clear that, although rain is the immediate reference made, the metaphor also contains the idea that, like water, God's presence is everywhere. Thus, he affirms: "Life itself is an indication of God's omnipotence 'bringing forth the shoots' or supplying 'rain to mankind.'"[68] In the rest of the paragraphs under this article "The Omnipotence of God," he discusses similar metaphors which other various African peoples use to express this intrinsic attribute of God.[69]

If God is perceived in this way by the African, it is no wonder that the Dagao, for instance, is most often focally aware of God's presence in all events, and in all his or her own life's activities. Kuukure attests, in discussing the transcendence and immanence of God among the Dagaaba, saying: "God himself is around, near, attentive and active. He hears us when we invoke him, when we swear by his name, he accompanies the traveller, etc. ... we are ever before his presence."[70]

We shall now consider more closely a couple of the insights we have obtained through the above theoretical discussions on inspiration and vertical interformation. We shall reflect briefly on how they apply to the religious subject of our primary formation event.

Integrative Reflection

When we reflect more deeply on the decision of the religious subject in the original formation event after his meditative response to the question about a particular ancestor in his faith tradition, it seems clear that the ancestor' life-story had a strong impact on him in his own current life situation. After he had discerned – appraised – certain details of the life

---

[68] Opus cit.

[69] See also John Mbiti, *African Religions and Philosophy*, 31.

[70] Edward Kuukure, opus cit., 46.

form of the ancestor, which he so meditatively apprehended in the narrative of his life story, the religious became greatly influenced by them.

These details in the ancestor's life-form are what Formation Science theory calls 'life-directives.' They are dynamics from the life form of the ancestor which have become *spiritual ideals* for the religious. As such, they are transcendent, and "they appeal to him from the beyond." They have become life-directives, which inspire and influence the religious' current life-form, thus leading him to submit his previous willfulness to the transcendent will of God in imitation of his ancestor. In this way, the religious' ancestor, as a vertical interformative pole, gives formation to the religious through inspiring the latter's current form of life with consonant life-directives. These come from his own life-form which the religious so well apprehended in the narrative of his life story through meditating on it.

In the life story of Thérèse of Lisieux, such vertical interformation, especially with regard to her vocation to the Carmelite Order, is evident. Her mother, who died when Thérèse was only about four and half years old,[71] continued *from the beyond* to be the great inspiration and encouragement to her in her desire to become a Carmelite nun. As she writes with regard to her youthful lonely struggle her vocation:

> I found only one soul to encourage me in my vocation, that of my *dear mother*. My heart found a faithful echo in hers, and without her, perhaps, I would not have reached the blessed shore which received her five years before on its soil permeated with the heavenly dew. Yes, I was separated from you for five years, dear Mother, and I believed I'd lost

---

[71] While Marie-Francoise-Therese Martin was born on January 2, 1873, her mother, Madame Zelie Martin, died on August 28, 1877; See, *Story of a Soul: The Autobiography of St. Thérèse of Lisieux* (Washington, D.C.; ICS Publications), 279.

you forever; at the moment of trial your hand pointed the way I should follow.[72]

The above passage taken from Thérèse's autobiography can also be recognized in the life-stories of many other people who lived before us. In it, it becomes clear that *inspirational vertical interformation* is always available to us if only we appreciatively appraise and hence discern the life stories of others who lived before us. Therese received her original inspiration of simplicity and love from Jesus whom she regarded as having set before her "the book of nature" with its beauty in the little flowers.[73] This primary inspiration is what her mother continued to nurture in her with her own life-form even after her death. They are similar to the life-directives, from the life-form of Aloysius, which inspired the religious subject of our original formation event, and led him to submit himself, like his ancestor in the faith, to the transcendent will of God.

OBSTACLES TO, AND FACILITATING CONDITIONS FOR, RELIGIOUS FORMATION

In this Coformant on the foundational religious horizon, one main obstacle to consonant human formation is the absence of any more trust in the visiting other, and eventually in God himself whom the subject regards as having abandoned him. The religious can no longer believe, nor accept as anything good for him, what the other may now say to him. Another obstacle is the illness itself which has debilitated the vital life forces of the religious subject, and so, has affected his *function ability*.

---

[72] St. Thérèse of Lisieux, opus cit., p. 106. See also pp. 33 & ff. about details of Madame Martin's life which had become life-directives for her daughter's current form of life.

[73] Ibid, p. 14.

With regards to facilitating conditions for religious formation and reformation of the subject, we would like to mention among others, the following three conditions which could facilitate his consonant formation: 1) The persevering compassionate presence of the other who remains by the subject, even after the obvious desperation of the subject; 2) the religious form tradition narrative which the subject had learnt of earlier in his life; and 3) the ability of the other to question the subject formatively in his religious form tradition so that he could be led to formative reflection and meditation on the life-directives from his ancestor, and so, eventually to submit himself to God's divine will.

Transition to Chapter Seven: Christian Ministers

The foregoing research sought to elucidate the dynamics of foundational religious presence in formation tradition narratives of religious. Such dynamics seem to have the power to give consonant direction to religious subjects, thereby making them focally aware of the Radical Mystery of Formation and thus lead them to submit themselves to God and to experience peace in themselves. The following research will appraise the Inbreaking directives which come from the faith tradition narratives of subjects. On the foundational Christian level of presence, it will explore how life-forming directives may be revealed and applied through Kataphatic contemplation, a concept which will be explained in the following chapter.

CHAPTER SEVEN

REVELATION AND APPLICATION OF LIFE-FORMING DIRECTIVES THROUGH KATAPHATIC CONTEMPLATION

INTRODUCTION

The last chapter which elucidated Inbreaking form-directives of the formation event under investigation examined how these directives are discerned by the subject on the foundational religious level of presence. This chapter will study, on the Christian level of presence, the revelation of these directives through Kataphatic contemplation. The Coformant is formulated as follows:

> As these Christians are formatively questioned in their faith tradition, they may contemplate a story therein. Aided by Kataphatic contemplation, life-forming directives may be revealed to them from the story. Such directives may inspire Christians to renew their faith in Jesus Christ and begin to humbly abandon themselves to the pneumatic will, and enjoy peace.

As it is now the pattern, we shall elucidate two remote foundational statements contained in the Coformant. We shall explore in the first remote foundational statement how *the life-forming directives in one's Christian faith tradition become revealed*, and in the second statement we shall examine the process of incarnation of these directives in the Christian's life-form.

PART ONE

THE REVELATION OF FAITH TRADITION LIFE-FORMING DIRECTIVES

This part of the chapter will seek to illumine the following remote foundational statement:

Through formative questioning, aided by Kataphatic contemplation, life-forming directives from a story in their faith tradition may become revealed to Christians.

The elucidation will be done in two sections. Section A will explore the dynamic of contemplating a life-story in the Christian faith tradition. And following on this, Section B will study how Kataphatic contemplation by the Christian may enhance the revelation of life-forming directives.

SECTION A: CONTEMPLATING A LIFE-STORY IN THE CHRISTIAN FAITH TRADITION

A formative questioning by a competent other on a story in his faith tradition may evoke in the Christian the disposition of contemplation. As his visitor questions him whether he remembers the life-story of a saint, which he narrated to him when he was still young, the Christian subject is suddenly reminded of the particular saint's life-story. He apprehends in detail the story, especially the dispositions which the saint had towards his imminent death and begins to appraise them contemplatively. In this area of Christian presence, our research will focus on the dynamics of Christian contemplation.

Chapter 7: Revelation and Application of Life-Forming Directives

<u>From the SFHF</u>: Approaching Contemplation

In his response to the question concerning the life-story of his ancestor in the Christian faith tradition, the Christian in the primary formation event feels strongly evoked to enter into the very depths of his interior. There, as Keith Barron asserts, he may rediscover his transcendent self-presence.[1] This seems to be the reason why Richard Byrne also considers 'praying' for the Christian to be a response to an invitation by a *crisis to go beyond and to focus on the transcendent*. As he says, "Praying, like every other Christian activity, is drawn into the central fact of our existence."[2] In their book, *The Power of Appreciation*, Adrian van Kaam and Susan Annette Muto strongly affirm the appealing power of crisis with respect to prayer: "This invitation is not a mode of coercion but one of appeal. It is as if we are being asked to go beyond or more deeply into some of the ways in which we were disposed to look at life previously,"[3] they say.

In the light of the above attestation, prayer is indeed a form of meditation. For the process of going beyond, or more deeply into oneself appreciatively, is **meditation**. Such meditation leads us into relationship with the very ground of our existence. One can therefore affirm that the true Christian prayer of meditation is that critical awareness which brings us to focus on the transcendent reality which is the ground of our existence. It is in this sense that *meditation* becomes practically the same as *contemplation*.

---

[1] Confer Keith Barron, Unpublished lecture notes in "Christian Formation and the Life of Prayer." (Pittsburgh: Duquesne University, IFS), February 8, 1993.

[2] Richard Byrne, "Approaching prayer as Mystery: Some Basic Assumptions," in *Spiritual Life* (Spring, 1988), 16.

[3] Adrian van Kaam & Susan Muto, *The Power of Appreciation* (opus cit.), 104.

In *Pathways of Spiritual Living*, Muto defines contemplation by describing in actionable language what *approaching contemplation* means. She writes:

> We approach contemplation the moment we make an act of faith in the omnipotence of God. To contemplate means to be in the temple of the Lord, sensing, believing and experiencing that we are actually in his presence, that he is in us and we are in him. This basic union never changes, whatever obstacles we may place on the contemplative path.[4]

In this definition, it is clear that contemplation is the centering of our awareness on the reality beyond us yet deep within us. It is a recollection of our focal awareness to centre all of our being on the unconditionally loving Father of Jesus Christ as Jesus himself did in his lifetime here on earth. Hence, in this respect, as Muto says, "Contemplatives are no different in essence from ordinary people."[5] This means that the disposition of contemplation is not the prerogative of only a privileged few. For, if contemplation is to be the temple, the presence of God who is the very ground of our being, then it should be within the grasp of all humans, especially the Christian who believes himself or herself *to be in the temple of the Lord*. It is the faithful practice of the spiritual disciplines which prepare us to abide in this contemplative presence of God who gives us his peace.[6]

From the SFHF: Joy and Contemplation

---

[4] Susan Muto, *Pathways of Spiritual Living*, 127. See "*Philo*, on the Contemplative Life." Trans. Gail Paterson Corrington, in *Ascetic Behavior in Greco-Roman Antiquity*, ed. Vincent L. Wimbush.

[5] Ibid., 128. See also her *John of the Cross Today: The Dark Night* (Notre Dame, Indiana: Ave Maria Press, 1994), 85-6.

[6] Ibid., 128.

Chapter 7: Revelation and Application of Life-Forming Directives

If in the dissonance of his current life form, the Christian of our original formation event does not seem to experience any joy, this may be blamed on the internal turmoil which expresses itself in his depression, feelings of rejection by God and anger at him. He could not appreciatively go beyond himself; hence, he could not enter more deeply into himself in order to abide in a contemplative presence of his unconditionally loving God. As van Kaam has very well established:

> Reinforced appreciation gives rise to joyousness. [And] the deeper one's appreciation is rooted in spiritual participation in the Mystery of Formation, the more profound is the joy one experiences when the consonant disposition is activated.[7]

Hence, our Christian of the primary formation event, who was unable to enter deeply into himself to encounter and participate spiritually in the Mystery of Formation – the ground of his being – could not experience any joy. Because, as it appears clear, joy and contemplation are essentially bound to one another.

In his book *The Roots of Christian Joy*, Adrian van Kaam affirms in a more categoric manner this bond between joy and contemplation. At the beginning of the fifteenth chapter, he attests to this bond in these terms:

> Joy may no longer be ours because we have lost the ease of contemplation. This presence in wonder was our birthright as little children. Becoming again like little children, we may enter the heaven of simple presence. The Lord filled our fields of life with forms beautiful to behold. Created forms reflect His goodness, truth, and beauty. Too busy with accidentals, we may be unable to delight in the splendor of the form of

---

[7] Adrian van Kaam, *Human Formation*, 13.

our own life and in the loveliness of the forms that surround us in pristine simplicity.[8]

From this insight, it is clear that the fruits, which are revealed through contemplating the life-forming directives in a particular life-story of one's Christian faith tradition, include not only deep internal peace but also profound Christian joy. In the following paragraphs, we shall further explore what the Spiritual Masters understand by the contemplative disposition. We shall briefly discuss, with Thomas Merton, what contemplation is.

Thomas Merton: Contemplation as Awareness of the Reality of the Source

In Formation Science theory, we learnt from van Kaam and Muto that contemplation is, indeed, the centering of our awareness on the reality beyond us.[9] In this perception of contemplation, Formation Science is following the Christian spiritual masters and their classics.[10]

Thomas Merton, after several affirmation of contemplation as the highest expression of the human being's spiritual life, asserts: "Contempla-

---

[8] Adrian van Kaam, *The Roots of Christian Joy* (Denville, New Jersey: Dimension Books, 1985), 134.

[9] Confer footnote #3 above.

[10] See for example, Teresa of Avila, *Way of Perfection*, chapters 16-8; John of the Cross, *The Ascent of Mount Carmel*, Book Two, Chapter Eight #6. Throughout the Collected Works of both Teresa and John of the Cross, contemplating the Divinity in this sense can be said to be conspicuously the principal theme running through them. Also in his book, Contemplative Psychology, Han F. de Wit speaks of contemplative knowledge very much in the same understanding of Christian contemplation.

Chapter 7: Revelation and Application of Life-Forming Directives

tion is, above all, awareness of the reality of that source."[11] The Source Merton refers to here is what he calls the invisible, transcendent, and infinitely abundant Source from which life and being in us proceeds.[12] He regards contemplation to be "the response to a call;[13] and also as "a religious and a transcendent gift."[14] After further defining contemplation as "the awareness and realization, even in some sense, *experience*, of what each Christian obscurely believes," Merton concludes:

> Hence, contemplation is more than a consideration of abstract truths about God, more even than affective meditation on the things we believe. It is awakening, enlightenment and the amazing intuitive grasp by which love gains certitude of God's creative and dynamic intervention in our daily life. Hence, contemplation does not simply "find" a clear idea of God and confine Him within the limits of that idea, and hold Him there as a prisoner to whom it can always return. On the contrary, contemplation is carried away by Him into His own realm, His own mystery and His own freedom.[15]

It is in this sense that contemplation can be truly called "a kind of spiritual vision."[16] This spiritual vision is that of the very reality of our Source and Origin which the contemplative experiences.

The above discussion, both on the level of formation theory and of the spiritual classics, offers us some valuable insights into Christian contem-

---

[11] Thomas Merton, *New Seeds of Contemplation* (Abbey of Gethsemani: A New Direction Book, 1972), 1.

[12] Ibid., 1.

[13] Ibid., 3.

[14] Ibid., 4

[15] Ibid., 5.

[16] Ibid., 1.

plation. In the section following, we shall look into the quality which Kataphatic contemplation may bring to the revealed life-forming dispositions – or directives – contained in the Christian's faith tradition.

SECTION B: *ENHANCING THE APPREHENSION OF THE REVEALED LIFE-FORMING DIRECTIVES FROM ONE'S FAITH TRADITION THROUGH KATAPHATIC CONTEMPLATION*

The vivid life-forming directives contained in the story from the faith tradition of the Christian are stimulated by his imagination. Thus, these contents of the story become powerful images. Apprehended as such, these revealed contents engage the subject more intensely. Hence, his contemplation of the story is enhanced **kataphatically**. Here in this area of the research, we shall examine the nature of Kataphatic contemplation and how it can foster and nurture consonant revelation of form directives within a life-story of one's Christian faith tradition.

From the SFHF: The Apophatic and Kataphatic Dispositions in the Light of the Functional-Transcendent Dimension[17]

---

[17] In chapter one, we spoke of the dimensions of the formation field. There we made mention of the *functional-transcendent dimension* which van Kaam, in his more recent writings, lists more consistently as dimension of the field in its own right (See chapter one, footnote #14). In the volume of **Transcendent Formation** (New York: Crossroad, 1995), 214, he explains the existence of *the functional-transcendent dimension* in these terms: "There is no abrupt passage from the dynamics of a lower dimension to those of a higher one. Our initiation into the beginnings of a more explicit transcendent dimension of life gives rise initially to a new crossover phase. This phase is still functional, yet it is more explicitly touched by a nascent awareness of the deepest potency of human life, that of full and focal transcendence. I conceived this as the functional-transcendent dimension."

Chapter 7: Revelation and Application of Life-Forming Directives

In his very enlightening discussion on the functional-transcendent dimension, van Kaam warns of the "always-limited expression" that myths, symbols, archetypes, and dreams or images are, by their nature, in relation to the more complete transcendence of which they may be only pointers.[18] Referring to the educational traditions which foster a rather subtle prevalence of the "practical and vitally pleasant over the higher facets" of the intrasphere of the functional-transcendent, he says: "They try to make transcendent symbols and ideals the servants of our self-actualization, individuation, and aesthetic pleasure."[19]

However, it is important to underline, at the same time, that van Kaam recognises all these myths, symbols, archetypes, and images as being pregnant with the potency of being pointers to what he calls the *fuller transcendence*.[20] In this sense they serve the purpose of contemplation, aiding the individual in a more or less concrete and incarnate manner to apprehend and to focus upon the transcendent form directives which may be revealed to him or to her in this functional way in a story from his or her faith tradition. It is in this dimension that contemplation may become ***apophatic*** or ***Kataphatic***.

In an article in *Studies in Formative Spirituality*, James Price makes one of the most clear summary distinctions between the *apophatic* and *Kataphatic*.[21] Speaking of the ages-long distinction between apophatic and the Kataphatic in Christian theology, which he claims is well known, he asserts that they are the traditional ways by which Christian spirituality

---

[18] Adrian van Kaam, *Transcendent Formation* (opus cit.), p. 218.

[19] Ibid.

[20] Ibid.

[21] James R. Price, III. "Transcendence and images: The Apophatic and Kataphatic Reconsidered," *Studies* XI (May, 1990), 195-201.

articulates the relationship between images and transcendence.[22] Within the theological perspective, therefore, Price goes on to define the two, contrasting them in this manner:

> ***Apophatic theology*** is the way of negation. Here the claim is that God can only be talked about by negation and denial, and truly experienced only in a divine darkness which transcends the operation of sense, image and concept. ***Kataphatic theology*** in contrast is the positive way. Here the claim is that God's attributes can be positively designated in images and doctrines, and that God is in fact encountered through images and stories in the realm of history.[23]

However, as traditional and clear as this distinction may be, Price himself points out the danger that it may conceal within its very self.[24] As he admits, such a distinction has a metaphysic as its ground. Thus, as such, it becomes, itself, a radical ground for the separation and eventual dichotomy of the natural and the supernatural. Hence, metaphysically, it suggests that God, who is being contemplated is up and beyond there; while we, who contemplate God, are down here below. Price contends that such formulation of the relationship between images and transcendence masks or conceptually obscures the functional connection between them. And so, in the rest of the article, he attempts to reformulate the functional relationship between images and transcendence in such a way that the traditional distinction is maintained, while at the same time, the foundationally functional connections between them are better revealed.

---

[22] Ibid., 195.
[23] Ibid.
[24] Ibid., pp. 195-6

Chapter 7: Revelation and Application of Life-Forming Directives

From the SFHF: Imagination in Contemplation and the Divesting of Power

From our discussion so far, it would seem obvious that the ***Kataphatic***, which is considered by Christian spiritual tradition to be a consonant form of contemplation, has very much to do with the auxiliary formative power of imagination. For the images through which God may be encountered, according to the traditional concept of *Kataphatic theology*, are the products of the imagination. However, Muto in her book, *John of the Cross for Today: The Ascent*, draws attention to the Saint's reservation concerning imaginative apprehensions. As she sums up the Saint's perception, "Natural imaginative apprehensions, however blissful, he says, are inadequate means for attaining union with God."[25]

Yet it is not all imaginative apprehensions, by means of which God may be contemplated, that John of the Cross would consider as "harmful impediments." For Kataphatic contemplation, which uses formative imaginative apprehensions, is a largely accepted traditional form of prayer through which some contemplatives reach union with God.[26] Muto attests to John of the Cross' reservation about the imaginative contemplation in the following carefully worded observation: "In his calm, methodical fashion, the saint invites us to think twice about what constitutes real, as opposed to imaginative contemplation."[27] In this observation, it may be surmised that what the Saint is truly suspicious of here, regarding the imaginative, are images produced by audiovisual aids which our world, dependent on mass-media, uses for some sensual stimulation of people, as Muto herself pointed out earlier.[28] So, John of the Cross' reservation would not include the pro-

---

[25] Susan Muto, John of the Cross Today, the Ascent, (opus cit.), 62.
[26] See James Price's definition of the *Kataphatic*, above.
[27] Ibid.
[28] Ibid.

ducts of truly formative imagination – that auxiliary power which can foster and lead to the consonant contemplation of, and eventual union with, God. In other words, John of the Cross is referring to fantasies which, as we already remarked above, are considered by formation theory as dissonant imaginations.[29]

In her perception which agrees with and is based on John of the Cross' understanding, Muto regards contemplation as "a divesting process." She describes it in the following terms:

> The movement to contemplation is neither a matter of exterior stimulation not of satiating the imagination with interior phantasies. The opposite must occur. A process of "denuding" or "divesting" sensate powers of their natural apprehensions and appetites through the active "night of the senses" is essential.[30]

This concept of contemplation as a process of gradually divesting oneself of one's sensate powers of their natural, also supernatural apprehensions, make evident the limited role of imagination, even formative, as a discursive power. As such it only enables and helps the contemplative, through Kataphatic meditation, to reach the fullness of contemplation which is union with God. As Muto indicates, the trouble is that many mistakenly stagnate at the products of the imagination as if they were the union itself with God, or at least, proximate means to this union.[31] In the spiritual classics of the Christian tradition, we shall further discuss, with Harvey D. Egan, Kataphatic contemplation as the *"via Affirmativa,"* which is also known as the *"via positive."*

---

[29] See chapter six, under 'Fantasy and Imagination.'
[30] Susan Muto, John of the Cross Today: The Ascent (opus cit.), 62-3.
[31] Ibid.,p. 63.

Chapter 7: Revelation and Application of Life-Forming Directives

Harvey D. Egan: The *Via Affirmativa* in the Ignatian Spiritual Exercises

The spirituality of St. Ignatius of Loyola has definitely had a great influence in Christian spirituality due to the long standing and widely spread practice it has enjoyed. In Egan's view, St. Ignatius of Loyola's (1491-1556) spiritual exercises

> have played a significant role in Catholic spirituality since their composition in the sixteenth century. For over four hundred years, they have fed the spiritual lives of countless Jesuits, religious orders of men and women whose spirituality is Ignatian, and numerous others who for various reasons came into contact with this form of spirituality.[32]

What we want to discuss here is to determine the principal form of prayer by which the Ignatian spirituality may be identified. In this regard, we deem it helpful to point out that, although Christian spiritual writers have tried to maintain a distinction between mysticism and contemplation, basically they agree that the two refer to the same religious experience as their objective.[33] They agree that union with God, only possible through God's own grace, is the objective of both mysticism and *infused*

---

[32] Harvey D. Egan, *Christian Mysticism; The Future of a Tradition* (New York: Pueblo Publication Company, 1984), 30.
[33] Ibid., 4.

contemplation.³⁴ In this light, the contemplative or mystic is only but the passive recipient and beneficiary.³⁵

Although the objective of contemplation or the mystical form of prayer is the same – union with God – Christian spiritual writers have identified two principal forms by which the contemplative or mystic can arrive at this union. At the beginning of the discussion in his chapter on "The Spiritual Exercises of St. Ignatius of Loyola," Egan clearly indicates these two Christian traditional forms of prayer as Christian apophatic mysticism and Christian Kataphatic mysticism. He then describes the two traditions thus:

> The apophatic tradition, the *via negative*, emphasizes the radical difference between God and creatures. God is best reached, therefore, by negation, forgetting, and unknowing, in a darkness of mind without the support of concepts, images, and symbols. God is "not this, not that." Kataphatic mysticism, the via affirmativa, emphasizes the similarity that exists between God and creatures. Because God can be found in all things, the affirmative way recommends the use of concepts, images and symbols as a way of contemplating God.³⁶

---

[34] Egan indicates the existence of a qualitative distinction between *infused* and *acquired* contemplation in these terms: "Many mystics and mystical theologians distinguish sharply between an 'infused' or mystical, form of prayer totally beyond the capabilities of the person and requiring a special grace, and 'acquired' contemplation, or the highest form of prayer within the reach of all Christians endowed with 'ordinary' grace;" (opus cit. 11). The mystical union is what Paul, the mystic, talks about in 2 Cor. 3: 18; Gal 2: 20; and Rom 6: 5-6. He also urges the Philippians to dispose themselves well for such a mystical union with God (Phil 2: 5 & ff).

[35] This reality is what Teresa of Avila in *The Interior Castle*, consistently points out as God's grace, and, therefore, gift for which the *privileged soul* should, nevertheless, incessantly pray; opus cit. pp. 289, 332, 336, 340, 388, etc.

[36] Harvey D. Egan, (opus cit.), 31.

Chapter 7: Revelation and Application of Life-Forming Directives

Egan later points out that, though the two traditions may be two different ways of reaching union with God, they are both orthodox ways of contemplating; one form, furthermore, always contains elements from the other.[37] This is, indeed, the healthy balance between the two which would make, for the contemplative, the best form of prayer, the single-mindedness of Mary combined with the "busy-ness" of Martha: (Jn. 10: 38-42). And this can be seen as the way to *the Jesus prayer* which the Desert Fathers sought so ardently.[38] However, the style of the individual contemplative for arriving at this union with God is influenced and characterized by whichever of the two traditions is most prominent with him or with her. It is in this light that Egan characterizes the mysticism of St. Ignatius as radically Kataphatic.[39] And as if at the other end of the continuum of the mysticism of Ignatius, he sees the mysticism of his compatriot, St. John of the Cross, to be very strongly apophatic. The following are his comments in this regard:

> John's apophatic mysticism contends that when compared to God, all creatures are nothing. In fact, "all the goodness of creatures in the world compared with the infinite goodness of God can be called evil" (AMC, I. chap. 4, no. 4, p.79). The main problem is that our appetites are disordered and frequently misdirected. Therefore, John advocates a radical mortification of the appetites to redirect them towards their true goal, which is God.[40]

---

[37] Ibid.

[38] See Kallistos Ware, "The origins of the Jesus Prayer: Diadochus, Gaza, Sinai," in *The Study of Spirituality*, eds. Cheslyn Jones, Geoffrey Wainwright and Edward Yarnold, S.J. (New York: Oxford University Press, 1986), 175-84.

[39] Harvey D. Egan (opus cit.), 51.

[40] Ibid., 173. This is what Muto also observes of John of the Cross' mysticism. See 282-4.

Despite such a sharp contrast which John of the Cross' *apophatic mysticism* seems to portray in comparison with the *Kataphatic mysticism* by which Ignatius of Loyola's form of contemplation is identified, the two can never be considered as exclusive of one another. On the contrary, as Egan makes us to understand after he has taken a walk through the works of Teresa of Avila and highlighted her mystic affinities with those of Ignatius of Loyola, *The Cloud of Unknowing* and of John of the Cross, her well renown mysticism has far more affinities with that of Ignatius.[41] Yet Teresa and John of the Cross, who were both Carmelites committed to the reform of their respective communities, were great friends in spite of their two basically different traditional ways to union with God. They collaborated so closely in their two different approaches to this union in their task of reforming the male and female communities of their Order – the Discalced Carmelites – that the complementarity of the two ways became evident.

Thanks to the light of the insights which the above discussions offer, we shall now reflect on the life-forming directives which are revealed in the faith tradition of the Christian in our initial formation event.

Integrative Reflection

As the form of St. Aloysius Gonzaga becomes revealed in greater detail to the Christian of our original event, the **unconditional love** of God for him becomes evident, as seen in narrative of the event. Hence, before such compelling love and goodness towards him, he feels himself overwhelmingly persuaded, even in his death-threatening illness, to respond unequivocally to it with great abandonment of himself to the Source itself of such love and goodness. He, indeed, trustingly abandoned himself in a serenity

---

[41] Ibid., 152.

which could only come from a peace experienced as the fruit of self-abandonment to the Source of such compelling consonance.

If the Christian of the original formation event was able to arrive at such self-abandonment to God's will, as God's overwhelming love for him paradoxically yet so clearly revealed in the situation of his life-threatening illness, it is due to the compelling images which the life form of Aloysius presented to him as he appraised its dynamics. For as these dynamics of Aloysius' life form became such concrete images to him, they persuasively, yet compellingly, gave directions to his life through the consonant life forms they thus offered to him.

This way through which the Christian appraised the dynamics of the Saint's life form is what we may, basically, characterize as Kataphatic contemplation. For in gazing at these images of love in the Saint's life form with such trust, he also encounters God's presence and unconditional love and goodness.[42] It is therefore this form of appraising the life-directives from the Saint's life form "in the temple of the Lord," with the help of his formative imagination through Kataphatic contemplation, that the subject of our primary formation event made such a significant approach towards union with God.

In the life-story of Saint Aloysius, P. Virgilio Cepari, his principal biographer, has brought to light the many life-forming dynamics which were actual in the Saint's current life form.[43] In his narration of the Saint's behaviour in his death-bed – his practice of humility, obedience, patience, and voluntary mortification in particular – he comes to the following conclusion among others on him:

---

[42] Susan Muto, *Pathways of Spiritual Living*, (opus cit.), 127; see also Price, in, Studies XI (May 1990), 195; and Egan, *Christian Mysticism*, 31.

[43] See "His Last Illness and Death." In the American Edition of *The Life of St. Aloysius Gonzaga of the Company of Jesus* (New York and Philadelphia: P.J. Kenedy & Sons, Publishers to the Holy Apostolic See, n.d.), 284-314.

It needs scarcely be observed, after all that has been said, that the patience, equanimity and obedience which Aloysius manifested during the languishing illness which was gradually wasting his life away, offered a pattern in which not a flaw could be discerned of the way in which a religious should bear sickness. From the moment he was laid in his bed he would give ear to no conversation but such as has the things of God and eternal life for their immediate object.[44]

From this summary of Aloysius' disposition in his illness, it appears clear how he, in all these images and archetype symbols coming from his practice of virtue, is directed more surely towards union with God. In spite of all his suffering in illness, the Saint saw these images and archetype symbols in his consonant disposition towards his illness as the way in which he was attaining union with God. Hence, "he would give ear to no conversation but such as had the things of God and eternal life for their immediate object."

That Aloysius' life form, particularly in his terminal illness, was an image and an archetype symbol, which had the potency to give formative direction to many who encountered him, is attested to by the Cardinal della Rovere and the Cardinal Scipione Gonzaga who visited him so often. As Cepari informs us, the Father Rector, who wanted to spare the two cardinals the trouble of coming so often to visit the saint, assured them he would send them regular information about his health. But, "they replied that they could not resist coming on account of the edification they received."[45] Also, the mutual edification that Aloysius and Father Corbinelli were to each other in their self-abandonment to God's will is clearly manifested nowhere else

---

[44] Ibid., 292.
[45] Ibid., 294.

Chapter 7: Revelation and Application of Life-Forming Directives

than in their last visit with one another before their death. As we are informed:

> The joy of the old man was inexpressible; for a while, they conversed together of that glorious heavenly home to the threshold of which they were both so nigh, and mutually exhorted each other to patience and resignation to the Divine will.[46]

This manner of "being in the temple of the Lord" is also very strongly attested to in our times. Bernard Häring, in one of his most recent books, confirms such manner of being in the presence of the Lord. In the second chapter of his book, *I have Seen Your Tears*,[47] Häring gives two concrete experiences he had with people in grave sickness, live in the presence of God, and in this way become a radiation of joy and consonance to others.

After he had narrated about his eventual deep respect for a poor, old, and blind lady whom his mother took care of and used to give him bread to carry to, Häring also tells the story of a parish in which, as a young priest, he was invited to preach a Religious Week. The faith of the parishioners struck him very much. So, he asked the pastor what the secret of their conspicuous concern for spiritual things may be. The pastor directed him to visit a sick woman in the parish who was bedridden for many years and was then afflicted with gout and could not even raise her hand to feed herself. After complying with the pastor's invitation, Häring informs his readers of his visit thus:

> I visited her in her blessedly poor apartment, and it struck me that she glowed like a warm light. Her face was not distorted with pain, but

---

[46] Ibid., 295

[47] Bernard Häring, *I Have Seen Your Tears*, trans. Robert Hodge (Great Wakering Essex: McCrimmon Publishing Co. Ltd., 1995.

rather one with shining eyes and radiating goodness. I can still remember her exact words: "Father, one cannot thank God enough that our sickness and our sorrows are redeemed and that we can co-operate in the work of redemption."[48]

As he makes his readers understand, Häring came away from his visit with an indelible image of this woman who considered the love of God in the work of redemption to be a gift received – a grace. He had this confirmed by the pastor who said to him after his visit with the gravely ill woman: "It seems to me that this woman has become the focus for proclaiming the good news for our parish, a proclamation without the wordiness of preaching."[49] This is, indeed, a focus on a life form directive which is so concretely *enshrined* in such a formative image that it has the potency to engage the entire parish and to draw it towards the object of the Good News – towards the eventual union with God.

Transition to Remote Foundational Statement Two

The research in the above remote foundational statement on the Christian level of presence sought to investigate the dynamics of contemplation. It also examined the Kataphatic form of contemplation which may enhance the revealed life-forming directives coming from a life story in the subject's faith tradition. In this second part, we wish to focus on the ability of such directives to inspire and to lead the Christian to self-submission to God in joy and peace.

---

[48] Ibid., 12.
[49] Ibid.

PART TWO

THE INSPIRATIONAL POWER OF FAITH TRADITION DIRECTIVES

This second remote foundational statement may be formulated in the following manner:

> Such directives may inspire Christians to begin to humbly abandon themselves to the will of God and also to experience joy and peace.

We shall make our investigations of this remote foundational statement in two sections, A and B. Section A will study the beginnings of a humble abandonment to God, thanks to the pneumatic inspiration while Section B will focus on the peace and joy experienced in this self-abandonment to the Divine Will.

SECTION A: BEGINNING TO HUMBLY ABANDON ONESELF TO GOD THANKS TO PNEUMATIC INSPIRATION

As the Christian contemplates the form directives from the life-story of a saint in his faith tradition, he becomes inspired and begins to apprehend the greater unconditional love God seems to have for him, compared with the saint whose life-story he contemplates. At this revelation, he begins to humbly abandon himself to God. The investigation here will focus on the dynamic of pneumatic inspiration which is so able to move the Christian towards this humble self-abandonment to God.

From the SFHF: The Pneumatic-Transcendent Dimension of the Formation Field

In an earlier discussion on opening oneself to God's graced communion in Christ, we arrived at the understanding that the pneumatic-transcendent of the individual's formation field is that dimension of him or her, which enables him or her as a distinctively human person, to participate in the *graced power of formation*.[1] Adrian van Kaam maintains, and with good reason, that it is in the light of the pneumatic-transcendent presence that graced formation has the potency to incarnate congenial and compatible life forms which are appropriate expressions of the foundational Christ-Form in individuals.[2] Reviewing various potentials relative to human formation, he describes the *pneumatic formation potential* as: "The infused potency and tendency to be transformed by and to serve the transformation of inspiration of the Holy Spirit.[3]

Compared with his description of transcendent formation potential which he gave just before it, the pneumatic does not only enable us "to be formed by and to give forms to aspirations emerging from the transcendent nature of [our] human life," but it is an infused power which transforms us. This means that, while the purely *transcendent formation potential* comes from the "preformational given" which makes us distinctively human and so innately ensures our distinctively formation, the *pneumatic formation potential* is a super-added gift. It is a potential which is freely infused in the individual by the Holy Spirit and which serves the transformation of our human life form through transforming the inspirations of the Holy Spirit in us.

---

[1] See chapter three.

[2] Adrian van Kaam, "Provisional Glossary," *Studies in Formative Spirituality* 1 (May, 1980), 298.

[3] Adrian van Kaam, "Provisional Glossary," *Studies* 1 (February, 1980): 147.

One thing which becomes gradually evident, therefore, is the all-transforming power of the pneumatic-transcendent presence. Adrian van Kaam has earlier undergirded this concept of the pneumatic dimension in formation theory when, in discussing *the pneumatic phase of personal-spiritual formation*, he insists:

> The articulation of the Christian form tradition by the science of formation emphasizes that it is impossible for people to attain this transcendence in a consistent and pure way. Grace is needed, and, hence, so is the *pneumatic dimension*.[4]

In this light, therefore, the pneumatic does not only limit itself to transcendent presence, but it speaks of the formation potential of the Purely Transcendent Other, whose influence in our distinctively human formation is a free gift to us. It is Grace. It is what inspires us and makes it possible for us to be formed and, indeed, to journey towards our transforming with the Christ-Form, which is the *inexhaustible mystery of graced transformation*,[5] as our ultimate exemplar. It is in this Christ-Form that can be found the ultimate self-submission and humble abandonment of oneself to God the Father, after the example of Christ.

From the SFHF: Cooperation with Divine Grace

Although the pneumatic-transcendent presence in us opens us to the free gift of the Holy Spirit which is grace, this grace cannot effect, alone, our distinctively human formation and transformation without our free cooperation. If as Christians the ultimate objective of our formation is to

---

[44] Adrian van Kaam, *Fundamental Formation* (opus cit.), 144, 181-4, and 305.
[5] See Adrian van Kaam, "Preliminary Glossary of Christian Articulation of Formation Science" TS, Epiphany Association, Pittsburgh, PA, 59-65.

receive and maintain the Christ-Form which will eventually bring us to union with God,[6] we can attain this objective only if we cooperate with Divine grace for which task we have the potential in our pneumatic-transcendent dimension.

The necessity of this cooperation with Divine grace for truly human transcendent formation is underscored by formation theory. In their *Formation Guide to Becoming Spiritually Mature*, van Kaam and Muto point this out when they say:

> The Father ultimately intends for us lives that are whole, complete, at peace; this happiness and harmony for which we all long can only be ours if we follow the lead of the Holy Spirit; we must strive, with the help of grace, to fix our eyes on Jesus, to follow him; this is what it means to be a disciple.[7]

Following the lead of the Holy Spirit in fixing our eyes on Jesus, so that we may become his disciples means our free cooperation with the Holy Spirit. For the Spirit, which is of God, is working in us so that we may receive the Christ-Form, long before our formation ever began. Hence, we only need to cooperate with this Holy Spirit which has already been working in us, all the while, for our formation and transformation in the Christ-Form and image.[8] Under the next paragraph-head, we will seek with Karl Rahner to understand the dynamic of grace which the Holy Spirit so freely gives to us for our distinctively human formation.

---

[6] Ibid., 61–3.

[7] Adrian van Kaam and Susan Muto, Formation Guide to Becoming Spiritually Mature (opus cit.), 166.

[8] See chapter three.

Chapter 7: Revelation and Application of Life-Forming Directives

Karl Rahner: The Dynamic of Grace

In a sermon edited and later turned into an article entitled "*You are accepted*,"⁹ Paul Tillich surveys, in contrast to the notion of sin, different ways in which people understand grace. After sampling different understandings of grace, Tillich, in the fifth paragraph of the article, goes on to present in a very dense language his own understanding of grace in these terms:

> In grace something is overcome; grace occurs "in spite of" something; grace occurs in spite of separation and estrangement. Grace is the reunion of life with life, the reconciliation of the self with itself. Grace is the acceptance of that which is rejected. Grace transforms fate into a meaningful destiny; it changes guilt into confidence and courage.¹⁰

Tillich concludes this out-pouring of his understanding of grace by underlining the insurmountable power of grace, saying: "There is something triumphant in the word, 'grace:' in spite of the abounding of sin, grace abounds much more."¹¹

Such an understanding of grace is certainly one of the best expressions denoting the reality of Divine grace. However, a close look at one of Karl Rahner's perceptions of grace does not only complement Tillich's understanding of it but takes one to the very Source itself of grace. In his book entitled *Grace in Freedom*, Rahner, reflecting on the paragraph-heading: "Freedom and Grace," asserts:

---

⁹ Paul Tillich in *The Shaking of the Foundations* (New York: Charles Scribner's Sons, 1948), 153–63.

¹⁰ Paul Tillich, Ibid., 155.

¹¹ Ibid.

Our historical transcendence depends on God's offer to communicate himself; for our spiritual transcendence is never merely natural, but always surrounded and carried by a dynamic of grace that points towards God's nearness; in other words, God is not only present as the horizon of our transcendence that ever refuses itself, but also offers himself as our direct possession in what we call deifying grace.[12]

Here, Rahner sees grace as necessary for our [very] transcendence. That means, we depend absolutely on grace for our growth and transformation as distinctively human beings. Its dynamic surrounds our spiritual transcendence always, and it is God's infinitely precious offer to communicate Himself to us. Grace, therefore, as God's communication of Himself to us, has its foundation in God. Thus, as it comes into our life and surrounds us in our spiritual transcendence, it points to us the nearness of the source from which it comes – GOD. In this sense, grace becomes in us that power which deifies us, and so becomes *deifying grace*, as Rahner would call it. Deifying grace, and *sanctifying grace* in the Catholic tradition, both refer to the same thing. For the nearness of God, which such a dynamic communication would point to, would also sanctify and make holy the person to whom it has been communicated.

These theoretical discussions, both on the levels of formation anthropology and Christian theology, help us to understand better the formative disposition of humble self-abandonment to God as the work of pneumatic inspiration, which comes from the Holy Spirit. Before we go on to reflect on the self-abandonment of the Christian in our original formation event against this background, it is proper that we examine first the ***peace and joy*** which seem to flow as its fruits.

---

[12] Karl Rahner, *Grace in Freedom* (New York: Herder and Herder, 1969), 209-10.

Chapter 7: Revelation and Application of Life-Forming Directives

SECTION B: PEACE AND JOY IN THE ABANDONING OF ONESELF TO THE WILL OF GOD

Subsequent to abandoning himself to the will of God, the Christian apprehends the feeling of peace and joy in himself. He no longer experiences the anger, frustration, restlessness, and the despair, which previously characterized his current life form. As he submits *his functionalistic and willful self*, with all its projects to the divine will of God, he begins to feel peace and joy welling up within him. In this section, we will explore the dynamics which seem to effect the peace and joy, making them come forth as the direct fruits of the self-abandonment of the Christian to the divine will of God.

From the SFHF: Fullness of Peace and Joy

In the original formation event, we observed the beginning of the experience of peace on the Christian as he appraised the dynamics of the life form of Aloysius in his complete self-submission to the will of God.[13] He had remarked how content – joyful – and serene the saint was in the face of

---

[13] Aloysius' self-submission to the will of God can be perceived in every page of his biography, no matter what edition one refers to. However, it seems to be most manifest in the event of his dearly beloved father's death. As his biographer, Cepari, tells us, "He himself confessed that had he regarded the loss of his parent simply in itself, no doubt it would have been a severe grief to him; but that he was unable to feel sorrow for any dispensation of God, or for any event which he knew to be agreeable to the Divine will." See *The Life of Saint Aloysius Gonzaga*, American edition (New York and Philadelphia: P.J. Kennedy & Sons, Publishers to the Holy Apostolic See, n.d.), 172. See also M. Basil Pennington, "Aloysius Mystic?" in, *Aloysius*, eds. Clifford Stevens and William Hart (Huntington, Indiana: Our Sunday Visitor Inc., 1993), 118.

death as he abandoned himself to the will of God.[14] Peace and joy, therefore, are what seem to be the main form directives from the saint's life-form, which the Christian in the primary formation event appraised and applied to his own current life form.

Discussing the *Primordial Act of the Formation Will*, van Kaam asserts it as being prior to the option for any specific form disposition in a person, and then describes in these terms the ultimate objective of human formation:

> The final aim of all human formation may not be clearly known to us. In most instances, it is only implicitly apprehended. This vague apprehension or basic intuition is proper to our embodied transcendent mind. It is the vailed intuition that we should try to attain a fully consonant form of life. It follows that we should try to ratify or initiate and develop only dispositions that will help us to realize that consonant form[15]

Van Kaam points out the impossibility for our formative will in its primordial act to desist from willing this fully consonant life form. As he argues; "There is an intrinsic connection between the ultimate aim of formation – to attain full peace and joy, [in union with God] – and the necessary means of a fully consonant life-form that leads to that fulfillment."[16] He then goes on further to specify, in relation to such peace and joy, what a fully consonant form of life is; and this fully consonant form of life, he says: "is the ultimate necessary means to this fullness of peace and

---

[14] See Formation Event, Preface viii-xii.

[15] Adrian van Kaam, *Human Formation* (opus cit.), 71.

[16] Ibid.

joy." He adds, "The fullness of peace and joy is the universal and absolute good necessarily striven after by the will."[17]

From the SFHF: Longing for Peace; the Human Foundation

In *Blessings That Make Us Be*, Susan Muto perceives the inherent longing for Peace in all human beings as foundational. After she has described the symptoms and also the consequences indicative of the absence of the fullness of peace in the hearts of people, she comes to the conclusion that inner peace is the *conditio sine qua non* for the making of outer peace.[18] She goes on to intuit and so, affirm:

> There seems to be in our nature a kind of restlessness that is at the same time a longing to rest. This inner dynamism is characteristic of the human being as spirit-in-the-flesh. Our transcendent nature accounts for this continual emerging, striving, aspiring tendency. In short, for our always being in some way, restless. By the same token, we long for what the poet T.S. Eliot called "the still point of the turning world."[19]

---

[17] Ibid.,Elsewhere Adrian van Kaam describes this *Fullness of Peace and Joy* in these still more straight forward terms: "Human formation is dynamically moved by an inherent aspiration to attain a form of life that assures the fullness of peace and joy. In congenial formation the Divine Source of formation is progressively experienced and lived as the Fullness of Peace and Joy. The final glorious form fully participates – within its specific, communal and unique form limits – in the Peace and Joy that is divinity;" see, *Studies* 1 (May, 1980): 296. For further discussions on *Joy* as gift of the Holy Spirit, see also Adrian van Kaam *The Roots of Christian Joy* (Denville, N.J. Dimension Books, 1985), 30-5.

[18] Susan Annette Muto, *Blessings That Make Us Be* (Petersham, Massachusetts: Saint Bede's Publications, 1982), 86.

[19] Ibid.,Muto makes reference to van Kaam's definition of *Foundational Dynamic of Human Formation* in *Studies* 1 (1980): 293; and also T.S. Eliot's poem,

For Muto, all these contrarieties of life built around the longing for peace and actual chaos – rest and restlessness – define the nature of peace; they form together the "foundational dynamic of the human formation," as she intimates above. Hence, she sums up all these opposing dynamics in the individual, which she considers as peace and asserts:

> Peace is the strange blend of rest and restlessness. It is not a static condition but a dynamic quest of harmony between apparent opposite forces which in reality belong together. Life unfolds within this rhythm of being still and moving on. It is like the ebb and flow of night and day, of sleep and awakening, of inhaling and exhaling, of finding peace and making it. The goal of formation is not to lead one polarity to the detriment of the other, but to live within the creative tension between them.[20]

It is this insight to what peace is for us human beings, who are spirit-in-the-flesh, which seems to have led Muto to conclude that the true peace which "we long for is not quite within our power to attain, and hence, we seek some Ultimate Source of peaceful integration.[21] From this conclusion therefore, it appears clear why it is only through our willing cooperation with the pneumatic-transcendent inspirations that we may attain this peace in its fullness. In our next set of paragraphs, we shall discuss, with the spiritual masters, the achievement of true peace and the experience of true joy which relates to it.

"Burnt Norton," in *Four Quartets* (New York: Harcourt, Brace & World, Harvest Book, 1943), 15.

[20] Susan Muto, *Blessings That Make Us Be* (opus cit.), 86.

[21] Ibid., 87.

Chapter 7: Revelation and Application of Life-Forming Directives

John of the Cross: The Nature and Experience of Joy

Before he goes on to distinguish the various objects of joy for the will of the mystic on his or her journey to union with God, and to discuss how best it may respond to each of them,[22] St. John of the Cross defines *joy* as *the first emotion of the will*. In the very opening paragraph of chapter seventeen of *The Ascent of Mount Carmel*, he writes:

> The first passion of the soul and the emotion of the will is joy. Joy – to give a definition suited to our purpose – is nothing else than a satisfaction of the will with esteem for an object it considers fitting. For the will never rejoices unless in something which is valuable and satisfying to it.[23]

The will, therefore, experiences satisfaction in an object which has been clearly apprehended and which it regards as appropriate. John of the Cross calls this experience of the will, *active joy*; i.e., joy in which "a person understands distinctively and clearly the object" over which his or her will freely chooses to rejoice. His contra-distinguishes this joy from what he calls *passive joy*, in which the will, as he says, "finds itself rejoicing without any clear and distinct understanding – though at times it has – of the object of its joy."[24]

---

[22] Saint John of the Cross, *The Ascent of Mount Carmel*, in *The Collected Works of St. John of the Cross*, trans. Kieran Kavanaugh, O.C.D., and Otilio Rodriguez, O.C.D. (Washington, D.C. ICS Publications, 1980), 240-73. These pages cover chapters 18–33 in which the saint discusses what he describes as six various objects of joy with which the will has to deal. They are temporal, natural, sensory, moral, supernatural, and spiritual goods.

[23] Ibid., 239.

[24] Ibid.

Here in our research, it is the first kind of joy which seems to be of particular interest. And now we shall explore in brief, "the fullness of peace" which seems to characterize especially the last three dwelling places of *The Interior Castle* of St. Teresa of Avila.

Teresa of Avila: Understanding the Fullness of Peace

Keith R. Barron summarizes the basis of the spirituality of St. Teresa of Avila in seven foundational dispositions. He identifies the second of these as hope in the direction of history, and he explains it as the disposition on account of which nothing could disturb her "inner peace."[25] In fact, in *The Interior Castle*, inner peace or the fullness of peace, is one of the fruits which Teresa identifies in the soul that enjoys spiritual union, especially spiritual marriage, with God, as it is evident in the last three dwelling places.[26]

Although the complete union between the soul and God – the point of no return – takes place only in the seventh dwelling places of *The Interior Castle*, Teresa already points out in the fifth dwelling places how the trials which the soul endures in them give rise to peace. As she describes the restlessness that can still beset the souls in this stage of their journey towards union with God, the *unitive stage*, she is quick to point out the presence of peace even in the midst of these trials. "I don't mean to say that those who arrive here do not have peace; they do have it, and it is very deep. For the trials themselves are so valuable and have such good roots that although very severe, they give rise to peace and happiness."[27] However, it is in the final dwelling places that this peace attains its fullness. It is there that "one

---

[25] See Keith R. Barron, Unpublished lecture notes, on, "The Spiritual Classics," (Pittsburgh: Duquesne University, IFS), March 18, 1992.

[26] Teresa of Avila, opus cit., 335-450.

[27] Ibid., 345.

Chapter 7: Revelation and Application of Life-Forming Directives

delights in God's tabernacle." For as Teresa, addressing Jesus concerning the peace he gives to the souls that inhabit these dwelling places, says:

> For, in the end, people must always live with fear until you give them true peace and bring them there where that peace will be unending. I say "true peace," not because this peace is not true, but because the first war could return if we were to withdraw from God.[28]

With the illuminations offered by the above discussions on the power of inspiration and the formative directions that it can give in one's faith tradition, we shall now reflect on the self-abandonment, and the fruits thereof, of the Christian in the original formation event.

Integrative Reflection

It is evident that the question which the concerned visitor asked the Christian of our initial formation event being investigated inspired in him highly formative ideals. As we have observed in the narration of the event, the question led the subject gradually to a self-abandonment to God in imitation of St. Aloysius whose life the question made him to reflect upon and to appraise appreciatively.

This eventual abandonment of himself to God was made possible by the dynamics of the formative directives in the life-form of Aloysius. They contained the potency to inspire the Christian and to enable him to imitate the saint. For it was in his contemplation of the saint's life-story that he was able to perceive how immense the love of God for him is and how this love of God for him is not bound to any condition whatsoever. It is, therefore, a love which is not tied to anything that he could have done in the past to merit.

---

[28] Ibid., 443.

The current life-form of Aloysius which the Christian had just appraised demonstrated, on the contrary, that the disposition of the saint towards God, in spite of what he was suffering in his final days, was not determined by any conditional relationship established between him and God. If what he was physically suffering was to be considered as a return reward from God for his disposition of complete self-abandonment to him, by the same human logic, it would be impossible to explain why Aloysius could have continued to maintain such a disposition of trusting self-abandonment to him. In fact, in the last visit Aloysius had with Father Corbinelli, as we are told, the two of them, oblivious of the sufferings from their illnesses, were rather preoccupied with the glorious heavenly home which they perceived was soon to be theirs. They felt their mutual impatience for the arrival at this glorious home was so strong that they realized the need to exhort "each other to patience and resignation to the Divine will."[29]

The formation of such a disposition in the individual is, therefore, certainly not possible unless it is inspired. Nothing less than the inspiration of God Himself can lead a person to eventually abandon his own will and his cherished willful projects to God. This is what Formation Science recognizes as *pneumatic-transcendent presence* and which the Christian tradition calls *grace*. It is precisely this dynamic which Aloysius recognized working constantly in his current life form, particularly as death drew nearer him. His biographer tells us that one day during his last illness the saint revealed to his beloved Cardinal Scipione Gonzaga, who exerted a great interest in his vocation, how immense special graces he was receiving from God. Father Cepari relates:

With Cardinal Scipione particularly, who by reason of his gout had to be carried thither and who seemed as though he could not leave his side,

---

[29] See American Edition, *The Life of St. Aloysius Gonzaga of the Company of Jesus* (opus cit.).

Aloysius discoursed upon his approaching death and of the goodness of God calling him to himself at that early age.[30]

In "Living with Brother Death," Häring narrates of the joy and peace demonstrated by his Roman colleague, Father Dressino, at the approach of his death. In his admiration for such peace in his colleague's death, he testifies:

> What peace I saw on his face! A couple of hours after receiving the sacraments for the dying, he turned to me and asked: "What is the name of the priest who wrote that fine book, *'Yes, Father?'*" When I answered: "Richard Graf" he said in a low voice: "Now I am saying this prayer for the last time: '*Yes, Father!*'" Then early in the morning when the nurse found him and asked him how he was, he replied: "I am blissfully happy!" These were his last words.[31]

Häring asserts that they are such memories that have healed his soul of serious wounds inflicted by his witnessing to so much violent death during World War II in which he was enlisted for service with the German medical corps.

It seems as evidence to confirm that peace and joy are the inalienable fruits of self-abandonment to the will of God, even in the face of suffering and death self. This is what the life-form of Aloysius, and also that of Father Dressino, teach us. And this seems to be what the Christian, in our primary formation event, experienced. As is the pattern, we shall, in conclusion

---

[30] Father V. Cepari, S.J., *Saint Aloysius Gonzaga*, ed Rev. Francis Goldie, S.J. (New York: Benziger Brothers, 1801), 224. In the American Edition quoted above, the formulation "special grace which God vouchsafed him in calling him thus early to himself," is used, (confer the referred to edition, 294).

[31] Bernard Häring, *I Have Seen Your Tears* (opus cit.), 22.

briefly indicate some obstacles, and also conditions, which can prevent, or facilitate consonant formation of the Christian in the Coformant we have just elucidated.

OBSTACLES TO AND FACILITATING CONDITIONS FOR FORMATION ON THE CHRISTIAN LEVEL OF HUMAN PRESENCE

In this Coformant of the primary formation event, several obstacles can be identified. A primary obstacle to consonant formation and reformation of the Christian who has been contemplating new directives from his faith tradition, could be 1) idolization of the ideals contained in the Inbreaking directives. An idolization of even the best ideals is capable of hindering the eventual transformation of the Christian. For, the ideal which becomes an idol is absolutized, and in this way, loses its original power of inspiration since by becoming an idol and an absolute, it becomes rigid and inflexible; and sight may even be lost of its Absolute Source. 2) Another obstacle is the difficulty of abiding in the presence of God epiphanically manifested through the saint in his life story. Agitation, impatience, and the earlier proclivity to despair may continue to be stumbling blocks, hindering the Christian from maintaining his contemplative gaze on the presence of the loving God in the Inbreaking directives.

There are, however, also present some facilitating conditions for consonant growth and transformation of the Christian. Although we do not intend to discuss them presently, we can certainly list three major ones here. These could be listed as 1) the awareness of God's unconditional love; 2) the perception, however analogous, of images of the life story of the saint; and 3) the actual feeling of peace, and of joy. This latter facilitating condition can foster and promote, in further contemplation, greater abandonment of the Christian to the will of God.

Chapter 7: Revelation and Application of Life-Forming Directives

Transition to Chapter Eight: Christian Ministers

We have studied, rather extensively, the Coformant on the Christian level; elucidating it appreciatively, appraising the new Inbreaking directives from the life-story of a saint in the Christian faith tradition. We investigated how the dynamics of contemplating new directives may lead the Christian to self-submission to the divine will of God and to the beginning experience of peace and joy.

Now, the investigation that follows wishes to explore the true meaning of Christian ministry in the light of the deeper awareness of the Inbreaking directives which the Christian has gained through his faith tradition. This moves the study towards the true understanding of Christian ministry itself, which will be the task in the following chapter, Chapter Eight.

CHAPTER EIGHT

UNDERSTANDING CHRISTIAN MINISTRY IN THE LIGHT OF GRACED APPRAISAL OF INBREAKING DIRECTIVES

INTRODUCTION

While the last chapter elucidated directives received through Kataphatic contemplation in Coformant Two on the Christian level of presence, Chapter eight will explore these Inbreaking directives in the same Coformant, on the horizon of Christian ministers, formulated in the following terms:

> Christian ministers, when formatively questioned in their tradition, may recollect the heroic life-story of a minister-saint. Their formative imagination may help them to perceive, with greater clarity, the Christ-Form directives inspired by the life-story of the saint. As they incarnate these directives, they may be further inspired with new zeal and dedication to imitate, in their own lives, the example of true Christian ministry given to them in the narrative, and humbly abandon their own willful designs in obedience to the will of God who has called them to be ministers.

To elucidate the Coformant on this horizon of Christian ministers, two remote foundational statements will be drawn from it. The first foundational statement will investigate how a deeper awareness of Christian ministers' life-forming directives may be obtained through the help of formative imagination; while the second foundational statement will be to explore the incarnation of directives as the way to renew the true zeal and dedication of Christian ministers in their ministry.

PART ONE

DEEPENING CHRISTIAN MINISTERS' AWARENESS OF THEIR LIFE-FORMING DIRECTIVES THROUGH THE HELP OF FORMATIVE IMAGINATION

The first part of this chapter will investigate to elucidate the following remote foundational statement:

When Christian ministers are formatively questioned in their faith tradition, helped by their formative imagination, they may perceive with greater clarity Christ-Form directives inspired by the heroic life-story of a saint, and so become consonantly influenced by them.

This remote foundational statement will be studied in two sections. Section A will focus on the recreating of oneself through formative imagination; and in Section B, the focus will be on how Chris-Form-directives may be apprehended as they are inspired through the heroic life-form of a saint who is an ancestor in the Christian minister's faith tradition.

SECTION A: BEING REFORMED THROUGH CREATIVE IMAGINATION.

When Christian ministers, with the help of their imagination, respond to formative questions put to them in their faith tradition, they may become focally aware of directives therefrom. These directives, of which they are focally conscious, may lead them to reform their deformed dispositions as Christian ministers. So, this proximate area of research intends to explore the necessity for Christian ministers to maintain as much as possible focal consciousness of the consonant dispositions which are indispensable for their authentically true ministry.

From the SFHF: **Focal Consciousness**

In Chapter Five, we discussed the source of formative consciousness and its indispensability for the maintenance of our formation potency. We also observed how it is essentially connected with our life form as persons.[1] However, when we also consider the various dimensions of consciousness,[2] it becomes clear that consciousness means the awareness which the individual has of himself as a "person." It is in this sense, and in the light of our intrinsic freedom, that van Kaam speaks of the possibility we still have of denying or veiling our "consciousness as persons."[3]

Discussing the changes which we experience as the Divine Mystery of Formation becomes nearer to us, van Kaam describes thus the mysterious ambiance formed – a new way in which we begin to appreciate events, people, and things in our everyday life – which invites us in an ever-growing intimacy to true transcendence:

> The changes we experience first take place in our inner sphere of life. Therein resides an unacknowledged hidden awareness of our intimacy with the Mystery. This transconscious gift is a treasure hidden in what I have identified and named as the transfocal region of our consciousness. The difference now is that we become aware, however vaguely, of this gift. We let awareness of it seep into what in my theory is the prefocal

---

[1] See chapter five.

[2] Adrian van Kaam, *Fundamental Formation* (opus cit.), 262; see also *Transcendent Formation* (opus cit.), 100, 202, and 208.

[3] Adrian van Kaam, *Transcendent Formation*, 20

region of consciousness. If we create spaces of stillness, our focal awareness may be touched by moments of inner intimacy arising from our transfocal consciousness vis our prefocal consciousness. It does not come from a suppressed oceanic or symbiotic childhood feeling that some other personality theories speak about.[4]

In this light, the presence of the different degrees of consciousness in the individual person becomes evident. It seems also, indeed, clear that for a consonant formation to take place, this "unacknowledged hidden awareness of our intimacy with the mystery" – God – has to be made conscious to some degree, and to be allowed to enter into our prefocal consciousness, and eventually into our focal consciousness. It is in this process of becoming focally conscious of our growing intimacy with God that our imagination, which is one of our Intraspheric auxiliary powers of formation, can indeed play an important role in the appraising of the formative disposition present therein.

From the SFHF: Creative Imagination

Above all, when formative imagination is creative, the influence it exerts in the consonant reformation of dissonant dispositions is immense. In discussing this influence of creative imagination on the vital level, Adrian van Kaam demonstrates this immense power with the following example:

Take the case of a Person we shall call Peter who constantly suffered low back-pain due to the treatment of rectal cancer. The pain became so intolerable that only three options seemed open to him: effective treatment of the pain, commitment to a mental institution, or suicide. He was lucky enough to have become acquainted with an experienced, well-

---

[4] Ibid., 229.

trained formation counselor. This woman suggested that he should deactivate his present disposition toward pain, and develop a new disposition that would diminish his suffering. She proposed to him a project of vital disposition reformation by means of formative imaging. They would talk first through the object pole of the disposition he should reform. She helped him to address himself to the pain, not as an abstract concept or a simple perception, but to form an image of the pain that would express how it really affected him – an image that would not be made up by the mind in isolation but that would emerge from the source of the pain as concretely located in the vital dimension of his life. It should be an image that could tell him something about his suffering.

Van Kaam continues the narration of his example and discloses the success:

> Under her guidance, he was able to form an image of a vicious terrier chewing his spine. It was a nightmarish image, but it enabled him to give form to his pain experience. This visual image in turn made it possible for him to form a verbal image. In this form the pain became available to his appraisal. This appraisal had to be positive or appreciative. The image and the experience it represented had to be seen as a formation opportunity. Only then could he approach it as a point of departure for the initiation of a formative disposition. Then he could begin to work with it[5]

Van Kaam concludes this highly illustrative example by confirming that Peter was able to reach his formative decision: "Yes, I want to reform my disposition toward pain. I am resolved to work with this image, to see it as an opportunity for the improvement of my life."[6] This clearly demonstrates

---

[5] See Adrian van Kaam, *Human Formation*, 111.
[6] Ibid.

the powerful influence creative imagination can have in the appraisal process, and hence, in the reformation of dissonant dispositions of which a person may become focally conscious in his or her inner sphere of life.

In the above paragraphs, we have discussed about focal consciousness, and how creative imagination can contribute to the apprehension therefrom of dissonant dispositions, and so, the influence of such creative imagination in their reformation. Now with David Grandfield, we want to study the import of mystical consciousness; while with Meister Eckhart, the disposition of "letting go of attachments."

David Granfield: Mystical Consciousness

With Formation Science, we took note of the object of "the unacknowledged hidden awareness of our intimacy, which is the mystery" residing in the mysterious ambiance of our daily existence, and which invites us more intimately to its transcendence.[7] Formation Science, in its Christian articulation, calls this mystery, the Divine Mystery of formation, and also the Triune God who is the Source of our human consciousness. It is interesting to note that, here again, formation anthropology, in its Christian articulation, is perfectly in tune with the Christian faith tradition.

Speaking of what he calls, *mystical consciousness*, David Granfield distinguishes between *"radical theophany"* which he says, "is consciousness of the Holy Mystery," and defines *"common theophany"* as "consciousness of divine revelation."[8] Granfield perceives these two kinds of consciousness as what leads to the flowering of a third kind he calls *mystical theophany* or *mystical consciousness*. He reminds his readers that, in this mystical consciousness faith is still necessary, since, he says, "we do not, during this life,

---

[7] See footnote #4 in this chapter.

[8] David Granfield, Heightened Consciousness (New York: Paulist Press, 1991), 41.

pierce the veil and get a direct vision of God, who 'dwells in light inaccessible; whom no one has seen nor can see' (1 Tim 6: 16)."⁹ After taking a quick look at three other formulations of mystical consciousness in the Christian context, which he also calls a *peak spiritual experience,* he describes it thus:

> Mysticism is a heightened consciousness of a loving union with the transcendent and triune God, a many-leveled awareness of the divine presence, more intimate than usually afforded by graced reason and revelation.[10]

Though the above discussion on consciousness may be rather short, it makes clear that the concept of formation theory regarding formative consciousness comes from and is well supported by Christian tradition of which it is the articulation in the SFHF. In the paragraphs that follow, we shall explore, however limitedly, the meaning of the construct: "Letting go of Attachment" in the spirituality of Meister Eckhart.

Meister Eckhart: Letting Go of Attachment

We have discussed a great deal, especially in the second part of the last chapter, about abandonment of oneself and one's functionalistic willful

---

[99] Ibid.,Granfield concept of consciousness can be said to reflect very much van Kaam's expression of the same reality as we have observed above. See under *Focal Consciousness,* 309-10.

[10] Ibid., 41. Three other formulations come from i) William James: "Consciousness of illumination is for us the essential mark 'mystical' states;" ii) Joseph Marechal: "[Mysticism is] the feeling of immediate presence of a transcendent being" and iii) Reginald Garrigou-Lagrange: "The mystical life is Christian life, which has, so to speak, become conscious of itself."

projects to the Divine will. Under the above paragraph-heading, we want to find out if what Meister Eckhart formulates as 'letting go of attachments' may not, indeed, of the first experience of abandoning oneself to the will of God – detachment from oneself in view of a more free attachment of the same self to God, sinking deeper into him.

In his book entitled *The Recovery of Love*, Jeffrey D. Imbach discusses in Part IV – Coming Home to Ourselves – three themes in the spirituality of Eckhart. Together these themes of Eckhart converge with those of three other spiritual masters on what Imbach calls "The Vision of Passionate Love."[11] It is in the second theme – Our Essential Ground – that Imbach discusses Eckhart's construct of "*Letting go of Attachments*." It is clear that, in speaking of "Letting go of Attachments," Eckhart is speaking of '*detachment.*' To introduce his discussion on Eckhart's "let go" and "sink down," Imbach writes:

> It is somewhat double-edged to discover that life does not come from outside! It is exhilarating to contemplate the fact that I have such depth of being that in some indescribable way I am one with God. On the other hand, the journey to my centre requires that I let go of my persistent belief that I will find my meaning in some outside person or experience. Returning home means leaving the "far country."[12]

This appropriately introduces and describes the reason for "detachment of myself from myself." I detach myself from all that keeps me away from returning and reaching home to where I belong; to be one with my center,

---

[11] Jeffrey D. Imbach, *The Recovery of Love* (New York: Crossroad, 1992), 87-111. The three other spiritual masters Imbach lists in this convergence on *the Vision of Passionate Love* are: Julian of Norwich, John Ruusbroec, and Dante Alighieri.

[12] Ibid., 104.

Chapter 8: Understanding Christian Ministry

my ground; to be united and to be one with God. As Imbach defines, "Detachment is the refusal to buy into any outside experience as my source of life."[13]

In this light, the fullness of the concept of detachment manifests a two-way movement, a double-edged [reality], as Imbach calls it, of which the first movement home consists of "letting go," and the second, of sinking down." It is in his own explanation of such detachment that, as Imbach says, "[Eckhart] speaks often about 'letting go' our attachment to external things in order to sink down into this union with God."[14] By the constructs "let go" or "go out" as Eckhart sometimes would say, he refers not to some external place, but "to the infinite depth into which we emerge when we "go out" through the center of our being and emerge into God," Imbach suggests. As he quotes from Eckhart's explanation in his Sermon on this theme:

> That is why I say that if a man will turn away from himself and from all created things, by so much will you be one and blessed in the spark of the soul. … This spark rejects all created things, and wants nothing but its naked God. (German Sermon, #48. p. 198).[15]

Imbach likewise explains Eckhart's imagistic use of the construct, 'sink down' as "the simplicity of relaxing into God."[16] Hence, after we "let go" all those created things which hamper and prevent us from reaching home to our souls' naked God, they become free from all such unnecessary baggage, and so, are able simply to sink home into God our Ground, Centre, and Home.

---

[13] Ibid.
[14] Ibid, 105.
[15] Ibid.
[16] Ibid.

Integrative Reflection

In his initial dissonance, the Christian minister in the original formation event had identified his own willful projects and their goals, and he believed, they were willed for him by God who called him, in and through the Christ-Form, to be minister of them.[17] This making of his own will God's made it impossible for him to consonantly recognize God's true will when it presented itself in what seemed to be his approaching death. This is because his disposition of *"willing abandonment"* to God's Divine will was currently deformed. It needed to be reformed in order to allow him to consonantly apprehend and appraise, even his approaching death, as part of God's will for him as his true minister in the Christ-Form.

This is what happened when, through his appreciative appraisal of the life-story of St. Aloysius – a true minister of Christ – he was eventually able to perceive and recognize the unconditional love God has for him.[18] He was then able to perceive, even his own imminent death, as part of God's plan for him in the ministry to which he had been called in and through Christ.

In coming to accept even his looming death as the will of God, and to abandon himself, therefore, to God, the Christian minister in the original formation event was following the example of Saint Aloysius, the contemplation of whose life-story, in the first place, had led him to do the same. It is Aloysius' disposition of complete abandonment of himself to the will of God in his approaching death which so immensely inspired the Christian minister, with its pneumatic dynamic of transcendent presence. As he was able to say after his consonant appraisal of the life of St. Aloysius, "God! You have certainly shown more love to me than you [even] seem to have done to poor Aloysius and others like him."[19]

---

[17] See chapter four.
[18] See Formation event, Preface to this Book, viii-xii.
[19] Ibid.

Chapter 8: Understanding Christian Ministry

It seems evident that what led St. Aloysius to such total abandonment of himself to God, even in his approaching death, was his focal consciousness of God's presence in him and with which he was very intimate.[20] He was already focally conscious of God's nearness to him, for instance, through his daily meditations which virtually and effectively occupied most of his day.[21] This vivid reality made him to so trustingly abandon himself evermore completely to the infinitely loving care of God.

In the maintenance of this focal consciousness of God's intimate presence with him, St. Aloysius' creative imagination must have had a great influence. The imagery of the Crucifixion in his contemplations,[22] his mental images of the Passion,[23] and other images, such as images of the self-maceration of his great founder, St. Ignatius of Loyola out of love for Christ his King,[24] all helped to maintain more concretely, clearly, and so, more intimately the object of his focal consciousness – the presence of God – defined by Granfield as: "the heightened consciousness of a loving union with the transcendent and triune God."[25]

As it will be recalled, it is when the Christian minister began to "let go"[26] of his own previous willful projects to which he was attached – deformatively considering them as God's will – that he began his journey back home. This detachment from his previous willful projects that were

---

[20] Adrian van Kaam, *Transcendent Formation*, 229.

[21] Virgilio Cepari, *The Life of St. Aloysius Gonzaga of the Company of Jesus*, American Edition (New York: P.J. Kenedy and Sons, n.d.), 195. These chief subjects of the Saint's meditation – The Passion of the Lord, the Divine attributes, etc. – certainly kept God focally consciously ever nearer and closer to him in his life.

[22] Ibid., 53.

[23] See footnote #21 above.

[24] Virgilio Cepari, (opus cit.), 223.

[25] David Granfield, (opus cit.), 41.

[26] Jeffrey D. Imbach, *The Recovery of Love*, 104-6.

mistaken as God's will began to see its completion when, after "letting go of these attachments," he could return to "sink down" home into God – the object of his focal consciousness, the Ground and Centre of his being, the Triune God. All this has become possible, thanks to the *re*-formation and *re*-creation of his disposition of self-abandonment to the will of God.

If then Christian ministers, who due to deformative dispositions such as the one of self-abandonment, are able to reform them and to acknowledge and return to consciousness of their intimacy with God, it may be thanks to the inspired, heroic life-directives contained in the life-story of a saint-minister. In the section that will follow, we will investigate to discover how the Christian minister may apprehend and discern the Christ-Form-directives which are essential for his ministry through an inspired life-story of a saint.

SECTION B: APPREHENDING AND BEING INFLUENCED BY CHRIST-FORM DIRECTIVES THROUGH AN INSPIRED HEROIC LIFE-STORY OF A SAINT

Christian ministers who appraise and are influenced by Christ-Form directives through an inspiring and heroic life-story of a saint may become renewed, reformed, and even transformed in their ministry. These Christ-Form directives, made focally conscious by their formative imagination, may draw Christian ministers to imitate Christ the High Priest and Good Shepherd of his flock of which he invites them to be ministers. In this proximate area of research, we will want to concentrate on the Christ-Form which is the model for all human beings, especially for those who are called to Christian ministry as pastors.

Chapter 8: Understanding Christian Ministry

From the SFHF: The Transcendent Love-Will

We have spoken at length of the Christ-Form in Chapter Three of this research. Here we want to focus more on what Adrian van Kaam identifies as "the transcendent *love-will*," which he explores in the *characteristics of formation conscience,*[27] and which should be one of the foundational characters in especially Christian ministers.

In chapter twenty-eight of the manuscript of his sixth volume in his magisterial series on **Formative Spirituality**, van Kaam discusses the quality of the articulation of what he calls 'theistic formation anthropology.' In this chapter, which he regards as the transition between "a well-formulated pretheological Formation Science" undergirded by "an empirical formation anthropology" and "a systematic formation theology," he discusses, among others, a number of philosophical-theological constructs.[28]

After he has carefully described what he calls 'the more than' – the transcendent dynamic deep in us – as "the *love-will* of the Mystery at work within us," van Kaam reminds his readers that this Mystery is what he refers to throughout his series in Formative Spirituality, as the Radical Mystery.[29] It is in articulating the ground-source of this Mystery and its '*love-will*,' deep in every human being, that he points out some of the basic different views people have of this Radical Mystery – Divine Mystery, God – as it manifests itself in their daily life and world.

Earlier in Chapter Nine of *Transcendent Formation*, van Kaam, discussing the existential character of *conscience formation*, succinctly points

---

[27] Adrian van Kaam, *Transcendent Formation*, MS, Sixth volume of Formative Spirituality series, Epiphany Association, Pittsburgh, 1994.

[28] Adrian van Kaam, "Transcendent Formation," MS, Sixth Volume of Formative Spirituality series, Epiphany Association, Pittsburgh, 1994.

[29] Ibid., chapter twenty-eight, 1.

out that this existential character shares in the basic quality of the human personhood.[30] This basic quality of the human personhood, which he also calls a disposition, is what he designates as "the love-will." After explaining the origin of this construct, which has found its way into his formation theory, he goes on to describe its formative task in this way: "The love-will inspires in depth of one's soul, at the very root of one's founding life form, an unconditional willing of love."[31] Thus, it seems right that this love-will, which originates from the Mystery of Formation, itself should, as van Kaam has argued earlier, be "the ground of our personhood."[32] It is in this way that our primordial will to love shares in the love-will of the Mystery itself and strives to love and to do what the love-will of the Mystery of Formation wills and directs us to implement for our consonant formation.

In order that the primordial love-will, which undergirds the personhood of the unique-communal individual be activated in his or her formation, it has to pass through the different phases of the person's formation journey. These phases, as van Kaam points out, are the vital-parental functional-collective and individual, functional-transcendent, transcendent unique-communal, and transcendent-functional.[33] It is in them that the current shifts which take place in the ongoing formation or unfolding of the individual's unique-communal founding life-form can be empirically observed. They are what the SFHF calls the *dimensions of forming presence*,[34] and they are truly the *"loci observandi"* of the operations of this basic characteristic – the love-will – of the human personhood.

Although our intuition tells us that the love-will of our personhood gives us form through the dimensions of forming presence, how may one

---

[30] Adrian van Kaam, *Transcendent Formation*, (opus cit.), 95.

[31] Ibid.

[32] Ibid., 96.

[33] Ibid., 99.

[34] Adrian van Kaam, *Fundamental Formation* (opus cit.), 57-61.

know that this Love-will effectively operates in one dimension of the forming presence or other? De Wit's concept of the two types of knowing helps us to address this question.

Han de Wit: Conceptual Knowing and Perceptual Knowing

In his book *Contemplative Psychology*, de Wit, in chapter three, under paragraph-heading, "A Contemplative Epistemology," explores in depth the concept of *knowing* in the contemplative traditions. After he has distinguished the areas of epistemology; cognitive psychology and methodology, in the development of which the two first ones cooperate, Han de Wit observes the difficulty of making such clear distinctions among the three in the contemplative traditions' approach to *knowing*.[35] However, after making this observation, he indicates that the absence of such clear distinctions – as in the three areas of the mental processes above - instead of making us consider knowing in the contemplative traditions as vague, naïve or beside the point, rather challenges us to look for answers appropriate within the contemplative traditions themselves. For such answers, as he says, "may clarify the particular approach which contemplative traditions take with regard to the concepts of *mind* and *knowledge*.[36]

With the conviction that de Wit has about a different approach to "knowing" that the contemplative traditions must possess, he points out an important reality in that respect. He writes: "[They] are not interested in knowledge but in producing good *knowers*. They are not interested in *having knowledge*, but in *being wise.*"[37] As he further clearly affirms:

---

[35] Han de Wit, *Contemplative Psychology*, trans, Marie Louise Baird (Pittsburgh, PA: Duquesne University Press, 1991), 82-3.

[36] Ibid, 83.

[37] Ibid.

Differences in emphasis and detail notwithstanding, the contemplative traditions work with two types of knowing: a conceptual way of knowing and a non-conceptual way of knowing. These two ways to knowledge are again based on the central thesis that we cannot only think clear about experience but also clearly experience our thinking.[38]

Hence, with these insights, de Wit indicates the two basic types of knowing which he identifies in the contemplative traditions; they are conceptual knowing (being good knowers) and perceptual knowers (being wise knowers).

Conceptual form of knowing according to contemplative traditions, as de Wit understands, "results in discursive, conceptual knowledge in the sense of information that one can acquire, possess and transmit. This knowledge is the result of *thinking abou*t something, whether concept or experience."[39] On the other hand, perceptual knowing, as he defines it, "involves *sharpening* our experience of mindfulness, attentiveness, awareness, or intuition."[40]

It is therefore clear that, whereas in the contemplative traditions of knowing, ***conceptual knowing*** is considered connected with the human intellectual faculty or reasoning mind, ***perceptual knowing*** is regarded as being connected with the human soul or heart.[41] In the contemplative traditions therefore, knowledge – thought – or experience is regarded as the fruit, not only of one's intellectual faculty of the mind, but also of one's heart or soul. Hence, in this light, the contemplative is not only able to think clearly about his or her experience, but he or she is also able to experience clearly his or her thoughts.

---

[38] Ibid., 84.
[39] Ibid., 84.
[40] Ibid., 85.
[41] Ibid., 86.

Chapter 8: Understanding Christian Ministry

Integrative Reflection

In his appraisal of the disposition of Aloysius life form, the Christian minister in our original formation event arrived at the decision to take the Saint's life form as his model. This decision is implicit in what his inner voice said as it addressed God: "You have certainly shown more love to me than you seem to have done to poor Aloysius and others like him. I am ready to die [as Aloysius was] if you want to have me come to you now."[42]

It is evident that if the Christian minister had finally come to abandon himself to God and was ready to die if that was the will of God, it is because he was inspired by the formative disposition which he perceived in the heroic life form of Aloysius, particularly during his terminal illness and moments of death. Such a life form became for him a consonant model and example which he could follow. He discerned in the life form of Aloysius, which was similar to his own current life form, the presence of transcendent dispositions which enabled the saint not only to accept his conflicted situation but even to seem to be impatient to embrace it because he perceived that it was the will of God.[43]

The fact that Aloysius was always so ready to give up his own plans in favour of God's and seemed to enjoy such profound peace as a result was so gently compelling an inspiration that the Christian minister could not resist imitating the saint. The influence of such consonant directives on him, coming from the saint's form disposition, was so immense. Aloysius' demonstration of his disposition of peace, even just moments before his death, is another example of such transcendent dispositions. As it is recorded, "P. Guelfucci gazed at him but could see no sign of imminent death

---

[42] See Formation event, Preface to this Book, viii-xii.
[43] See *The Life of St. Aloysius Gonzaga*, (opus cit.), 295.

on the calm and placid face before him."[44] This is clear evidence of the profound and transcendent peace he enjoyed then.

It must be pointed out that Aloysius himself was a faithful imitator of the image that Christ was to him, and he submitted himself, to a heroic degree, to the directives of the Christ-Form of which he had such clear perceptual knowledge in and through constant contemplation. As P. Cepari repeatedly made very clear, foremost among the chief subjects of Aloysius' contemplation were the Most Holy Eucharist, the Passion of Our Lord, and the scene of the Crucifixion.[45] One can say that it was his contemplation of these images of Christ and the form dispositions which he so clearly perceived therein as directives that inspired him with the form of Christ the High Priest (Heb 3 – 10:18) who came among us as the Good Shepherd (Jn 10:11) to do the will of God (Jn 4:34; 5:30; 6:38-40).

Aloysius' biographer recorded his greatest desire to imitate Christ in every way, and at the end, to be united with him: *"Cupio dissolve et esse cum Christo"* (I desire to be dissolved and to be with Christ).[46] All this is a clear demonstration of how profoundly Aloysius sought to be formed, in every way possible, in the image of the Christ-Form. Christ himself who is God's beloved Son (Mt 3:17; 12:18-21), came into our world as a human being and the servant of God to do God's will (Mt. 6:10; 26:42; Lk 22:42). He is, therefore, the epiphany of the Divine love-will to us. Hence, in his disposition to live this Christ-Form, Aloysius was open to the influence of the dynamics of all these primordial dispositions in the Christ-Form. When, therefore, the Christian minister in our primary formation event, after appraising these dynamics in the life form of Aloysius, decided to apply and

---

[44] Ibid., 311.

[45] Ibid., 195; see also pp. 51-5. Even in his youth, as we are informed, "[Aloysius] exercised a little Apostleship at home, going to teach the children in the schools of Christian Doctrine." (54).

[46] Ibid., 303.

incarnate them in himself, he was being influenced by the Christ-Form directives through the life-form of St. Aloysius.

Transition to the Second Remote Foundational Statement

The investigations in the first remote foundational statement in this chapter sought to elucidate the dynamics of focal consciousness of the consonant dispositions that the Christian ministers need to cultivate and maintain in view of their ministry. To exercise true Christian ministry, ministers have to make the Christ-Form their model (Phil. 2:5-11). The second part of the chapter will seek to discover how incarnating the Christ-Form directives may lead ministers to renewed zeal and dedication in their ministry.

PART TWO

INCARNATING CHRIST-FORM DIRECTIVES AS THE WAY TO RENEWED ZEAL AND DEDICATION IN CHRISTIAN MINISTERS

The second remote foundational statement which needs to be elucidated is the following:

As Christian ministers incarnate these directives, they may further be filled with new zeal and dedication which may lead them to imitate, in their own lives, the true example of Christ in their ministry as Christian leaders. They may thus humbly abandon their own will in obedience to the will of God.

This remote foundational statement will explore two proximate directives. The first proximate directive, which will be explored in Section A, will study how *incarnating Christian life-directives may inspire ministers to imitate Christ more*; while the second proximate directive in Section B, will focus on *humble self-abandonment and obedience to God's will as essential part of Christian ministry.*

<u>SECTION A</u>: *INCARNATINNG CHRISTIAN LIFE-DIRECTIVES AND FURTHER INSPIRATION TO IMITATE CHRIST*

As ministers incarnate these Christian life-directives in themselves, they may further be inspired to imitate Christ in their ministry with greater zeal and dedication. In this section, we wish to examine more closely how Christian ministers may incarnate in themselves these Christ-Form directives so that they may become source of further inspiration to more fervent imitation of Christ.

<u>From the SFHF</u>: Applying and Incarnating Form Directives

In Chapter thirteen of *Fundamental Formation*, Adrian van Kaam discusses at length the form potency of the transcendent dimension. In this, he asserts that spiritual ideals are transcendent. For, as he reasons, "they appeal to us from the *beyond*; they are not made by us but are given to us."[47] Hence, as such, these ideals are transcendent directives – inspirations – which have as their ultimate source the Divine Mystery. As the person appraises these directives thus received, he or she eventually applies them to him- or herself. It is, however, the incarnation of these form directives in the person's life form which brings to a consonant completion their appraisal process.[48]

---

[47] Adrian van Kaam, *Fundamental Formation*, opus cit., 168.
[48] Confer chapter four, under *Mind and Will in Formative Appraisal*. For a graphic explanation of the entire appraisal process, see Adrian van Kaam & Susan Muto, *Formation Guide for Becoming Spiritually Mature*, opus cit., 118.

Chapter 8: Understanding Christian Ministry

Adrian van Kaam, discussing how transcendent ideals may be translated into functional projects, writes:

Inspirations have to be translated into manageable, enfleshed, and situated projects. This process implies an ongoing dialogue with concrete reality as disclosed both in the self and in the environment. As human persons, we live in and through our body in a formation field. We have to incarnate abstract ideals into concrete projects, strategies and tactics.[49]

In this light, the incarnation of the transcendent directives in the human life form does not only bring their appraisal process to a consonant conclusion, but it also makes empirically observable the changes which manifest that formation has actually taken place. When incarnation of spiritual ideals has taken place, the changes that this brings about are marked by, and also can be observed as van Kaam makes it evident, the "attendant ambitions, moods, feelings, perceptions, memories, thoughts, and attitudes" of the person.[50]

Furthermore, speaking about the *dynamic principles of formation theory in the formation of dispositions* towards the end of chapter seven in *Human Formation,* he underlines the relevance of the principle of *incarnational formative tendency.* He asserts:

This principle maintains that any act of formative transcendent or functional appraisal and volition tends to incarnate itself in our life as a whole. This penchant results in form directives, which tend to form in

---

[49] Adrian van Kaam, *Fundamental Formation*, 168.
[50] Ibid.

turn suitable images, memories, and anticipations, with their attendant feelings and strivings.[51]

All the above affirmations make it abundantly clear that incarnation of form directives, even of transcendent inspirations, is necessary in order to claim that formation has actually taken place. It is when these form directives, in the form of spiritual ideals or inspirations, have been incarnated in the life form of the person, that they in turn may become new form directives in the form of "suitable images, memories, and anticipations."

When inspirations which come to a person through dispositions in the life form of another are appreciatively appraised, they may lead the person to decide to imitate this other who may be only their immediate source and eventually to imitate their original source itself. In the following paragraphs we want, with the help of the author of *The Imitation of Christ*, to draw attention to formative inspirations which may come to us either directly from the life-story of Christ or through the life-form of others who have been his fervent followers.

Thomas À Kempis: "The Imitation of Christ"

To understand the message of *The Imitation of Christ*, "a timeless work" which has been attributed to Thomas À Kempis as its author,[52] it is important to recall here briefly the world in which it was written. Written in The Netherlands between the years 1420 and 1427 by an anonymous author, and autographed in 1441 by Thomas à Kempis, it is a spiritual classic of devotional literature, as William Creasy indicates.[53]

---

[51] Adrian van Kaam, Human Formation, opus cit., 136.

[52] Thomas à Kempis, *The Imitation of Christ*, trans., with an introduction, by William C. Creasy (Notre Dame, Indiana: Ave Maria Press, 1989).

[53] Ibid., 11 and 13-5.

Chapter 8: Understanding Christian Ministry

The world of the fifteenth century into which *The Imitation of Christ* was so welcomed was a world in deep conflict at all levels of human existence. It was a world shattered and crumbling. With the death of Pope Gregory XI in 1378, the papacy was in shambles, quickly leading to the Great Schism and the "Babylonian Captivity" of the popes in Avignon. This ecclesiastical drama brought with it its attendant spiritual confusion among the people, and the subsequent decadence in all of Europe.[54] The Black Death which had begun sweeping through Europe in 1348, had already killed, as Creasy estimates, a third of the population. This had such immense horrible ramifications in the economic, social, and political fields that it left the population in utter desperation, and nowhere to turn to for any solace and true purpose of their lives.[55] Such, in a nutshell, was the background of the world in which *The Imitation of Christ* was written.

In crises of such proportions and of all levels of life, there, in turn was unleashed a general decadence of similar immensity in the lives of people. Hence, they began to turn to God, taking God as the centre of their lives, and seeking to cultivate intimate relationship with him in whom alone they could have hope to find meaning and the fulfillment of their lives and existence. It is in this shift of their lives, looking for its meaning and fulfillment in God, which gave birth to the various movements of reform, such as the '*Devotio Moderna*,' begun by Gerard Groote. As Creasy tells us about people in the little communities of "Brothers and Sisters of the Common Life" who were shaped by the *Devotio Moderna*:

[They] strove to imitate the lives of the early Christians. They had little interest in philosophy, scholastic theology, or Church politics; rather, through simplicity, humility and great faith they were intent on

---

[54] Ibid., 20-1.
[55] Ibid., 21.

developing an intimate relationship with God and on nurturing a personal piety grounded in devotion to prayer and meditation.[56]

This is the context out of which *The Imitation of Christ* was born. Its purpose was to help and to guide people, through the example of Jesus Christ and his earlier followers, back to intimate and loving relationship with God. Hence, Creasy in his introduction, would call *The Imitation of Christ* "a guidebook to a life of holiness whose end is God." Anticipating the spiritual rewards everyone can draw from reading *The Imitation of Christ*, he writes as part of the conclusion to his introduction:

> Following Jesus' example, we might teach and heal and rebuild our world during the day, but at night we should retreat into the quiet of our own hearts for deep, intimate prayer; with God at the center, all we do will flow from him, and all we do will be for love of him.[57]

In this respect, it is clear that the example of Jesus' disposition towards the Father is what inspired the countless people, either directly through the Gospel or indirectly through the lives of others who had themselves been inspired by this disposition of Jesus, to seek intimate relationship with God, and to make God the centre of their lives. This is what À Kempis consistently indicated to his audience as the objective of *The Imitation of Christ*. In Chapter Eighteen of Book One, for instance, À Kempis presents to his readers the life-form of the early Fathers (and Mothers) of the Church as examples which had the power to inspire them in their quest for intimate relationship and, ultimately, to attain union with God. They themselves, having been inspired by the example of Christ, were led to imitate him in

---

[56] Ibid., 22.
[57] Ibid., 27.

Chapter 8: Understanding Christian Ministry

their lives. Thus, after urging his readers to "look into the lively examples of the holy fathers," he explains:

> Saints and friends of Christ, they served the Lord in hunger and thirst, in cold and nakedness, in toil and weariness, in vigils and fasts, in prayer and holy meditation, in persecution and in many scornful insults. Oh, how many grave troubles they suffered, the apostles, martyrs, confessors, virgins and all the others who resolved to follow Christ! They did not care about their lives in this world, as long as they might possess them in eternal life.[58]

If the saints, friends of Christ, were prepared to suffer all these hardships so that they might possess their lives in eternal life, it is because they were inspired by the example of Christ himself who was disposed and willing to experience all this because it was the will of his Father. All these saints and friends of his, therefore, saw no other way by which they could eventually attain union with the same Father and God, other than the way Christ himself has shown them by his own life-form and its dispositions towards the Father.

Before we go on to reflect on the relevance of all the above discussions on the incarnation and further inspiration of Christian life-directives in ministers, and the examples of the Imitators of Christ by many in the fourteenth century and following, we shall first explore, in Section B, two essential dispositions for true Christian ministry.

---

[58] Ibid., 46.

SECTION B: THE CHRISTIAN MINISTRY IN HUMBLE SELF-ABANDONMENT AND OBEDIENCE TO THE WILL OF GOD

In their imitation of Jesus Christ, Christian ministers may make it their primary preoccupation to seek to carry out their ministry in humble self-abandonment and obedience to the will of God. They may recognize that the ministry they do is not their own personal project but Christ's, in which he continues to carry out his eternal mission of reforming and transforming human beings in his own image and likeness. This area of the research will seek to examine the theological assumption that Christian ministry is the participation in the continuous formation, reformation, and transformation of people by Christ inn his own image – *donec Christus in vobis formabitur* (Gal 4:19).

From the SFHF: The Radical Trinitarian Formation Mystery

In Division One of this research, we discussed at some length the Divine Formation Mystery, or the Radical Mystery of Formation – God.[59] Formation theory asserts that this Mystery is "revealed as the Holy Trinity of Father, Son, and Spirit,[60] and calls it the *Eternal Formation Event*. In a glossary entry in Studies, van Kaam defines it as "The Eternal Trinitarian Formation Event in which the Father forms the unique personhood of the Son, and the Father and the Son form the unique personhood of the Holy Spirit."[61] It is the likeness of this *Eternal Radical Trinitarian Mystery of Formation* which the SFHF asserts our life-form to be only a uniquely limited, but true participation in. For as van Kaam affirms, "The Christian form tradition implies that we are called beyond this limited form to parti-

---

[59] Confer chapter three.
[60] Adrian van Kaam, *Formation Guide for Becoming Spiritually Mature*, 36.
[61] Adrian van Kaam, "Glossary," Studies I (Feb. 1980), 141.

cipate in the 'eternal formation event' that is the mystery of the Trinity, emanating from the dark and formless divinity."[62]

Van Kaam's designation of God as the Divine or Radical Forming Mystery in Formation Science comes from his discovery that God is the unfathomable mystery in which all of creation exists. He asserts that it is from this unfathomable mystery that all of creation is sourced and formed. This fully concords with what Paul said to the Areopagites in Athens in his discourse to them. Towards the end, Paul concludes his argument for the existence of the God he was speaking to them about, who, he told them, is the origin and source of everything: "In him we live and move and have our being" Acts 17:28 – NRSV). It is also this God, in Paul's discourse, which formation theory designates as the Eternal Radical and Trinitarian Formation Mystery.

From the SFHF: Basic Christian Character Dispositions

Discussing character formation rooted in the transcosmic mystery, van Kaam writes: "Our character form consists of a more-or-less integrated set of dispositions that define our enduring basic stands in our formation field, whether they are consonant or dissonant."[63] As he further says concerning our character, which he affirms is partly given and partly acquired:

> The basic disposition of a consonant or virtuous character is one that inclines us to disclose and implement our founding life form or, dynamically speaking, our unique-communal life call. This sustaining ground is symbolized for us by our faith and formation traditions. The founding life form in our unique-communal expression, image, or

---

[62] Adrian van Kaam, *Fundamental Formation*, opus cit., 212.
[63] Van Kaam, Transcendent Formation, (opus cit.), 111.

mirror of the transcosmic formation mystery. Most deeply we *are* that unique image.[64]

Hence, it becomes clear that a basic consonant character disposition in the SFHF is what Christian tradition calls virtue. As Adrian van Kaam once more holds in his Christian articulation of consonant character dispositions and directives:

> The Christian formation tradition provides us with graced directives and dispositions or virtues for a transcendent formation increasingly consonant with the Gospel. Some of these are ultimate, others are proximate directives and character dispositions. Evangelical formation directives and dispositions or virtues do not invalidate truly consonant, albeit analogous, pre-Christian formation directives and dispositions. They deepen and elevate them by Christian articulation. A Christian formation directive or corresponding virtue or character disposition elevates a pre-Christian consonant formation directive.[65]

Now we shall discuss two of such basic Christian character dispositions, the virtues of "humility" and "obedience" in the *Writings* and *Rules* of Francis of Assisi and Benedict of Nursia, respectively.

---

[64] Ibid., 113.

[65] Adrian van Kaam, Preliminary Glossary of Christian Articulation of Formation Science (PGCA), TS, Epiphany Association, Pittsburgh, PA., 73. In chapter three, we discussed, under the Christ-Form, the basic Christian character as "modelled after the heart or character of Christ."

Chapter 8: Understanding Christian Ministry

Saint Francis of Assisi: The Virtue of Humility

In our discussions on *The Imitation of Christ*, by Thomas À Kempis, we came to the conclusion that its primary objective was to guide people to intimate relationship with God through the following of the example of Christ made manifest in his basic character dispositions towards the Father. The most popular known saint today, at least since the Middle Ages, who seems to have empirically imitated Christ the closest, is Saint Francis of Assisi. As Regis Armstrong and Ignatius Brady tell us in their introduction of their book entitled *Francis and Clare,* "the life of the Poor Man of Assisi is characterized best by his identification with the mysteries of Christ." Shortly after saying this, they add:[66]

> His biographers tell of his intense devotion to the mystery of the Eucharist, in which Francis saw the Lord of all creation assume poverty and humility each day so that all men and women might be reconciled with God and one another. The crucified Christ, however, absorbed the saint's attention to a great degree so that the last years of his life became caught up in the mystery of the Cross. On September 14, 1224, while Francis was immersed in a long period of prayer, he received the stigmata, which he carried until his death.[67]

It is while Francis was working, on February 24, 1208, in the Portiumcula near the Church of St. Matthias, that he overheard a sermon on the missionary discourse of Jesus to the Twelve from the tenth chapter of Matthew's Gospel. It struck him so deeply that it resulted in his characteristic following of Jesus in complete and utter poverty, which became his

---

[66] Regis J. Armstrong and Ignatius C. Brady, trans. & intro, *Francis and Clare: Complete Works* (New York: Paulist Press, 1982), 4.

[67] Ibid.,

central vision of the discipleship of Christ. From that time on, Francis unreservedly embraced "Lady Poverty" together with humility. It is these two virtues which he "saw the Lord of all creation assume each day" in the Mystery of the Eucharist.

For Francis, all the virtues seem to have value and are in imitation of Christ only when they are practiced in humility and, indeed, have humility as their soul. This is evident throughout his *Writings*. Thus, for instance, in his *admonitions*, commenting on the virtue of patience, he writes: "The servant of God cannot know how much patience and humility he has within himself as long as everything goes well with him."[68] Again, in his *Letter to the Faithful*, he says: "Let us then have charity and humility." And in his salutation of the virtues, he sees humility as essential in the practice of poverty.[69] If all the virtues are to be practiced with the Christian character disposition of humility, it is because, for Francis, humility is one of the basic character dispositions expressed most evidently in the Christ-Form. This is clear in his *Writings* and in *The Rules*. The hymn to the humility of Christ, into which he burst in a letter to the entire Order, makes evident this basic character disposition which he perceives so clearly and cherishes so deeply in the Christ-Form.[70]

Benedict of Nursia: Obedience to the Father

If Francis, in his discipleship of Christ, saw the value of all the virtues in terms of their relationship to humility which seemed for him to characterize most the Christ-Form, Benedict, who lived from 480 to 547,[71] discovered

---

[68] See Francis and Clare, opus cit. pp. 32 and 35.

[69] Opus cit. See pp. 69 and 151 respectively.

[70] Ibid., 58.

[71] Anthony C Meisel and M.L. del Mastro, trans. And intro, *The Rule of St. Benedict* (New York: Image, Doubleday, 1975), 25.

obedience as the key character disposition to be imitated in the Christ-Form. For him, Christ's absolute obedience to the Father is what characterized all the other character dispositions which could be perceived in him. It is important to remember that although The Rule of Benedict was clericalized in the Carolingian reform,[72] Benedict did not address it to hermits or clerics, but to lay people. He considered his Rule the most perfect instrument which would help them in their struggle to attain intimate relationship with God. He saw it as the best way by which laymen and women of his time – confused, worried, and hopelessly destitute[73] - could live best their committed discipleship of Jesus.

If Benedict therefore saw obedience as the basic character disposition by means of which the Disciples of Christ were to reach intimacy and eventual union with God, it is because he perceived in the Christ-Form absolute obedience to the Father, the basic character disposition by means of which Christ himself remained in intimate relationship and union with the Father. Hence, obedience became for Benedict the basic character disposition in Christ through the imitation of which people could attain intimate relationship and union with God.

Integrative Reflection

When the Christian minister of the primary formation event made the decision to abandon himself consonantly to God, he was incarnating in

---

[72] Gerald A. Arbuckle and David L. Fleming, eds., Religious Life: *Rebirth through Conversion* (New York: Alba House, 1990), 6.

[73] See Gerald A. Arbuckle and David L Fleming, opus cit., 6-9. The historical period in which Benedict lived is known as The Dark Ages. It is during this time that feudalism was rife in Europe, reducing most of the people to practical slavery and untold misery. It can be said to be the precedent to the Middle Ages proper, the period in which Francis of Assisi lived. See also Anthony Meisel and M.L. del Mastro, opus cit., 25-39.

himself the formative directives which he had so appreciatively discerned and appraised in the life-form of St. Aloysius. These life form directives which were inherent in St. Aloysius were Christ-Form directives with which he had been inspired, especially through contemplation of the basic character dispositions of the Christ-Form expressed in the Holy Eucharist, the Passion, and the Crucifixion, as we have observed earlier. Hence, when the Christian minister in our original formation event incarnates in his own life-form such life directives from St. Aloysius, he is inspired with, and incarnates in his basic character disposition the Christ-Form expressed through the life-form of the saint.

For St. Aloysius to be able to abandon himself to the Radical Trinitarian Formation Mystery – God – he had to possess the basic Christian character dispositions of humility and obedience. Without a certain degree of the humility which Christ so abundantly manifested in becoming human and further giving himself to us as food and drink in the Holy Eucharist, Aloysius, who was an aristocrat and heir to his father as Marquis of Castiglione della Stiviere in Lombardy, would never have submitted himself to any authority of the degree and eagerness as he did. His biographers observe the following:

> Amongst the many heroic virtues which he was enabled to practice with more consummate perfection in religion may be noticed his humility and his exactness. We have seen him in the world rejecting and even abhorring all the distinctions of his rank, and, as much as possible in his condition, choosing the lowest place, the meanest dress, the plainest fare.[74]

Concerning the consonant character disposition of obedience of St. Aloysius, it will be further enlightening to quote more extensively the com-

---

[74] *The Life of St. Aloysius Gonzaga* (opus cit.), 164.

ments of his biographers on it. It is indeed a paradox considering his noble birth:

> Moreover, what he now did was no longer by the movement of his own free election, but was performed simply in virtue of obedience; and unreflecting observers might therefore judge that his actions had lost something of their grandeur, and something also of their merit, by submission to direction, and that Brother Aloysius was not so marvelous a prodigy of grace in the Company as was the Prince Aluigi in the paternal castle. But a slight consideration will suggest the immense increase of perfection and the merit which this very submission of obedience conferred, for we all know, however apt we may be practically to forget it, that it is not the matter of a work which gives it its value in the eyes of God, not even the energy with which it is performed: it's worth wholly comes from its being done for God and in God; so that not only is the end supernatural, but the motives from which it springs and the spirit in which it is carried out remain equally so. But it is much harder to exclude self from intermeddling when the act is one of our own choosing; the humility inseparable from true obedience embalms our good deeds, and excludes the secret corrupting influence of self-love; not to speak of the fresh merit imparted by the exercise of an additional virtue, and one of such intrinsic excellence that of Christ it is emphatically said He was "obedient;" summing up in that one word the transcendent merit of His sacrifice. Certainly in the humble and docile Lewis we at no time find a trace of self-love, yet his strong desire to be placed under obedience shows the estimation in which he held it, and the profit which he hoped to derive from it.[75]

---

[75] Ibid., 163-4.

Saint Aloysius' heroic practice of these basic consonant character dispositions, inspired in him through the Christ-Form, was not only admired by so many, including his superiors in and out of his community, but it inspired all around him to incarnate the same Christian character dispositions in themselves. As we learnt earlier from the period of his illness leading to his death, two of his relatives, the Cardinal della Rovere and the Cardinal Scipione Gonzaga, always went to visit him and would not be persuaded to go less often because of the edification they always received from him.[76] Thus, for example, during one of such visits Saint Aloysius told the Cardinal Scipione Gonzaga of how much he, Aloysius, felt indebted to him. At this, the Cardinal began to weep, protested, and spoke of how much he rather was to the saint. The saint's biographers record the Cardinal's response thus: "despite the difference of age, it was he who recognised in Aloysius a *father* and *spiritual master*, on account of the great profit and consolation he had always derived from his words and example."[77]

This seemed to be what happened to the minister of our primary formation event after the inspiration he received and his subsequent appraisal of the Christian character dispositions in Saint Aloysius' life-form. He did not only affirm these life directives, but also incarnated them in his own life-form. This renewed in him his zeal and dedication as a Christian minister. And, in this respect, he became an encouraging example for others, who desired to attain more intimate relationship and union with God, to imitate.

---

[76] Ibid., 294.
[77] Ibid.

OBSTACLES TO, AND FACILITATING CONDITIONS FOR THE FORMATION OF CHRISTIAN MINISTERS

There are several potential obstacles to consonant formation and reformation of the human form of life on the segmental level of Christian ministers in this Coformant. However, we would like to point out one principal obstacle here which could have much ramification. This is the ambition which Christian ministers may have to make of their ministry their own personal project in life. This personalization of the ministry makes them functionalistically willful and transcendently blind. They become unable to perceive that the success of the ministry they are doing does not depend on them. And they are blind to the need to humbly follow the directions of the One to whom the ministry belongs by mission from all eternity.

Facilitating conditions for consonant formation and transformation on this level are several. One of the most obvious of such conditions is the concrete example of saintly Christian ministers such as St. Aloysius Gonzaga who, in their humble obedience to God's will, perceive even conflicted situations in their current life-forms, not as contrary to, but rather as essential part of the ministry to which they have been called. Above all, another such condition is the model of humility before and obedience to the Father which the Christ-Form is, especially to Christian ministers. It may proffer the most facilitating condition for the consonant formation of the Christian ministers, as it enables them to abandon themselves completely to God in the reality of his omnipotent care.

TRANSITION TO DIVISION THREE

The investigations in Division Two sought to examine the Inbreaking form directives from tradition simultaneously in the four horizons of human presence. It focused on the "letting go" of the resistance of subjects and opening up of their intrasphere when formatively questioned in their form tradition. Thus, it explored the roles of memory and imagination in the appraisal of directives coming from the form tradition of subjects and also examined the beginning of appreciative abandonment of themselves to the Radical Mystery of all Formation.

Thus on the universal level, the research sought to explore and illumine the dynamics contained in the Inbreaking directives through the help of formative questioning; on the foundational religious level, it concentrated on the discernment of Inbreaking religious faith directives; on the Christian horizon, it examined how contemplation helps Christians to discover and apply these directives in their lives; and on the segmental horizon, it investigated the authentic understanding of Christian ministry, which the Inbreaking directives from tradition made possible. This represents, in the four horizons, a definitive and consonant shift which subjects could make towards the fullness of their formation.

On all the four levels of human presence under study here, Division Three of our research intends to focus on this self-abandoning of subjects to the Radical Mystery of Formation, as the process of self-abandonment grows, deepens, and becomes fuller. It will seek to examine the dynamics of a more complete self-abandonment to the Mystery and will study the empirical manifestations of these dynamics which may lead subjects towards the fullness of ***formative healing.***

DIVISION THREE

SELF-ABANDONMENT TO THE MYSTERY AS FULNESS OF FORMATIVE HEALING

INTRODUCTION

RESEARCH ON THE STATEMENT OF THE BASIC FORMATION QUESTION

Although people who are inflicted with a life-threatening illness and impending death may become, formatively speaking, impotent, they may be able to be positively influenced by a narrative from their faith and formation tradition. After consonantly and appreciatively appraising directives from the narrative in question, they may abandon themselves to the Radical Mystery of Formation and make a shift from their previously dissonant current form of life to one that is more congenial with their FLF. Although such people may remain gravely ill, and still threatened by imminent death, they may experience in themselves a profound feeling of being formatively healed as they abandon themselves to the Mystery.

The basic formation task to be carried out in this division is to shed light on how the dynamics of self-abandonment to the Mystery, which lead people to the fullness of formative healing, may become empirically manifest, and so, become observable. Just as in the two preceding divisions, this formation question will be studied simultaneously in the four horizons of the human presence.

ARTICULATION OF COFORMANT THREE

The third Coformant of the initial formation event is articulated in this way on the four levels of human presence of the Division:

1) **Universal Human Presence**: As subjects transcend their vital-functional dissonance, they may now abandon themselves more fully to

the Mystery, become grateful, and seek more reformation of their dissonant dispositions. While still feeling peaceful, they may also desire reconciliation with others.

2) **Foundational Religious Presence**: As religious subjects overcome their self-seeking weakness and feel more purified, they may receive greater inspiration to abandon themselves more completely to the Divine Mystery – God. They may also feel grateful to God and their ancestors. And in their greater self-abandonment, may humbly desire to attach themselves more faithfully to God in deep peace and in reconciliation with others.

3) **Foundational Christian Presence**: Christians who surrender their prideful willfulness may become inspired and drawn by grace to submit themselves more humbly to God. They may become appreciative of all the love they receive and in humility and meekness may seek Christian perfection in obedience to the will of God, even if that includes death.

4) **Segmental Presence of Christian Ministers**: When Christian ministers who have submitted themselves to the will of God desire ardently to overcome their functionalistic zeal and subsequent frustration in the fear of imminent disruption of their ministry, they may be inspired and drawn by grace to greater self-abandonment to the will of God. They may feel grateful, and with a transformed sense of their ministry, experience more congenially, in meekness and greater fidelity to God's will, their unique-communal call to follow Christ in their vocation to Christian leadership.

CHAPTER NINE

MOVEMENT TOWARDS A MORE COMPLETE SELF-ABANDONMENT TO THE MYSTERY

INTRODUCTION

In this chapter, we will research on the level of foundational human presence the movement towards fuller self-abandonment to the Mystery manifested in Coformant Three of the initial formation event. The Coformant is articulated in these terms:

> As subjects transcend their vital-functional dissonance, they may now abandon themselves more fully to the Mystery, become grateful, and seek more reformation of their dissonant dispositions. While still feeling peaceful, they may also desire formative reconciliation with others.

The investigation in this Coformant will be carried out in two remote foundational statements which will be drawn from it. The first statement will study the transcending of *vital-functional dissonance as subjects abandon themselves to the transcendent Mystery – incarnating such self-abandonment*. Then, in the second statement, it will examine the *inner peace and the desire for reconciliation with others* which this self-abandonment to God will have inspired.

PART ONE

MOVEMENT TOWARDS A MORE COMPLETE SELF-ABANDONMENT TO THE MYSTERY

The first part of this chapter will investigate the following remote foundational statement:

Subjects who transcend their vital-functional dissonance may more fully abandon themselves to the Mystery, become grateful, and seek further reformation of their dispositions.

The elucidation of this foundational statement is carried out under two sections – A and B. Section A will investigate *the transcending of the vital-functional dissonance* while Section B will study the *ongoing reformation of dispositions* which take place *through increasing self-abandonment to the Mystery of Formation*.

SECTION A: TRANSCENDING VITAL-FUNCTIONAL DISSONANCE

In willingly abandoning himself to the Mystery, the subject apprehends a change in himself. He no longer feels the depression under which he was until then, nor does he feel any more anger and resentment towards anyone. The fear of death which preoccupied him has also disappeared. The focus of investigation in this proximate area of research will be to identify the dynamics by means of which the subject transcends his vital-functional dissonance.

Chapter 9: Movement Towards a More Complete Self-Abandonment

From the SFHF: Incarnational Sources of the Empirical Life Formation

In the original formation event, it is observed that, as the subject appreciatively abandoned himself to God, he began to feel the recession of his anger and other dissonant dispositions associated with it. In its place is welling up in him sentiments of gratitude towards God and all the caregivers in the health facility. It is further observed that he also began at this point to feel yet more deeply the peace which he initially experienced at the moment he first abandoned himself to the Radical Mystery. In the face of such sudden experiences going on within the subject, the following question arises: From where do all these empirically-experiential sentiments – such as gratitude and peace – come?

The response to this question seems to lie, at least partly, in the integrational structures of the foundational life-form of the person,[1] but more especially in what van Kaam calls *the five incarnational sources of empirical life formation*. After his discussion about the structural effects of human formation in his summary of the theory of foundational formation, van Kaam underlines the transcendent as the source of empirical life formation.[2] Not only is transcendence the ultimate source of formation potency in the human being,[3] but through its primary formative centres – mind and will – the FLF of the person is able to empirically manifest the consonant unfolding of itself; i.e. it makes observable the formation it has effected in the embodied spirit. This empirical manifestation is done through **incarnation** of the formation received, thereby making empirically

---

[1] See chapter one; under "The human formation field."
[2] *Fundamental Formation*, opus cit., 250-2.
[3] See chapter one, under "Transcendent Form Potency."

observable in the four integrational life forms – the core, current, apparent, and actual[4] - the growth in formation.

This formation which becomes thus incarnated, and so observable in the person, has as its sources the primary transcendent powers of formation, the mind or intelligence and the will. But besides these two primary transcendent centres of the human formation, such incarnated formation in the person can also be attributed to the three secondary or auxiliary powers of formation as its other sources: the formative memory, imagination, and anticipation.[5] Hence, discussing the sources of empirical life formation, van Kaam lists all five – the two primary and the three secondary or auxiliary sources – as incarnational. As he identifies them and explains: We speak of incarnational sources because they assist the implementation of transcendent ideals in daily life. The incarnational sources are functional formative intelligence, will, memory, imagination, and anticipation."[6] After this statement, van Kaam goes on to describe the role each plays as source of the formational incarnation of the ideals or form directives in the person.

From the SFHF: Transcendent and Functional Volition

We pointed out above what the incarnational sources of the empirical life form are. Now we want to explore, in the SFHF, what *transcendent and functional volition* may mean. In a chapter on *Appraisal and Formative Striving*, van Kaam speaks of *transcendent willing* and *functional willing* as, respectively, primary and secondary kinds of *willing*. After affirming the necessity of both for the formation of concrete spiritual dispositions, he says this of the *transcendent willing*:

---

[4] For a detailed discussion on the four integrational life forms, see *Fundamental Formation*, 253-61.

[5] See chapter two.

[6] *Fundamental Formation*, opus cit., 252.

Chapter 9: Movement Towards a More Complete Self-Abandonment

At times we refer to the first kind as receptive or appreciative volition: *receptive*, because it is an answer to inspirations and aspirations that the will receives from the power of transcendent appraisal; *appreciative*, because it is an affirmation by the will in appreciation of a spiritual form directive and the dispositions it implies. Such form directives and dispositions are disclosed by the appreciative spirit to us as willing persons.

Adrian van Kaam then goes on to describe *functional willing* in these terms:

Functional volition is sometimes called executive, or managing, willing by Formation Science: executive, because we will the execution of concrete acts that engender in our life the dispositions disclosed to us by the appraising mind and the transcendent appreciative will; managing, because the functional will manages concretely the acts and dispositions that form our daily life in the unique and communal image of the Mystery we are called to be.[7]

With this explanation, it seems evident that both kinds of volition – *transcendent* as well as *functional* – are indeed indispensable for the consonant completion of the appraisal process although *transcendent willing* is primary and essential for consonant formation.[8] Incarnation of the form directives or dispositions, which completes the consonant form reception in the appraisal process, cannot take place without a functional willing of these directives. Hence, transcendent volition alone is not sufficient for formation to be observed as having taken place. Does *wish fulfilment*, according to Freud, mean the same as any of these two? And what does Kushner mean when he says that *God leaves us room to be human*? We shall briefly discuss these two questions in the following paragraphs.

---

[7] *Human Formation*, opus cit., 101.

[8] See chapter four.

Sigmund Freud: The Three Divisions of the Adult Mind and the Sources of Reflex Action and Wish-fulfilment

In Freud's theory of personality, the mind of the mature adult has what we may call three components. These are the *id*, the *ego*, and the **superego**.[9] While Freud defines the *ego* as "[t]he executive of the personality whose job it is to satisfy the needs of both the *id* and the **superego** by engaging in appropriate environmental activities,"[10] and the **superego** as "[t]he moral component of the personality that has two parts: the conscience and the ego ideal,"[11] he defines the *id* as "[t]he component of the personality that is completely unconscious and contains all the instincts."[12] Because of its instincts, the *id* compartment is regarded as the animal part of the human personality, which is governed by Freud's famous *libido* – the pleasure principle.

According to Freud, the id has two ways by which it may satisfy our bodily needs. These ways are the *reflex action* and the *wish fulfilment*. For Freud, the *reflex action* of the id is "the automatic reflexive response" of a person which aims to remove a source of irritation; for example, blinking one's eye to remove something from it. On the other hand, he considers *wish fulfilment* as "the conjuring up of an image of an object or event" which

---

[9] See any of the following works of Freud: *The Psychology of Everyday Life* (New York: Norton, 1901); *Civilization and its Discontents* (New York: Norton, 1930); *The Future of an Illusion* (New York: Norton, 1927), and especially *The Interpretation of Dreams* (New York: Norton, 1900). Freud himself, and many others, consider the latter as his most important work. See also Anna Freud's work, *The Ego and the Mechanisms of Defense* (New York: International Universities Press, 1936).

[10] See B.R. Hergenhahn, *An Introduction to Theories of Personality*, 3rd ed. (Englewood Cliffs, New Jersey: Prentice Hall, 1990), 54.

[11] Ibid., 56.

[12] Ibid., 54.

has to power to satisfy a biologic need; for instance, the hungry person who thinks of food-related objects.[13]

While the *id* is incapable of distinguishing between its images and the external reality, the *ego* eventually "develops and attempts to match the images of the *id* with objects and events in the real world." But as even these two together are still unable to explain moral processes in the individual person in Freud's anthropology, he introduces the concept of the *superego* which, he explains, "develops from the internalized patterns of reward and punishment that the young child experiences."[14] In this way, these three divisions of the mature adult mind would become the sources responsible for all human actions and behaviour, according to Freud's theory. Within the context of such anthropology, can one ever be able to speak of transcendence in one's *reflex actions* or *wish fulfilment*? The response seems to lie evidently in the negative.

Harold S. Kushner: "God Leaves Us Room to be Human"

In his national bestseller, 'When Bad Things Happen to Good People,' Kushner, a rabbi, contends that God leaves us humans to be truly human. In the fifth chapter of his book, Kushner, after evoking what Genesis (1-3) says concerning creation and the fall, to support his claim that "One of the most important things that any religion can teach us is what it means to be human," goes on to repeat the traditional interpretation of this story in Genesis, and then to declare:

I think there is more to the story than a simple case of disobeying God and being punished for it. My interpretation may be very different from

---

[13] Ibid., 29; See also pp. 55 and 56 where Hergenhahn summarizes respectively the two constructs of Freud.

[14] Ibid., 29-31.

the ones you have grown up with, but I think it makes sense and fits the biblical context. I think the story is about the difference between being human and being an animal, and the key to understanding it is the fact that the "forbidden" tree is called the Tree of the Knowledge of Good and Evil.[15]

He then goes on to apply his own hermeneutics to the Genesis story of creation and the fall, and he comes to the conclusion that Adam and Eve became human in the process which led to their fall – the act of their freedom in choosing:

> This is what it means to be human "in the image of God." It means being free to make choices instead of doing whatever our instincts would tell us to do. It means knowing that some choices are good, and others are bad, and it is our job to know the difference. "Behold, I have set before you the path of good and the path of evil, the way of life and the way of death. Choose life (Dt 30: 19."

As Kushner comments on what he has just said, "That could not be said to any other living creature except Man, for no other creature is free to choose."[16] This freedom to choose between good and evil, the power of which actually makes us human, is one of the essential characters of every human being. In his response to the question of whether we could say that someone like Hitler *chose* to be destructive, or say that it is his historical background that made him the person he was, Kushner is very clear:

---

[15] Harold S. Kushner, *When Bad Things Happen to Good People* (New York: Schocken Books, Inc. 1981), 74-5.

[16] Harold S. Kushner, *opus cit.*, 79.

Chapter 9: Movement Towards a More Complete Self-Abandonment

I can only say that the cornerstone of my religious outlook is the belief that human beings are free to choose the direction their life will take. Granted, some children are born with physical or mental capacities which limit their freedom of choice. Not everyone can choose to be an opera singer, a surgeon, or a professional athlete. Granted further that some parents mishandle their children badly, that accidental events – wars, illness – traumatize children so badly that they may not be able to do something they would otherwise be qualified for, and that some people are so addicted to habits that it is hard to speak to them as being free. But I will insist that every adult, no matter how unfortunate a childhood he had or how habit-ridden he may be, is free to make choices about his life.[17]

With such insights as are raised in this anthropology, Kushner's assertion, that *God leaves us room to be human*, becomes purposeful in the light of formation theory. The Radical Mystery indeed leaves us room to transcend the animal part of our being, with all its vital-functional dissonance, and to freely choose the image and likeness of God in which he created us. These insights from the above discussions prepares us now to examine, in Section **B**, how increasing self-abandonment to the Mystery may lead to further reformation of dispositions.

SECTION B: ONGOING REFORMATION OF DISPOSITIONS THROUGH GREATER SELF-ABANDONMENT

As the subject abandons himself more appreciatively to and trust more deeply the Mystery, he feels gratitude towards the same Mystery. At the same time, he also becomes more regretful of his earlier deformative disposition of depression and anger, and functionalistic willfulness. This

---

[17] Ibid., 83.

increase of self-abandonment to the Mystery reveals in the subject the primordial disposition of awe for the Mystery. This proximate area of research proposes to study disposition reformation in relation to increasing abandonment to the Mystery.

From the SFHF: Disposition Reformation and Transcendent Appraisal

In chapter two of the current research, we discussed at some length the nature of the disposition of awe. As we quoted van Kaam's definition, it is perceived as a mysterious force in the core of our being; a principle of consonance and of unity.[18] Here we want to investigate how, being already in a disposition of awe before the Mystery to whom one has begun to abandon oneself, one may keep on reforming one's dispositions.

Discussing disposition reformation and transcendent appraisal, van Kaam makes it unequivocally clear that, although both functional and transcendent appraisals are necessary for disposition reformation, transcendent appraisal is primary.[19] Functional appraisal of our dispositions may be an excellent way by which we may functionally assess the concrete implications of our inner directives and acts. But alone and as an exclusive approach in the appraisal process, it can never bring such a process to a consonant end. As van Kaam warns in formation theory, after pointing out its irreplaceable role in the appraisal process:

> Functional appraisal becomes destructive, however, if it excludes a priori any transcendent appraisal. For it implies that we do not acknowledge the primary importance of the transcendent meanings, life direc-

---

[18] See chapter two.
[19] See *Human Formation*, 96-7.

tives, and dispositions that may have something to tell us in regard to our decisions.[20]

If functional appraisal can be exclusive, divisive, and thus destructive, transcendent appraisal not only completes and directs it in the appraisal process, but operates unitedly, as it attunes and guides us towards the mysterious unity of our life. All of this is what van Kaam implies in his succinct and analytic description which he gives of transcendent appraisal:

> Appraisal is transcendent when it enables us to go beyond the manifold dispositions [that] rise from our pulsations, and ambitions. It pushes us beyond the limited meanings of childhood traumas, sensitivities, faults, and projects that give rise to dissonant dispositions. In and beyond all of these, it integrates our lives contextually in the whole of the formation field and its all-pervading source. It brings us in touch with our primordial form of life, which as such is always open to realization in consonant dispositions. It unites us with the primordial movement of our transcendent will, which strives spontaneously after the fully consonant life-form. It is this life-form that leads to the fullness of peace and joy in participation with others in the Mystery.[21]

This understanding of transcendent appraisal makes it evident that consonant disposition reformation can never be accomplished in a person without it.[22] For although functional appraisal in view of the reformation of

---

[20] Ibid., 95.

[21] Ibid., 96.

[22] For concrete detailed actual reformation of directives and dispositions (leading to transformation), see Adrian van Kaam, *Human Formation*, 93-5; see also *Formation of the Human Heart*, 338-41, 346, and 348. In *Transcendence Therapy*, van Kaam discloses how form traditions, twisted by family, may be

dispositions has its purpose and so is necessary, it is transcendent appraisal which completes the process and discloses our founding life form in its primordial form of unity with the Mystery. This therefore makes it evident that the person who is in a disposition of awe – as he has already begun to abandon himself to the Mystery – will perceive more readily and be drawn more compellingly to the reformation of any dissonance and deformity in dispositions that may still be in the way of his growing desire for greater self-abandonment to the Mystery. Disposition reformation at this level is what can eventually lead a person to **transformation** and is what van Kaam intuits and even asserts, as he discusses the inner repletion sessions of eroded social presence: "We must resign ourselves (again in the sense of the reassignment of meaning) to a life readiness for patient reformation of deformed directives and dispositions in the hope that we may be led by the Formation Mystery to a deeper, more enduring transformation."[23]

The above paragraphs, as intended, have disclosed and made clear to us as possible, the mutual *ongoing fostering of formation*[24] between self-abandonment to the Mystery and disposition reformation through transcendent appraisal. We now want to examine briefly, under a light which is different from that of formation theory, the complementarity of the functional and the transcendent in the appraisal and reformation of form directives and dispositions. The insights in this different light seem to be proffered in Viktor E Frankl's concept of *determinism* and *humanism*.

---

reformed. He suggests: "In the beginning of the reformation process, one may need idealized figures that model, if not one's unique-communal life call, then at least fidelity to that call as lived in the light of one's chosen, basic tradition (109)."

[23] Adrian van Kaam, *Formation of the Human Heart*, opus cit., 338.

[24] See "the Principle of Ongoing Formation" in 21-22, under "Dialogue with the Principles of Formation Science."

Chapter 9: Movement Towards a More Complete Self-Abandonment

Viktor E. Frankl: Determinism and Humanism

In a lecture which he delivered at the occasion of the 600th anniversary of his alma mater, the University of Vienna, in 1968, Viktor Frankl spoke on the two perennial problems of the human person which, he is convinced, cannot be solved. He identified the two issues as "the problem of body and mind, and the problem of free choice." In other words, the unsolvable problem comes down to determinism versus indeterminism.[25] Although Viktor Frankl does not believe that the two problems can ever be solved, he is, nevertheless, convinced of the possibility of at least identifying the reason why they cannot be solved. This is the task he set out to accomplish in his article, *"Determinism and Humanism."*

After presenting an analogy of the seeming contradictions of different cross sections of the same cylinder to demonstrate the different ways in which individual sciences may portray the same reality, Frankl summarizes thus the results of the two main different depictions of the human being by individual sciences:

> He [the human being] too, is sometimes portrayed as if he were merely a closed system within which cause-effect relations are operant such as conditioned or unconditioned reflexes, conditioning processes or responses to stimuli. On the [other] hand, being human is profoundly characterized as being open to the world, as Max Scheler, Arnold Gehlen and Adolf Portmann have shown. Or, as Martin Heidegger has said, being human is "being in the world."[26]

He then goes on to describe what he himself considers to be the undergirding principle of the human being:

---

[25] Viktor E. Frankl, "Determinism and Humanism," *Humanitas* VII (1971): 23.
[26] Ibid., 25.

What I have called the self-transcendence of existence denotes the fundamental fact that human being means relating to something, or someone, other than oneself, be it a meaning to fulfill, or human beings to encounter. And *existence* falters and collapses unless this self-transcendence quality is lived out.[27]

Frankl points out that this capacity of existence – the human being – to transcend itself, to be open to something or someone other than the self, is touched by one cross section of the same reality – existence – and missed by another. He considers this to be understandable because, paradoxical as it may seem, *closedness* and openness, he claims, have become compatible.

In the *closedness* of the human being, which is the portrayal of *existence* as seen in its biological-psychological cross-section, Frankl perceives the presence of **determinism**. However, thanks to the *openness* of the same existence, he perceives *freedom* depicted in its nooloical – spiritual, intellectual – dimension. It is in the latter perception of the human being, his or her *freedom*, that Frankl identifies the **humanism** of *existence*. Hence, he can affirm that, while within the problem of determinism there is "unity in spite of diversity." In the problem of humanism there is "freedom in spite of determinism."[28]

Frankl honestly asserts the finitude of human freedom. But he also states emphatically that, although the human being may not be free from conditions, he or she remains, nevertheless, free to take a stand to them. As he writes, "The conditions do not completely condition him. For within limits it is up to him whether or not he succumbs and surrenders to the conditions. He may as easily rise above them and by so doing open up and enter the human dimension."[29] Frankl further uses his concrete experience in the

---

[27] Ibid.
[28] Ibid.
[29] Ibid., 25-6.

concentration camps, of which he had been in four, to argue against Freud's assumption that, putting a number of people under the same condition would blur all individual differences. For Frankl's experience in the concentration camps demonstrates that the reverse is true: "In concentration camps," he attests, "people become more diverse. The beast was unmasked – and so was the saint. The hunger – [the condition] – was the same but people were different."[30]

In the rest of the article, Frankl continues to consolidate the reasons why the problem in determinism and indeterminism or humanism of *existence* will remain unsolvable. However, the insights already offered here on the issue are many and relevant to this part of our research. They help us to understand that reformation of our dispositions in view self-transcendence must be ongoing, lest we *falter* and *collapse*. For our *humanism*, in this light, equips us with the potency for transcending our *determinism* in which is always present our vital-functional dissonance. This should lead us to an ever-greater apprehension of that, something other Than Our self to whom we may eventually entrust, with greater appreciative self-abandonment, the process of our growing ever more and more towards transformation and the fullness of our humanism.

Integrative Reflection

If the subject of our original formation event no longer felt the anger, depression, and the resentment which he experienced earlier in his conflicted situation, it becomes evident that all this is the result of his self-abandonment to the Mystery of Formation. Not only did these vital-functional dissonant dispositions recede from his current life-form, but in their place there welled up consonant dispositions.

---

[30] Ibid., 26.

When he followed the example of Aloysius' abandonment of himself to the Radical Mystery of formation, the subject became inspired to transcend these vital-functional deformative and dissonant dispositions which previously stood in his way to a similar abandonment of himself to the Mystery. Hence, thereafter, he was able to enjoy within himself the realities of no longer being depressed, no longer feeling resentment, and no longer feeling any anger against God and others. In fact, he felt grateful to God for the numerous manifestations of the unconditional he enjoyed, including the care that was being given him by others there in the health facility. As long as he remained immersed in the dissonance of his vital-functional disposetions and did not transcend them, he could not appreciatively apprehend all these consonant directives, which surrounded him in his everyday life, even in his life-threatening illness.

Therefore, transcending the vital-functional deformative dispositions, which manifested to a certain degree his life-sufficiency in his **willfulness**, did not only lead the subject to self-abandonment to the Radical Mystery. It also marked the beginning of the process of an ongoing reformation in which the disposition of self-abandonment to the formation Mystery in turn triggered in him the reformation of other dispositions. Hence, this becomes a mutual and reciprocal chain of an ongoing reformation of the dispositions of self-abandonment to the Mystery and other consonant dispositions in him, such as the disposition of gratitude. For as these dispositions become incarnated after having been appreciatively appraised, they become yet greater transcendent invitations, proffering still more compelling transcendent directives which have the power to lead them to further reformation of themselves and that of other dispositions, eventually leading to the transformation of the life-form of the subject.[31]

In *Cancer and Faith*, John Carmody underscores in a powerful way the spiraling realization which ought to be taking place within the bosom of the

---

[31] See paragraph *"The Formative Action Pattern"* above, xx.

Chapter 9: Movement Towards a More Complete Self-Abandonment

Church. In the 35th of his "Reflections on living with a Terminal Illness" which has led him to appraise appreciatively so many dispositions in his own life form, Carmody perceives vividly how the Church could be reformed. From his experience in the reformation of his own life dispositions and directives in the wake of the dissonance caused by his terminal illness, he reflects, with regard to the reformation of the Church, in these terms:

> It is easy to criticize the Church and terribly hard to reform it. We Christians are the Church, all of us believers, and we are a stiff-necked people. Divided for centuries, we have come to love our divisions, thinking them necessary to our sense of ourselves. Who would we be, if we were not different from Baptists or Orthodox, if they were more like us than different? How would we remain the apple of God's eye if Buddhists and Muslims could be saved? The ecumenical movement stalled when Church leaders realized what consummating it would ask of them, but stalling struck man a responsive chord in the pews of the different denominations.

After making explicit these deformative dispositions which stand in the way of reformation of the Church in both leaders and their respective faithful, Carmody goes on to suggest where such needed reformation of the Church could begin and then spiral towards transformation:

> So, now, we have to ask again what it means to call ourselves "the people of God," what reforms that image imposes. The Church is always to be reformed, if Protestant theology is perceptive. The holiness of the Church come only from God – all human ordinances are imperfect. I have been most saddened by the unwillingness of Church leaders to cash

out the central theology of Christian faith so as to maximize the freedom of their people.[32]

If the Church has to reform and to spiral in this reformation to that perfection of unity in which it was founded and for which Christ prayed so earnestly (Jn 17: 20-23), its current deformative dispositions, made empirically manifest in its leaders and down to the faithful in the pews, will have to be reformed. This reformation can only come about, as Carmody's observation implies, through the transcending of the individual and personal interests which the leaders in particular are usually unwilling to relinquish. The individuals in the Church will have to reform their dissonant dispositions in this regard, and so, move towards the fullness of their transformation in "humanism."[33]

The transcendent directives which can make this reformation of the Church possible are especially the assumption that we are "the people of God." And the reality that "the holiness of the Church come only from God." If God would be truly and appreciatively appraised as the source of the holiness that should be embodied in the Church, this would lead to the incarnation of the holiness of the Church, making this manifest and, indeed, as the unique, universal, and Catholic. The dissonance of divisiveness would greatly recede, leading in its place a diversity in unity. But this will only be a reality in the Church when its individual members, especially its leaders, are able to transcend, like Carmody, their personal vital-functional dissonant dispositions. In so doing, they will abandon themselves to God who is the source of the holiness and the essence of the Church, which it should genuinely incarnate and make manifest to all.

---

[32] John Carmody, Opus cit., 87.
[33] See Viktor Frankl's concept of *humanism* above.

Chapter 9: Movement Towards a More Complete Self-Abandonment

Transition to Remote Foundational Statement Two

The research in Remote Foundational Statement One above focused on the transcending of vital-functional dissonance in relation to the increasing self-abandonment of the subject to the Mystery. It sought to demonstrate that the more subjects are able to transcend their vital-functional dissonance, the greater their self-abandonment to the Mystery becomes, and the more in turn they may transcend their vital-functional dissonance. This spiraling process, which results from the mutual relationship between transcending one's vital-functional dissonance and abandoning oneself to the Mystery, incarnates the relative formative dispositions in subjects. It is on the transformative core dispositions of *peace* and *reconciliation* that the research in the Second Remote Foundational Statement now intends to concentrate.

PART TWO

INNER PEACE AND THE DESIRE FOR RECONCILIATION WITH OTHERS

Our Second Remote Foundational Statement may be formulated in the following manner:

Subjects who feel peaceful in their self-abandonment to the Mystery may also seek formative reconciliation with others.

The elucidation of this remote foundational statement will be done in two sections. Section A will seek to give illumination for exploring the deeper peace in the appreciative self-abandonment of the subject to the Mystery, and Section B will study the disposition of reconciliation with others in the subject.

SECTION A: PEACE EMERGING FROM SELF-ABANDONMENT TO THE MYSTERY

Besides the awareness of the diminishing effects his deformative dispositions, and his feeling of gratitude towards God and others, the subject also feels a greater surge of peace and serenity pervading his entire being as if from an unquenchable source deep from within him. Also, an atmosphere of gentleness seems to surround him.

This proximate area of the research will concentrate on exploring the deeper peace which increases in the appreciative self-abandonment, of the subject, to the Mystery.

From the SFHF: Seeking Deeper Peace

The initial peace, which took hold of the subject of our primary formation event after he first appraised the life story of Aloysius, deepened in the spiraling reformation of his form dispositions. As he submits in the gush of his feeling of gratitude, "In this deep feeling of gratitude towards God, I feel deeply within me such peace as I have never felt at any moment during the two and one-half months I have been in the hospital." [34] He felt himself enveloped by a deeply peaceful and serene moment.

At the very beginning of chapter 28 of his initial manuscript of transcendent formation, Adrian van Kaam made the following declaration:

> Our longing for peace, poise, potency, wholeness, and happiness cannot be fulfilled by social security, vital pleasure, functional satisfaction or functional-transcendent excitements alone. Deep down we want more than that. Sooner or later we may experience that by themselves alone

---

[34] See narrative of formation event, Preface to this Book, viii-xii.

Chapter 9: Movement Towards a More Complete Self-Abandonment

they are never enough for us. This awakens us to our hidden desire to go beyond them to something more.[35]

Van Kaam makes this declaration about these dispositions for which we strive focally, prefocally, or infrafocally for the purpose of introducing the transcendent dynamic – the love-will of the Mystery – which is represented in us by this deepest desire and its striving force.[36] However, this also serves to point out that, as embodied spirits, our quest for and striving to attain these dispositions can always go only deeper and deeper. Although we shall never be able to attain the fullness of them in our human life form, we have the potency to always keep advancing, even if only *'ad infinitum'* towards that fullness.

After they have observed the illusive nature of genuine peace and inner tranquility, and the poor substitute which society presents and persuades us to accept, van Kaam and Muto in their book *The Power of Appreciation* present their readers with the nature of true peace.[37] The genuine peace which all human beings desire deeply in them and seek is infinitely deeper than what our consumer and pleasure-seeking society, supported by the mass-media, sells to us. This genuine peace has its source in the *More Than*. Hence, it is this peace, the source of which is the More Than, that deep down in us, we seek. We seek that lasting peace which is only possible with "steady attunement to the restlessness of our heart for the 'More Than.'"[38]

Describing and giving examples of how fallacious directives of pre-transcendent desires for self-fulfillment can bring depreciative effects and

---

[35] Adrian van Kaam, *Transcendent Formation, MS*, (Sixth volume of Formative Spirituality Series. Epiphany Association, Pittsburgh, 1994.

[36] Ibid.,

[37] Adrian van Kaam and Susan Muto, *The Power of Appreciation*, opus cit., 69.

[38] Ibid.

not genuine peace to us, van Kaam and Muto makes the following conclusion:

> Unless your attitude changes, depreciation, not peace-loving presence, is bound to guide your appraisal. You begin to see others only as potential threats. You become more tense and aggressive. You place yourself in a fight-or-flight posture. Your heart beats faster. Your power of appreciation grows dim. Your struggle to cope with the imagined threat of others keeps you on the defensive. Your overriding goal of self-protection results in bouts of rage, acrimony, and aggravation. You become irritable and hard to live with whenever things fail to go your way. You feel the slumbering tiger of resentment about to leap any time your anxious self-concern runs into resistance or contradiction.[39]

From the above insights, it is abundantly clear that true peace can only be attained through appreciative appraisal of events, even of depreciative emotions. Such appreciation will turn them into inspirations, thereby enabling the person to overcome greater obstacles to transcendence and the Mystery which is the very source of true peace. And the deeper the appreciation of such inspirations, the deeper the peace that one strives for.

From the SFHF: Gentleness and Presence to the Mystery

In the primordial disposition of the peace we have just discussed above, other core dispositions such as gratitude, serenity, tranquility, and gentleness come to the surface. Here, we would like to make one or two observations about the core disposition of gentleness in the light of Formation Science.

---

[39] Ibid., 70-1.

Chapter 9: Movement Towards a More Complete Self-Abandonment

As I sought to deepen my understanding of gentleness, I read the book by Adrian van Kaam entitled – *Spirituality and the Gentle Life*.[40] Afterwards, I found it a more daunting task to give a single comprehensive, and yet coherently satisfying definition. to the term gentleness. This is because I discovered that it is so embracing that it defies any one single such definition. To use an analogy: as a disposition, gentleness is like salt, the value of which becomes more evident and appreciative as it permeates food, preserving it and giving taste to it. So does the essentially valuable nature of gentleness manifest itself as it becomes the background from which we encounter others, listen to ourselves, and respond to our surroundings and events in our everyday life. However, in what van Kaam entitles "Listening and the Gentle Life," he describes gentleness in these terms:

> Gentleness makes me more aware of the spiritual dimension of life. It shows me the Origin beyond the manifest practical meanings of my everyday existence. It keeps me in touch with the Whole and Holy. Gentleness creates openness for the spiritual side of people, things, and events. In gentleness, the framework of practical and vital interpretations is not denied or destroyed; it only gains its rightful place in the eternal scheme of things.[41]

After he has linked the disposition of firmness to that of gentleness, without which, he claims, firmness deteriorates into severity and becomes a debilitating weakness, and thus he affirms: "The gentle disposition is a facilitating condition as well as a fruit of the consonant life." Then he declares in all certainty: "Gentleness is the royal road of presence to a

---

[40] Adrian van Kaam, *Spirituality and the Gentle Life* (Denville, NJ: Dimension Books, 1974).

[41] Ibid., 35.

mystery that cannot be compelled or controlled."[42] Later on, as he further elucidates this presence of gentleness to the Mystery, he underscores its transcendent nature, even though it can be regarded as one form of the incarnation in us of the primordial disposition of peace, the Source of which is the Radical Mystery. As he writes:

> Presence to the mystery is a most precious gift. It transcends our analytical modes of thought. In functional thinking we tend to isolate what we are pondering from the larger scene in which people, events, and things appear. This horizon is the whole of our formation field. This field itself points to a wider, as yet not fully known horizon out of which it consonantly emerges. This is the mystery of formation and its epiphanies.[43]

This is what the disposition of gentleness is. Hence, van Kaam could assert: "Gentle presence is a return to our original form of loving consonance with the mystery from which we emerge."[44] And such a disposition of gentle presence to the mystery also lends much meaning to van Kaam's claim when he says: "The disposition of gentleness is linked with that of abandonment. When we live in appreciative abandonment we can let go. We can give ourselves to the calming climate of a gentle life style."[45] With Mary Fidelis Tracy, we now want to find out how we can make meaning out of "abandoning the familiar for the unknown."

---

[42] Adrian van Kaam, *Formation of the Human Heart*, (opus cit.), 83.
[43] Ibid., 87.
[44] Ibid., 88.
[45] Ibid., 86.

Chapter 9: Movement Towards a More Complete Self-Abandonment

Mary Fidelis Tracy: "Abandoning the Familiar for the Unknown"

In her article, "Man Responding to Changes: The Movement to Mend the Disruption of the Familiar,"[46] Mary Fidelis Tracy systematically and succinctly outlined how, as follows:

Insofar as a man is able to move thoughtlessly through his taken-for-granted world, we refer to him as a common-sense self. Insofar as he is concerned in handling the world, we could refer to him and his world as an ego-mass. When referring to man as able to enjoy and live from the world, we call him a complaisant self.[47]

The problem arises when one finds oneself in a world with which one is no longer familiar. One becomes insecure, because one no longer feels oneself so embedded in this new and unknown world. The expertise in which one took pride, in the familiar world before, gives way to unskillfulness and even ignorance. Thus, one becomes altogether uncomfortable and shaken out of one's previous complacency.[48] Hence, this new and unfamiliar world becomes a challenge to the familiar way of living of the person.

This challenge is not just to one particular area of the lifestyle of the person, but to the total *existent being*. And if the person has to continue to live and function, growing towards his goals as a human being, he has to accept the change affecting his entire being as *existence*; i.e. he will have to adapt to his new world, befriending it and growing familiar with it. He will

---

[46] Mary Fidelis Tracy, "Man Responding to Changes: the Movement to Mend the Disruption of the Familiar." *Humanitas* X (1974), 171-88.

[47] Ibid., 172.

[48] Ibid., 174-5.

have to feel himself *belonging*[49] to this new world. And while *surrendering* thus himself in this relationship to his new world, he learns to master it. This process of surrendering and mastering one's new, and until then, unfamiliar world is what Tracy considers "*abandoning the familiar for the unknown;*" and she describes the nature of this movement in these terms:

> Involved in abandoning the familiar for the unknown is a risk that touches the existence of man. To be human is to be related and giving up the familiar modes of relating in order to allow new ones to develop involves the fear of unrelatedness or final dissolution. "Since growth requires breaking of old patterns, willingness 'to die' is a precondition of living." It is the security of being linked with all reality that gives man courage to face the insecurity of the new and to risk the loss of particular relatedness.[50]

There is self-consistency in all of this, as Tracy makes very clear. For in this way of *abandoning the familiar for the unknown*, I make manifest "my experience of being significantly related,"[51] able "to retain self-consistency and to move toward mastery and surrender when I say, 'I feel at home.'" She explains.

Before we reflect on the rich insights proffered here above in this section and ponder on their relevance to the subject of our initial formation event we have been investigating, we want to discuss the desire that such subjects may have, to reconcile themselves with others.

---

[49] Ibid, 179

[50] Ibid., 181. The text in quotation marks is taken from Andras Angyal's book: *Neurosis and Treatment*, eds. E. Harfmann and R.M. Jones (New York: John Wiley and Sons, 1965).

[51] Ibid., 188.

Chapter 9: Movement Towards a More Complete Self-Abandonment

SECTION B: DESIRE OF RECONCILING AS INTERSPHERIC EXPRESSION OF SELF-ABANDONMENT TO THE MYSTERY

As the subject abandons himself to the Mystery and feels more peaceful and serene within himself, he also becomes aware of the desire in him to make peace with others. This self-abandonment which leads him towards "at-one-ment" with – attunement to – the Mystery may further disclose the directive also to seek to be "at-one" with others. The investigation in this section will focus on the nature of the relationship between self-abandonment to the Mystery and striving for "at-one-ment" – reconciliation – with others in the interformative sphere.

From the SFHF: Epiphanies of the Mystery and Interformation

Universal Interformation or Cosmic Epiphany: In his discussion about the epiphanies of the Mystery of formation, Adrian van Kaam indicates universal interformation as one of the principal assumptions of Formation Science. As he writes:

> A central presupposition of the science of formation is the unity and interformation of all people, things and events, which share in some measure in the cosmic epiphany of the formation Mystery. This science insofar as it offers a universal synthesis of all foundational factors of human formation, draws much of its inspiration from the world view of modern physics, wherein new models and theories support a vision of a universe that is a web of interformative interactions.[52]

In the light of such description of this central presupposition of the SFHF, the unity in interformation of all people, things, and events which

---

[52] Adrian van Kaam, *Fundamental Formation*, 190.

share in the cosmic epiphany of the formation Mystery is, indeed, universal and all embracing.

Personal and Social Epiphany: However, universally interformative and all-embracing as the cosmic epiphany may be, *personal-social epiphany of the formation Mystery* manifests yet a by far closer participation in the mystery of formation. In this epiphany of the formation mystery, we who participate in the cosmic epiphany of the mystery, in virtue of our human spirit, transcend the cosmic and are an epiphany of the formation mystery in a most special way. After this consideration of the cosmic epiphany of the formation mystery, van Kaam, turning to what he identifies in formation theory as the transcosmic appearance of human life in the cosmos, affirms: "Human life, as spiritual, transcends the cosmic while participating in it. It spiritualizes its own participation in the macro- and microcosmic dance of the universe. Human life is spiritualizing, both as individual life and as the life of the human community.[53]

Transcosmic Epiphany: This transcosmic epiphany of the mystery that we are, both as individuals and as the human community, manifests to a very high degree, even in our embodied limitations, the unlimited and eternal *dynamic of living consonance* of the Mystery of formation. As the Mystery calls us to a transcosmic life beyond the mere cosmic, and beyond even a life socially determined, it draws us in *personal freedom and insightful apprehensions, appraisals, and options*, towards union with it in its own unconditioned *dynamic of loving consonance*. As van Kaam is led to affirm in the transcosmic life to which we are so transconsciously called and drawn by increased personal freedom and insightful awareness:

> Corresponding to this formative call is the inherent aspiration of the human person to become in some way like the mystery of formation

---

[53] Ibid., 208. Van Kaam quotes Albert Einstein in support of his orderly vision of the universe.

itself in a union of consonance or, what is the same, of love and likeness, for there is a likeness between the person formed in human consonance, or love, and the mystery forming him or her in both cosmic and transcosmic consonance of love.[54]

Considering the same reality with a Christian eye, van Kaam articulates: "The Christian form tradition implies that we are called beyond this limited form to participate in the 'eternal formation event' that is the Mystery of the Trinity, emanating from the dark and formless divinity." Several realities, which represent various ways in which the same basic transcendent reality of our call to *union of loving consonance* with the formation mystery expresses itself, become evident. This call to formation in this manner is a call to attunement – "at-one-ment" – in our current life form with the eternal dynamic of the loving consonance of the formation Mystery.[55] It is in response to this "at-one-ment" with the Mystery that our core form, endowed with its preformational freedom, can *move towards, away from, against, or with*[56] this goal to which we have been called uniquely and in common.

Interformative Relationship: In this light, therefore, our unique-communal call to transcend the mere cosmic and even social, presupposes preformational harmony and consonance which is a share in the eternal formation event, and which enables us to move uniquely and together, and towards union with the Mystery. In such consonance and harmony, we are able to relate also to one another interformatively besides the interformative relationship which we already have with the Mystery.[57] Hence, it becomes

---

[54] Ibid., 211-2.

[55] Ibid., 192.

[56] Confer Ibid., 254-5.

[57] Adrian van Kaam, discussing the possibility of personal interformative relationship between the Mystery and the human life form, explains *interformative*

consequential that, when the disposition of such harmony and consonance between individuals for the *attunement* of the eventual union with the Mystery is disturbed, the individual, in whom the dissonance exists and threatens this form disposition, would seek to restore it if his unique, but also communal, calling is to be consonantly responded to.

With the Freudian psychoanalyst, Karen Horney, we want to discuss the import of the movements towards, against, and away from people. This will allow us, on this universal level of human presence, to perceive more clearly what more the *movement with*, in Formation Science, could imply.

Karen Horney: Aspects of the Basic Conflict – Neurosis

In her book. *Our Inner Conflict*,[58] Karen Horney, who came to understand the significance of neurotic hopelessness, was thus led to discover the meaning of sadistic trends in people. These trends, which she asserts "represented an attempt at restitution through vicarious living, entered upon by a person who despaired of ever being himself,"[59] further led her to see evolved a theory of neurosis. She declares, after she has clearly observed that the need in a person for destructive exploitation was not some different neurotic trend: "Thus a theory of neurosis evolved whose dynamic center is a basic conflict between the attitudes of 'moving toward,' 'moving against,'

---

relationship thus: "We call the relationship interformative in the sense that the transcosmic mystery can allow the free acts of the human life form to influence its own transformative acts and modes of presence in relation to this life-form and its conditions." Later in the same discussion, he describes interformative relationship between persons as the effective encounter which "presupposes the acceptance of the unique intrasphere of the other with its preformative roots, without transgressing this line of personal uniqueness." See *Human Formation*, 242-3.

[58] Karen Horney, *Our Inner Conflict: A Constructive Theory of Neurosis* (New York: W.W. Norton & Company, 1945).

[59] Ibid., 18-9.

and 'moving away from' people."[60] After this declaration, Horney discusses and describes more systematically in chapter two this basic conflict which she identifies as the dynamic center of neurosis. Then in chapters three, four, and five, she discusses in detail the *movement towards*, *against* and *away from*, which together constitute the dynamic center of the basic conflict in the person in neurosis.

Explaining the attitude of the neurotic *moving towards people*, Horney writes: "When ***moving toward*** people he accepts his own helplessness, and to lean to them." As to what implied in the neurotic's ***movement against*** people, she asserts: "When he *moves against* people, he accepts and takes for granted the hostility around him, and determines consciously or unconsciously, to fight. He implicitly distrusts the feelings and intentions of others toward himself." And finally, Horney explains what attitude the neurotic expresses when he or she ***moves away from*** people: "when he *moves away* from people he wants neither to belong nor to fight, but keeps apart. He feels he has not much in common with them, they do not understand him anyway. He builds up a world of his own – with nature, with his dolls, his books, his dreams." Horney points out that, in each of these movements, one of the elements involved in the basic anxiety is usually over-emphasized. Hence, in the first movement, it is **helplessness** which is over- emphasize, in the second, **hostility**, and in the third, **isolation**.[61]

That Horney does not make any allusion to "moving with" people is so obvious. Although the reason for such ignorance of this attitude here can be left to conjecture, my intuition is that she has limited such attitudes, constituting neurosis in a person, to what comes from the person alone. She seems to preclude any other dynamic, such as is the transcendent, by which

---

[60] Ibid., 18.

[61] Ibid., 42-3. Here Horney explains the three movements of the self as attitudes.

the person may be inspired to ***move with*** others. The Mystery which is our common origin, even in the uniqueness of the individual, seems absent when considering what she [Horney] has come to regard as the dynamic centre of basic conflict in a person.

Integrative Reflection

The insights from the above exploration proffer us a good understanding of the greater inner peace and the desire for reconciliation which the subject of our original formation event experienced after he has abandoned himself to the formation Mystery.[62] As it seems obvious, the deep inner peace which the subject enjoyed would be only superficial – like the peace offered by social security – if his disposition of harmonious relationship with others, with whom he shares in common his unique founding life call, remained deformative.

However, in this situation of peace characterized by serenity and gentleness, the subject was still able to apprehend the deformation of his previous interformative relationship with others, especially with his visitor. So, he became worried, and regretted his deformation. As he attested: "Presently looking at my Bishop, I feel ashamed and sorry for having been angry at him. Innocent instrument of God that he is, he has always loved me and been good to me since the first moment I knew him, when he was still a seminarian. How then can he intentionally wish me any harm in life?"[63] This clearly shows how the subject sought to reform this disposition, lest it block and become a lasting obstacle to the deeper inner peace which he has been seeking consciously or otherwise, and now seemed to begin to enjoy it.

In the same light, the subject also perceived that the reformation of such a deformed disposition can only be achieved through reconciliation. So, he

---

[62] See Formation event, Preface to this Book, viii-xii.
[63] Ibid.

Chapter 9: Movement Towards a More Complete Self-Abandonment

desired to reconcile himself with, and to allow his heart to *move with* the others, *against* whom he has been *moving* in his alienated situation. Hence, in this moment, he felt himself "at-one-ment," at home, and belonging together with the others, as he could more readily surrender himself to the formation Mystery.

John Carmody, in his *Reflection on Living with Terminal Illness,* manifested similar dispositions, especially that of interformative relationship with others, in the reflection he entitles "Finding my Way to God, Addressing God," in his desire to find and draw closer to him, to abandon himself to him, and to eventually be united with him, Carmody tells God this: "*I want my heart to speak to your heart, my being to cling to your being, far below the level of mind or emotions, in a colloquy or embrace of love that makes you and me.*"[64] He then remarked to God about how the author of *The Cloud of Unknowing* reminded him of the type of spirituality he has always loved the most – apophatic – which, however, is *pregnant with **liquid love**.* Later, he goes on to tell God how his terminal illness, which he now considers as part of his *unique founding life call,* demands of him a relationship with friends, acquaintances and others, which should help them – interformatively – to respond to their *communal founding life call.* He makes his reflection audible and addressed to God in the following lengthy soliloquy:

> Formidable indeed are my unbridled mind, my self-satisfaction, my enjoyment of singular status. Part of me likes being special, standing out from the crowd. I find myself conceding to the awkwardness of others and so making cancer into business as usual, even comedy. To be sure, some of this is healthy. You want us to demythologize the principalities and powers. Yet some of my collusion in distraction is also cowardly.

---

[64] John Carmody, Cancer and Faith (opus cit.), 50.

Teach me the difference between minimalism and distraction, and give me the guts to honour it.

I find being unusual strange, and so have much to learn about how to use my peculiar kind of privilege ("he has bone cancer, you know") to make other people more thoughtful. I don't want to become sententious or self-important. Yet, even more, I don't want to turn my back on the gift you have made me. You have forced me to think of each day as one of a dwindling few. On all sides, friends and acquaintances need to hear this message. I'd like to get it under their skin without being too irritating. Otherwise, I'm just another bit of news, flashy today but ignorable tomorrow.

More than my pride is hurt when the reality of my condition is ignored. Hurt as well is the core of Christ's message: "The time has come. The Kingdom of God is at hand. Repent, and believe in the good news." Yes, the fate of Christ's message, the acculturation of the gospel, is a pervert comfort, as well as a continual horror. If they have disregarded the Master who died and rose for them; if even he has become old news; what should I expect but quick relegation to familiarity and innocuousness? No servant is greater than his Master, can avoid his Master's fate.[65]

The fact that Carmody is apprehensive that others might ignore his consonant disposition of interformative relationship, has not deterred him from resolving to use his current life situation to help them find the way to respond to their communal founding life call – even though each has his or her own unique founding life call – and of which the Christ-Form is the exemplar *par excellence*.

No one can ever make the necessity of disposition clearer than Christ in his *Sermon on the Mount*. After he told the multitudes that the Old Law only

---

[65] Ibid., 50-1.

forbade their ancestors to kill another, he made it clear that such a standard was rather very low (Mt 5:21-22). He taught that even to be angry with another is already a serious deformation which needs some redress. Hence, he urged his followers saying: "So then, if you are bringing your offering to the altar and there remember that your brother has *something against you*, leave your offering there before the altar, go and be reconciled with your brother first, and then come back and present your offerings" (Mt 5:23-24). Jesus therefore demands that his followers be the first to seek reconciliation with the other, even when the deformative relationship is not initiated by them. The subject of our original formation event therefore followed a universal form directive in desiring reconciliation.

OBSTACLES TO, AND FACILITATING CONDITIONS FOR UNIVERSAL HUMAN FORMATION

Several major obstacles to consonant human formation dynamics can be identified in this Coformant on universal level of human presence. We intend to mention just three of them here. The first is putting limits to the process of self-transcendence. This is the case when the subject does not trust in innate potency to reform his dispositions. The second obstacle may be the mistaking of comfort effected by the feeling of peace and serenity as the goal itself of formation. And the third may be the limiting of one's striving towards "at-one-ment" to only the Mystery. This can block, or even ignore completely the formative disposition of reconciliation with others.

Several principal facilitating conditions for consonant human formation and reformation also emerge. Some may be identified as follows: First, the awe-filled silence which inspires the immediate situation; second, the corresponding peaceful, gentle, and relaxed presence to the Mystery; third, the continuing transcendent volition to appreciatively abandon oneself to the Mystery; and fourth, the deepening of dispositions for interformation, and of genuine and loving respect for the others, the disposition of *moving* one to desire and strive for at-one-ment with others.

Transition to Chapter Ten – Religious Presence

The foregoing investigations have been on the foundational human level of presence, focused on self-abandonment to the Mystery as leading to fullness of formative healing made manifest in deep feeling of peace. For as subjects open their intrasphere to directives coming from a narrative in their form tradition and subsequently abandon themselves to the Mystery, they feel a deepening of inner peace and joy, though they may still experience the physical – empirical – reality of their illness with the looming threat of death. Chapter Ten will study in the Coformant, how more complete self-abandonment to the Divine Mystery may be manifested through the disposition of gratitude of religious subjects.

CHAPTER TEN

DISPOSITION OF GRATITUDE AS A MANIFESTATION OF GREATER SELF-ABANDONMENT TO THE DIVINE MYSTERY

INTRODUCTION

As we indicated at the end of the last chapter, Chapter Ten will focus on the disposition of gratitude as an expression of greater self-abandonment to God. It will first elucidate how religious may seek purification of their dissonant dispositions in the willfulness of their projects. Thus, purified and also reconciled to others, they may become more faithfully attached to God. The Coformant will therefore be stated in the following terms:

> As religious subjects overcome their self-seeking weaknesses and feel more purified, they may perceive greater inspiration to abandon themselves more completely to the Divine Mystery – God. They may also feel grateful to God and their ancestors. And, in their greater self-abandonment, they may humbly desire to attach themselves more faithfully to God in deep peace, and to true reconciliation with others.

Like the others before, the elucidation of this Coformant will also be done in two parts. Each part will present a remote foundational statement, drawn from the Coformant.

PART ONE
GREATER SELF-ABANDONMENT TO GOD THROUGH PURIFICATION

In this first part of the Coformant, the remote foundational statement is articulated in the following terms:

> As religious subjects overcome their moral weaknesses and are more purified of their faults, they may receive further inspirations to abandon themselves more completely to the Divine Mystery.

This remote foundational statement will be investigated in two sections A and B. Section A will study how self-*purification* is reached effectively *through repentance and penance*. Meanwhile, Section B will focus on *the acceptance of one's faults as the way to greater submission* of oneself to God.

SECTION A: PURIFYING ONE'S MORAL FAULTS THROUGH OVERCOMING THEM IN REPENTANCE AND PENANCE

Religious subjects may acknowledge their moral guilt and seek to abandon themselves more completely to their God. They may further nurture the desire to purify themselves of their moral faults and hope thereby to become more acceptable to their God as they continue to abandon themselves to Him. In this proximate statement, area of research, we wish to examine in what moral guilt and its purification, through repentance, may consist.

From the SFHF: Dynamics of Transcendent Guilt-Formation

Although the religious subject may feel deeply peaceful within himself and grateful towards God and others around him, he may however feel some shame for his earlier disposition of anger towards his visitor who is still at his bedside. He may feel guilty conscience for such an attitude towards his Bishop, for which guilty conscience he is now remorseful and feels sincerely sorry. The formation dynamics at work here are evidently guilt and repentance.

The dynamic of guilt which the religious experiences is one which is transcendent and comes as a fruit of his self-abandonment to God, the Radical Mystery of formation. In his discussion on what he calls *Dynamics of Transcendent Formation Guilt*, Adrian van Kaam describes how transcendent guilt comes to be formed in a person. He observes that one may experience transcendent guilt after, first, distancing oneself periodically from one's immediate inclinations; second, weighing, in a wise and relaxed appraisal, each of one's lower conscience directives[1] "until we see what should be our direction in the light of transcendent conscience as enlightened by our consonant faith and formation traditions;" and, third, retreating from the din of society thereby creating moment of silence.[2] Transcendent formation guilt is, indeed, a guilt of an illuminating experience. Hence, van Kaam describes it in these terms:

> This guilt is like a beacon of light on our journey into the darkness of an unknown destiny. Subduing the noise of exclusive, individualistic functional dynamics of conscience, we may grow in transcendent self-presence. We may be able to distinguish between mere functional guilt experiences and the recognition of having failed the dynamic direction of our transcendent formation conscience.[3]

---

[1] The lower directives leading to conscience formation are parental, functional-collective, and functional-individual. They will be found discussed in detail in Adrian van Kaam: *Transcendent Formation*, 81-5.

[2] Adrian van Kaam, Ibid., 88-9.

[3] Ibid., 89.

This transcendent formation guilt is in contrast to what van Kaam asserted earlier concerning *functional formation conscience*.[4] As he perceives the difference between the accompanying guilt of mere functional formation conscience, and the transcendent formation guilt, he describes thus the dynamic of guilt in the former: "Dominated by functional formation conscience, our guilt may have been shallow. We may have felt guilty mainly about mistakes in the functional execution of our collective and technical-ethical obligations." He however goes on to point out the inadequacy of such mere functional guilt for human formation. As he observes, "While this was important, it told us little about our failures to be faithful to life as a whole, to respond to the disclosure of our distinctive destiny by the formation Mystery. We may have lacked a sense of guilt when failure to live up to our unique, inmost formation responsibility."[5]

This contrasting difference between the two – transcendent formation guilt and mere functional guilt – leads van Kaam to summarize them in this crisp and clear conclusion: "Functional guilt is merely issue-oriented; transcendent formation guilt is not only issue-oriented but open toward life in its mysterious unfolding wholeness and in its rootedness in the sacred."[6] Hence, it seems clear that deeper insights of transcendent guilt lead us to knowledge of our guilt which comes, not only from our parental, or collective, or individual conscience, but **in the distinctively human apprehension of our failure in the task of transcending our life call**. To put it in the words of van Kaam, "We are guilty in the distinctively human sense of failing our transcending life call. The dynamics of transcendence make us

---

[4] Ibid., 86.

[5] Ibid., 88.

[6] Ibid., 89.

sense that we have violated the call we most deeply are, that we have betrayed the source of our true nobility.[7]

From the SFHF: "Making up for the Wrong done" – Expiation

As the religious appreciatively appraises the wrong he has done, and for which he experiences such a transcendent formation guilt, he feels his heart drawn to amend the wrong he has committed. Discussing *Sin and Forgiveness* in her book, *The Journey Homeward*, Susan Muto, under the paragraph-heading, "Gift and Challenge of Forgive-ness," underscores this reality.[8] Articulating in the Christian tradition the fullness of amends for a wrong committed and return to consonant formation again by an individual, she writes:

> Though our sins are forgiven due to the merits of Jesus and the grace of Baptism, full remission of our sins committed after Baptism, together with restoration of friendship with God, requires a sincere conversion of heart and amends made for the injustice committed against his goodness. Such restoration is accomplished through confession and repentance for sin, making up the wrong done, and freely accepting the punishment demanded by an all-wise and loving Lord. This action is meant to impress upon us the folly and gravity of sin and its harmful consequences to mankind.[9]

---

[7] Ibid., See also van Kaam, *Fundamental Formation*, 64; *Human Formation*, 152; and *Traditional Formation*, 73-4.

[8] Susan Muto, *The Journey Homeward* (Denville, New Jersey: Dimension Books, 1977), 163-9.

[9] Ibid., 164.

Such full reformation, and eventually, transformation after a wrong committed through deformation of one's form disposition or other is possible, thanks to transcendent formation guilt which the religious is able to apprehend in himself. For through the apprehension of such guilt, the religious is able to appraise appreciatively the wrong he has committed, ultimately against the Mystery of formation – his God. In so appraising the wrong he has committed, such a religious is led to affirm and to apply the transcendent directive to seek forgiveness, through incarnating his sincere repentance in the penance that he freely accepts from his God, and so, reform. Formation Science perceives this carrying out of the penance as essential to the full purification of the religious from the wrong he has done. As Muto rightly articulates again in the Christian faith tradition:

> After the fall into sin, man was obliged to repair the bridge between himself and God, but on his own merits he was incapable of doing so. Therefore God took expiation if sin upon himself in the person of Jesus. By his suffering and death, Jesus rendered to the Father vicarious atonement for the sins of men. The redemptive action of Jesus not only granted remission from sin; it also bestowed the grace that leads to heaven.[10]

In the light of all of this discussion in the view of Formation Science, it is clear that the feeling of the transcendent formation guilt, and the expiation of the "distinctively human sense of failing our transforming life call" are essentially linked together. It is thanks to the former that we, as religious beings, can be led to purify: Hence, to reform and even to transform our distinctively human failings in the ongoing consonant response to our founding life call, and thus eventually towards the full and consonant disclosure of our Foundational Life Form.

---

[10] Ibid., 163.

Formation theory associates transcendent formation guilt with transcendent conscience, of which the formation Mystery is its ultimate source and origin,[11] and so, is the basis of all human morality. In the following paragraphs, we shall discuss the basis of the African concept of morality and shall try to indicate how a breach of the moral code demands ritual purification.

Origin of the African Moral Code and the Purification of Guilt

Many researchers: social anthropologists, ethnologists, missionaries, and researchers in other related fields, including African researchers themselves in this century, have written much on African cultures, customs, and religions and morals.[12] It is generally agreed by all serious researchers,

---

[11] Adrian van Kaam, *Transcendent Formation*, 86-8.

[12] The following is a rather very short list of the so many who have researched substantially on various peoples of Africa: Maurice Delafosse, Haute-Senegal-Niger, 3 vols (Paris: Emile Larose, 1912); The Negoes of Africa, trans. F. Fligelman (Port Washington, N.Y.: Kennikat Press, Inc., 1931); Jack Goody, *Death Property and the Ancestors* (London: Tavistock Publications, 1962); The Myth of the Bagre (Oxford: Clarendon Press, 1972); Henri Labouret, "La Divinisation en Afrique Noire." *L'Anthropologie*, 1922); J. Laesourd, *En Afrique Occidentale* française :*Les Dagaris,* Paris, 1939 ; D. Westermann, Die Sudansprachen, eine Sprach-vergleichende Studie, Homburg, 1913 ; Die Westlichen Sudansprachen und ihre Beziehungen zum Bantu, Berlin, 1927 ; John Mbiti, African Religions and Philosophy, 2nd. Ed. (Oxford: Heinemann, 1969); Concepts of God in Africa (New York : Praeger Publishers, 1970); Peter K .Sarpong Ghana in Retrospect: Some Aspects of Ghanaian Culture (Accra- Tema: Ghana Publishing Corporation, 1974); Gregory Kpiebaya, "God in Dagaaba Religion and in the Christian Faith," (Diss. Universite Catholique de Louvain, Belgium, 1973); Edward Tengan, *The Land as Being and Cosmos* (New York: Peter Lang, 1991); Albert A. Kuuire, "*The Christian Faith in the Dagarti Culture,*" (Licentiate Thesis Lumen Vitae, Louvain,

that the origin and source of the African morality is God; and after God, is the ancestor.[13] As God is considered to be remote from his daily life,[14] which cannot be conceived other than religious, the ancestor becomes the basis and, indeed, the *norm of morality* for the African. As Ray has rightly claimed after delineating what the African considers to be the degree of involvement of God with him, including particularly the eschatological world, for which he now lives and hopes:

> God, however, rarely intervenes in the moral life of men on earth; for the most part, it is the ancestors who act as the official guardians of the social and moral order. This is especially true of small scale, stateless societies whose sociopolitical rules are almost entirely governed by a descent system based on genealogical frameworks. In such societies ancestors become the focus of religious activity. This is not because of a special "fear" of the dead or because of an especially strong "belief" in souls, but rather because of the importance of the descent system in defining moral relations.[15]

Elsewhere, I have discussed more extensively the entity that the ancestor is in the African society – his making, and the central role he plays in the morality of both society and the individual – with particular reference to the

---

Belgium 1972); Diss. *Dagaati Solidarity and Salvation in Christ in the Light of 'Gaudium et Spes,'* Pontifical Lateran University, Rome, 1976.

[13] See for example, John Mbiti, *African Religions and Philosophy*, 1969; and Benjamin C. Ray, *African Religions*, 1976. As it can be observed, in most authors in this field, African morality is so bound up with the *Problem of Evil* that it is practically impossible to think of morality apart from concrete evil which is a constant reminder to the African of the moral injunctions that have been handed down to him, and which he has to observe meticulously.

[14] See chapter two.

[15] Benjamin C. Ray, *African Religions*, 146-7.

solidarity of his descent group.[16] Any breaking of the injunctions of the moral code handed down by the ancestors, brings evil – physical as well as spiritual or mythical – upon the perpetrator, and the guilt therefrom may affect the entire family or even clan. Unless such a breach to the moral code is repaired through purification and the guilt thus taken away, the evil, which is regarded as punishment for the offence, will remain as a constant reminder that the offender and his or her family or clan, depending on the nature of the offence, have been alienated from his or her ancestor(s), and ultimately from God.

This is the reality which Mbiti asserts and expresses when he writes: "Most African peoples accept or acknowledge God as the final guardian of law and order, and of the moral and ethical codes. Therefore the breaking of such order, whether by the individual or the group, is ultimately an offence by the corporate body or the society.[17] And he goes on to reiterate: "The people believe that if a person does wrong, God will sooner or later punish him, and the punishment affects not just the individual alone, but the corporate group of which he is only a part."[18]

In his discussion on *The Concepts of Evil, Ethics and Justice*, Mbiti also discusses, to a good extent, the different kinds of punishment that may come upon the offender in this life.[19] These punishments serve two goals. As we have already said, they serve as a reminder to the individual or group concerned that a wrong, of which one may not have focal awareness at the time, has been committed. They may also serve as part of the process of *purification* which would culminate in ritual sacrifice of one kind or other, after a diviner has been consulted, and both the wrong committed and its

---

[16] See S.T.D. diss. Opus cit. Here, the problem of evil is also largely presented and contrasted with the concept of evil in Christian theology, 170-9.

[17] John Mbiti, African Religions and Philosophy, opus cit., 201. See also p. 40.

[18] Ibid., 201-2.

[19] Ibid., 205-7.

purification rite identified and determined respectively.[20] The offender will then have to confess the wrong he has committed: i.e., by accepting and owning up what has been brought to focal consciousness through divination, and also accepting to offer the sacrifice determined by the diviner, both as an inner and an external sign of his sincere repentance. It is only then that the guilt may be considered "lifted" from the offender – from the individual sinner and all who might have been affected.

Before we try to find out how the insights from this section of our research may apply to the religious of our primary formation event, we shall explore immediately where this acceptance and repentance of one's faults lead one to in one's relationship with God.

SECTION B: ACCEPTING ONE'S FAULTS AS THE WAY TO GREATER SUBMISSION TO GOD

When religious subjects appreciatively appraise their faults and seek to be purified of them, they may open the way to greater submission to God's will, and thus further abandon themselves to Him. This proximate area of our investigations will seek to find out in what the acceptance of one's faults may consist.

---

[20] See Divination and Soothsaying in chapter two. In his book, *The Myth of the Baghre*, Jack Goody, after a very substantial introduction, presents the entire religious initiation rite of the *Lobr* and the *Dagara*, which people and less major and less major point of the year-long ritual. See also Jack Goody, *Death, Property and the Ancestors*, 39-41, 56-60. Here Goody speaks in great detail of the ritual purification of the dead as well as living persons from one category of 'dirt' (deghr) or other. Immediately after death has occurred. Also subject to this ritual purification are the habitations. "Deghr" is moral dirt.

Chapter 10: Disposition of Gratitude

From the SFHF: Repudiated Memory and Guilt

In section A above, we observed that formation anthropology regards *transcendent formation guilt* as a distinctively human apprehension of the failing of our ***transforming life call***. Such a failure can be due to a repudiation of one's formative memory by the disposition of guilt itself. This means the transcendent formation guilt which one experiences may be so present because of the fact one resisted and suppressed the formative memory which could otherwise have led to an apprehension and subsequent appreciative appraisal of the transforming life call in the particular situation of one's current life form.

The reality is clearly captured by van Kaam in his presentation of what he calls *Stilted Formation Disposition and Stilted Memories*. After describing how our stilted formation disposition may affect our formation memories, he says of the formation memories made impotent in the process: "Memories may be more or less available to our appraisal power. They may be repudiated and hence, insulated in the infrafocal realm of life formation, or they may be refused and hence, exiled in the transfocal realm."[21] He gives an example of how people may have repudiated infrafocal consciousness because of threats they might have had from unwise formation persons earlier in childhood. He then goes on to give the following analysis of such repudiated formation memory, effected by a stilted formation disposition:

> As long as this repudiated memory is not apprehended and appraised one cannot deal effectively with the fear disposition that feeds on it. Others may have refused a transfocal aspiration or inspiration to create room in their lives for presence to others in transcendent love and respect. This refused aspiration or inspiration, with the memories attending it, remains blocked in the transfocal realm of life. It gives rise

---

[21] Adrian van Kaam, *Human Formation*, 152.

to *an unacknowledged guilt disposition,* which is activated when one's formation field invites such presence. In this case, refused memories are evoked that are no longer available to one's apprehension and appraisal power.[22]

In the light of the above explanation, it is very clear how a stilted formation disposition may cause the repudiation of a formation memory. Once the formation memory is thus repudiated, and so, suppressed, transcendent formation guilt disposition will remain unacknowledged, apprehended, and therefore, cannot be appreciatively appraised.

From the SFHF: "Acceptance of My Unique Limitations

To deal effectively with any guilt or fear disposition, such a disposition must be, indeed, available for appraisal. It is this which should lead eventually to the acceptance of one's limitations, one's faults. Under the paragraph-heading which he titles '*Choice and Commitment*' in his discussion on "Spiritual Identity and Modes of Incarnation," van Kaam explains the absolute importance of accepting one's own limitations in view of one's formation. Speaking about the choice of a spiritual way of life in which one can commit oneself, he writes:

> Choosing a spiritual path implies necessarily foregoing the possibilities of other paths. Incarnation means accepting my limits; it means affirming the reality of foregoing ways of life because I am called to another lifestyle, of offering up talents never to be realized, places and persons never to be met. Without the experience and acceptance of my unique limitations, spiritual life is bound to remain formless, floating, and ethereal. In other words, it will not be a real spiritual life. The true spiri-

---

[22] Ibid.,

tual life in man is always an incarnated one, for man is essentially an incarnated spirit.[23]

From this explanation of the absolute importance of accepting one's unique limitations, it has become evident that, without accepting one's unique limitations, it will not be possible for one to ever submit oneself to the Divine Mystery of formation, much less to entertain any desire of reaching any greater degree in such self-submission. As one refuses to accept one's unique limitations, one would be refusing to acknowledge, and so, to apprehend and appraise transcendent formation guilt dispositions which may arise from the essentially incarnated spirit that we are as *existent beings*. Hence, the formation disposition which directs us to seek to abandon ourselves to God – because of our unique limitations which make it impossible to form ourselves – will never be effectively appraised so as to give us adequate formation.

In the remaining paragraphs of this section, we shall devote them to the investigation of what the African religious does with his moral limitations which he discovers, be it through divination or other means.

John S. Mbiti: Discovery of Moral Faults through Means other than Divination

For the religious African, a person's life, which is always before God and his ancestors, most especially so, when he carries out a religious rite – death being the highest such moment – should always be free from all "dirt."[24]

---

[23] Adrian van Kaam, *In Search of Spiritual Identity* (Denville, New Jersey: Dimension Books, 1975), 142.

[24] "Dirt" here refers to infringement, focal or prefocal, of the moral code of life handed down by the ancestors. See Jack Goody, *Death, Property and the Ancestors* (Opus cit.): for the ritual removal of all "dirt," confer 40-1 and 56-60; purification

Hence, such a person should be cleansed and purified of all moral faults. Otherwise, his filth would arouse God's anger and call upon him rejection by and punishment from his ancestors. However, in Mbiti's discussion about *Restitution and Punishment*, following upon an establishment of an offence, it will seem that in the African moral code for living, there is not much distinction between a legal offence and a purely moral one. As he asserts:

> Each community or society has its own set form of restitution and punishment for various offences. Both legal and moral. These range from death for offences like practicing sorcery and witchcraft, committing murder and adultery, to paying fines of cattle, sheep or money for minor cases like accidental injury to one's companion, or when sheep escape and eat potato vines in a neighbour's field.[25]

If there seems to be no distinction between what may be regarded as legal offence and a purely moral one for an observer, it is precisely because the African does not make any dichotomy between the legal and the moral order. All belong to the ancestors, and ultimately to God. And the entire code of law regulating the lives of people comes from God through the ancestors who have the duty to see to it that their descent groups observe all of this moral code in their lives. But to the observer, it may seem that this one moral code of law for the African is the purely legal common law, as Mbiti presents it in the rather narrow context of restitution and punishment: "It is generally the elders of the area who deal with disputes and

---

of a defiled soul, confer 58-60, also 305. However, not all such *dirt* from which a dead person and others living are ritually purified, such as dirt incurred through sexual relations between spouses, may be considered as having been moral infringements.

[25] John S. Mbiti, *African Religions and Philosophy*, 206.

Chapter 10: Disposition of Gratitude

breaches arising from various types of moral harm or offences against custom and ritual. Traditional chiefs and rulers, where these exist, have this duty of keeping law and order and executing justice in their areas.[26]

However, as we remarked earlier, it is the ancestors who are the official guardians of both moral and social order.[27] It is in the establishing and finding out of the guilty that different means may be used. These means include not only divination, but also the common law governing the society; and curses, especially in cases where there is evidence that the moral code has been violated but no particular individual has owned up to the guilt. Mbiti himself affirms: "There is one form of justice administered through the use of the curse. The basic principle here is that if a person is guilty, evil will befall him according to the words used in cursing him. By the use of good magic, it is believed a person can curse an unknown thief."[28]

When the offence is established and disclosed, the guilty person who thus has to accept his fault will also have to make amends for his offence. It is here that, besides the punishment which may come directly to the guilty person from the ancestors – and ultimately from God – in one form or another, different communities and societies may have their own set forma of making these amends, as Mbiti indicates. They may be in the form of restitution and/or further punishment from the society for the offence committed.[29]

In all cases where the guilt of the religious African has been established and accepted by him, and for which he has made amends by restitution and undergoing other punishments, he still has to repair and to re-establish his relationship with God and his ancestors. This is what he does through the making of sacrifice. Although there are several reasons for which the reli-

---

[26] Ibid.,

[27] Confer under paragraph: "Origin of the African Moral Code," 387-9.

[28] John S. Mbiti, opus cit., 206.

[29] See footnote #25, 393.

gious African makes frequent sacrifices, there are two main goals for this particular sacrifice – reparation and reconciliation. Such a sacrifice is usually determined by a diviner, if it is not already prescribed in the common law of the society.[30] Through this sacrifice, the religious is again purified and has become once more the true child and descendent of his ancestors, and through them, he is again acceptable to God, and enjoys a certain relationship of union with him.

Integrative Reflection

The insights gained from the above discussions in this part of our research – self-purification through repentance and penance, and greater submission of oneself to God made possible by the acceptance of one's faults – make quite understandable the current disposition of the religious of our original formation event to abandon oneself in a greater degree to God. To begin with, as long as the religious refused in the first place to abandon himself to God, he could only see, though falsely, that his present compassionate visitor merited his anger for a wrong he believed the latter to have done to him.[31] He was totally blind to the unjustifiableness of his claim that "his own will be accomplished." However, now that, through an initial abandonment of himself to God, he achieved what he has been infraconsciously striving for,[32] he apprehends that the more he could be purified of his remaining

---

[30] Bekuone Some Der Joseph-Mukassa very well describes such a sacrifice among the Dagara of West Africa, after divination, in these terms: "La consultation divinatoire (Bawr-buwfu) mene automatiquement au rite sacrificiel (bawr-maalu) de reparation, de consecration ou d'action de grace, etc.

[31] The whole of chapter two of this research has been devoted to the investigation of this refusal of the religious subject to abandon himself to God, and of the dynamics that have been responsible for this refusal.

[32] As the religious subject abandons himself to God, he achieves, as fruit of his abandonment, inner peace and formative healing; confer chapter six.

Chapter 10: Disposition of Gratitude

willfulness, the more he would allow God to take control of his will and direct him.

In the understanding of the working of the dynamic involved in this, the SFHF's *dynamics of transcendent guilt-formation* offers in particular, a great insight. As it reveals, the dynamic of this transcendent formation guilt is the distinctively human apprehension of our failure in the consonant transforming of our founding live call. It is this transcendent realization that he was failing to respond consonantly to his foundational life call, which ignited in the religious of our original formation event the desire to continue, and eventually to submit himself more completely to God. But this could not be possible unless he was first purified of his deformative willful dispositions through the acceptance of the transcendent formation guilt which they imposed on him.

Although the faith tradition of our religious is no longer that of his traditional ancestors, nevertheless, insights from that religious faith, not his Christian faith tradition, lend immense support to him in his search for that peace, which only the formative healing he has been looking for but infrafocally, can give. The fact that every of the individual's life in that faith tradition is perceived to be governed by the one moral code – the observance of which the ancestors are responsible – makes it clearer why the religious should submit, even his personal willful projects, to God. And subsequently, it also makes sense why he should seek to make amends, through repentance and penance, for the purification of his guilt. For in accepting his guilt, he is thus able to return to God, purified of his previous faults, and can abandon himself in a greater degree to God.

I am persuaded that this dynamic of taking the necessary means to abandon oneself to God in an ever-greater measure, and consequently, obtaining the healing and peace that God alone can give is what Anthony de Mello intuits in his story about *The Temple Bells*. Built on an island, the symphonic peals of the thousand finely crafted bells of this temple were able to bring raptures to the heart of their hearer. De Mello continues the narration of his story:

> But over the centuries the island sank into the sea, and with it, the temple bells. An ancient legend said that the bells continued to peal out, ceaselessly, and could be heard by anyone who would listen. Inspired by this legend, a young man travelled thousands of miles, determined to hear those bell. He sat for days on the shore, facing the vanished island, and listened with all his might. But all he could hear was the sound of the sea. He made every effort to block it out. But to no avail; the sound of the sea seemed to flood the world.
>
> He kept at his task for weeks. Each time he got disheartened he would listen to the village pundits, who spoke with unction of the mysterious legend. Then his hear would be aflame ... only to become discouraged again when weeks of further effort yielded no results.
>
> Finally he decided to give up the attempt. Perhaps he was not destined to hear the bells. Perhaps the legend was not true. It was his final day, and he went to the shore to say goodbye to the sea and the sky and the wind and the coconut trees. He lay on the sand, and for the last time, listened to the sound of the sea. Soon he was so lost in the sound that he was barely conscious of himself, so deep was the silence that the sound produced.
>
> In the depth of that silence, he heard it! The tinkle of a tiny bell followed by another, and another and another ... and soon every one of the thousand temple bells was pealing out in harmony, and his hear was wrapped in joyous ecstasy.[33]

As can be remarked in this beautiful story, it is only when the young, determined man abandoned his own willfully crafted means for hearing the

---

[33] Anthony de Mello, *The Song of the Bird* (New York: Doubleday, 1982), 22-3.

symphonic pealing of the temple bells and abandoned himself to listening to the sound of the sea that he was able to begin to hear the peals of the bells. And the more he abandoned himself, the greater the harmonious peals of the thousand bells reached his ears and wrapped his heart in joyous ecstasy. He had become *purified* of his previous willful listening disposition and had thus reformed it through an ongoing abandonment of himself to the very mystery he was now contemplating.

Transition to the Second Remote Foundational Statement

In the Remote Foundational statement above, we concentrated on the aspiration and inspiration to greater self-abandonment which religious subjects may experience as they are purified of their faults. In their desire for such purification, they may also feel grateful particularly towards God, and in humility, are able to attach themselves more faithfully to God. In the second remote foundational statement, we will now explore the disposition of gratitude.

PART TWO

DISPOSITION OF GRATITUDE IN THE CONTEXT OF SELF-ABANDONMENT TO GOD AND RECONCILIATION WITH OTHERS

This second remote foundational statement to be elucidated in this part of our research is formulated in the following manner:

Religious subjects may feel grateful to God and their ancestors. And in their greater self-abandonment, they may humbly desire to attach[34] themselves more faithfully to god in profound peace, and in reconciliation with others.

Although we already discussed, in the preceding chapter, reconciliation on the universal level of human presence, in this remote statement, we want to explore, in two sections, the disposition of *gratitude* and also that of *reconciliation within the context of purification of moral faults.*

SECTION A: FEELING GRATEFUL TOWARDS GOD, ANCESTORS, AND OTHERS

Religious subjects who desire purification from their moral faults may feel welling up in them gratitude towards God, their ancestors, and others as they regret their earlier deformative disposition of ingratitude among these others. Here, we wish to explore the core disposition of gratitude.

From the SFHF: An Attitude of Gratitude

In *Webster's Third International Dictionary*, the terms **gratefulness** and/or **gratitude** are defined thus: "The quality or state of being grateful;" "warm and friendly feeling toward a benefactor prompting to return a favor." Earlier, it defined the word ***grateful*** in these terms: "Appreciation of

---

[34] As embodied spirits, attachment of the human being to God is not possible without detachment from one's dissonant dispositions, such as willfulness and anger, which may keep one away from God. This disposition of detachment from all that is self-willed will be discussed at greater length in chapter eleven, on the horizon of Foundational Christian Presence.

benefits received: willing or anxious to acknowledge and repay or give thanks for benefits."[35]

In this light, we can say that **gratitude** or **thankfulness** is therefore a core disposition of the *existent being*. It is that character in every human person which disposes one to express one's appreciation for some good or favour that has been freely bestowed and received. In the book *The Power of Appreciation*, van Kaam and Susan Muto, discussing *pride,* which they argue should be rejected because it is an obstacle to appreciation, describe appreciative living in these terms:

> Living appreciatively means being grateful for all that is – from its source in the divine forming mystery to its outflow in every sphere of our life and world, in every disposition and directive we embody, in every act and affirmation we make. To live appreciatively means to co-operate with grace not only when we feel blessed but also when we have to bear life's many burdens.[36]

When we consider this description of *appreciative living*, it is nothing other than a basic, comprehensive description of gratitude. Indeed, gratitude as a disposition in the human being comes, not just as some vital quality, but a quality which is innate to the *existent being*. It therefore comes from the very core of our being: from the depth of our human spirit. It belongs to our founding life form, to our *preformational given*. As such, gratitude or thankfulness has its origin in the Divine Forming Mystery. This is why van Kaam and Muto can assert the following:

---

[35] "Grateful, Gratefulness, Gratitude," *Webster's Third International Dictionary.*

[36] Adrian van Kaam and Susan Muto, *The Power of Appreciation*, opus cit., 99-100.

To live appreciatively is to rely on the Transcendent despite setbacks and failures. It is to believe that our days on earth unfold like pages of an infinitely trustworthy text. It is to acknowledge humbly God's eternal yes to our well-being and to make this promise the main dynamic principle of our life on earth.[37]

In this sense, therefore, Formation Science regards gratitude as a core disposition which is not only to be appraised and incarnated horizontally between existent being as acknowledgement of favours from them. In its incarnation, it finds its perfection in the vertical acknowledgement of the eternal favours – grace – which we receive every moment of our lives from God, the Radical Mystery of formation. Thus, even what may seem to be the many burdens of life become, in the final analysis, formative blessings allowed by the Divine Mystery.

From the SFHF: The Primordial Triad and Parental Benediction

The discussion on the core disposition of gratitude, and other similar core dispositions, leads one to the basic question concerning how they come to be awakened in the early stages of an individual's *existence*. According to Formation Science theory, two primordial dispositions begin to develop early in the core form of every child's life. Van Kaam identifies these initial formation dispositions and describes them when he writes: "These two dispositions are **sensibility** and **responsibility**, which refer to the ability to sense vitally or to feel, and to thee ability to respond." He further describes them thus:

> **Responsibility** could also be called *felt-consciousness*. Sensibility refers to the vital excitability of human life. Responsibility in childhood is a

---

[37] Ibid., 100.

primordial, elementary, affective capacity to experience some responsibility for certain acts or omissions. It also implies some pristine ability to act upon that germinal feeling of responsibility.[38]

Formation anthropology considers the pair as foundational. As van Kaam clearly asserts: "This fundamental sensibility and responsibility is the subtle fruit of a first implicit spiritual formation."[39]

This initial and fundamental pair of dispositions is what gives rise to core dispositions like gratitude which we have just discussed above, gentleness, firmness, and the host of other core dispositions which van Kaam discusses in great detail in the third volume – *Formation of the Human Heart* – of his series of **Formative Spirituality**. This pair is what gives rise to the *primordial triad* of faith, **hope**, and **consonance** or **love** which conform in turn to these core dispositions.[40]

Although these core dispositions may be primordial, initial or foundational in the child, they need to be nurtured and awakened in it as the child sets out on its formation journey to maturity. These primordial, pristine form dispositions in the child are awakened by what formation theory calls **parental benediction**. In chapter four of *Human Formation*, Adrian van Kaam indicates how the first rudiments of form dispositions are awakened in the child. Based on the assumption that the human life form is a substantial entity, and so describing it as an embodied-spirit, formation theory teaches that elementary occurrences in early childhood influence the formation of dispositional life form of each human being. Intuited by the well-founded presupposition, van Kaam asserts: "If the first interformative reaction with the mother is satisfactory, it gives rise to an elementary dispositional triad of faith, hope, and love. This fundamental triad, awakened

---

[38] Adrian van Kaam, *Human Formation*, 58.
[39] Ibid.
[40] Ibid., 9. See also p. 192.

in the early mother-child relationship, is significant for the wholesome formation of the child's distinctively human or spiritual life."[41]

This early mother-child interformative relationship is what is all important for the consonant awakening of this dispositional triad of faith, hope, and love which the *existent infant* needs for the consonant unfolding of its foundational life form. For it is what gives rise to especially the adequate formation of the rudiment of **appreciative abandonment** which we call ***trust***. Both this foundational triad and the rudiment of trust are rooted in the bodily interformative interaction with the mother or substitute, or simply the primary care givers. Van Kaam points out that, "This earliest meeting in mutual faith, hope, and love, no matter how vaguely and implicitly it is experienced, no matter how elementary its level, is the beginning of the child's spiritual formation."[42] Hence, van Kaam is led to call such early interformative relationship of parents with the child, *'parental benediction,'* which is expressed both inwardly and outwardly through the dispositions of attention, affection, appreciation, and confirmation.[43]

This disposition of gratitude seems not only to be present in the African form tradition, but more especially so in their faith tradition – in their relationship with the Divine Mystery and with their ancestors. We shall discuss this form disposition in the African in the last paragraphs of this section.

Edward Tengan: Gratitude in the Harvest Festival among the Sisala

The ritual celebration of the harvesting of the farm produce, and also game that has been hunted, is something which is very common among the

---

[41] Ibid., 52.
[42] Ibid., 53.
[43] Ibid., 59-60.

different people of Africa.[44] Most African societies will not eat the newly harvested fruits, nor eat of the game that has been brought in from the hunting expedition, until due gratitude has been expressed to God who sends his rain to water the crops to fruition and bless the hunters with the game they bring in.

In his book *The Land as Being and Cosmos*, Edward Tengan discusses what he describes as, "The Harvest Ritual," among the Sisala of Northwestern Ghana. After describing the ritual ceremony over the first fruits, he remarks the following:

> As my informants explain, all the supra-humans within the house have contributed in one way or the other, to the success of the farming. It would thus be an unpardonable ingratitude to deny them the right of tasting the first produce. Besides expressing the gratitude of humans to these aides, this offering also consecrates the rest of the yield. They take care to offer the best of the yield to these beings. For, as superior beings, they could be angry if they were to find out something other than the best was given to them.[45]

---

[44] See John S. Mbiti, *African Religions and Philosophy*, 24, 71. Discussing about rainmakers (174-7) Mbiti gives other reasons why celebrating the harvest of the crops is such an important thing among various African societies. But he makes it evident that the people, who always regard the rain "as a great blessing," rejoice when it comes. Hence, it is clear that they will, first and foremost, use the celebrating of harvesting of the first-fruits to express their bounded gratitude to God who lets the rain water the crops and bring them to fruition. As Mbiti remarks, a good lot of Africa lies in the tropics. This gives rise to the division of the year into just two main seasons: the dry season when the prolonged absence of rain leaves everything dried up; and the raining season during which the people are able to cultivate their crops. See also Jack Goody, The Social Organization of the LoWiile, 2nd ed. (London: Oxford U, Press).

[45] Edward Tengan, *The Land as Being and Cosmos*, opus cit., 152.

If it seems that not much is said directly in reference to the Divine forming Mystery in this expression of gratitude, it has to be remembered that in most African societies, God – the Radical Mystery of formation – is generally considered inaccessible to humans. Because of that, the day to day life and activities of human beings are left to the ancestors and the intermediaries between God and the humans. They become God's "vicars" in all human activities.[46] As Tengan himself remarked earlier, the Sisala believe that God (*Wiise*), after he created the land, gave it to the humans to tend.[47] It is understood that they do this under the supervision of the ancestors and the intermediary deities who have been given this responsibility by God. So any gratitude expressed to them is understood to be intended for and destined ultimately to God the creator of all.

Besides the elaborate expression their gratitude to God, the ancestors and the realm of the minor deities for the fruits of the land, and for the game of the wilds, African societies have very many other occasions in which exuberant appreciation is expressed to God and the ancestors. One such occasion is the end of the initiation into The *Bagre* Association among the Dagaaba of West Africa.[48] Kuukure describes the final rites as consisting mainly in sacrificing of the remaining fowls, which the initiates received during the year-long ceremonies of initiation, to the God of life through the ancestors and the minor deities as usual.[49] As much as this can be taken to be for the many other reasons for which sacrifices are offered, the fact that these sacrifices in the ritual of the Bagre Myth, together with the exuberant expression of joy in endless drumming and dancing, and are an expression of gratitude to God for the success of the events, cannot be missed.

---

[46] See chapter two, under *Dagaaba Beliefs about God*.

[47] Edward Tengan, opus cit., 34.

[48] Confer Edward Kuukure, *The Destiny of Man*. Opus cit. pp. 95-102. See also especially Jack Goody, *The Myth of the Bagre,* opus cit.

[49] Edward Kuukure, *opus cit.*, 102.

Chapter 10: Disposition of Gratitude

We shall come back to reflect on the gratitude which the religious of the primary formation event felt towards God and the care givers in the hospital in the light of the insights obtained from the above discussions. However, we now wish to cast a quick regard at the reconciliation with others which such religious may desire for the purpose of greater attachment of himself to God.

SECTION B: SEEKING RECONCILIATION WITH OTHERS

As religious subjects feel grateful towards their God and their ancestors, they may also be led to desire to be reconciled with others, especially with their care givers. We have already discussed the disposition of reconciliation in so far as it promotes self-abandonment to the Mystery and deeper inner peace.[50] We shall now take a closer look at the reconciliation with others which the religious may desire as an expression of genuine gratitude towards these others; i.e. we shall endeavour to identify the dynamic of reconciliation in the context of gratitude and its links with the formation tradition of the religious.

From the SFHF: Pyramids of Formation Tradition

As we demonstrated in the very first chapter of this research, formation anthropology affirms that the individual human being is fitted out from his or her preformation with various characteristics or dispositions which dynamically give direction for the consonant ongoing disclosure of his or her founding life form – formation.[51] Such an individual in the human society is considered by Formation Science to be at the very peak of a pyramid, as it were, of generations of a formation tradition. Introducing the

---

[50] See chapter nine.
[51] Confer, 40-6.

concept of *form traditional pyramid* in his formation anthropology, Adrian van Kaam says: "It [form tradition pyramid] expresses for me that we all live by personal and shared 'pyramids' of form traditions, for we live in pluritraditional societies. Many of their directives affect in different intensities our daily existence."

This pyramid of each the individual is the peak, and which has as its basis what is distinctively human – hence, ultimately God – consists of layers of traditions. This is precisely the concept which van Kaam describes in Formation Science in these terms:

> At the base of my pyramid I situated the basic form tradition to which we are committed as a congenial and compatible expression of our faith tradition within our formation field. Above this base, I located ever smaller, less intensively influential form traditions. We try to integrate their form directives with our basic form tradition. One of the fundamental criteria of this integration is that they are consonant with our form as well as our faith tradition.[52]

Continuing his explanation of the pyramid, van Kaam asserts that the peak of the pyramid represents the individual person in this shared field of formation, as we have just remarked above. In poetic language, van Kaam describes this top of the pyramid in these terms: "It images a kind of lived synopsis of all our form traditions as more or less integrated into our basic tradition at the base of our pyramid. The top of the pyramid thus stands for our actual life form."[53]

Adrian van Kaam, discussing *sociohistorical form traditions and the expression of the transcendence dynamic*, makes it unequivocally clear as to how presuppositions of our individual pyramids of form traditions coform

---

[52] Adrian van Kaam, *Traditional Formation*, opus cit., 34.
[53] Ibid.

not only the sociohistorical dimension of the individual person's life form, but also his or her intrasphere of life – the heart – and its transcendent dispositions or characters. As he clearly affirms, after describing how the sociohistorical transforms the individual through language, for example:

> The inner form of our life and its transcendent dynamism has thus been coformed by the presuppositions of our pyramid of form traditions. Among all the traditions we formationally receive in and through language, those that are transcendent should prevail. The intraform of our life is influenced by the particular traditions that are lived in the socio-historical inter- and outerspheres of our formation field. Our intraform unfolds in continual interformation with these spheres.[54]

If we therefore consider our pyramids of formation traditions in this light, their indispensable role in the awakening, reformation, and even transformation of our inner character-dispositions, including reconciliation, gentleness, firmness, gratitude, etc., become evident. This has led van Kaam to come to the conclusion that; "The disclosure of our unique transcendent life call and its transcendent dynamic occurs simultaneously with the disclosure of the living truth of the presuppositions of our faith tradition as sociohistorically and experientially implemented in our formation tradition.[55]

This is what makes it easy to understand how a religious' disposition of reconciliation with God, and also with the *neighbour*, is so well embodied in humanity's history. For as van Kaam points out with regard to the history of Christian love, which essentially implies reconciliation with God, "In loving we actualize the golden thread that makes history one in its tending toward the final destiny of humanity." And this integrating historical

---

[54] Ibid., 187.
[55] Ibid.

orientation towards the destiny of humanity, he asserts, "has been realized in Jesus' reconciliation of man with God."[56] Hence, it becomes evident that formation theory perceives the dynamic of reconciliation as being present in all of the pyramids of the various formation traditions all of which tend historically and ultimately towards the same unique and final destiny of humanity.

How much role does the dynamic of reconciliation play the religious' pyramid of form tradition? This is the question we shall briefly endeavour to respond to in the last part of this section.

Edward Kuukure: Reconciliation with God, Ancestors, and Fellow Humans

Most researchers admit that the disposition of reconciliation between God and humans, and also between humans, is peculiarly present in the life form of the individual and in the formation traditions of every African society. Such a disposition is so strong in their faith tradition that it is a source of daily preoccupation and constant ritual celebration. Focally conscious of the fallen condition before God,[57] the African will incessantly endeavour to maintain good relationship with not only God, nor only the intermediaries and the ancestors, but also his fellow humans, especially members of his descent group.

---

[56] Adrian van Kaam, *In Search of Spiritual Identity*, opus cit. p. 319; see also 15.

[57] See John S. Mbiti, *African Religions and Philosophy*, opus cit. pp. 94-7. See also Benjamin C. Ray, *African Religions*, opus cit. pp.135-46. Even though Ray does not speak of creation and fall as many do, the fear and dependence of the human on God, the intermediaries and the ancestors, make him always desire to maintain a good relationship with them. So, he [man] would actively seek reconciliation with the many time the good relationship with them would be, or even seem strained or disturbed.

Chapter 10: Disposition of Gratitude

Speaking about other religious rites most common among the Dagaaba of West Africa in which sacrifices may be offered or not, Kuukure mentions the **confession** of the various wrongs which a person may have committed and from which he or she would be seeking purification. After he has indicated the fact that purificatory rites are many and common place among the Dagaaba, he writes: "Confessions are called for in various occasions, such as for a woman in difficult labour, an unmarried woman in labour, a witch when diagnosed by the diviner, and neophytes throughout the period of their initiation ceremonies."[58] In all of these confessions, the wrong committed is always, in the first instance, against a fellow human being, especially against a member of one's own descent group. In which case, it is regarded as being against one's ancestors whose authority as custodians and overseers of the moral law given to their descent group by God that has been violated.[59] And so, ultimately, it is God himself, the origin of the injunction which has been violated, against whom the wrong has been done, as we have remarked several times above.

All these three categories of persons are the ones with whom one has to maintain good relationships. The reasons for maintaining such good relationships with the last two – God and the ancestors – are obvious from our previous discussions. The reason for maintaining a good relationship with one's fellow humans, especially with members of one's descent group, should, however, also be obvious, as all human beings come ultimately from God, and are therefore all subject to the same moral code which he has given to them through their ancestors. Hence, for instance, making someone's wife pregnant is a violation of the moral code which does not only strain one's relationship with God and one's ancestors, but also strains one's relationship with the spouse of the pregnant woman, and his family, whose

---

[58] Edward Kuukure, *The Destiny of Man*, 95.
[59] Ibid., 67.

right to sexual union with her was sanctioned in marriage, witnessed to and blessed by God through the ancestors.

Hence, any restoration of the ardently desired good relationships – reconciliation, which does not include a restoration of relationship with the spouse of the violated woman, cannot be considered a genuine reconciliation on any of the other two levels. Thus, the guilt will eventually catch up with the violator, and he will have to make the proper amends and so, reconciliation.

Integrative Reflection

In conclusion to his beautiful reflection on reforming the Church, John Carmody openly manifested his core disposition of gratitude to God when he affirms:

> I want to die as a child of the Church, and I know that only I myself can prevent this. I want to keep the faith so long handed down, so beautiful to the great crowd of witnesses. The Church has been my home, spiritually more than politically or physically. Much as I've despised churchiness, Uriah Heep in cassock or preacher's gown, I've learned to pray, and love, and laugh in the Church, and so to sense what a healthy view of death requires. For all these reasons, when I pray for the Church I first pray, "Deo gratias": "Thanks be to God."[60]

In spite of all the physical as well as moral pain and hurt which he suffered and was still suffering, something deep down in Carmody made him able to transcend all his pain and to appreciate and thank God for his "favours" in his current life form. This, we may say, is the dynamic of gratitude which has made this expression – incarnation of his appreciation

---

[60] John Carmody, *Cancer and Faith*, 89.

of God's goodness and favours to him in his conflicted life – possible. Because of this dynamic of gratitude, he is able to apprehend, appraise, and graciously appreciate all God's favours, which have come down to him through "the great cloud of witnesses" in his faith and from the tradition pyramid at the top of which he now is. He had learnt in the primordial triad, and with the "blessings of his parents," to trust in God's goodness – even on seemingly hopeless situations – for which he is now grateful.

In Holy Scripture, Luke's Gospel tells us of the cure which Jesus performed victims of skin-disease (Lk 17:11-19). Out of the ten, only one who found himself, indeed, cured of his disease returned to express his gratitude to Jesus. As Luke observes, this man who went back "and threw himself prostrate at the feet of Jesus and thanked him" was a Samaritan (v.16). The comment Jesus made, commending the man for coming back to express his gratitude in praise of what God had done for him, clearly manifests the transcendent value of the disposition of gratitude in us humans. Jesus' comment is a demonstration of divine approval us as distinctively human when we do not only affirm this core disposition which he indicates as primordial, but incarnate if in our current life form. It is therefore no wonder that the Old Testament, particularly the Book of Psalms,[61] is so full of instances of expressions of gratitude to God for his numerous gifts to individuals, communities, and in fact, to all of his creation.

The disposition of gratitude in humans towards God cannot be genuine without the parallel desire to be "at-one" – reconciled – with God. As the religious of our primary formation event appreciatively praises God's goodness towards him and incarnates this appreciation through the expression of his gratitude to God, he seemed to quickly understand that any strained relationship between him and others would adversely affect the genuineness of his relationship with God, and thus also of his gratitude to him. Hence,

---

[61] See especially *Psalms* 18, 28, 30, 65, 66, 136, 138 and 139.

as he apprehended that he had strained relationships with others, he desired and sought to be reconciled with them.

The desire for reconciliation in religious subjects is not only to reestablish good and harmonious relationship with God alone, but also with others. Insights from our discussions on the desire for purification of oneself in view of maintaining good relationship with God and the ancestors in the African faith traditions have confirmed this reality. Above all, Jesus has taken the essential character of the disposition of reconciliation with others to beyond any doubt. Instructing his large number of followers in *The Sermon on the Mount*, he told them of the obligation of being reconciled to one's brother (or sister) before presenting one's offering to God (Mt 5: 21-26).

If therefore the religious subject of our original formation event sought to be reconciled with the care givers of the health facility in which he has been for all those months, he was at least infrafocally conscious that a genuine reconciliation, and any hope of good relationship and eventual union with God in the ancestral *congregation*, would be a delusion.

OBSTACLES TO AND FACILITATING CONDITIONS FOR RELIGIOUS FORMATION

As our investigations of the Coformant has adequately revealed, at least two main obstacles to consonant human formation on the religious horizon, have become exposed. One such obstacle is the creation of the religious subject's own *willful projects* for his life. Influenced by his autarchic pride form, he may find it difficult either to express gratitude or to actively seek reconciliation, especially on the level. Hence, *his willful projects* may continue to make it difficult for him to submit himself completely to God. The other primary obstacle may be *the lingering moral guilt* of having wronged his God. This guilt-feeling may make him not to feel completely

Chapter 10: Disposition of Gratitude

acceptable to his God; and like cancer, could gnaw at his core disposition of gratitude, and of the desire to reconcile, until he gives up in despair.

On the other hand, facilitating conditions for consonant human formation on this horizon include, first of all, the atmosphere of peace which now surrounds the subject; second, the disposition of gratitude towards his God, ancestors, and others; and thirdly, the desire to reconcile and to be "at-one" with others whom he believes he hurt in his previously dissonant current form of life.

Transition to Foundational Christian Presence

The preceding research concentrated on the foundational religious horizon of human presence. It endeavoured to discover how greater abandonment of self to God may lead religious towards a fuller formative healing through purification in reconciliation and, in deeper peace, may make them become grateful. On the Christian horizon of human presence, the Coformant, in the following investigation, will focus on how a Christian may attain perfect healing even in death.

CHAPTER ELEVEN

ATTAINING CHRISTIAN PERFECTION THROUGH DETACHMENT FROM ONE'S WILLFUL PROJECTS

INTRODUCTION

In this chapter, we intend to elucidate Coformant three on the horizon of foundational Christian presence. As the Christian abandons himself to God and is purified and reconciled to Him, he may further seek perfection through detachment from those functionally willful projects, the failure of which initially made him feel abandoned by God. The Coformant is formulated in the following terms:

> Christians who surrender their prideful willfulness may be inspired and drawn by grace to submit themselves more humbly to God. They may become appreciative of all the love they receive. And, in humility and meekness, they may seek Christian perfection in obedience to God's will, even if that includes death.

As we have done in all the levels elucidated so far, this Coformant will also be elucidated in two parts. The first part will study how the Christian, in *surrendering his pridefulness*, may be led to a greater *self-submission to God*. Part two will focus on obedience to the will of God as the way to Christian perfection.

PART ONE

SURRENDERING ONE'S PRIDEFULNESS AS THE WAY TO SELF-SUBMISSION TO GOD

This first remote foundational statement of the Coformant is formulated in the following terms:

Christians who endeavour to surrender their prideful willfulness may become inspired and drawn by grace to submit themselves more humbly to God.

In this first part of the chapter, we will explore the above statement in two sections. Section A will study *how Christians may surrender their prideful willfulness to God*, while section B will explore *the role that grace may have to play in the Christian's self-abandonment to God*.

SECTION A: OVERCOMING ONE'S PRIDEFUL WILLFULNESS

The Christian who seeks complete abandonment of himself to the will of God, so that he may follow Christ's example of total submission to his Father's will, may realize that this is not possible without an effective desire to overcome his prideful willfulness. In this area of our research, we intend to find out in what prideful willfulness may consist and how it may be overcome through self-detachment of the Christian.

Chapter 11: Attaining Christian Perfection

From the SFHF: Willfulness, Willlessness, and Willingness

In chapters one and three of this research, we discussed at some reasonable length the concepts of *willingness* and *willfulness*.[1] Here we would like to recall what Formation Science intends by these concepts and also what it means by *willlessness*. This should help us to understand better in what the construct prideful *willfulness*, which the Christian desires effectively to overcome, consists.

In *Religion of Personality*, Adrian van Kaam devotes to a great extent the third chapter of his discussions to these three connected concepts.[2] He regards *willfulness* and *willlessness* as two extremes of *willingness*. To introduce this discussion on *willfulness*, he writes: "Willfulness emerges in man when he loses the experience of his unity. He separates his will, as it were, from other elements of his personality, such as his past history, his inclinations and passions, his imaginations, his anxiety, and the power of his habits and customs."[3] In indicating in this way the origin of the willfulness which may manifest itself in a person, van Kaam defines comprehensively at the same time its meaning. In this sense, it affirms that my willfulness, especially as a Christian, is the ignoring of the working of grace in me in the belief that I alone, by my will power, can make things work the way I want them to do. The result of such willfulness is that I refuse, as van Kaam says, "to take into account all the other aspects of my life." This refusal includes, unfortunately, the transcendent potency – God, the Divine Forming Mystery.[4] The task at hand thus becomes relegated to execution by only my functional will.

---

[1] See chapter one and chapter three.

[2] Adrian van Kaam, *Religion and Personality* (Pittsburgh, PA: Epiphany Association, 1991); see especially 92-113.

[3] Ibid., 92.

[4] Ibid., 98.

While *willfulness* makes me believe that I can always master, direct, control, and eventually manipulate my own existence at will, *willlessness*, which is the opposite of *willfulness*, is an insidious denial of the power of the working of grace in me to effect the good willed by God. In other words, it is the denial of the God-given powers in me to effect the innate consonance in my founding life form. After having described willfulness as above, van Kaam appropriately makes evident, in the following terms, its extreme opposite – willlessness:

> On the other hand, while admitting the influence of the other aspects of my life, I should not exaggerate these either. I should not declare for example, that I can do virtually nothing, that my passions and the influence of my past are stronger than I am. Nor should I claim that grace should do all for me because I am too weak and evil to cooperate with grace in any significant way.[5]

From this clear contrasting critique which he makes of the two, van Kaam is right to conclude thus: "In both cases I fall from my imaginary absolute will power to an equally imaginary lack of will. I fall from willfulness into willlessness."[6]

With these insights from the notions of willfulness and willlessness, willingness becomes evidently the consonant experience of the human will. This is what van Kaam calls the *existential and religious will* of the human person. He is convinced that as a human being, I can take a stand in the situation of sin, even of organic affliction and neurosis. As he explains:

> I can do so because my will has an existential or dialectical nature. My will is not, as we have seen, the absolute ruler imagined by the will-

---

[5] Ibid., 98-9.
[6] Ibid.

power Christian. Nor am I the will-less product of my past, my impulses, passions, or environment. My will is my ability to respond to reality as it reveals itself to me in a situation, even when I am not able to change this reality in all its factual aspects.[7]

Hence, willingness, which is my religious will, opens me up to the Divine presence of God. This is why van Kaam can appropriately affirm: My religious will becomes unconditional commitment and surrender to His mysterious design.[8]

From the SFHF: Detachment and Openness

As one might have observed in our discussion on willfulness, the human pride form, which is the quasi-foundational life form and is isolationist, obviously has much dissonant influence in its emergence, however insidiously it might seem to present itself. However, we shall not discuss the pride form here, as we have already done so earlier.[9]

In an article on 'Transcendence Crisis as an Invitation,' published in *Studies in Formative Spirituality*,[10] I reechoed the invitations asserted by van Kaam and Muto, which transcendence crisis offer to people generally in their mid-life. One of these invitations, they had pointed out is de-idolization.[11] They succinctly point out how *mid-life crisis*, or better, *transcendence*

---

[7] Ibid., 105-6.

[8] Ibid., 106.

[9] See chapter one; Adrian van Kaam, *Fundamental Formation*, 54-6.

[10] Albert A. Kuuire, "The Event of Physical Weakening: A Transcendence Crisis as an Invitation and an Opportunity to Foster Formative Anticipation," *Studies in Formative Spirituality XIV* (November 1993): 367-80.

[11] Adrian van Kaam and Susan Muto, Unpublished lecture notes on *Developments in Formation Science* (Pittsburgh: Duquesne University, IFS, Spring Semester, 1992). See especially Adrian van Kaam, *The Transcendent Self*, 55-79.

crisis, invites us to de-idolize all the things: career, material things, ideals, and ideologies, even persons we made idols of in the height of the most successful period of our life.[12] For in the process of idolizing them, we attach ourselves to these things and give God little or no place at all in our life form.

Hence, this profess of de-idolizing, as van Kaam and Muto assert, is nothing other than detachment from these things to which we had become so attached. In this way, we may be liberated to attach ourselves to God. For now that all the glamour, which we experienced in our attachment to these idols of our most successful period in life, is vanishing in the wake of our deteriorating current form of life, it becomes an opportunity for us to make effective a consonant detachment from them and to attach ourselves to God. It is an invitation to what van Kaam calls **active detachment**, which he describes as "a spirit-guiding giving up of the inner attachment to what we have been deprived of." This differs from **passive detachment**, which "involves God depriving us of something sufficiently significant in terms of our current life form to affect its structural strength."[13]

In this sense, detachment becomes *openness*. It becomes a liberating force which opens us up in *willingness* to embrace the mystery with its limitless possibilities. It opens us up to God and even to the host of other possibilities which we may have locked out in the very idols to which we had attached ourselves. This seems to be what van Kaam implies when he writes:

---

[12] This is the period when the person can be at the height of his or her vital-functional potential. Van Kaam describes this phase of the human development in the following terms: "To be successful in this phase is to enjoy the experience of our expanding skillfulness. We feel the power of our ambitions, the effectiveness of our actions" (*The Transcendent Self*, 39-40). This period is usually considered to be within the ages of 30 and 40. However, Transcendence crisis, of which van Kaam speaks here, is not restricted to any particular period in the human development as psychologists define for the mid-life crisis. Transcendence crisis can occur at any time in a person's lifetime; See my article mentioned in footnote #10 above.

[13] Adrian van Kaam, *Religion and Personality*, opus cit., 185.

This detachment gives rise to a more expansive presence to self and surroundings. It is rooted in the trust that every situation the Lord allows is potentially rich. Daily life may become less of a drain on our energy. Lived in the Lord it may even recharge our powers. Each task and problem may present itself as an opportunity to flow with the Divine will.[14]

This is so because we have broken open and become liberated from our selfish encapsulated presence to the idols we created for ourselves. For as van Kaam rightly estimates:

When we focus on exalted experiences, we block out the divine tidings in and around us in the everyday. Our spirituality is no longer incarnated in daily life. We try to fit the situation into our schemes and projects instead of asking what the situation itself directs us to regardless of self-centered inclinations and past stereotypes.[15]

We shall now explore further the dispositions of humble self-detachment and surrender in attachment to God in the mystic, Teresa of Avila.

Teresa of Avila: Self-Detachment in Humility and Surrender in Union with God

Throughout her classics, Teresa of Avila has consistently come back on the theme of "detachment." It is clear indication that, for her, the union with God, which is the ultimate objective of all spirituality and mysticism, is

---

[14] Adrian van Kaam, *The Dynamics of Spiritual Self-Direction*, 44-5.
[15] Ibid., 44.

impossible without a complete detachment of the person (soul) in humility from everything that is created. This assumption seems implied in every step the soul takes on its way to this union with God which takes place in the Seventh Dwelling Place of *The Interior Castle*.[16] For example, admonishing her sisters of the little security we have in this life, and urging them to stand deprived and thus naked before the Lord, she reassures them: "There is no doubt that if a person perseveres in this nakedness and detachment from all worldly things, he will reach his goal."[17] And again she reaffirms:

> I really believe that whoever humbles himself and is detached (I mean in fact because the detachment and humility must not be just in our thoughts – for they often deceive us – but complete) will receive the favor of this water from the Lord and many other favors that we don't know how to desire.[18]

In all of the detachment that Teresa urges her sisters to make, humility seems the most essential, as can be observed from the above. As Teresa leaves it clearly implied, even evident, if a soul has become detached from everything that is worldly (pp. 426, 436, 439, 440), and has become so attached to the Lord and ardently seeks union with him (pp. 408, 274, 337, 353, 360, 379, 395, 429-30), so that it becomes His slave (446-7), it is because

---

[16] Teresa of Avila, *The Interior Castle*, in *The Collected Works of St. Teresa of Avila*, vol. 2, trans. Kieran Kavanaugh and Otilio Rodriguez (Washington, D.C.: Institute of Carmelite Studies, ICS Publications, 1980). See especially from the Third to the Seventh Dwelling Places. See also p. 274, in the Introduction. Also in *The Way of Perfection, in the Collected Works*, particularly chapter four (53-8 of vol.2), she discusses love of one another, detachment from all created things, and true humility, as the "three things that are important for the spiritual life.

[17] Ibid., 308.

[18] Ibid., 326-7.

of the high degree of humility that it has attained. For no soul can reach any detachment whatsoever from all things, including the idols of things and persons that it might have created for itself, without a humble openness of itself to the Infinite Majesty of the Lord before which it stands naked. Hence, Teresa expresses the importance of humility for detachment when she cries out in wonder of those who would consider rather lightly the overcoming of spiritual dryness without humility: "Oh, humility, humility! I don't know what kind of temptation I'm undergoing in this matter that I cannot help but think that anyone who makes such an issue of this dryness is a little lacking in humility."[19]

For Teresa there is no other way to the soul's union with God in the *spiritual marriage*[20] except through complete detachment of oneself, in humility, from everything created. This liberates the soul so that it can in turn freely surrender itself in union with God – His Majesty. In the next section, we shall examine what role the grace of God plays in this surrender of the soul (or person) for its union with God.

SECTION B: SUBMITTING TO THE WILL OF GOD THROUGH GRACE

In the desire to conquer one's prideful willfulness, and to humbly submit oneself to the will of God, the Christian may find himself or herself powerless to do so all alone. However, through the help of divine grace he

---

[19] Ibid., 307.

[20] In the *Seven Dwelling Places*, Teresa describes the union between the soul and God as a *spiritual marriage*. It is how John of the Cross also regards this complete surrender and attachment of the soul in union with God as it is evident in especially his *Spiritual Canticle*; confer *Collected Works of St. John of the Cross*, trans. Kieran Kavanaugh and Otilio Rodriguez (Washington, D.C.: ICS Publications, 1977), 399-402, 458, 488-99, 512-3, 550-1, etc.

may overcome his prideful willfulness and become able to submit himself to the will of God in greater humility. The research in this proximate area intends to study the dynamics of divine grace.

From the SFHF: Pneumatic Anticipation

Earlier, we discussed the nature of grace and its formative power.[21] Before even the Christian begins to desire and to actively work towards the submission of himself or herself to the will of God, grace is considered to have already preceded his or her very desire and is what actually inspires him or her this desire to surrender himself or herself to the will of God.

Such grace which inspires even the Christian's very desire to submit and surrender himself or herself to God seems to be what formation theory calls ***pneumatic anticipation***. In his glossary entries in *Studies in Formative Spirituality,* van Kaam describes *Pneumatic Anticipation* as:

> The availability degree, meaning and configuration of pneumatic revealed and infused formation truths and events, both shared and personal, that form one's inspired life-anticipation and that may prophetically influence present Christian formation. This anticipation enables one to surmise tentatively by the power of grace some probable aspect of the divine direction of one's life-formation in the near and distant future.[22]

Even from such an empirical description of pneumatic anticipation, it appears evident that this same reality is what *informational theology* would consider as one kind of **"actual grace;"** i.e. insofar as "*Conversion*" [as grace] is the opening of a human person to God's love," and "'Actual grace' is that

---

[21] See chapter three, part two.
[22] Adrian van Kaam, "Provisional Glossary," Studies 2 (Feb 1981): 122.

help of God which enlightens our mind, and moves our will to shun evil and to do good'"[23] It seems clear that such pneumatic anticipation, as described above, is that actual grace which is sometimes called more specifically "*gratia preveniens.*" That means, pneumatic favours or free gifts of the Holy Spirit which come beforehand to a person to inspire and to prepare him to receive the grace of conversion itself to God's love – *sanctifying* or *justifying grace.*

Understood in this light, pneumatic anticipation will be that preceding action of the Holy Spirit in the formation centres of the Christian – mind and will – in order to prepare him for full surrender to, and union with God.

From the SFHF: Grace and Detachment

In his book *The Woman at the Well*, Adrian van Kaam devotes an entire chapter to *Grace and Detachment.*[24] Here, with an empirically formative disposition, van Kaam discusses the interaction between grace and the Samaritan woman's disposition of detachment which became manifest in the event of her encounter with Jesus at the well. After pointing out how willing Jesus was to grant the request of the woman for "living water," van Kaam also immediately indicates how the woman was not yet prepared to receive what she was requesting. The "living water" which she asked for is grace. But she was not yet ready to receive it. Van Kaam gives the reason for her unpreparedness to receive what she herself had asked for, as he explains:

---

[23] See Quentin Quesnell, "Grace," *The New Dictionary of Theology*, eds. Joseph A. Komonchak & Co. (Collegeville, MN: The Liturgical Press, 1991), 437-50. See also Stephen J. Duffy, "Grace," *The Modern Catholic Encyclopedia*. Eds. Michael Glazier & Monika K. Hellwig (Collegeville, MN: Liturgical Press, 1994), 349-55.

[24] Adrian van Kaam, *The Woman at the Well* (Denville, New Jersey: Dimension Books, 1976), 65-75.

To become ready for grace, we need a growing awareness that our search for fulfillment outside of God has been in vain, that it has wounded us. We need the insight that idle pursuits have led us to idolize people and things. We substitute them for God, displacing him as the ultimate source of joy and meaning.[25]

Van Kaam is convinced that it is this awareness that we are striving for fulfillment in the wrong direction, which may give rise to two consonant directives in us: humility and repentance. They are these two dispositions which, if constantly awakened in us, will effectively ready us for the reception of the graces we request from God. As he succinctly points out, "Humbleness must pervade our wounded self as a fine fragrance, making us attractive to God as a demure bride is for her groom. An atmosphere of repentance must create and gently maintain a movement of inner distancing from self-created idols and frenzied agitation they evoke.[26]

In order that the grace we ask for from God and which God freely gives to us may be effective for our formation, we must, in repentance, distance ourselves from anything that we created to take God's place in us. For as long as we do not distance ourselves from them, they remain as obstacles which will block the dynamic of grace from God coming into our "hearts." This *distancing* of ourselves from these idols of our own creation is what is best known as *detachment.*

Before we consider the relevance of all these insights from the above discussions to the Christian of our primary formation event, we want to dwell for a moment with Saint John of the Cross, on the gratuitous nature of grace.

---

[25] Ibid., 65.
[26] Ibid., 65-6.

Chapter 11: Attaining Christian Perfection

Saint John of the Cross: "Ah, the sheer Grace!"

In the earlier discussion on the *refusal of grace*, we took note of the definition which the recent *Catechism of the Catholic Church* has given to it. In essence, the *Catechism* defines grace as "a participation in the life of God." We also observed the Church's declaration about grace which she also calls "God's free initiative."[27] Further on, the same Catechism describes the nature of grace and also its source in these terms: "Grace is first and foremost the gift of the Spirit who justifies and sanctifies us. But grace also includes the gifts that the Spirit grants us to associate us with his work, to enable us to collaborate in the salvation of others and in the growth of the Body of Christ, the Church."[28] All this points unequivocally to the gratuitous gift that grace truly is. It is something which is not merited in any way by the recipient who so greatly benefits from it.

This reality about grace seems to be what St. John of the Cross so eloquently proclaims when, in the very first two stanzas of his great poem, *"A song of the soul's happiness in having passed the dark night of faith,"* he bursts out in deeply appreciative sentiments: "Ah, the sheer grace!"[29] In Book One of *The Ascent of Mount Carmel* in which he explains the first stanza of his poem, St. John of the Cross exposes, in chapter fifteen, the gratuitous nature of the soul's escape or liberation from prison expressed metaphorically in this third line of the stanza. In St. John of the Cross' own words.

> The soul uses as a metaphor the wretched state of captivity. It is a sheer grace to be released from this prison without hindrance from the jailers. The soul through original sin, is a captive in the mortal body, subject to

---

[27] See chapter three.
[28] *Catechism of the Catholic Church*, 485 (2003).
[29] St. John of the Cross, Collected Works opus cit., 68.

passions and natural appetites; when liberated from this bondage and submission, it considers its escape, which is unnoticed, unimpeded, and unapprehended by its passions and appetites, a sheer **GRACE**.[30]

In the explanation which St. John of the Cross gives to this metaphorical escape of the soul from the prison of its own body – the jail and its passions and appetites – the gratuitous help which the soul receives for such an escape cannot remain hidden. The reality, that it can escape from such a prison in which it has been so heavily incarcerated and confined, is a sheer favour given to the soul. The soul has done nothing which merits for it such an escape. It is a gratuitous liberation and freedom that it receives. *A sheer grace.*

One may begin to wonder what relevance all the above insights may have for the Christian of our primary formative even. The relevance of all this for the subject of our original formation event is what we shall now try to point out in the following paragraphs of our integrative reflection.

Integrative Reflection

Although the Christian of the original formation event experienced some inner peace, and felt grateful to God, and also to his care givers, after having eventually abandoned himself to God, as we observed, he felt there was still more of this his recent past that he needed to distance himself from. In the serenity of his newly found peace, he still had reason to feel ashamed of and sorry for dissonant dispositions in which he was till then, imprisoned. For as he admits, "Presently looking at my Bishop, I feel sorry and ashamed for having been angry at him."[31]

---

[30] Ibid., 105. Emphases, mine.
[31] See Formation Event, Preface to this Book, viii-xii.

Chapter 11: Attaining Christian Perfection

If the Christian of our primary formation event became angry at his Bishop for which he is now ashamed and sorry, it is because of the personal willful projects which he created for himself. In his insidious pridefulness, he had idolized the functional ambitious projects of his formation field. His functionalistically willful projects had thus taken the place of God as what would bring him fulfilment and satisfaction. Hence, when they began to fail him woefully, he blamed this failure in part on another. For in the blindness of his deformed disposition of exaltation in these projects, he thought that this other would have been the one to help him realize them. So, disappointed, our Christian became angry with this other.

However, thanks to the life-story of Aloysius Gonzaga, the Christian could appreciatively appraise God's unconditional love for him, and as a result, be able to abandon himself in surrender to God. Now he perceives that greater self-abandonment, leading to union with God, can only be realised in the measure that he detaches and distances himself from those functionalistic and prideful projects. He will have to overcome them all since they had taken the place of God within his *heart*. He will have to conquer all these deformative dispositions which lead him to move, not only away from and against god, but also away from and against his neighbours.

Though the Christian might have come to realize that his greater self-abandonment to and union with God depends on his self-detachment from his functionalistic willful projects, he also realises that, alone and by himself, he cannot do it. He is aware of the luring power of what St. John of the Cross identifies as the passions and appetites to which the soul fell victim and prisoner after original sin. Hence, it is through his cooperating with "sheer grace," as St. John says, that he can ever arrive at some significant degree of self-detachment, and that God may favour him in his self-surrender to God, with the grace of union between them. Thus, with the blessing which the Bishop gave him before leaving was already, for the Christian a confirmation, however remotely, of the donation of the pneumatic favours which would direct him in this task of self-detachment from his own created idols.

Besides St. John of the Cross' poetic explanation of such a mystical expression in which the human person – more specifically so the Christian – is called to surrender his pridefulness and to submit himself to God, St. Teresa of Avila also makes this reality of detachment in her spiritual classics. In *The Way of Perfection,* discussing what she considers as the "three things that are important for spiritual life," Teresa writes: "The first of these is love for one another; the second is detachment from all created things; the third is true humility, which, even though I speak of it last, is the main practice and embraces all the others."[32] Because of our limitations as *existent beings*, we can never be able to attach ourselves to God and to be in union with Him in whom is the fulfilment of our being while we remain attached to some created beings of our free choice.

Further in *The Way of Perfection*, Teresa, instructing her sisters about favours which God may give in contemplation, expresses her conviction of the necessity of detachment from even small things, to dispose ourselves for the embrace of God:

> Oh, blessed care, my daughters! Oh, blessed renunciation of things so small and so base that reaches so high a state. What would it matter, when you are in the arms of God, if the whole world blamed you? He has the power to free you from everything, for once He commanded that the world be made. It was made; His will is the deed.[33]

In the above quote, Teresa seems to be echoing Holy Scripture, both the Old and the New Testaments. In the New Testament, for example, Jesus taught incessantly that we should always seek to distant ourselves from all that is worldly and to attach ourselves to things willed by "the Father." Thus

---

[33] Ibid., 97.

for instance, as the disciples wondered at one time, if someone had brought Jesus some food because he did not seem to care for the food which they brought back from the town but was busy attending to people, he told them this: "My food is to do the will of the one who sent me to complete his work" (Jn 4:34).[34] Again, in revealing himself and the source of his mission to the disciples, Jesus humbly told them:

> By myself I can do nothing;
> I can judge only as I am told to judge,
> And my judging is just,
> Because I seek to do not my own will
> But the will of him who sent me (Jn 5:30)

When, therefore, the Christian of our original formation event appraised God's unconditional love for him in deep appreciation and sought union with God through self-surrender and attachment to God, there was no other way for him than to detach and to distance himself from all his willful self-created idols. It is only in this way that he can then hope to advance towards the perfection of the heavenly Father to which Jesus invites us all in his *Sermon on the Mountain*.

Transition to Remote Foundational Statement Two

In the foregoing remote foundational statement, our attention has been concentrated on the exploration of the way through which the Christian may conquer his prideful willfulness more effectively and be able to submit himself in greater humility to the pneumatic will. Such a Christian may be

---

[34] See also Mt 6:10; 7:21; 11:26; 12:50; 26:42; Lk 10:21; 22:42. The instruction of Jesus, that we should submit and abandon ourselves to the will of God rather than our own, is expressed most consistently in St. John's Gospel.

following the Christ-Form as an example and thus may be seeking Christian perfection and not his own functionalistic willful *perfection*. In the following remote foundational statement, we will focus on the disposition of gratitude and obedience as the way to Christian perfection.

PART TWO

SEEKING CHRISTIAN PERFECTION IN GRATITUDE AND IN OBEDIENCE

This remote foundational statement of the Coformant on the Christian level of presence is formulated in the following terms:

In appreciation for all the love they receive, Christians may develop increased gratitude, and in humility and meekness they may seek perfection in obedience according to the example of Jesus Christ.

In this part of our research, we shall, in two sections, explore the above foundational statement. We shall investigate, respectively, how gratitude and obedience are necessary dispositions for Christian perfection.

SECTION A: APPRECIATION AS ESSENTIAL TO GROWING TOWARDS CHRISTIAN PERFECTION

Under the influence of divine grace, the Christian's desire to submit himself to the will of God grows ever closer to, and becomes a more perfect imitation of, the Christ-Form to which Jesus invites all: "Be perfect, therefore, as your heavenly Father is perfect." This growing desire to completely submit oneself to God in imitation of the Christ-Form may be manifested in the Christian's core disposition of appreciation – gratitude. Here we want

Chapter 11: Attaining Christian Perfection

to explore the transcendent disposition of gratitude as a sign of growing in perfection as Jesus ordained us to do.

From the SFHF: **Hallmarks of an Appreciative Heart**

In the preceding chapter, we discussed at some length the disposition of gratitude. We did so within the framework of self-abandonment to God and reconciliation with God and neighbour. We discovered in this process that gratitude and appreciation express the same core disposition in the existent being which we may describe as "consonant acknowledgement of favours we have received."[35] However, as we observed, this disposition, which is a primordial core character, is also transcendent and has as its origin the Christ-Form after which it is modelled. Hence, in our expression of gratitude to God, either directly or indirectly, we not only acknowledge our appreciation for the divine favours we have received, but we also incarnate in ourselves the Christ-Form character by which Jesus is eternally grateful to God – the Father.

In their book *The Power of Appreciation*, van Kaam and Muto perceive the disposition of appreciation as having the potency both to mirror through our service to others, God Himself who is Eternal Love, and to transform God's creation which includes ourselves. After observing the dynamic of the transforming power of appreciative presence and its competence, they underscore the two goals of the disposition of appreciation mentioned above in these words:

> Our pursuit of the good is sustained by a disposition deeper than functional competence. It has to do with **mirroring** our service to others the love of God for all people. Our human care, in other words, begins to reflect the care of the Creator. We see ourselves as channels of care

---

[35] See chapter ten.

through whom the love of God touches and **transforms** every epiphany of creation. We become more sensitive to the pain and brokenness of humans everywhere.[36]

Therefore, while appreciation as a transcendent character mirrors in us God's Eternal Love and care for His creation, it also gradually transforms us into what we mirror to others, the image of God after which we are created. In this light, the four principal personal hallmarks of a caring heart which van Kaam and Muto identify as congeniality, compatibility, compassion, and competence make recognition of the true disposition of appreciation possible.[37]

From the SFHF: Self-Appreciation and Self-Depreciation

Earlier, we took note of what van Kaam and Muto consider living appreciation. "[It] means being grateful for all that is – from its source in the Divine Forming Mystery to its outflow in every sphere of our life and world."[38] In order that one may live appreciatively in this way, one has to start by appreciating "incarnationally" all favours – divine gifts, human as well as cosmic – which one receives. In this way, one's character of appreciation is gradually reformed and being transformed.

In a glossary entry which van Kaam makes on "self-appreciation" and "self-depreciation" in connection with *con-formation* and *co-formation*, he says this of the experience of *form effectiveness*: "This experience nurtures a deeper *self-appreciation* and the potential appreciation of the Formation Mystery in which one's deepest unique life call is rooted. The experience of form ineffectiveness or impotency, on the contrary, would give rise to

---

[36] Adrian van Kaam and Susan Muto, *The Power of Appreciation*, opus cit., 121.
[37] Ibid., 122. See also 123-6 for secondary hallmarks of the caring heart.
[38] See chapter ten.

dispositions of *self-depreciation*."³⁹ From this description of the two concepts of *self-appreciation* and *self-depreciation,* it implies that one cannot be appreciative of God's gifts in all of creation, unless one has learnt to appreciate favours bestowed on oneself by God either directly or indirectly through creation. So, living appreciatively, as van Kaam and Muto rightly perceive, will not be possible for one who has not learnt to live appreciatively for all favours received personally. With Karl Rahner, we shall now examine the disposition of gratitude which all *existent beings*, particularly the Christian, who is supposed to understand better, should have for the Cross of Jesus Christ.

Karl Rahner: "Gratitude for the Cross"

Divine favours, or transcendent directives, which are given to us in one way or another for our ongoing formation, and transformation, are not always perceived by us as acceptable and, therefore, appreciable. Most often, in our hedonistic cultures, we do not consider things which do not bring us immediate comfort as things which we should appreciate, and so, be eager for.

However, as Stanley Hauerwas correctly observes with a certain poignancy about genuine love, "[It] can only be authentic when it faces honestly the conditions under which we must love in this existence."⁴⁰ He makes this observation precisely in connection with (Christian) love for the Cross. If this is so, the manifestation of love, we can infer, always involves pain which hurts, unless if it is that "cheap love" which is often said to be blind.⁴¹ In this sense, therefore, the Cross of Jesus must be the absolutely

---

[39] Adrian van Kaam, "Provisional Glossary," *Studies* IV (May 1983), 272-3.

[40] Stanley Hauerwas, *Vision and Virtue* (Notre Dame, Indiana: Fides/Claretian, 1974), 117.

[41] Ibid.

authentic manifestation of love when we consider honestly the conditions under which he had to manifest his love for us in that manner.

The love which Jesus manifested thus on the Cross presents to us the Cross, with all its pain and hurt, a divine favour which should evoke in us the utmost of the disposition of gratitude of which we are capable. This seems to be the point which Rahner makes in his book *The Content of Faith*.[42] In the article entitled "Gratitude for the Cross," Rahner, after he had recalled what Christian spiritual literature has often affirmed about the *pious* accepting their "cross," remarks and comments on the incomprehensibility of such an affirmation and the demand it makes. He then goes on to affirm comprehensively from everyday experience the gratitude Christians should have for the Cross:

> It would appear that in life we can only give thanks through life for life and not for death, but that in fact is what both the cross of Jesus and our cross primarily are. In this rather hopeless situation we might at least take consolation in the thought that when nothing further can be done, we are free from all obligation. This, obviously would include gratitude for the Cross. To Christians, however, and to those who in the depth of their being are anonymously but truly Christians, a great and finally incomprehensible promise has been made. In death they will not only be saved, as it were, from without by God's power, but this saving act of God will enable them to save themselves. Through an act that is both theirs and God's, they will be able in death to abandon themselves and thus and thus experience gratitude for the Cross. Such gratitude consists ultimately in the acceptance, through God's gift, of Christ's cross and our own. The Christian hope is that God himself with His power will be with us in the abyss of our powerlessness at the moment of death so that not only will life follow death but death itself through God's power

---

[42] Karl Rahner, *The Content of Faith* (New York: Crossroad, 1992).

becomes our own act by which life is created. Willing self-abandonment is a deed that creates eternity.[43]

Although, admittedly, this affirmation of Rahner is definitely very comprehensive, dense and profound, a number of elements still come readily to the fore. One of such elements is the paradoxical nature of the gratitude that Christians should have for the cross. It is a gratitude in which there is pain, culminating in death itself. Yet it is precisely out of this pain and death that fullness of life comes forth to the Christian believer. Gratitude in this understanding therefore brings the fullness of life – formative healing – to the Christian in perfect salvation.

It is clear that more could be said here with regard to Rahner's affirmation above concerning the Christian's gratitude for the cross of Jesus. However, the observation we have just made with respect to it in the context of Christian perfection is sufficient for our goal in this research. Hence, we shall now go on to examine in section B, how obedience, after the model of the Christ-Form, essentially leads the Christian towards perfection.

SECTION B: SEEKING CHRISTIAN PERFECTION IN MEEK AND HUMBLE OBEDIENCE

As Christians, in their desire to submit themselves completely to God, seek to imitate the Christ-Form as perfectly as they can, they are aided in this by the Christian character of meek and humble obedience. This gives to the core form of life of Christians the disposition of Christ-Form docility to

---

[43] Ibid., 309-10. The Christian spiritual literature's affirmation and demand which Rahner find incomprehensible, holds that "the pious must and indeed can accept with gratitude and even joy the bitterness of their life, its disappointment, pain, and hopelessness, the slow and yet inexorable approach of death, as their "cross." (309)

the Father in the Holy Spirit. This area of the research intends to study the Christian virtue of Christ-like obedience which may lead to Christian perfection.

From the SFHF: Obedience as Total Openness

We studied in an earlier Chapter the virtue of obedience and discovered its basic character which is essential for true Christian ministry. As we may recall, the Christian minister who has been called to help accomplish the mission of Christ his Master has no authority of his own. Therefore, to be congenial and to respond consonantly to his unique and communal life calling, he has to obey and carryout, like Christ himself, the will of the one who called him to minister.[44] Here, however, we want to investigate and to find out what Formation Science considers to be the essence itself of the Christian character or disposition of obedience.

In what we may call a truly profound discussion on *The Emergence of Religious Life in the History of Human Unfolding*, Adrian van Kaam in his book **The Vowed Life** offers a comprehensive definition of the disposition of obedience in human beings. This definition is indeed comprehensive because it takes into consideration, not just the human being out of any context and by himself, but in relation to the cosmic epiphany out of which he emerges as a transcosmic being, thanks to his *free will*. This is what truly makes the human being a religious being.[45]

After he identified *freedom and insight* as the "new element" in the human being, which makes the qualitative difference between human life and that of animals,[46] van Kaam asserts: "Man is no longer dominated by

---

[44] See chapter eight.

[45] Adrian van Kaam, *The Vowed Life* (Denville, N.J.: Dimension Books, 1968), 24.

[46] Ibid., 23.

that instinctive animal appreciation of what happens around him."[47] Because of this difference provided by human "freedom and instinct" between the human and the other animals with which the human shares what he calls "instinctive obedience,"[48] van Kaam defines the character of obedience in humans thus: "Obedience in the widest sense is the total openness of the whole man to the meaning of all events in his life."[49] He explains:

> Because man is spirit, freedom and insight, his obedient listening to events attains a depth and variety incomparably richer than the instinctive obedience of animal life. Animal obedience is pre-set in advance, fixed, and focused in few directions. Man's obedience is dynamic. Man's ability to listen to the hidden meanings and potentialities of natural and historical events is never and finished but ever ongoing and expanding.[50]

It is in this light that the character of human obedience is perceived as total *openness*. This total openness of the human being to what happens and affects the human life form, which is foundationally called in a unique and communal manner, is due to the human spirit. Hence, this total openness which characterizes the human dynamic of obedience finds its origin in the Divine Forming Mystery, and more precisely, in the Christ-Form after which we are created.

From the SFHF: Meekness as Gift

---

[47] Ibid., 24.
[48] Ibid., 21.
[49] Ibid., 25.
[50] Ibid., 25-6.

Elsewhere in this research, we demonstrated the close link that exists between the disposition of humility and all the basic Christian character dispositions among which is obedience,[51] like the essentially inseparable relationship between humility and obedience, formation theory perceives a similar closeness between the Christian characters of meekness and humility. So closely are they linked that the presence of one instantaneously implies or suggests the presence of the other, as Susan Muto seems to suggest in her book, *Blessings that Make Us Be*.[52] The heart which is meek is also considered to be humble.

After a few attempts at explaining what the promise of the third Beatitude – *Blessed are the meek, for they will inherit the earth* (NRSV Mt 5:5)[53] – could mean, Muto discusses three main realities which she considers pertain to the foundational meaning of the disposition of *meekness*. *Meekness* is a gift; it is God-molded; and it is the way by which we can articulate our foundational Christian character.[54]

Because of its foundational human character geared towards our formation, meekness is, indeed, a gift. Again, Muto brings out this reality very

---

[51] See chapter eight.

[52] Susan Muto, *Blessings that Makes Us Be* Petersham, MA: St. Bede's Publications, 1982), 74. *The New American Bible* translates the Greek term IIpaeic, in Mt 11:29, as "meek." Others – see the *New Revised Standard Version*, the *Revised English Bible*, and the New Jerusalem Bible – translate it as "gentle;" see *The Interlinear Greek-English New Testament*, ed. n & trans. Jay P. Green (Peabody, Massachusetts: Hendrickson Publishers, 1985). See also A. Patristic Greek Lexicon, ed. G.W.H. Lampe Oxford University Press, 1961); here the Greek term: IIpaoc (IIpauc), is rendered *gentle, mild*, in English.

[53] The New Jerusalem Bible, which translates this beatitude, using the term, "gentle" in place of "meek," lists it as the second beatitude, and takes what the others list as the second beatitude for the third.

[54] Susan Muto opus cit., 75-80.

clearly when she explains the beatitude referred to above in the following terms:

> Contemporary language resists words like *gentleness* and *meekness*. *Confrontation, self-assertion, bold outward comportment* – these phrases push out words that acknowledge human limits. Yet this beatitude insists on praising all who are lowly. It seems to imply tender acceptance of our unique gifts, another word for "limits." We are not to measure who is more or less important in worldly terms, but to encourage one another to be on the basis of our true worth.[55]

It is in this light, therefore, that Muto sees the "giftedness" of meekness. For in this sense, meekness becomes essential for our interformation based on respect for the uniqueness of the individual other. As she affirms: "When we respect our own gifts, we can listen with docility to others who serve as our teachers."[56]

We have discussed the concepts of meekness, humility, obedience, and gratitude in the language of Formation Science as **dispositions** or **basic Christian characters**. These are what informational theology also designates as **virtues**. In these last paragraphs of the section, we will now discuss, in *The Catechism of the Catholic Church*, what Christian faith tradition understands by "**virtue**."

Catechism of the Catholic Church: **The Virtues**

The Catechism of the Catholic Church defines virtue in general as follows:

---

[55] Ibid., 75.
[56] Ibid.

A virtue is a habitual and firm disposition to do the good. It allows the person not only to perform good acts, but to give the best of himself. The virtuous person tends toward the good with all his sensory and spiritual powers; he pursues the good and chooses it in concrete actions.[57]

Following upon this definition of virtue, the Catechism tells us that "human virtues are firm attitudes, stable dispositions habitual perfections of intellect and will that govern our actions, order our passions, and guide our conduct according to reason and faith." This clarification of what the human virtues are recalls to mind formation theory's definitions of the *core form* of the human life as "the relatively enduring ground form of life,"[58] and form dispositions which are equally lasting dynamic directives coforming the actual human life-form.[59] The *Catechism* regroups all such human virtues under four major ones which serve as pivots for the rest. It calls these, "the Cardinal Virtues." They are Prudence, Justice, Fortitude, and Temperance.[60]

The *Catechism* teaches that these human virtues are "acquired by education;" and it adds that through "deliberate acts and by perseverance ever-renewed in repeated efforts [they] are purified and elevated by divine grace." As it further teaches, because the human being has been wounded by sin and, therefore, cannot easily maintain the moral balance with the strength of his own virtues alone, "Christ's gift of salvation offers the grace necessary to persevere in the pursuit of the virtues."[61]

---

[57] *Catechism of the Catholic Church* (opus cit., 443 (1803)),
[58] Adrian van Kaam, *Fundamental Formation*, 299.
[59] Adrian van Kaam, *Human Formation*, 1 and 166.
[60] *Catechism*, 443-5.
[61] Ibid., 445 (1810).

Chapter 11: Attaining Christian Perfection

Besides the human virtues, which are elevated by divine grace through Christ's gift of salvation which helps them to maintain the moral balance of the Christian, the *Catechism* distinguishes and describes in the Christian the presence of a by far superior category of virtues, which it calls theological. These are the virtues of *Faith, Hope,* and *Charity,* and they are the grounds in which our human virtues are said to be rooted. Originating directly from God, they are infused in us and thus become the foundation of our Christian moral activity.[62]

In connection with the virtues, acquired and infused, the Catechism instructs Christians that their moral life – which is to grow towards the perfection of the Father to which Jesus invites all – "is further sustained by the gifts of the Holy Spirit." These gifts are identified and listed as follows: ***wisdom, understanding, counsel, fortitude, knowledge, piety, and fear of the Lord.***[63]

If these seven gifts and fruits of the Holy Spirit are not directly also called virtues, we may say it is because they are perceived more especially as results, fruits of the theological virtues. However, as fruits, and therefore, gifts of the Holy Spirit, they dispose the Christian's life form in an enduring manner and so enable the Christian to sustain consonantly the unfolding of his or her founding life form as the image and likeness of God. The following paragraphs will endeavour to reveal to us how all this, together with the rest of the insights gained in the second part of the chapter, reflect on our Christian seeking perfection, and ultimately, if granted the grace, transcendent transformation.

Integrating in reflection, the ideas obtained

---

[62] Ibid., 446 (1812-29).
[63] Ibid., 450 (1830-2).

As we can conclude from the observation of the actual life form of the Christian in the original formation event at the time his concerned and caring visitor left him, his life form has changed from one of dissonance to one of consonance. He has grown ***from*** a life-form plagued by deformed and dissonant dispositions of prideful willfulness, despondency, anger, ingratitude, in short, a general dissonant disposition of fullness of self and self-sufficiency; ***through*** abandonment of himself to God; ***to*** the consonant foundational disposition of full appreciation of God's unconditional love for him, which he manifests in gratitude, and in humble and meek obedience to God's will.

In this process of change, the Christian of the primary formation event seems to have had his focus well on the Christ-Form, even if this focus was only prefocal. For example, the gratitude which he manifested after he was able to apprehend and to appreciatively appraise God's unconditional love for him, seems to come from nowhere else but from the Christ-like gratitude towards God the Father. The gratitude of Christ to the Father, like his humble and meek obedience to the Father's will, permeates all of the New Testament. In Christ's public life, as the gospels reveal to us, he was constantly giving thanks to God the Father for the so many favours that he regarded as coming from Him.[64] The Greek term: ευχαριστιών which is translated "thanksgiving," "gratitude," and is eventually called "the Eucharist" in the *re-enactment* of the Last Supper that Jesus had with his Apostles,[65] is the "*locus excellens*" in which is manifested Christ's ***grateful*** or ***thankful character*** to God. For in the Eucharist, Christ gives himself completely to the Father in ***thanksgiving*** for us.

---

[64] See Mt 11:25; 15:36; 26:27; Mk 8:6; 14:22; Lk 10:21; 22:17, 19; Jn 6:11, 23; 11:41.

[65] See a Patristic Greek Lexicon, ed. G.W.H. Lampe (Oxford University Press,1961).

Chapter 11: Attaining Christian Perfection

St. Paul, "the least of the Apostles" (1 Cor. 15:9), never ceased to make this character of the Christ-Form his own. This is very indicative in all of his letters. For example, he tells the Romans in the opening paragraphs of his letter to them, of how immensely grateful he is to God for their sake: "First I give thanks to my God through Jesus Christ for all of you because your faith is talked of all over the world" (Rom 1:8).[66] As we have also remarked in the last chapter, the psalmist in particular consistently manifested a disposition of profound appreciation and gratitude to God for God's immeasurable favours to them and to Israel His Chosen People.

As the Christian of our original formation event effectively seeks to distance himself from his prideful willfulness – his self-created life projects – so that he may approach perfection, he is aware that his own dispositions by themselves alone will never be able to bring him there, however virtuous they may be. Hence, his appreciation of the blessings which the Bishop gives him as he prepares to take his leave of him. Infraconsciously for the Christian, it is a calling of God's grace upon him. This grace is what he believed would help him and sustain him in his growth towards the Christian perfection to which Jesus has invited all his followers.

Christ promised his Apostles before his passion and death: "I shall not leave you orphans; I shall come to you" (Jn 14:18). Before that, he had already told them of how he would ask his Father to send the Paraclete to them (Jn 14:16-7). The coming of the Paraclete to them will be, indeed, God's immeasurable and free gift to them - *Grace*. This Paraclete would make clear to them all that Jesus himself has taught them, and it would sustain them in every way so that they may eventually attain the perfection willed by the Father, which consists of the fullness of the healing and salvation, that Jesus offers to all through his Passion, Death and Resurrection (Jn 16: 5-15).

---

[66] Also see Acts 27:35; Rom 6:17; 7:25; 16:4; 1 Cor. 1: 4, 14; 14:18; 15:27; 2Cor. 1:11;8:16; Eph. 1:16; 5:20; Phil 1:3; Col 1:3, 12; 1 Th 1:2; 3:9; 2Th 1:3; 2:13 Heb 12:27.

OBSTACLES TO AND FACILITATING CONDITIONS FOR CHRISTIAN FORMATION

The principal obstacle to consonant growth towards Christian perfection and therefore, towards formative healing, is functionalistic willfulness. It is the manifestation of the quasi-foundational life-form – the pride form. For the pride-form may insidiously give dissonant directives to the functional will of the Christian and thus hinder it from apprehending and appraising consonantly directives, especially from the transcendent will – the will of God. Its influence may even block the working of grace which God gives to help the human being to reach the fullness of perfection for which He created him. From this basic obstacle, therefore, may emerge a host of other obstacles on the way of the Christian's growth towards perfect imitation of the Christ-Form. They may also impede eventual union with God in which the Christian may find the total and formative healing he is looking for.

However, two primary conditions in particular seem to facilitate the Christian's growth towards perfect imitation of the Christ-Form which will lead him to formative healing and union with God. They are divine grace, which alone can successfully fight the dissonant influence of the pride form, and the Christ-Form which is ***Absolute Grace*** made incarnate for us, and which will always remain the inspiring model of perfect submission to, and union with God.

Transition to Segmental Presence: Christian Ministers

In the foregoing horizon of self-abandonment to God the Divine Forming Mystery of true formative healing, the research focused on how Christians may reach perfection. It explored how Christians may seek perfection, which includes, or is ultimately the formative healing of all distinctively human illnesses, through the surrendering of their functionalistic willfulness.

In the following horizon of appreciative self-abandonment, the segment of Christian ministers, we wish to bring our research to conclusion as we investigate to find out how Christian ministers, by effectively desiring to overcome their functionalistic zeal, may attain congeniality with their foundational life form in their ministry.

CHAPTER TWELVE

CONGENIALITY IN MINISTRY THROUGH OVERCOMING FUNCTIONALISTIC ZEAL

INTRODUCTION

The last chapter of our research investigated the third Coformant of our original formation event on the level of foundational Christian presence. It elucidated what is involved in the seeking of Christian perfection. While assuming as valid also for the Christian minister all that has been discussed of the Christian in the preceding chapter, we shall seek in this chapter to illuminate how Christian ministers may become truly congenial to their foundational life form in their ministry. The Coformant in this segmental horizon is stated in these terms:

> When Christian ministers, who have submitted themselves to the will of God, ardently desire to overcome their functionalistic zeal, and its previous subsequent frustration and despair in the fear of imminent disruption of their ministry, they may be inspired and drawn by grace to greater self-abandonment to god's will. They may feel grateful, and with a transformed sense of their ministry, may experience more congenially, in meekness and greater fidelity to god's will, their unique-communal call to follow Christ in their vocation to Christian leadership.

Just as we have followed the same method of investigation the Coformant in all the foregoing chapters, we shall elucidate the Coformant in two parts. Part one will study how the Christian minister may overcome *his functionalistic zeal through greater self-abandonment.* In the second part, we will endeavour to study how the same Christian minister may *become congenial with his unique-communal life call in his ministry.*

PART ONE

GREATER SELF-ABANDONMENT IN THE DESIRE TO OVERCOME FUNCTIONALISTIC ZEAL AND FRUSTRATION

The first part of this Coformant which will be elucidated, will be formulated in the following terms:

Christian ministers, who desire and work to overcome their functionalistic zeal and subsequent frustrations which arises from their perception of imminent disruption of their ministry and may lead them to despair, may be further inspired to greater self-abandonment to God's will.

This remote foundational statement will be studied in two separate sections. The first section, A, will examine how Christian ministry may be exercised with rather purely functionalistic zeal. The second section, B, will explore how the Christian minister may overcome frustration and despair which may arise as a result of apprehension of imminent disruption of his ministry.

SECTION A: EXERCISING CHRISTIAN MINISTRY WITH FUNCTIONALISTIC ZEAL

In the exercise of their role in ministry, Christian ministers may become functionalistically zealous. This zeal may be for their personal willfully crafted projects of life which they may make of their ministry. They may perceive in the ministry their own personal and willful goals which may neither be congenial nor compatible with the true Christian ministry to which they have been called. In this section of the research, we intend to study the deformative functionalistic zeal which Christian ministers may have in their ministry, which they may have to work to reform, and even to transform.

From the SFHF: Mere functionalistic and Exalted Dispositions

We have already discussed the necessity of form directives – hence, form dynamics which come from the formation dispositions inherent in the three form dimensions of the individual as a formation field – for the consonant formation of the person.[1] Although we observed that appreciative appraisal of all directives from the three dimensions is necessary for true and consonant formation to take place, we underlined the indispensable role played by the transcendent dimension.[2] However, here we want to discuss those directives which may come only from functional dispositions of the individual as a Christian minister.

Discussing about dispositions which may be merely functional, Adrian van Kaam states the following in contrast to the beauty that transcendent dispositions disclose:

> Some people live lives of mere routinization. They may develop an exalted fantasy life to break the tediousness of an existence that is not uplifted by transcendent presence. This fantasy life is fed by unappraised pulsions, flamboyant ambitions, and popular pulsations. To escape meaningless routines, people develop a deformative disposition for the

---

[1] See chapter one. See also chapter four.
[2] See chapter one.

novel, the grandiose, the latest, and the newest, for fads that emerge within and without their religious or ideological form traditions.[3]

Such dispositions, which are evidently taken as ends in themselves, are therefore nothing but mere functional dispositions. They stop short the appraisal process and do not lead to any consonant formation of the person.

These dispositions, which are merely functional, are exalted dispositions. Rooted in the exalted pride form of the person's life form, they are mere functional ambitions with dominate the person's life. In this way, they direct the person away from his or her goal of consonant formation, and thus alienate his or her founding life form. Adrian van Kaam makes the following clear observation in that regard:

> Because these dispositions in their[4] exaltation are **uncongenial**, they alienate persons from their foundational life-form. For the same reason, they are often incompatible with one's life situation, and they lack compassion for the vulnerability of self and others. Exalted dispositions estrange people from their own foundational life-call and potentialities, from daily reality, and from others.

Exalted Aspirations and Inspirations: The insights from the above observation by van Kaam discloses to us the true nature of exalted aspirations. They are disguised exalted ambitions which come from mere functional dispositions. In a presentation on *The Six Phases of the Ebb and Flow of Social Presence*, van Kaam describes the first of these phases thus: "First of all, there occurs an initial phase of exalted aspirations and ambitions. This phase is strongly influenced by the pride-form and its aggrandizing in-

---

[3] Ibid., 88.
[4] Ibid.

fluence on our imagination."[5] In the next phase, he indicates that there is a difference between exalted aspirations and ambitions, and realistic aspirations and ambitions.

This is where we get our intuition from; that exalted aspirations are simply disguised **mere functional dispositions**. This means that such aspirations are dynamics which do not really come from the transcendent dimension as they may seem to pose themselves, but from the mere functional dimension in which the object of the aspiration is taken as the goal in itself. Hence, such aspirations are not truly transcendent dynamic but exalted ambitions in disguise.

From the SFHF: Beyond Functionalism

From the above conversation, it appears clear that exalted aspirations, like exalted ambitions, come from an illusion isolated self. Dominated by the pride-form, such encapsulated and insulated self is convinced that he or she can attain "genuine formation" – a merely functional ambitious goal – all by himself.

As it appears, the transcendent dimension, and its dynamics, is absent in such a field of formation. But as we recalled above, the attainment of genuine formation is not possible without the dynamic which comes from the transcendent. Van Kaam again underscores the absolute necessity of the element from "beyond functionalism" – the transcendent. He explains in the following assertion:

> Transcendent dispositions cannot be based on the illusions of our isolated self. This self is imaged as a lonely rock arrogantly and defiantly arising from the sea of reality. It is illusory self, out of touch with its formation field and its transcendent source. We should center ourselves

---

[5] Adrian van Kaam, *Formation of the Human Heart*, 301.

instead in our hidden form of life, emerging as it does from the mystery within, generating dispositions of presence to its epiphanies in mundaneness of daily duties.[6]

This latter affirmation by van Kaam is, indeed, what the individual will experience if the dispositions by which he or she lives daily are not based on an isolated self-dominated by the pride-form but on dispositions which are transcendent. Hence, the Christian minister whose zealous daily ministry is not based on transcendent dispositions, but on illusions of his or her isolated self, dominated by his or her pride-form, will be exercising a ministry with functionalistic zeal fed by empty flamboyant ambitions, and popular pulsations.

In the paragraphs following, we shall explore, together with M. Basil Pennington who by the way of contrast demonstrates how Christian ministry can become a mere functional personal project for some ministers.

M. Basil Pennington: "Aloysius Mystic?"

As Basil Pennington illustrates very well by way of contrast in the ascetic practice of the life disposition of St. Aloysius, the daily ministry of a Christian leader can become a merely functionalistically willful personal project. In his article, "Aloysius Mystic?"[7] in which he discusses the ascetic practice of the Saint, he describes the mystic in these terms:

The mystic is the one who allows the Holy Spirit to act in his or her life through the gifts of the Holy Spirit received at Baptism. Our role in the

---

[6] Adrian van Kaam, *Human Formation*, 100.

[7] M. Basil Pennington, "Aloysius Mystic?" In *Aloysius*, eds. Clifford Stevens and William Hart McNichols (Huntington, IN: Our Sunday Visitor, Inc., 1993), 115-24.

mystical life lies in allowing the Spirit the freedom to act. The role of the ascetical life, which is not wholly prior but indeed concomitant with the mystical life, is to free ourselves from what prevent us from allowing the Spirit to act in us: the domination of our false self with its projects, its possessions and its self-centeredness.[8]

However, as he immediately acknowledges following upon this description of the mystic, "Unfortunately our ascetic practice can become a project in itself and end up binding us instead of freeing us."

After some in-depth analysis of the basis of the ascetical practice of Saint Aloysius, Pennington concludes that he was a true mystic. As he claims:

Aloysius was a mystic in the authentic sense in which each of us is called to be a mystic. He lived out the potential of his baptism. He let the indwelling Spirit form and led him, and he courageously listened and followed, no matter what the cost. God did seem to be in a hurry with him. That corresponded to his intense nature: Grace builds on nature, the nature God gives us.[9]

To demonstrate that Aloysius allowed the Spirit the freedom to act in his life, Pennington gives an example of an episode in the Saint's life in which, as he was playing cards during recreation, the group was asked by one of the novices what each would do if they knew they would die in five minutes' time. Aloysius, as Pennington says, is reported to have replied in words such as these: I would go right on playing cards. God is where his will

---

[8] Ibid., 117

[9] Ibid., 123. Earlier in the article, Pennington had observed Aloysius' ardent longing for death. He remarked: "Aloysius certainly overdid it and severely injured his health" (117). This seems to be what he alludes to as God being in a hurry with Aloysius.

is. He won't be found elsewhere. And that is where He wants to find us, not only at the moment of our death, but all the time."[10] To this, Pennington adds that the activity of the gift [of transcendence presence] was also evident in the manner Aloysius would get into worldly affairs to act as an effective mediator in family disputes.

Pennington finds this disposition of Aloysius to be based on the fact that "[he] had come to passionately love our Lord."[11] This is evidently an example to be emulated by the Christian minister who has sincerely come to passionately love Christ who is the Master, and who has called him or her to be his minister. Unfortunately, exactly like in the case of mysticism to which we are all called but some of us refuse to allow the Spirit the freedom to act in us, Christian ministers may turn their ministry into their own willfully crafted project, and so may refuse to allow the Spirit the freedom to act in them.

However, as the Christian minister in our formation event seems to have demonstrated, Christian ministers who may initially refuse to allow the holy Spirit the freedom to act in their lives may, through eventual abandonment of themselves to the same Holy Spirit, yet overcome the previous frustration and possible despair arising from their refusal to allow the Spirit to act in them. In section B which will follow, we shall explore how Christian ministers may overcome the frustration, and even the looming despair, which could be the end-result of their prefocal refusal to allow the Spirit freedom to act in their lives.

---

[10] Ibid., 118.
[11] Ibid., 119.

SECTION B: OVERCOMING FRUSTRATION AND DESPAIR ARISING FROM THE IMMINENT DISRUPTION OF ONE'S MINISTRY

As Christian ministers overcome their frustration which originated from their mistaken personal life projects as the divine project to which they are called, they become more liberated and inspired to abandon themselves to God with zeal which transcend their functionalistic ambitions. For in this way they may perceive illness and even death not as a disruption of their ministry but as the will of God through which their call to ministry may be fulfilled. Here, we will examine the nature of the frustration and possible despair which may arise from the functionalistic ambitions of such Christian ministers.

From the SFHF: Vital-functional Disposition of Frustration

In a discussion under the caption *Integrating Formation*, van Kaam points out the benefits which psychotherapy could reap if it would always take into account the transcendent as the centre in the dimensions of the human life form. He indicates freedom from social pressures and frustration as one of the benefits which such a compromise would bring. As he affirms, "The source of [such] misery is our insulation within the vital-functional constellation of life."[12] In this light, van Kaam observes that the frustrations, which the individual may suffer, come from the reality that such individuals have encapsulated themselves in their vital-functional dimensions and are thus cut off from the liberating directives of the transcendent dimension which is the centre of the dimensions.

---

[12] Adrian van Kaam, *Fundamental Formation*, 64.

Frustration as Vital-Functional Expression of Unfulfilled Ambitions

One of the realities which consistently returns in this research is the indispensability of the transcendent in the human life form. Whenever this dimension is shutout, be it focally or prefocally, we head for some disaster in our formation. Van Kaam in discussing *Communality and Privacy in the Human Formation Field,* underscores the necessity of a healthy dialogue between *creative distance-taking and creative encounter* among people if they are to receive a life dorm which is both **congenial** and **compatible**. He considers this dynamic to be a source of human culture and civilization. Hence, when it is absent from a society or from a particular crowd of people, the result is ***dehumanization***.[13] However, as he asserts: "Distinctive humanness (or *spirituality*) resides in the intrasphere as personality touched by the Formation Mystery in its ongoing and unique preformation of each human life."[14]

Therefore, what essentially happens to people when consciously or preconsciously the transcendent dimension is shutout of their formation field is that they become ***dehumanized***. It is this exclusion of the transcendent from their lives, and hence, the encapsulation of themselves within their vital-functional dimensions alone, which leaves them inevitably **hopeless**. For they are bound to run up against the limits of their vital-functional dimensions which will leave them, among other dissonant dispositions, ***frustrated***. The process of *dehumanization* will have been complete in them, and they will have no other potency to turn to within those two dimensions, "in their current life form," for the fulfillment of their personally crafted goals in which they do not take into account the transcendent. Van Kaam gives a very cogent illustration of such loss of one's *humanness* in the area of sexual promiscuity when he writes: "Frantic sexual

---

[13] Adrian van Kaam, *Formation of the Human Heart*, 161-2.
[14] Ibid., See also chapter six.

promiscuity, for instance, can be a symptom of a desperate search to enter the intrasphere of others and to share one's own interiority, which has been repudiated or closed off in anxiety, hostility, or frustration."[15]

A person therefore becomes desperate and will eventually become frustrated in his or her search to enter the intrasphere of others because his or her own intrasphere has been encapsulated in his or her vital-functional dimensions alone after he or she has shutout the transcendent, and so, has become *dehumanized*. In this case, true human encounter becomes impossible, because, having been dehumanized, the person becomes unable to meet and to communicate with another on a truly distinctively human level.[16] The reality which is therefore confirmed by the above insights is that *frustration* is the expression of a person's unfulfilled willful ambitions.

Still more, as the dehumanized person feels frustrated because of the non-fulfillment of his or her willful ambitions, **despair** may take-over, as the hopelessness of even having these ambitions fulfilled deepens and becomes more and more a stark reality beyond what the vital-functional dimensions alone of the person can handle. In the second part of this section, we will seek to re-examine with Søren Kierkegaard the concept of despair which he discusses in his work: *The Sickness unto Death*.

Søren Kierkegaard: Understanding Despair as "The Sickness unto Death"

In connection with the refusal of God's graced communion, we already discussed in chapter three Kierkegaard's contention that *despair is the sickness unto death*. We discovered what he means when he says, "Despair is the sickness unto death." As we noted, the *despair* that Kierkegaard envisions is not some mortal illness that would lead to mortal death of a

---

[15] Ibid.

[16] See chapter one.

person. As he explains despair as sickness unto death in the strict sense, it is "one in which the last thing is death, and death the last thing."[17]

If in this sense despair is considered to be the last thing, then it means that after despair has set in, there is nothing more that the person can do to salvage himself or herself. The final door has been closed to *hope*, and, therefore, to the possibility of any reformation of the despairer's life form. All is over, and nothing else can ever be done to remedy such a condition of the *existent being*. This situation is what we sometimes express, *in common parlance*, as "hoping against hope." The fate is sealed and cannot be changed again.

If **despair** is to be understood in this way, we may pose the following question: "Is it still possible then to speak of overcoming one's despair?" In the above sense that Kierkegaard understands *despair as sickness unto death*, we can answer in the affirmative. As Kierkegaard clearly points out the context in which he uses such a phrase, if despair were literally that mortal sickness which is synonymous with a sickness unto death, then despair could not be said to be sickness unto death. He regards *despair* as sickness unto death **only within the Christian context in which mortal death is understood not as an end**, but a *transition* into life."[18]

This understanding of *despair* gives a completely new dimension to it as sickness unto death. It becomes a concept which can only be well understood within the context of **transcendence**. As Robert Bretall makes clear in his introduction to *The Sickness unto Death*: "[It] an investigation of this corruption (man not being yet a self – the dramatic letdown of man) in human nature, which of course, is what the Church calls *sin* but which

---

[17] See chapter three.

[18] Søren Kierkegaard, *Sickness unto Death*; in, *A Kierkegaard Anthology*, ed. Robert Bretall (Princeton New Jersey: Princeton University Press, 1973), 341. See also the Preface in the Eucharistic Celebration for the Dead in the Catholic rite of Mass for the Dead.

Kierkegaard, in accordance with the 'psychological' view point here adopted, chooses to call despair."[19] In fact, Kierkegaard clearly made the point himself when he supports his claim of *despair* being sickness unto death with Socrates' proof of the immortality of the human soul. As he points out in *The Sickness unto Death*:

> Socrates proved the immortality of the human soul from the fact that the sickness of the soul (sin) does not consume it as sickness of the body consumes the body. So also we can demonstrate the eternal in man from the fact that despair cannot consume his self, that this precisely is the torment of contradiction in despair. If there were nothing eternal in a man, he could not despair; but if despair could consume his self, there would still be no despair.[20]

Hence, we cannot speak of overcoming despair in the Kierkegaardian sense, except with means which are transcendent. Since despair, being synonymous with sickness of the soul, *sin*, exists only on the transcendent level. This means is none other than **grace** which originates from the transcendent-pneumatic and can empower us to overcome such *despair*. As we reach that level of frustration which definitively marks the utmost limits of the vital-functional, and so makes every other effort by these dimensions alone hopeless, it is grace alone which can take over, and help us to overcome despair if we allow the Spirit to act in us. It is only grace which can still give the despairer the transcendent potency to overcome his or her despair.

How may we then relate the above insights to the Christian minister of our formation event who may seek to overcome his functionalistic zeal

---

[19] See *Introduction* to *The Sickness unto Death*, in *A Kierkegaard Anthology*, 340.

[20] Søren Kierkegaard, 'Sickness unto Death,' in *A Kierkegaard Anthology*, 344.

through greater self-abandonment to the will of God? This is what we intend to do in the integrative reflection that will follow.

Integrative Reflection

As we may recall, the frustration and feelings of despair which the Christian minister of our original formation event experienced came from his apprehension of the imminence of his death.[21] This signaled the brutal disruption of all the personal willfully crafted projects which he dissonantly appraised as belonging to the ministry to which he believed he has been called.[22] He had applied himself, with such great zeal, to the realization and thus the fulfillment of his personal projects which, under the influence of his **exalted pride form** in the insidious form of the exalted disposition of zeal, were crafted by his mere functional ambitions.

However, aided by consonant form directives from the life-form of Saint Aloysius, the Christian minister eventually appraised appreciatively what he initially believed to be the imminent end of his personal projects disguised as ministry, and so abandoned himself to God. In so doing, he experienced in himself the receding of his negative feelings, which included his frustration and despair. These two latter dissonant dispositions came as the result of the fact that he would not see his projects fulfilled. However, he perceived, either focally or infrafocally, that he could only overcome, to a greater extent, his previous frustration and despair the more completely he abandoned himself to God.

On the other hand, greater self-abandonment, as we discovered in the preceding chapter, cannot be achieved without a more complete detachment of oneself from one's own willful projects which have become one's ideals and idols. It is precisely the fact that the Christian minister could

---

[21] See Proximate Background to Formation event, Preface to this Book, ix.

[22] Confer chapter four.

neither realize nor attain fulfillment of these ideals that became the origin of his frustration and subsequent despair, Hence, overcoming these dissonant dispositions necessarily implies self-detachment from their source and origin – the personal willful projects – and attachment to God through greater self-abandonment. But as we also observed in the same preceding chapter, this process is bound to failure if grace – transcendent-pneumatic directive – does not intervene. It is only when grace comes to empower him that he is able overcome his previous frustration and despair. And this is what is implicitly acknowledged, in a vital way, in his grateful acceptance of the Bishop's blessings before the latter left him.

The overcoming of the functionalistic zeal and its subsequent frustration and despair of the Christian minister of our original formation event under investigation seems to mirror, to some extent, the life of moral corruption and depravity of Saint Augustine of Hippo and his subsequent **conversion**. In his Introduction to *The Confessions of St. Augustine*, in which he underscores the *timelessness* of it, John K. Ryan, after having remarked in a bird's-eye-view the comprehensiveness of Augustine's perennial work, summarizes it thus:

> In brief, the thirteen books of St. Augustine's *Confessions* were written by a man who had great emotional powers along with great powers of intellect and will, who had lived a life of conscious depravity as a quasi-pagan and had turned to a life of austerity as a Catholic, who was genius in philosophy, theology, and psychology, who was a pioneer in scriptural studies, who was extraordinary as a master of language, and who had strong personal attraction to others and marked qualities of leadership.[23]

---

[23] John K. Ryan, trans. *The Confessions of St. Augustine* (New York: Images Books, Doubleday, 1960), 17.

In view of all this depth of Augustine's life which, thanks to the Saint's mastery of language, springs forth in every page of his *confessions*. Ryan is right when he says: "To become familiar with St. Augustine's *Confessions* is to make one's own, to some extent at least, an inexhaustible source of intellectual stimulation, of esthetic delight, of moral help, and of spiritual enlightenment."[24]

However, what stand out in Augustine's life form as relevant to this part of our research are the depths of *moral corruption and depravity* to which he went in his "passion-to-shine," and the heights of sanctity to which rose in his *Conversion*. Directed by his vital pulsions and his functional ambitions alone, he zealously sought knowledge in the Greek philosophies, salvation or self-fulfillment in Manicheism, and pleasure in concubinage. He went wherever he thought he could attain these ends: he went from Carthage to Rome, and from Rome to Milan. But all was to his frustration and despair, for he could not find the fulfillment for which he so passionately roamed the world. As he himself reveals in the third chapter of the eighth book of his *Confessions*, his joy for the salvation, which faith in God and abandonment of himself to God brought him, but of which he had earlier despaired:

> O God the good, what goes on within a man that he should rejoice more over the salvation of a soul that had been despaired of, and was then set free of a greater peril, than if there had always been hope for him, or if his danger had been less? Merciful Father, you too rejoice more over one man who does penance than over ninety-nine just men who do not need penance.[25]

---

[24] Ibid., 18.
[25] Ibid., 185.

Here in this expression of joy for having found faith now in God and having abandoned himself to Him, Augustine's previous despair of his salvation is also clearly expressed. He expresses joy that he could come out of such despair which he experienced during his passionate quest for fulfilment in the wrong direction, to renewed hope and salvation in self-abandonment to God and detachment from his dissonant past ***through grace***.

If Augustine overcame his frustrations and despair in his zealous search for fulfillment of what he may call his personal projects, it is, indeed, thanks to grace. For instance, commenting on the fact that Augustine eventually did come to see the absurdities of the Manichean doctrine, Ryan points out the inevitable role divine grace played therein: "In time, by divine grace," Ryan says, "He was able to break loose from the sect and to become its greatest opponent and a principal source of knowledge with regard to its teachings and practices."[26] Through the tearful prayers of his mother, Monica, and the influence of the saintly Bishop of Milan, St. Ambrose, Augustine eventually received the grace of his Conversion which he describes so eloquently in especially chapter seven to eleven of the eight book of his *Confessions* appropriately entitled "*The Grace of Faith.*"[27]

In the light of all this, the Conversion of St. Augustine from his "passion-to-shine" in life could, therefore, not have been possible unless grace came to his rescue. The pursuit of his "passion-to-shine" in life encapsulated him in his vital pulsions and functional ambitions. But as these have no power of their own to bring him genuine fulfillment, they kept him imprisoned within themselves, and thus in endless frustrations and even despair. Therefore, perceiving Augustine's Conversion in this light, the overcoming of the functionalistic zeal, frustration and despair of the Christian minister of our original formation event through grace, mirrors, to a certain extent, the

---

[26] Ibid., 21.
[27] Ibid., 193-203.

Conversion of St. Augustine which he himself so eloquently narrates in his *Conversion*.

Transition to the Second Remote Foundational Statement

The first remote foundational statement above has studied how Christian ministers who endeavour to overcome their functionalistic zeal and frustration in the sudden perception of the end of their mistaken objectives in ministry are able to submit themselves more readily to God. In the second statement, we shall investigate the hypothesis that ministers who understand better the ministry to which they are called may more easily overcome the deformed dispositions of vital-functional dispositions in themselves. Then, in meekness and greater fidelity to the will of God, they may exercise their ministry in congeniality with their unique-communal life call and vocation to Christian ministry.

PART TWO

CONGENIALITY WITH ONE'S UNIQUE-COMMUNAL LIFE CALL IN VOCATION AND MINISTRY

As it is already indicated, the second part of this chapter will seek to illuminate the second foundational statement of the Coformant formulated in the terms here below:

> With a better understanding of their ministry, Christian ministers may experience congeniality in meekness and, in greater fidelity to God's will, their unique-communal life call and vocation to leadership in it.

In this remote foundational statement, which will also be elucidated in two sections, we will first explore the meaning of Christian ministry, and then, secondly, seek to find out how best the Christian minister may experience congeniality with his unique-communal life call in his vocation to ministry and leadership.

SECTION A: BETTER UNDERSTANDING OF THE MEANING OF CHRISTIAN MINISTRY

When Christian ministers consider their own functionalistic and personally crafted life projects to be what God has called them to realize in their ministry, it may be because they lack a better understanding of Christian ministry. This lack may be what gives rise to the deformative directive of zeal in the ministry which serves only their functionalistic will. To abandon themselves more completely to God in their ministry, such ministers may need to understand better the ministry to which they have been called. In this section, section A, we shall focus our study to understand better the true nature of Christian ministry.

From the SFHF: "Send Me on My Mission in Gentleness"

When the Christian minister of our primary formation event initially perceived in his grave illness that death was imminent and became convinced that this marked the abrupt end of his ministry, he blamed it on God and became angry with Him. He consequently became frustrated and despaired, convinced that God has abandoned him since his ministry would thus be unaccomplished – unfulfilled. This brutal confrontation of him by the Ultimate at that age made him question his very *existence*.

Infraconsciously, the reality is that the Christian minister was not frustrated and despairing because of the non-fulfillment of the ministry which is part of his preformation. He was frustrated, angry, and despairing rather because he became aware that, with the abrupt end of his ministry, he was not going to see the realization of and fulfillment of his own **willfully**

crafted projects. Following the dissonant directives of his vital pulsions and functional ambitions influenced by his pride form, as we observed earlier,[28] he confused with and mistook these projects for the ministry to which God called him. His understanding of ministry became, therefore, deformed. If the Christian minister understood better what the true nature of the ministry which he has been called to exercise, he might have perceived, from the beginning, its abrupt end which he was convinced was imminent in a different light. He might have appreciatively appraised it to be the will of God, and as such, truly part and parcel of the ministry to which he has been called.

The Christian call to ministry is first and foremost a call to the discipleship of Christ. In her book *A Practical Guide to Spiritual Reading*, Susan Muto discusses the disciple of Christ in the background of Isaiah's response to Yahweh's quest for someone to send to his people to speak to them on His behalf.[29] The prophet's response, "Send me," is an acceptance to carry-out God's mission. That is, to do what God was calling him and sending him to do, and not to do nor say what he, the prophet, willed. In this light, it becomes evident that the disciple of Christ, and more so, the one whom Christ has called in a special way and sent to minister in his name is not called and sent to realize and accomplish his or her own willful projects, but the projects of Christ. Hence, Muto regards, in that respect, every Christian as one who is sent on a "mission in gentleness" by God. Every Christian is sent to carry out what Christ was sent out by the Father to do and which he did according to the Father's will and not his own will. As Muto therefore affirms: "once we sense that the work we do is not merely ours but God's,

---

[28] See chapter four.

[29] Susan Annette Muto, *A Practical Guide to Spiritual Reading*, 2nd ed. (Petersham, MA: St. Bede's Publication, 1994), 131.

we can become attuned to the sacred implications of each act."[30] She underlines that the Christian does all this with gentleness.

If this is what defines every Christian as true disciple of Christ, the more so will it define the one who has been specially called to continue Christ's own ministry in the human society. And if the Christian minister will understand his ministry within this context of the discipleship of Christ, he or she will accept appreciatively whatever happens, in his or her life form, as part of God's will for him or for her, and therefore, not being outside of the ministry to which he or she has been called.

Striving After Human Approval:

Part of the willful projects of the minister may be, insidiously, to gain the approval of others. As may have been observed to be implicit in the remote background of the original formation event, the Christian minister could draw some prideful satisfaction from the approval of others for having attained efficiency in his ministry within the rather short time he was in his first station.[31] Speaking about *Deviations of the Religious Personality*, van Kaam discusses the tendency that one may have in the spiritual life to strive after human approval. He points out the dangers in such a tendency in these terms:

> A spiritual life that is built on a striving after approval is bound to become a debacle. This longing for approval makes me extremely sensitive to rejection of any kind by anyone, but especially by persons who represent for me authority in religious matters. I may even be

---

[30] Ibid.

[31] See Remote Background of the Formation event, Preface to this Book, viii.

tempted to neglect what god desires of me for Himself and His Church if I feel that it might jeopardize the approval which I so sorely need.[32]

Such a striving of the Christian minister for approval may never be on the level of focal-consciousness. Yet, as a residue of the survival mechanism from childhood, it may remain infraconscious in him with all the power to unleash the debacle which van Kaam warns about and can lead him to the ignoring of the transcendent will, even in his ministry.

It seems that Christian ministry, in practice, can be best defined in terms of *service*. With Albert Nolan, therefore, we will discuss the Christian ministry as service within the framework of Kingdom and Power.

Albert Nolan: The Power of Service and Freedom

In the chapter *The **Kingdom** and Power*, Nolan makes three very lucid statements which build up to the affirmation of power exercised in the kingdom of God as one of *service*. After stating that the difference between the kingdom of God and the kingdom of Satan concerns power, he asserts, secondly, that power and its structures are what we call politics in our days. And thirdly, he affirms that in the time of Jesus, politics concerned primarily who would be king or queen. After making these three statements, Nolan proceeds to give an analysis of what the kingdom of God consists in and quotes amply from the Evangelist, Luke, concerning the power structure of the kingdom of God.[33]

Indicating in what the principal difference is between the kingdom of God and that of Satan, Nolan makes it clear that such difference lies in the use of power. As he points out: "The power of Satan is the power of

---

[32] Adrian van Kaam, *Religion and Personality*, 155.

[33] Albert Nolan, *Jesus Before Christianity* (Maryknoll, New York: Orbis Books, 1976), 83-4.

domination and oppression, the power of God is the power of service and freedom."[34] Hence, he observes that God's kingdom is only determined by **the power of spontaneous loving service** which we render to each other. To substantiate this assertion, Nolan quotes Jesus in Mark's Gospel and especially in the way power is exercised in the kingdom of God:

> There is no mistaking the two different ways in which power and authority are understood and exercised. It is the difference between *domination* and service. The power of this new society is not a power which has to *be served,* a power before which a person must bow down and cringe. It is the power which has an enormous influence in the lives of people by being of service to them. It is the power which is so unselfish that it will serve others even by dying for them.[35]

This is the true understanding of the Christian ministry to which someone may be called. If, therefore, the Christian minister could understand the ministry he or she is exercising as a service to others and according to God's will, there will be no room for personal projects in the exercise of it, especially as a leader. For the call to Christian ministry is a call to leadership in loving service to others in accordance to the will of God.

---

[34] Ibid., 84.

[35] Ibid., 85. In Mark's passage referred to, Jesus instructs his Apostles about the use of power in, and the structure of, the Kingdom of God: "You know that among the gentiles those they call rulers lord it over them, and their great men make their authority felt. Among you this is not to happen. No; anyone who wants to be great among you must be your servant, and anyone who wants to be first among you must be slave to all. For the Son of man came not to be served but to serve, and to give his life as ransom for many" (Mk 10:42-5).

Now, in the last section of this chapter, we shall examine how such an understanding and exercise of Christian ministry may be congenial with one's unique and communal life call.

SECTION B: EXPERIENCING CONGENIALITY WITH ONE'S UNIQUE-COMMUNAL LIFE CALL IN ONE'S VOCATION TO CHRISTIAN MINISTRY AND LEADERSHIP

As the Christian ministers understand better the ministry to which they are called, they may be led to exercise it in meekness and in greater fidelity to God's will. In this way they may experience the congenial unfolding of their unique-communal call in life through their vocation to leadership. This section of our research will examine how Christian ministers, in their vocation to ministry and leadership, may live congenially with their unique-communal life call.

From the SFHF: The Unique-Communal Life Call and Divine Vocation

In chapter one of the research, we referred to the unique-communal life call in Formation Science as the dynamic aspect of the *foundational life form* of the individual human person.[36] Such dynamic way of referring to the *preformation* of our foundational life-form is a call to (freely) participate in a truly **primordial option** or **foundational formation option** which, by virtue of the human spirit, is characterized by the preformational *give* of *freedom*. This option, therefore, demands a free response from the individual. It is this response that formation theory calls 'foundational for-

---

[36] Confer chapter one, footnote # 11. See also Adrian van Kaam and Susan Muto, *Formation Guide for Becoming Spiritually Mature*, 53-65.

mation decision,' as we have indicated already in chapter six of this research.[37]

This unique-communal foundational life call, which formation theory also regards as the *primordial option*, and which option the individual is invited to freely make, is what it calls *Divine vocation*. Adrian van Kaam asserts:

> The religious personality knows himself as a unique creation with an irreplaceable divine vocation. He knows that God has called him from eternity to be a unique expression of divine goodness, truth and beauty. If he is a Christian, he realises that Christ desires to live in him in an individual way. Every Christian personality is a new and special manifestation of Christ that did not exist before him and will not repeat after him.[38]

This foundational life form of the individual, dynamically expressed by formation anthropology as the person's founding life call or divine vocation, should not be confused with what is also often popularly referred to as "vocation." While the first is preformational and, therefore, is said to be foundational, the second – what is usually popularly designated as "vocation in life" – may be best described as secondary to the foundational – Divine vocation. This response to this vocation comes from the willing *openness* of the individual to the epiphany of God in a particular way in his or her life. Adrian van Kaam clearly expresses this when, after he affirms that "willing openness is the permanent source of the manifold moods, feelings, memories, imaginations, and perceptions which particularize, as it were, my fundamental openness." He further asserts:

---

[37] See pages 261-3. For a more detailed discussion, see Adrian van Kaam, *Fundamental Formation*, 221-31.

[38] Adrian van Kaam, *Religion and Personality*, 44.

The willing openness which pervades my existence grows toward a firm decision which is a response of my whole being to that which reveals itself to my openness. For example, I may be a willing openness for what God wants me to do in my life, whether it be marriage, the married state in the world, the priesthood, brotherhood or sisterhood.[39]

Therefore, although popularly this may be referred to simply as vocation, and may also be regarded as a preformational "given," it is only so because it is implicit in the individual's unique-communal foundational calling.

From the SFHF: Congenial and Compatible Life Form

In the very first chapter of the first volume of the series in Formative Spirituality, van Kaam speaks about congenial life form. Discussing what he captions "The Emergence of the Science of Formation," he writes:

> Sometimes a congenial and compatible form of life seems to emerge almost effortlessly. Formative aspirations, ambitions, impulses, and pulsations arise spontaneously in natural consonance with one another. We sense that we are growing wisely. We feel in harmony. Life flows easily. Formation is not problematic.[40]

What we may understand in this affirmation is that, sometimes we may feel that our life form grows harmoniously, and without problems, towards maturity and its fulfillment, because such a process of growth is congenial

---

[39] Ibid., 107.
[40] Adrian van Kaam, *Fundamental Formation*, 5.

and compatible with the goal itself towards which we are growing.[41] If that is so, it means that the directives, which we follow in our journey of growth and change towards maturity, are consonant, and, therefore, congenial and compatible with the final destination of our journey.

Again, discussing about *Formation Movements in Human Life*, van Kaam says of the vital form, in that regard: "Congeniality and compatibility of ongoing formation will lead to a more relaxed flow of organismic powers and energies.[42] Further, he summarizes succinctly the directives and the object of congeniality and compatibility of the human life form in this manner:

> The verbal and nonverbal expression form of the congenial life corresponds to the spiritual, functional, and vital form of the latter are congenial to the foundational form and compatible with the consonant communities and situations in which human life participates within its formation field. The more the ongoing formation of life is congenial and compatible, the more its expression form will become gracious, peaceful, and joyful. It will manifest openness and an inner relaxed attentiveness. Facial expression, language, gesture, movement, and bearing will become relaxed yet animated manifestations of our uniquely human, congenial life in its playful interaction with all the polarities of the formation field.[43]

Hence, when indications of consonant growth towards maturity are present in a particular human life form, Formation Science concludes that

---

[41] Ibid., Under *Formation Movements in Human Life*, van Kaam affirms, "The foundational unique preformation, in which one's congenial life form is rooted, animates and energizes one's consonant formation action," 267.

[42] Ibid., 268.

[43] Ibid.

such a life form is growing congenially towards the fullness of consonant disclosure of itself.

In the light of the above considerations, we may pose the question: How could a priest, for example, assure himself that he is growing congenially in his vocation as a Christian minister? And secondly, in which way could he regard leadership as implicit in his ministry? We shall discuss these two issues, particularly the first, in the following concluding paragraphs of the chapter.

The Catholic Catechism: Participation in the Ministerial Priesthood of Christ and Leadership

In the Catholic Church, at least, Christian ministry is associated most especially with the ordained priesthood, even though by virtue of Baptism all are called to ministry in the Church, each one like "another Christ"[44] when, therefore, we speak of Christian ministry, what comes first to mind is the ordained priestly ministry. Although Baptism confers on all Christians a participation in the ministerial priesthood of Christ, down the centuries, the ordained priesthood became more identified with it.

However, the recent *Catechism of the Catholic Church*, while maintaining the special vocation to the ordained priesthood as privileged and, therefore, closer to the ministerial priesthood of Christ,[45] very clearly indicates the difference of the two participations in this one priesthood of Christ as essential. The two ways by which Christians participate in the one

---

[44] See Gerard Austin, "Baptism," in The *New Dictionary of Catholic Spirituality*, ed. Michael Downey, 1993.

[4545] *Catechism of the Catholic Church*, 384-6 (para. 1539-1545). *The Catechism* itself has quoted amply from the Liturgy of the Church for the consecration of the Bishops and from the ordination of priests and deacons to demonstrate the special manner in which these groups share in the ministry of Christ's priesthood.

priesthood of Christ are, therefore, first: through baptism, as we have already pointed out (see *The Catechism,* paragraph 1546); and secondly, through ordination by which priests, in addition to the priesthood conferred on all the baptised, also participate in the ministerial priesthood of Christ. *The Catechism* distinguishes between the ministerial priesthood and the baptismal priesthood of all Christians in this way:

> The ministerial or hierarchical priesthood of bishops and priests, and the common priesthood of all the faithful participate, each in its own proper way, in the one priesthood of Christ." While being "ordered one to another," they differ essentially (confer Lumen Gentium, 10.2). In what sense? While the common priesthood of the faithful is exercised by the unfolding of baptismal grace – a life of faith, hope, and charity, a life according to the Spirit – the ministerial priesthood is at the service of the common priesthood. It is directed at the unfolding of the baptismal grace of all Christians. The ministerial priesthood is a means by which Christ unceasingly builds up and leads his Church. For this reason, it is transmitted by its own sacrament, the sacrament of Holy Orders.[46]

In the light of the above statement, therefore, not only is the ministerial priesthood essentially different from the priesthood of all the faithful by virtue of baptism, but it is also a participation in leadership in the Church.

The above discussions have certainly given us many insights into the true meaning of Christian ministry and also into the congeniality between such ministry and one's unique-communal life call. Now in the paragraphs that follow, we shall reflect on what relevance such insights may have on the Christian minister of our original formation event.

---

[46] Ibid., 386-7 (para. 1547).

An Integrative Reflection

From the insights gained from the above discussions pertaining the remote foundational statement elucidated therein, it seems evident that, initially, the Christian minister lacked, either focally or prefocally, a better understanding of Christian ministry. He confused his own personal projects with the will of God in the Christian ministry to which he has been called. Hence, when influenced by his autarchic pride-form he perceived that his personal willful projects would not reach their fulfillment, due to the looming immense of his death, he wrongly understood that it was God who was disrupting the realization of His own Divine Will – the ministry He has called him to exercise. Initially, therefore, the minister failed to understand that what seemed, to him, to be non-fulfillment of his ministry could be precisely the way God wanted it to be realized. In short, he, at least, did not focally apprehend his ministry as service of God and the Church, but rather as something which was to be self-serving to him – the realization of his own willful projects.

Perceived in this light, the minister's vocation to Christian ministry had become deformed, and so could not be said to be *congenial* with his *unique-communal foundational life call*. For if he understood his call to Christian ministry from the beginning to be truly a divine vocation in which he was called to participate in the ministerial priesthood of Christ, as the *Catechism* reminds all Christians, he might not have seen his imminent death as being outside of his vocation – as being a disruption of his ministry – and therefore, a non-fulfillment of his ministry. As we learnt earlier, the Christ-Form is the model after which the Divine Forming Mystery created us,[47] our foundational life form which, dynamically, is called our founding life call, can only find congeniality with itself in the Christ-Form. In this respect, therefore, the ministry of the one called to Christian ministry can

---

[47] See chapter three.

only be congenial with his unique-communal founding life call if it is, indeed, congenial and compatible with the ministerial priesthood which the **Word of God – CHRIST** – was sent from all eternity, to carry out.

However, as Christ made it abundantly clear, service to others in obedience to the will of the Father, ***even if that leads to death***, is the principal character of his ministerial priesthood. As he told his close followers whom he had specially chosen and called, but who were vying for positions of honour in the kingdom:

> You know that among the gentiles the rulers lord it over them, and great men make their authority felt. Among you this is not to happen. No; anyone who wants to become great among you must be your servant, and anyone who wants to be first among you must be your slave, just as the Son of man came not to be served but to serve, and to give his life as a ransom for many. (Mt 20: 25-28)

The congeniality in the self-realization or consonant self-unfolding of the Christian minister is, therefore, service to others according to the will of God in imitation of Christ, the ***Eternal High Priest***: and ***not*** according to the minister's own will. Living one's call to Christian ministry in this way means ***willingness even to die*** as part of the ministry itself to which one is called by God, and just as Christ the Eternal High Priest has demonstrated by ministering in this way ***even to his death*** on the cross. It is to this ministerial priesthood of Christ in which the Christian minister is called, in a special way, to participate. Therefore, carrying out this ministry according to the will of God, just as Christ did, assures the Christian minister that his ministry is in congeniality with his divine vocation, and is ultimately congenial with his *unique-communal foundation life-call*. This seems to be what the Christian minister of our formation event, at least, began to become focally aware of by the time the *concerned-other* had left his hospital room.

From Functionalistic Willfulness to Transcendent Willingness

OBSTACLES TO AND FACILITATING CONDITIONS FOR THE FORMATION OF CHRISTIAN MINISTERS

If just as the concerned-other was departing, the Christian minister seemed to be apprehending the true ministry to which he has been called, and so seemed to be experiencing some congeniality and compatibility in himself and his ministry, it must have been because he was beginning to have some difficulties that were blocking his way to formative recovery, being unblocked and overcome. These difficulties were, indeed, obstacles blocking consonant unfolding of his life call – true fulfillment of his vocation. Thanks that through the eventual encounter with the concerned other, he could get the help he needed to discover the means to overcome what was making his illness to defy treatment in the hospital.

From the above investigation that has been made, two main obstacles to genuine dedication to ministry, and so to transformation of Christian ministers, surface in this horizon of segmental human presence and are identified. **One such obstacle** is the functionally and willfully crafted set of life goals for the realization of which those called to Christian ministry may misdirect their ministerial zeal. For these functionally and willfully crafted false set of goals, which Christian ministers might think believe to be the will of God, would continue to block any recovery from their true illness. **The second obstacle** identified is the lack of understanding in what true Christian ministry is. They would have a functionally willful distortion of the true meaning of Christian ministry and would thus entertain and seek the service of their own prideful life goals, which are deformed, and so are both dissonant and non-congenial with the true goals of Christian ministry.

However, as has already been said, there do also surface and can be identified some facilitating conditions for the growth and gradual transformation towards becoming a true Christian minister. Two of such facilitating conditions can listed here. The *first* of these two is the *[pneumatic] inspiration* which the minister may receive' through **grace** to greater self-abandonment to God. The second identified, consists in the ***Christ-Form and its dynamic*** of ministerial priesthood with which the ministry of the Christian minister can, in his core dispositions of meekness and fidelity, be congenial. These together would foster and nurture the consonant shift needed in the Christian ministers towards the greater self-abandonment to the will of God. This would lead to the resulting experience of congenially responding to the unique-communal life call in their vocation to Christian ministry.

TRANSITION TO DIVISION FOUR

In the three preceding divisions of the research, each of the first three horizons or levels of human presence, sought consistently, either explicitly or implicitly, to apply the insights obtained from the investigations in them to the fourth horizon or the level – the specific segment of Christian ministers.

In the fourth and final division, our investigations will now focus more explicitly on the obstacles to, and facilitating conditions for, transcending functionalistic willfulness in life-threatening human illness. Hence, we will seek to discover the obstacles that will be preventing, or conditions that will foster and nurture, ***formative healing***. In this task, the findings in the three foregoing divisions will provide the basis for this fourth division, which will seek to be praxis-oriented.

DIVISION FOUR

SUMMARY OF RESEARCH INSIGHTS AND CONCLUSIONS

STATEMENT OF THE BASIC FORMATION QUESTION TO BE INVESTIGATED

In the fourth division of this research, the basic formation question will focus on the practical application of the findings which the entire investigation on the Christian minister, conflicted through grave and life-threatening illness, has yielded. In the light of *the science of foundational human formation*, this final division seeks to bring to greater light the insights provided by the findings of the research and their practical application to Christian ministers.

This final task of the research is threefold. First of all, it will re-examine more succinctly the *primary obstacles to, and facilitating conditions for*, formative healing, which have emerged from the research. Secondly, it intends to *formulate the major thesis – through affirmative denial testing* – which undergirds the entire research. And thirdly, in conclusion, it will endeavour to state the *contribution* which it will be making to this relatively new and growing *Science of Foundational Human Formation*, the importance of which, in this period of human history, can never be over-emphasized.

474

PART ONE

PRIMARY OBSTACLES TO AND FACILITATING CONDITIONS FOR THE FORMATION OF CHRISTIAN MINISTERS

INTRODUCTION

In the first three divisions of the research, a descriptive analysis of obstacles to, and facilitating conditions for, formative healing are disclosed in each of the four horizons or levels of the human presence discussed. In this last division, however, we want to re-examine more succinctly these obstacles and also facilitating conditions, especially insofar as they pertain to human presence on the segmental level of Christian ministers. We will seek to summarize them, refining and integrating them for their practical application to the distinctively human formation of Christian ministers as they are faced with imminent death through grave illness which they may contract in the exercise of their ministry. Because of the sudden disruption of what they may dissonantly perceive to be the goal of the ministry to which they are called, they may become frustrated, angry, and even despair of the consonant fulfillment of their unique-communal founding life call.

Here, practical application of these obstacles and facilitating conditions will be made, in particular, to the population segment of Christian ministers as we have indicated. However, from the insights offered by the entire research, it is evident that these obstacles and facilitating conditions also apply in appropriate and varying degrees to the other three horizons of human presence of which the segmental horizon is representative.

PRIMARY OBSTACLES TO THE FORMATION OF CHRISTIAN MINISTERS

With the help of the insights gained by our investigation of the formation event which has provided the project for our research, we have been able to identify a number of obstacles. These obstacles are able to hinder the consonant formation, and, therefore, true formative healing of the Christian ministers, as the findings of our research have very well demonstrated. Although such obstacles are many, we will point out five major obstacles which can be considered as the roots of the many others which we will not be able to enumerate here.

A. Obstacles Discovered in the First Division

In Division One of the research which concerns the self-encapsulation of Christian ministers conflicted by grave illness with looming imminent disruption of their ministry, two dissonant dispositions in particular emerge as obstacles to their consonant formation. The first of these is ***despair***. In the original formation event, for instance, the Christian minister, having confused his own willfully crafted plans with the will of God, and perceiving that these plans would not be realized and come to fulfillment, fell into ***despair***.[1] He saw the disruption of his ministry, through his imminent death, as the result of his being abandoned ***by God***. Hence, God, who has called him to the ministry having abandoned him, he had no more grounds in his life for any hope of self-fulfillment.

The second principal obstacle is the ***refusal to open oneself for human encounter*** with others, especially the neighbour who is concerned and sincerely wants to enter into dialogue with the conflicted Christian minister.[2]

---

[1] See chapter four.
[2] Confer 181-3, and 184-7.

As long as such a minister is not open to formative dialogue and human encounter with especially a concerned neighbour, the chances of consonant growth towards maturity, and hence, towards formative healing, are very slim.

B. Obstacles in the Second Division

Although there are several potential obstacles in this division, one single particular obstacle seems to be in the trunk to which many others are branched. This primary obstacle is the ***functional ambition*** which ministers may harbour within themselves.[3] It is this functional ambition which again, in the primary formation event, tempts the Christian minister to turn the ministry, to which he is called by God, into his own personal project. In this case, he makes appreciative appraisal of his conflicted current life form difficult, if not simply impossible. For as long as ministers are not able to appraise appreciatively the directives and see what is going on in their current life forms as part of the ministry to which God calls them, they are bound to remain blind to the need to humbly accept and follow God's directives, and so will not be able to grow towards maturity in consonance in their ministry.

C. Obstacles Emerging from the Third Division

The research in the Third division reveals, in particular, two main obstacles which militate against the consonant ongoing formation and eventual **transformation** of the Christian ministers. The first one is ***misdirection of their zeal and dedication*** to their own functionalistically and

---

[3] See chapter eight. If the Christian minister has been able to appraise and to assume dispositions similar to those of St. Aloysius, it is because he aban-doned his own functional ambitions.

willfully crafted set of goals in their ministry.[4] In such misdirection of their zeal, they dedicate all their energy to the service of their own created idols and so may only use the ministry to which God has called them for the realization of these willfully functionalistic goals of their own. Hence, they will not be able to abandon themselves to God so that they may receive from God *formative healing* in its fullness.

The second main obstacle revealed in this division is the *lack of a better understanding of true Christian ministry*. If a Christian minister does not understand what the ministry to which he is called truly is – if he does not know the true nature of the ministry he has been called to exercise – he will not be able by himself, to carry it out congenially. In fact, this obstacle may be considered as the origin of the other one we just identified above – misdirection of zeal and energy. For the inability – focally or non-focally – of the Christian minister in our primary formative even to understand the true meaning of Christian ministry, for instance, left him victim to the influence of his quasi-foundational life form, his autarchic pride form.[5] It influences him to dedicate all his zeal to the service of his own personal willful projects in the guise of the Christian ministry to which he is called.

PRINCIPAL FACILITATING CONDITIONS FOR THE FORMATION AND TRANSFORMATION OF CHRISTIAN MINISTERS

Besides the obstacles which our investigation of the project of our research has permitted us to identify scientifically, through the primary formation event, I have also been able to identify conditions which facilitate the formation and even the possibility of the transformation of Christian ministers. Here below, we present what we consider as principal facilitating conditions in each of the three Coformants of our original formation event,

---

[4] See chapter twelve.
[5] Ibid.

designated as the three divisions of the research project. In all, we indicate seven such facilitating conditions.

A. Facilitating Conditions for Formation in Division One

Among others, three facilitating conditions may be easily listed in the first Coformant of the original formation event. The first facilitating condition may be identified in the *formative presence of the concerned "neighbour."*[6] It is, thanks to such presence, girded by a strong disposition of loving patience on the part of the concerned "neighbour," which enabled him to remain compassionately with the conflicted minister, in his dissonant and encapsulated current life form, until the latter opened up for human encounter.

The second facilitating condition consists in the preformational *form potencies of mind and will*, inherent in all human beings. But these potencies are especially formed and brought to focal awareness in the Christian minister for his consonant formation in compatibility and competence for the exercise of his life call to ministry. It is through these primary form potencies, as Formation Science calls them,[7] that ministers can enter into formative dialogue with a neighbour, thus opening up the possibility for form reception.

This facilitating condition for formation, and transformation of Christian ministers presupposes another condition. This condition, which we would identify as the third in the Coformant, is the *consonant interformative sphere*. This condition facilitates the formative process undertaken

---

[6] See chapter one; and see especially chapter three. This facilitating condition is already evident on the level of universal human presence. However, it is so basic that we want to underscore its essential character as such for the Christian minister.

[7] Adrian van Kaam, *Scientific Formation*, 156. See also 194-7.

by the central or primary powers of formation.[8] For without a truly consonant interformative sphere, dialogue is impossible, and penetration of the minister's intrasphere through communication, will be futile. Thus, any appreciative appraisal process will be blocked before it could even ever get started.

B. Facilitating Conditions in the Second Coformant

In the second division, we identify in particular two main conditions which facilitate the formation of Christian ministers. The first of these is the ***Christian character of obedience to the will of God***.[9] This character, which is divinely exemplified in the Christ-Form, disposes the Christian minister in his ministry to do what God wants him to do, as God's com-missioned minister in the image of Christ, and not what *he, the minister*, wants to do.

The second facilitating condition is the ***Christ-Formed character of humility*** before God.[10] Like the Christian character of obedience, this very foundational disposition of the Christian minister permits him to perceive his ministry in humility and to humbly carry out the will of God as Christ himself did, even when it meant taking on our lowly human nature. This is what Paul the Apostle of the Gentiles points out to the Philippians, and encourages them in his letter when he writes:

> Nothing is to be done out of jealousy or vanity; instead, out of humility of mind everyone should give preference to others, everyone pursuing not selfish interests but those of others. Make your own the mind of Christ Jesus:

---

[8] See chapter four.
[9] See chapter eight.
[10] Ibid.

> Who being in the form of God,
> Did not count equality with God
> Something to be grasped.
>
> But he emptied himself
> Taking the form of a slave,
> Becoming as human beings are;
> And being in every way like a human being,
> He was humbler yet,
> Even to accepting death, death on a cross *(Phil 2: 3-8)*.

Humility, therefore, is the condition, the attitude, the disposition, which facilitates and opens up the Christian minister to greater and greater self-abandonment to God. In this way, he is on the path towards the fullness of the ***formative healing*** of which he stands in need like the rest of the People of God whom he is called and commissioned to minister to in the of Jesus the Eternal High Priest.

C. Facilitating Conditions in Coformant Three

We identify two principal facilitating conditions in this division. These are the ***inspiration of grace***,[11] and the ***dynamic of the ministerial priesthood of Christ***.[12] Although Christian ministers may eventually be disposed to seek, with great zeal, the consonant unfolding, and the genuine fulfillment of their human life form, they will never be able to attain it, unless they are helped by a ***transcendent-pneumatic dynamic – grace.*** For their vital-functional dimensions alone fall infinitely short when it comes to the attain-

---

[11] See chapter twelve.

[12] Ibid.

ment of the **formative healing** for which they are searching, even in ministering to others.

To help Christian ministers still more empirically, Christ offers himself as the eternal example which can effect in them the reality itself which his Form exemplifies. It is only the ministerial priesthood of Christ, as it is revealed, through the Judeo-Christian Holy Scriptures, which sacramentally[13] proffers both the model and the means to respond to the fullness of his founding life call – a call which is, indeed, to the foundationally formative healing of *all their grave and life-threatening illnesses.*

The above reflections on the obstacles to, and facilitating conditions for, the consonant formation and eventual transformation of the Christian ministers now help us to state in conclusion with the substantial intent of this research project through **affirmative-denial testing**. With the practical application already demonstrated and observed in our integrative reflections, the thesis here-researched does not remain any longer a mere hypothesis. It has become a thesis that has been demonstrated as real and practicable, and with genuine applicability to the population segment for which the research was made – **Christian ministers**. This segment of the human population, any one of whom may find him or herself in such similar situation, may with great profit, apply to himself or herself the findings of this research.

---

[13] The *Baltimore Catechism of the Catholic Church* defined a sacrament as, "An outward sign with an inward grace." Theologically, this means that a sacrament effects inwardly what it symbolizes outwardly. The recent *Catechism of the Catholic Church* defines sacraments more dynamically as, "'powers that come forth' from the Body of Christ, which is ever living and ever giving. They are actions of the Holy Spirit at work in his Body, the Church. They are 'the master-works of God' in the new and everlasting covenant" (289, para. 1116). In this sense, Christ himself is the Sacrament of God's salvation for all of humankind. See, for example, Edward Schillebeeckx, *Christ the Sacrament of Encounter with God* (New York: Sheed and Ward, 1963).

Summary of Research Insights and Conclusions

PART TWO

AFFIRMATIVE-DENIAL TESTING OF THE
THESIS OF THE RESEARCH PROJECT

The investigations throughout this research project sought to disclose the formation dynamics in the remote foundational statement of the Coformants, as well as in their proximate directives. This process of elucidating the dynamics took place through dialogical consultation between the relevant Formation Science constructs, its religious and Christian articulations, and with some auxiliary sources. Through this process, several major hypotheses were expounded and verified and thus have consolidated the thesis initially proposed for the research project.

In the light of the verification of the remote hypothetical statements and their proximate directives through the elucidation of their dynamics, the thesis of the research project can now be evermore firmly stated in the following terms as a conclusion to the truth that has been demonstrated therein:

The formative healing of all life-threatening illness may be expedited through submission of the subject's self-encapsulated functional will to the transcendent will in appreciative abandonment, which allows for the congenial unfolding of the person's foundational life form.

This truth thus stated can be verified through *affirmative-denial testing*; that is to say, through attempting to deny either part of this thesis by affirming its negative. Such an affirmation of the negative in the thesis would result in a statement which would contradict itself. If for instance such an affirmation of the negative of the first part of the thesis could be stated in the following terms:

> *The formative healing of all life-threatening illness <u>may never</u> be expedited through submission of the subject's self-encapsulated will to the transcendent will in appreciative abandonment.*

As it is immediately evident, such a statement fundamentally contradicts the very essence of formation. Formation is **_essentially_** the work of the transcendent. And unless one submits one to the transcendent will in appreciative abandonment, **_formative healing_**, which is the fullness of self-realization in formation, is in any way impossible. For without submission of oneself to transcendent directives which are expressions of the transcendent will, one remains a prisoner in one's functional and lower dimensions alone where true human formation can never take place.

The same reality applies to the second part of the thesis statement. Denying it also by affirming the negative may be stated as follows:

> *Appreciative abandonment to the transcendent will does not allow for the congenial unfolding of a person's foundational life form.*

Again, the contradiction in such an affirmative-denial in this second part of the thesis is obvious. The statement contradicts itself in that the congenial unfolding of one's founding life-form cannot be attained through any other way, except through accepting transcendent directives, in appreciative abandonment of oneself to the transcendent will. Hence, to deny that appreciative abandonment of oneself to the transcendent will enables the congenial unfolding of one's foundational life-form is a gross self-contradiction of such a statement which affirmatively negates this second part of the thesis.

From these above demonstrations, it is, therefore, quite evident that, according to the principles and concepts of the **science of foundational human formation**, the *antithesis* to the *thesis* negates and also contradicts the truth of the thesis which has been amply substantiated in the research. This is to say, the *thesis* thus formulated is one in which *the truth is foundationally sustained* by the empirical experience of **_formative healing_**. For in it the affirmation that the current life-form of people in a similar life situation are able to grow from *functionalistic willfulness* to a more consonant current life-form of *transcendent willingness* has been foundationally and empirically demonstrated.

PART THREE

CONTRIBUTION OF THIS RESEARCH TO THE SCIENCE OF FOUNDATIONAL HUMAN FORMATION

The research which has been undertaken here sought to demonstrate that distinctively human – formative – healing of illness, even bio-physical, is foundational and does not simply consist in the restoration of physical health. The underlying intuition has been that, this foundational and *formative healing* is what all human beings aspire to, and exert themselves for, whether with focal consciousness or with only prefocal and even infrafocal consciousness. To attain this *formative healing*, the individual has to relinquish and must go beyond his or her own functionalistic and willful projects in life and submit himself or herself to the Radical Mystery of all Formation – God.

In the task of demonstrating this principal hypothesis of the research with a view towards establishing it as a thesis, the assumption, principles, constructs, and concepts of the pretheological science of foundational human formation, initiated in 1944-45 by Professor Dr. Adrian van Kaam in the Netherlands, along with the formation theology he began earlier in 1935, also in the Netherlands, have been used to dialogue with its auxiliary sources. In this dialogue, the research examined and analyzed the other major hypotheses – the remote foundational statements – of the research project on *formative healing*, and it verified and affirmed the findings. One example of such hypotheses is the affirmation that:

> Religious subjects who are suffering grave illness and are depressed may anxiously fear rejection by the Mystery for some wrong they have done, and so may also remain closed up to encounter with another.

It is primarily in the light of these findings, made possible in this research mainly through the body and methods of the *pretheological science of foundational human formation,* that we see the contribution of this research to the expansion of the science itself. For it is my hope that the results of this research will augment the body of Formation Science in this area of the human formation field, particularly of the population segment of Christian ministers, through the translation and transposition of data which might have been before this somewhat unknown to it. In doing so, the research has also demonstrated empirically that **transcendent willingness,** and not *functionalistic willfulness*, is, indeed, the pathway to truly ***formative healing*** of the *existent being.*

BIBLIOGRAPHY

BOOKS:

À Kempis, Thomas. *The Imitation of Christ*, trans. William C. Creasy. Notre Dame, IN: Ave Maria Press, 1989.

Adler, Alfred. *Superiority and Social Interest*, ed. Heinz L. Ansbacher and Rowena R. Ansbacher. Evanston, IL: Northwestern University Press, 1964.

---, The Individual Psychology of Adler, ed. Heinz L. Ansbacher and Rowena R Ansbacher. New York: Basic Books, Inc., 1956.

Alfaro, Juan. "Christian hope and hope of Mankind." Concilium 9 (June 1970)

Ancel, Alfred. *"Libération de l'homme et Salut par la Foie n Jésus Christ."*
La Documentation Catholique 70 (1973) : 532-6.

Angyal, Andras. Neurosis and Treatment, eds. E. Harfmann and R.M. Jones. New York: John Wiley & Sons, 1965.

Aquinas, Thomas. *Summa Theologiae*. Madrid: Matriti, 1962.

Arbuckle, Gerald A. and David L. Fleming, eds. *Religious Life: Rebirth through*

Conversion. New York: Alba House, 1990.

Armstrong, Regis J. and Ignatius C. Brady, trans. *Francis and Clare; The Complete Works*. New York: Paulist Press, 1982

Augustine, Saint, Bishop of Hippo. *De Trinitate*: Corpus Christianorum Series Latina, 50, 50A. Turnhoti: Brepolis, 1968.

Barry, William A. Spiritual Direction and the Encounter with God. New York: Paulist Press, 1992.

Bascom, William. *Ife Divination: Communication between Gods and Men in West Africa*. Bloomington: Indiana University Press, 1969.

Beker, J. Christian. *Suffering and Hope: The Biblical Vison and the Human Predicament*. Grand Rapids, Michigan: William B. Berdmans Publishing Company, 1994.

Bekye, Paul K. *Divine Revelation and Traditional Religions: With Particular Reference to the Dagaaba of West Africa*. Rome: Leberit Press, 1991

Bemile, Paul. *The Magnificat within the Context and Framework of Lukan Theology*. Regensburger Studien zur Theologie. Frankfurt am Main: Verlag Peter Lang, 1986.

Bemile, Sebastian K. *'Dagara' Stories*. Heidelberg: P. Kivouvou Verlag. 1983.

Bretail, Robert, Ed. *A Kierkegaard Anthology*. Princeton, New Jersey: Princeton University Press, 1973.Brueggemann, Walter. *The prophetic Imagination*. Minneapolis: Fortress Press, 1978.

Buber, Martin. *Between Man and Man*, New York: MacMillan, 1965.

---, I and Thou. Edinburgh, 1971.

Buhlmann, Walbert. *La Terza Chiesa alle Porte*. Roma : Edizione Paulini, 1975.

Capps, Donald. *Agents of Hope: A Pastoral Psychology*. Minneapolis: Fortress Press, 1995

Carmody, John. *Cancer and Faith*. Mystic, Connecticut: Twenty-Third Publications, 1994.

Carothers, John Collin. *The African Mind in Health and Disease; A Study in Ethno psychiatry*. World Heal Organization. Monograph Series, no. 17. Geneva: World Health Organization, 1953.

Carr, Wesley. *Tested by the Cross*. London: Harper and Collins Publishers, 1992.

Carroll, David. *Living with Dying*. New York: Paragon House, 1991.

Cepari, Virgilio. *Life of Aloysius Gonzaga*. Ed. Francis Goldie. New York: Benziger Brothers, 1891

---, *The Life of Saint Aloysius Gonzaga of the Company of Jesus*. American Edition. New York: P.J. Kenedy & Sons, 1867 c.

Coombs, Theresa Marie, and Francis Kelley Nemeck. *The Spiritual Journey; Critical Thresholds and Stages of Adult Spiritual Genesis*. Wilmington, Delaware: Michael Glazier, Inc., 1985

Cragg, Kenneth. *Troubled by Truth*. Cleveland, OH: The Pilgrim Press, 1912.

Crom, S. On Being Real. *A Quest for Personal and Religious Wholeness*. Wallingford,

PA: Pendle Hill Publications, 1967.

Delafosse, Maurice. *Haute-Sénégal-Niger. 3 vols*. Paris: Emile Larose, 1912.

---, *The Negros of Africa*. Trans. F. Fliegelmann. Port Washington, New York: Kennikat Press, Inc., 1931.

De Mello, Anthony. *The Song of the Bird*. New York: Doubleday, 1982.

---, *One Minute Wisdom*. New York: Doubleday, 1985.

---, *One Minute Nonsense*. Chicago: Loyola University Press, 1992.

---, *More One Minute Nonsense*. Chicago: Loyola University Press, 1993.

De Wit, Han F. *Contemplative Psychology*. Trans. Marie Louise Baird. Pittsburgh, PA : Duquesne University Press, 1991.

Dieterlen, G. *Textes Sacres d'Afrique Noire*. Paris: Galimard, 1965.

Donne, John. No Man is an Island. Ed. Keith Fallon. Los Angeles: Stanyan Books, 1970.

Douglas, Mary and Phillis M. Kaberry, eds. *Man in Africa*, London: Tavistock Publications, 1969.

Dulles, Avery. *The Craft of Theology; From Symbol to System*. New York: Crossroad, 1992.

Ebner, F. *Das Wort und die geistigen Realitat*. Innsbruck, 1921.

Edwards, Dennis. *The Human Experience of God*. New York: Paulist Press, 1983.

---, *Wort und Lieber*. Regensburg, 1935.

Egan, Harvey D. *Christian Mysticism: The Future of a Tradition*. New York: Pueblo Publishing Company, 1984.

Eliade, M. *The Sacred and the Profane*. New York: Harcourt, Brace and World, 1959.

Eliot, T.S. *Four Quartets*. New York: Harcourt, Brace& World, Harvest Book, 1943.

Endo, Shusaku. *Silence*. Trans. William Johnston, New York: Taplinger Publishing Company, 1980.

Fairlie, Henry. *The Seven Deadly Sins Today*. Notre Dame: University of Notre Dame Press, 1980.

Feldman, Susan. *African Myths and Tales*. A Laurel original. New York: Dell, 1963.

Felman, Shoshana. *Jacques Lacan and the Adventure of Insight*. Cambridge, MA: Harvard University Press, 1987.

Ferder, Fran. *Words Made Flesh: Scripture, Psychology and Human Communication*. Notre Dame, Indiana: Ave Maria Press, 1986.

Field, Margaret Joyce. *Religion and Medicine of the Ga People*. London, New York, etc.: Oxford University Press, 1961.

---, Search for Security; *An Ethno-Psychiatric Study of Rural Ghana*. Northwestern University; African Studies, no. 5. Evanston, IL: Northwestern University Press, 1960.

Forde, Cyril Daryil. *West African Kingdoms in the Nineteenth Century*. London: Oxford University Press, 1967.

---, ed. *African Worlds: Studies in the Cosmological Ideas and Social Values of African Peoples*. London: Oxford University Press, 1954.

---, *The Study of Africa*. Eds. Peter McEwan and Robert Sutcliffe. London: University Press.

Fortes, Meyer. *African Systems of Thought*. London: Oxford University Press, 1949.

---, *The Dynamics of Clanship among the Tallinsi*. London: Oxford University Press,

---, *Religion Morality and the Person*. Ed. Jack Goody. New York: Cambridge University Press, 1987.

Fowler, James W. *Becoming Adult, Becoming Christian*. San Francisco: Harper & Row, 1984.

---. *Stages of Faith; The Psychology of Human Development and the Quest for Meaning*. San Francisco: Harper & Collins Publications, 1978.

---. *Life Maps: Conversations on the Journey of Faith*. Waco, TX: Word Books 1978.

Frazer, James G. *Totemism, 4 vols and Supplement*. London: Dawson Paul Mall, 1910.

Freud, Anna. *The Ego and the Mechanism of Defense*. New York: International Universities Press, 1936.

Freud, Sigmund. *The Psychology of Everyday Life*. New York: Norton, 1901.

---. "On the History of the Psychoanalytic Movement." Vol. 1 of *Collected Papers*. Ed. James Strachey. New York: Basic Books, 1959.

---. *Analysis Terminable and Interminable*. London: Hogarth Press, 1964.

---. *The Interpretation of Dreams*. London: Hogarth Press, 1900.

---. *Civilization and Its Discontents*. New York: Norton, 1930.

---. *The Future of an Illusion*. New York: Norton, 1927.

Fromm, Erich. *The Heart of Man*. New York: Harper & Row, 1964.

Gadamer, Hans-Georg. *Truth and Method*. 2$^{nd.}$ Edition New York: Continuum, 1994.

Gardner, John. *Self-Renewal*. New York: Harper & Row, 1965.

Goody, Jack. *The Social Organization of the LoWiili*. 2nd ed. London: Published for the International African Institute by Oxford University Press, 1967.

---. *Death, Property and the Ancestors; a Study of the Mortuary Customs of the LoDagaa of West Africa*. London: Tavistock Publications, 1962.

---. *The Myth of the Bagre*. Oxford Library of African Literature. Oxford: Clarendon Press, 1972.

Granfield, David. *Heightened Consciousness*. New York: Paulist Press, 1991.

Grant, Wilson Wayne. *The Power of Affirming Touch*. Minneapolis: Augsburg Publishing House, 1986.

Green, Thomas H. *When the Well Runs Dry*. Notre Dame, Indiana: Ave Maria Press, 1979.

---. *Darkness in the Market Place*. Notre Dame, Indiana: Ave Maria Press, 1981.

Greenson, R.R. *The Technique and Practice of Psychoanalysis*. New York: International Universities Press, 1967.

Gutiérrez, Gustavo. *We Drink from Our Own Wells: The Spiritual Journey of a People*. Trans. Matthew J. O'Connell. Maryknoll, N.Y.: Orbis Books, 1988.

Häring, Bernard. *My Witness for the Church*. English translation. Mahwah, New Jersey: Paulist Press, 1992.

---. *The Truth Will Set You Free*. Vol. 2 of *Free and Faithful in Christ*. New York: The Seabury Press, 1979.

---. *Morality is for Persons*. New York: Farrar, Straus and Giroux, 1971.

---. *This Time of Salvation*. New York: Herder and Herder, 1966.

---. *Faith and Morality in a Secular Age*. Slough, England: St. Paul Publications, 1973.

---. *Sin in the Secular Age*. New York: Doubleday and Company, Inc., 1974

---. *Evangelization Today*. Trans. Albert Kuuire. Notre Dame, Indiana: Fides Publication, Inc., 1974.

---. *Etica Cristiana*. Roma: Edizioni Pauline, 1973

---. *Hope is the Remedy*. Slough, England: St. Paul Publications, 1971.

---. *I have Seen Your Tears*. Trans. Robert Hodge. Great Wakering Essex: McCrimmon Publishing Co. Ltd., 1995.

---. *Heute Priester Sein*: Eine kritische Ermutigung. Freiburg: Herder, 1995.

---. *Ich habe mit offenen Augen gelernt: Meine Erfahrung mit einer anderen Kirche.* Freiburg: Herder, 1992

---. *Ich bete, um zu leben.* Graz Wien Köln: Verlag Styria, 1996.

Hall, Thelma. *Too Deep for Words.* New York: Paulist Press, 1988.

Hammarskjöld, Dag. *Markings.* New York: Alfred A. Knopf, 1966.

Harper, George Lea. Jr. *Living with Dying: Finding Meaning with Chronic Illness.* Grand Rapids. Michigan: William B Eerdmans Publishing Company, 1992.

Hauerwas, Stanley. *Vision and Virtue.* Notre Dame, Ind., Fides Publishers, 1974.

---. *Naming the Silences: God, Medicine, and the Problem of Suffering.* Grand Rapids, Mich.: William B. Eerdmans, c. 1990

---. *Character and the Christian Life: A Study in Theological Ethics. Trinity University monograph series for religion; vol. 3.* San Antonio: Trinity University Press, 1975.

---. And L. Gregory Jones, eds. *Why Narrative? Readings in Narrative Theology.* Grand Rapids, Michigan: William B Eerdmans Publishing Company, 1989.

---. *Truthfulness and Tragedy: Further Investigation in Christian Ethics.* Notre Dame, Ind.: University of Notre Dame Press, 1977

Heidegger, Martin. *Being and Time.* Eds. & trans. John Macquarie & Edward Robinson. San Francisco: Harper & Row, 1662.

---. "Existence of Truth." *Existence and Being.* Ed. W. Brock. London: 1949.

Hergenhahn, B.R. *An Introduction to Theories of Personality.* 3rd ed. Englewood Cliffs, New Jersey: Prentice Hall, 1990.

Hegel, G.W.F. *Phenomenology of Spirit.* Trans. A.V. Miller. Oxford: Oxford University Press, 1977.

Horney, Karen. *Our Inner Conflicts.* New York: W.W. Norton & Company, 1972.

---. *Neurosis and Human Growth; The Struggle Towards Self-Realization.* New York: W.W. Norton & Company, 1991.

Huebsch, Bill. *A Spirituality of Wholeness; The New Look at Grace.* Mystic, CT: Twenty-Third Publications, 1992.

Imbach, Jeffrey D. *The Recovery of Love.* New York: Crossroad, 1992

Johann, R.O. *The Meeting of Love.* Westminster, MD, 1959.

John of the Cross, St. *The Ascent of Mount Carmel.* The Collected Works of St. John of the Cross. Trans. Kieran Kavanaugh, O.C.D. and Otilio Rodriguez, O.C.D. Washington D.C.: Institute of Carmelite Studies, ICS Publications, 1979.

---. *The Dark Night.* The Collected Works of St. John of the Cross. Trans. Kieran Kavanaugh, O.C.D. and Otilio Rodriguez, O.C.D. Washington, D.C.: ICS, 1979.

---. *Spiritual Canticle.* The Collected Works of St. John of the Cross. Trans. Kieran Kavanaugh, O.C.D. and Otilio Rodriguez, O.C.D. Washington, D.C.: ICS Publications, 1979.

John Paul II, Pope. *Reconciliation and Penance: Post-Synodal Apostolic Exhortation.* Washington, D.C.: United States Catholic Conference, December 2, 1984.

---. *Crossing the Threshold of Hope.* Ed. Vittorio Messori. New York: Alfred A. Knopf, 1994.

Johnston, William. Ed. *The Cloud of Unknowing and the Book of Privy Counseling.* New York: Doubleday Image Books. 1973.

Jones, Cheslyn, Geoffrey Wainwrights & Edward Yarnold, eds. *The Study of Spirituality.* New York: Oxford University Press, 1986.

Kegan, Robert. *The Evolving Self.* Cambridge, MA: Harvard University Press, 1982.

Kenny, J.P. *The Supernatural.* Staten Island, New York: Alba House, 1972.

Kierkegaard, Søren. *Practice in Christianity.* Eds, and trans. Howard V. Hong and Edna H. Hong. Princeton University Press, 1991.

---. *Fear and Trembling; The Sickness unto Death*. Princeton, N.J.: Princeton University Press, 1968.

---. *Concluding Unscientific Postscript to Philosophical Fragments*. Princeton, N.J.: Princeton University Press, 1992.

---. *A Kierkegaard Anthology*. Ed. Robert Bretall, Princeton, N.J.: Princeton University Press, 1962.

Klein, Donald F. and Paul H. Wender. *Understanding Depression*. New York: Oxford University Press, 1993.

Koch, Robert. *Il Peccato nel Vecchio Testemento*. Roma: Edizioni Pauline, 1973.

Kushner, Harold S. *When Bad Things Happen to Good People*. New York: Avon Books, 1981.

Kuukure, Edward. *The Destiny of Man; Dagaare Beliefs in Dialogue with Christian Eschatology*. Frankfurt am Main: Peter Lang, 1985.

Larkin, Ernst. *Silent Presence: Discernment as Process and Problem*. Denville, New Jersey: Dimension Books Inc., 1981.

Laurentin, Rene. *Liberation, Development and Salvation*. Trans. Charles Underhill Quinn. New York, 1972.

Lawrence of the Resurrection, Brother. *The Practice of the Presence of God*. Trans. Donald Attwater. Springfield, Illinois: Templegate, 1974.

Lemaire, Anika. *Jacques Lacan*. Trans. David Macey. London: Routledge, 1977.

Lesourd J. En Afrique occidentale française : Les Dagaris. Paris, 1939.

Levenson, Edgar A. *The Fallacy of Understanding: An Inquiry into the Changing Structure of Psychoanalysis*. New York: Basic Books, 1972.

Libreria Editrice Vaticana. *Catechism of the Catholic Church*. English Translation for the United States of America Catholic Conference. Liguori, MO: Liguori Publications, 1994.

Lonergan, Bernard J.F. *Insight*. San Francisco: Harper and Row Publishers, 1978.

Luijpen, William A., and Henry J. Koren. *A First Introduction to Existential Phenomenology*. Pittsburgh: Duquesne University Press, 1969

McQuarrie, John, and Edward Robinson, trans. *Being and Time*, by Martin Heidegger. San Francisco: Harper & Row, 1962.

---. *Principles of Christian Theology*. 2nd ed. New York: Charles Scribner's Sons, 1977.

---. *In Search of Humanity; A Theological Philosophical Approach*. New York: Crossroad, 1985.

Maslow, Abraham. *Toward a Psychology of Being*. 2nd ed. New York: Van Nostrand Reinhold Company, 1968.

---. *The Farther Reaches of Human Nature*. New York: Viking Press, 1971.

Maus, Marcel. *The Gift*. Trans. Ian Cunnison. London: Cohen and West Ltd., 1970.

May, Gerald G. *Will and Spirit; A Contemplative Psychology*. San Francisco: Harper Collins Publishers, 1982.

---. *The Awakened Heart: Opening yourself to the Love you Need*. San Francisco: Harper Collins, 1993.

---. *Care of Mind Care of Spirit*. San Francisco: Harper Collins Publishers, 1982.

---. *Addiction and Grace*. San Francisco: Harper Collins Publishers, 1991.

Mbiti, John S. *The Prayers of African Religion*. Maryknoll, New York: Orbis Books, 1976.

---. *Concepts of God in Africa*. Praeger Publishers, 1970.

---. *African Religions and Philosophy*. Oxford: Heinemann Educational Books Inc., 1969.

McCoy, Remigius F. *Great Things Happen*. Ed. Rene Dionne. Canada: Society of the Missionaries of Africa, 1988.

Meisel, Anthony C., and M.L. del Mastro, trans. *The Rule of St. Benedict*. New York: Image Books, Doubleday, 1975.

Merton, Thomas. *New Seeds of Contemplation*. New York: New Directions Publishing Corporation, 1961.

---. *No Man is an Island*. New York: Harcourt Brace Jovanovich, 1978

Miller, David, ed. *Popper Selections*. Princeton, New Jersey: Princeton University Press, 1985

Miller, A.V. *Phenomenology of Spirit, by G.W.F. Hegel*. New York: Oxford University Press, 1977.

Montagu, Ashley. *Touching: The Human Significance of the Skin. 3rd ed.* New York: Harper & Row, 1986.

Muto, Susan Annette. *Pathways of Spiritual Living*. Petersham, MA: St. Bede's Publication, 1984.

---. *John of the Cross for Today*: The Ascent. Notre Dame, Indiana: Ave Maria Press, 1991

---. *John of the Cross for Today: The Dark Night*. Notre Dame, Indiana: Ave Maria Press, 1994.

---. *Meditations in Motion*. Garden City, New York: Image Books, 1986.

---. *Blessings that Make Us Be*. Petersham, MA: Saint Bede's Publications, 1982.

---. *The Journey Homeward*. Denville, New Jersey: Dimension Books, 1977.

---. *A Practical Guide to Spiritual Reading. 2nd ed.* Petersham, MA: Saint. Bede's Publications, 1994.

---. *Celebrating the Single Life*. New York: Crossroad, 1989.

---. *Approaching the Sacred*. Denville, New Jersey: Dimension Books, 1973.

---. *Steps Along the Way*. Denville, New Jersey: Dimension Books, 1975.

---. *Renewed at Each Awakening*. Denville, New Jersey: Dimension Books, 1979.

---. *Woman Spirit*. New York: Crossroad, 1991.

---. *Late Have I Loved Thee*. New York: Crossroad, 1995.

Muto, Susan, and Adrian van Kaam. *Commitment: Key to Christian Maturity*. New York: Paulist Press, 1989.

---. *A Workbook and Guide for Commitment: Key to Christian Maturity.* New York: Paulist Press, 1990.

Nemeck, Francis Kelly, and Marie Theresa Coombs. *O Blessed Night.* New York: Alba House, 1991.

Nicholl, Donald. *Holiness.* New York: Paulist Press, 1981.

Niebuhr, H.R. *Christ and Culture.* New York, 1956

Nolan, Albert. *Jesus Before Christianity.* Maryknoll, New York: Orbis Books, 1976.

Nouwen, Henri J.M. *The Wounded Healer.* New York: Doubleday, 1990.

---. *Show Me the Way.* New York: crossroad, 1992.

O'Connor, John Francis Xavier, ed. *Life of Aloysius Gonzaga of the Society of Jesus.* New York: Saint Francis Xavier's College, 1891.

O'Shaughnessy, Mary Michael. *Feelings and Emotions in Christian Living.* New York: Alba House, 1988.

Of St. Stanislaus, Father Germanus. *The Life of Gemma Galgani.* Trans. A.M. O'Sullivan, O.S.B. London and Edinburgh: Sands & Company, 1992.

Pannenberg, Wolfhart. *Jesus – God and Man.* Philadelphia, PA: The Westminster Press, 1974.

Parrinder, Edward Geoffrey. *African Traditional Religion.* 2nd rev. ed. Seraph. London: S.P.C.K., 1962.

---. *West African Psychology; A Comparative Study of Psychological and Religious Thought.* London: Lutterworth Press, 1951.

Paul the Apostle. *First Letter to the Corinthians.* (New Jerusalem Bible) New York: Doubleday, 1985.

Peters, Ted. *Sin; Radical Evil in Soul and Society.* Grand Rapids, Michigan: William B. Berdmans Publishing Company, 1994.

Polkinghorne, Donald E. *Narrative Knowing and Human Sciences.* Albany: State University of New York Press, 1988.

---. *Methodology for the Human Sciences; Systems of Inquiry*. Albany: State University of New York Press. 1983.

Prost, André. *Les Mission des Peres Blancs en Afrique Occidentale avant 1939*. Paris. 1970.

Quigley, Carol, ed. *Turning Points in Religious Life*. Westminster, MD: Christian Classics, Inc., 1988.

Radcliffe-Brown, A.R. *African Systems of Kinship and Marriage*. London: Oxford University Press, 1950.

Rahner, Karl. *The Content of Faith*. New York: Crossroad, 1992.

---. *Encounters with Silence*. Westminster, MD: Newman Press, 1960.

---. *The Practice of Faith*. Karl Lehmann and Albert Raffelt. New York: Crossroad, 1992.

---. *Foundations of Christian Faith: An Introduction to the Idea of Christianity*. Trans. William V. Dych. New York: Crossroad, 1993.

---. *Grace in Freedom*. New York: Herder and Herder, 1991.

---. *Theological Investigations; Volume XXIII*. Trans. Joseph Donceel and Hugh M. Riley New York: Crossroad, 1992.

Rattray, R.S. *The Tribes of the Ashanti Hinterland*. Oxford: Clarendon Press, 1969.

Ray, Benjamin C. *African Religions: Ritual and Community*. Englewood Cliffs: Prentice Hall Inc., 1976.

Ricoeur, Paul. *Fallible Man*. Revised Edition. New York: Fordam University Press, 1986.

---. *The Symbolism of Evil*. Boston, MA: Beacon Press, 1969.

---. *A Ricoeur Reader: Reflection and Imagination*. Toronto: University of Toronto Press, 1991.

Rohr, Richard. *Near Occasions of Grace*. Maryknoll, N.Y.: Orbis Books, 1993.

---. *Radical Grace*. Ed. John Bookser Feister. Cincinnati OH: St. Anthony Messenger Press, 1993.

Rondet, Henri. *Original Sin: The Patristic Theological Background*. Trans. Cajetan Finegan. Staten Island, N.Y. 1972.

Ruffing J. *Undercovering Stories of Faith*. New York: Paulist Press, 1989.

Ryan, John K., trans. *The Confessions of St. Augustine*. New York: Doubleday, 1960

Sarpong, Peter K. *Ghana in Retrospect: Some Aspects of Ghanaian Culture*. Accra-Tema: Ghana Publishing, 1974.

Schafer, Roy. *The Analytic Attitude*. Basic Books, Inc., Harper and Collins, 1983.

Schillebeeckx, Edward. *Christ the Sacrament of Encounter with God*. New York: Sheed and Ward, 1963.

Schoonenberg, Piet. *Man and Sin*. London: Sheed and Ward, 1972.

Schultz, Karl A. *Where is God when You Need Him?* New York: Alba House, 1992.

Seeburger, Francis F. *Addiction and Responsibility*. New York: Crossroad, 1993

Sellner Edward C. *Mentoring the Ministry of Spiritual Kinship*. Notre Dame, Indiana: Ave Maria Press, 1990.

Stevens, Clifford, and William Hart McNichols, eds. *Aloysius*. Huntington, Indiana: Our Sunday Visitor, Inc., 1993.

Tengan, Edward. *The Land as Being and Cosmos*. Frankfurt am Main: Peter Lang, 1980.

Teresa of Avila, Saint. *The Way of Perfection*. Vol. 2 of The Collected Works of St. Teresa of Avila. Trans. Kieran Kavanaugh, O.C.D. and Otilio Rodriguez, O.C.D. Washington, D.C.: Institute of Carmelite Studies, ICS Publications, 1980.

---. *The Interior Castle*. Vol. 2 of The Collected Works of St. Teresa of Avila. Trans. Kieran Kavanaugh, O.C.D. and Otilio Rodriguez, O.C.D. Washington D.C.: ICS Publications, 1980.

Thérèse of Lisieux, St. *Story of a Soul.* Trans. John Clarke. Washington, D.C.: ICS Publications, 1972.

---. *Thérèse of Lisieux: A Discovery of Love.* Ed. Terence Carey, O.C.D. New York: City Press, 1992.

Thomas, Louis Vincent. *Les Religions d'Afrique Noire.* Paris: Fayard/Denoël, 1969.

Tillich, Paul. *Dynamics of Faith.* New York: Harper Torchbooks, 1957.

---. *The Shaking of the Foundations.* New York: Charles Scribner's Sons, 1948.

Toffler, Alvin. *Future Shock.* London: Pan Books Ltd., 1971.

Tracy, David. *The Analogical Imagination; Christian Theology and the Culture of Pluralism.* New York: Crossroad, 1991.

Underhill. Evelyn. *Practical Mysticism.* Columbus, OH: Ariel Press, 1942.

---. *Mysticism.* London: Doubleday Image Books, 1990.

Van Kaam, Adrian. *Foundations for Personality Study.* Denville, New Jersey: Dimension Books, 1983.

---. *The Dynamics of Spiritual Self-Direction.* Pittsburgh. PA: Epiphany Association, 1992

---. *The Mystery of Transforming Love.* Denville, N.J.: Dimension Books, 1981.

---. *The Music of Eternity.* Notre Dame, Indiana: Ave Maria Press, 1990.

---. *Fundamental Formation. Vol. 1 of Formative Spirituality.* New York: Crossroad, 1989.

---. *Human Formation. Vol. 2 of Formative Spirituality.* New York: Crossroad, 1989.

---. *Formation of the Human Heart. Vol. 3 of Formative Spirituality.* New York: Crossroad, 1991.

---. *Scientific Formation. Vol. 4 of Formative Spirituality.* New York: Crossroad, 1987.

---. *Traditional Formation*. Vol. 5 of *Formative Spirituality*. New York: Crossroad, 1992.

---. *Transcendent Formation*. Vol. 6 of *Formative Spirituality*. New York: Crossroad, 1995.

---. *Transcendent Therapy*. Vol. 7 of *Formative Spirituality*. New York: Crossroad, 1995.

---. "Preliminary Glossary of Christian Articulation of Formation Science," *MS*. Epiphany Association, Pittsburgh, PA: 1994.

---. *The Transcendent Self*. Pittsburgh PA: Epiphany Association, 1991.

---. *Religion and Personality*. Pittsburgh, PA: Epiphany Association, 1991.

---. *In Search of Spiritual Identity*. Denville, N.J.: Dimension Books, 1975.

---. *The Art of Existential Counseling*. Denville, N.J.: Dimension Books, 1966

---. *The Roots of Christian Joy*. Denville, N.J.: Dimension Books, 1985.

---. *Spirituality and the Gentle Life*. Denville, N.J.: Dimension Books, 1974.

---. *The Woman at the Well*. Denville, N.J.: Dimension Books, 1976.

---. *The Vowed Life*. Denville, N.J.: Dimension Books, 1968.

---. *Fulfillment in the Spiritual Life*. Denville, N.J.: Dimension Books, 1966

---. *On Being Involved*. Denville, N.J.: Dimension Books, 1970.

---. *Looking for Jesus*. Denville N.J.: Dimension Books, 1977.

---. *Fulfillment in the Religious Life*. Denville, N.J.: Dimension Books. 1969.

---. *On Being Yourself*. Denville, N.J.: Dimension Books, 1972.

Van Kaam, Adrian & Susan Muto. *Formation Guide to Becoming Spiritually Mature*. Pittsburgh, PA: Epiphany Association, 1991.

---. And Susan Muto. *The Power of Appreciation*. New York: Crossroad, 1993

Vanstone, W.H. *The Stature of Waiting*. London: Darton, Longman Todd Ltd., 1982.

Volkl, R. *Selbstliebe in der Heiligen Schrift und bei Thomas von Aquin*. Munchen. 1956.

---. *Fruhchristliche Zeugnisse zu Wesen und Gestalt der Christlichen Liebe.* Freiburg, 1963.

---. *Botschaft und Gebot der Liebe nach der Bibel.* Freiburg, 1964.

Wesley, John and Charles. *Selected Writings and Hymns.* Ed. Frank Whaling, New York: Paulist Press, 1981.

Westermann, Dietrich. *Geschichte Afirkas; Staatenbildungen Suedlich der Sahara.* Köln: Greven-Verlag, 1952.

---. *The Languages of West Africa.* London: Oxford University Press, 1952.

---. *Die Sudansprachen, eine Sprachvergleichende Studie.* Hamburg, 1913.

---.*Die Westlichen Sudansprachen und ihre Beziehungen zum Bantu.* Berlin, 1927.

Whitehead, Evelyn Eaton & James D. Whitehead. *Seasons of Strength.* New York: Image Books, 1986

Wilber, Ken. No Boundary: Eastern and Western Approach to Personal Growth. Boston: Shambhala, 1985.

Wilkes, Paul. *These Priests Stay.* New York: Simon and Schuster, 1973.

Willoughby, W.C. *The Soul of Bantu.* Westport, Connecticut: Negro University Press, 1970.

Wimbush, Vincent L., ed. *Ascetic Behaviour in Greco-Roman Antiquity.* Minneapolis: Fortress Press, 1990.

Yonge, C.D. *The Works of Philo.* Peabody, MA: Hendrickson Publications, 1993.

Zahan, Dominique. *The Religion, Spirituality, and Thought of Traditional Africa.* Chicago: University Press, 1979

ARTICLES

Alfaro, Juan. "Christian Hope of Mankind." *Concilium* 9 (June 1970): 59-69.

Ancel, Alfred. "Libération de l'Homme et Salut par la Foi en Jésus-Christ. » *La Documentation Catholique,* 70 (1973) 532-6

Arupe, P. « Pluralismo delle Culture e Cristianesimo. » *Sapienza* 20 (1967) :7-16.

-----. « Culture and Mission. » *Christus* 13 (1966) : 395-405.

Baron, André Barral. « Libération en Jésus-Christ. » *Christus* 19 (1972) : 395-405.

Beatie, J.H.M. « Divination in Bunyoro. » *Ethnology* 3 (1964).

Boff, Leonardo. "Salvation in Jesus Christ and the Process of Liberation." *Concilium* 6 (October 1974): 78-91.

Byrne, Richard. "Approaching prayer as Mystery: Some Basic Assumptions." *Spiritual Life* 34 No.1 (Spring 1988): 12-9.

Carrington, P. and H. Ephron. "Meditation and Psychoanalysis." *Journal of the American Academy of Psychoanalysis 3* (1975): 43-57.

Dumont, C. "Education of the Heart." *Monastic Studies.* 12 (Michalmass 1976):191-206.

Ferret, H.M. "L'Amour Fraternel Vécu en l'Eglise et le Signe de la Venue de Dieu." *Concilium* 29 (1967) : 19-36.

Frankl, Victor. « Determinism and Humanism. » *Humanitas 7* (Spring 1971): 23-36.

Girault, Louis. "Essai sur la Religion des Dagara." *Bulletin de 'Institut Français d'Afrique Noire* (Bulletin I.F.A.N.) 21 (Juillet-Octobre 1959) :329-56)

Goody, Jack. « The Clarification of Double Descent Systems. » *Current Anthropology* 2 (1961): 2-25.

Gowan, J.C. "The Role of Imagination in the Development of the Creative Individual." *Humanitas* 14 (May 1978): 209-25.

Hogan, William E. "Leadership in Weakness." *Studies* 3 (February 1982): 63-74.

Husserl, Edmund. "Philosophy as a Rigorous Science." *Cross Current* 6 (1956): 227-46 and 325-44.

Kennedy, Eugene. "Religious Faith and Psychological Maturity." *Concilium* 9 (1973): 119-27

Knowles, R.T. "Fantasy and Imagination." *Studies in Formative Spirituality* 6 (February 1985): 53-63.

Kuuire, Albert A. "The Event of Physical Weakening: An Invitation and an Opportunity to Foster Formative Anticipation." *Studies XIV*, 3 (1993): 367-80.

Labouret, Henri. "La Divinisation en Afrique Noire." *Anthropologie*, 1922.

Levenson, E.A. «The Purloined Self» (Homeostatic Power of the Patient). *Journal of the American Academy of Psychoanalysis* 15 No. 4 (1987): 481-90.

Maisch, Ingrid. "Salvation Biblical Concept." *Sacramentum Mundi. Vol. 5*, 409-10.

Pennington, M. Basil. "Aloysius Mystic?" Aloysius Eds. Clifford Stevens & William H. McNichols. Huntington, Indiana: *Our Sunday Visitor*, Inc., 115-24.

Price, James R. III. "Transcendence and Images." The Apophatic and Kataphatic Reconsidered." *Studies* 11 (May 1990): 195-201.

Quesnell, Quentin. "Grace." *The New Dictionary of theology*, eds. Joseph A Komonchak and Co. Collegeville Minnesota: The Liturgical Press, 1991.

Ratzinger, Josef. "Heil." *In Lexikon fur Theologie und Kirche*, eds. J. Hofer and Karl Rahner. Vol. 5 Freiburg-im-Breisgau, 1960.

---. "The Dignity of the Human Person." *Commentary on the Documents of Vatican II*: vol. 5 115-63.

Robinson, H. W. "The Hebrew Concept of Corporate Personality." *Zeitschrift fur die Alttestamentliche Wissenschaft* 66 (1936).

Roustang, François. "La Rencontre des Autres." Christus 43 (1964) : 314-28.

---. « L'Amour Universel dans le Christ et l'Esprit. » *Christus* 18 (1958).

Shannon, William H. « Humility." *The New Dictionary of Catholic Spirituality*. Ed. Michael Downy. Collegeville, Minnesota: The Liturgical Press, 1993.

Sutich, Anthony J. "The Emergence of the Transpersonal Orientation: A Personal Account." *Journal of Transpersonal Psychology VIII*. (1976): 5-19.

Tracy, Fidelis. "Man Responding to Changes." *Humanitas* 10 (May 1974): 171-88.

Van Kaam, Adrian. "Provisional Glossary of the Science of Foundational Formative Spirituality." *Studies I. No. 1* (1980): 137-54.

---. "Provisional Glossary." *Studies* IV No.3 (1983): 409-24.

---. "Provisional Glossary." *Studies* I. No.2 (1980): 287-304.

---. "Provisional Glossary." *Studies* II. No.3 (1981): 499-540.

---. "Provisional Glossary." *Studies* II. No.1 (1981): 117-26.

Walsh, J.P.M. "Vocation." *The Modern Catholic Encyclopedia*. Eds. Michael Glazier and Monika K. Hellwig. Collegeville, Minnesota: The Liturgical Press, 1994.

Ware, Kallistos. "The Origins of the Jesus Prayer: Diadochus, Gaza, Sinai." *The Study of Spirituality*, eds. Cheslyn Jones Geoffrey Wainwright and Edward Yarnold. New York: Oxford University Press, 1986, 175-84.

DOCUMENTS AND REFERENCE WORKS

A Patristic Greek Lexicon. Ed. G.W.H. Lampe. Oxford University Press, 1961.

Catechism of the Catholic Church. Libreria Editrice Vaticana: Liguori Publications, 1994.

Cassel's Latin Dictionary: Latin-English, English-Latin. New York: Macmillan, 1968.

Encyclopedia of Catholicism. Ed. Richard P. McBrien. San Francisco: Harper-Collins, 1995.

Interlinear Greek-English New Testament. Ed. & trans. Jay P. Green. Peaboy, MA: Hendrickson Publishers, 1985.

Pastoral Constitution on the Church in the Modern World: "Gaudium et Spes," in Vatican Council II: The Post Conciliar Documents. Ed. Austin Flannery. Dublin: Dominican Publications, 1975.

The American Heritage Dictionary. 2nd College Edition.

The Chambers Dictionary. Chambers Harrap Publishers Ltd., 1993.

The New Dictionary of Catholic Spirituality. Ed. Michael Downy. Collegeville, Minnesota: The Liturgical Press, 1993.

The New Dictionary of Theology. Eds. Joseph A. Komonchak and Co. Collegeville. Minnesota: The Liturgical Press, 1991.

Webster's Third International Dictionary.

UNPUBLISHED SOURCES

Barron, Keith Reeves. "The Spiritual Classics." Class Lecture Notes. Pittsburgh, PA: Duquesne University, IFS, Spring Semester, 1992.

---. "Christian Formation and the Life of Prayer." Class Lecture Notes, Pittsburgh, PA: Duquesne University, IFS, Spring Semester, 1993.

Van Kaam, Adrian & Susan Annette Muto. "Christian Articulation of Formation Science." Class Lecture Notes. Pittsburgh, PA: Duquesne University, IFS, Spring Semester, 1994.

DISSERTATIONS

Baird, Marie Louise. "The Role and Dynamics of Conversion in Human and Christian Formation." Ph.D. diss., Duquesne University, 1993. Ann Abor: UMI, 1993.

Bekuone Some-Deri, Joseph-Mukassa. "Les Dagara: Leur écosystème et son fonctionnement interne face a la modernité. » 3 vols. PhD. diss, Institut Catholique de Paris, 1989.

Byrne, Richard. "The Science of Foundational Human Formation and Its Relation to the Christian Formation Tradition." Ph.D. diss., Duquesne University, 1982.

Kloepfer, John W. "The Art of Formative Questioning: A Way to Foster Self-Disclosure." Ph.D. diss., Duquesne University, 1990. Ann Abor: UMI, 1990.

Kpiebaya, Gregory E. "God in the Dagaaba Religion and in the Christian Faith." Licentiate Thesis in Theology, Universite Catholique de Louvain, Belgium, 1972.

Kuuire, Albert A. "The Christian Faith in the Dagarti Culture." Licentiate Thesis in Pastoral Theology and Catechetics, Institut "Lumen Vitae," Universite Catholique de Louvain, Belgium, 1972.

---. "Dagaati Solidarity and Salvation in Christ in the Light of 'Gaudium et Spes.' S.T.D. diss., Academia Alfonsiana. Pontificia Universitas Lateranensis, Roma, 1976. In micro-film at Ann Abor, UMI, 1996.

Note: Present book for publication; the original was a dissertation, stored in micro-film by Anne Abor, UMI: 1996.

www.ingramcontent.com/pod-product-compliance
Lightning Source LLC
Chambersburg PA
CBHW081343230426
43667CB00017B/2702